CHRISTIAN THEOLOG

CW00556298

SERIES EDIT

Timothy Gorringe   Serene Jo

CHRISTIAN THEOLOGY IN CONTEXT

Any inspection of recent theological monographs makes plain that it is still thought possible to understand a text independently of its context. Work in the sociology of knowledge and in cultural studies has, however, increasingly made obvious that such a divorce is impossible. On the one hand, as Marx put it, 'life determines consciousness'. All texts have to be understood in their life situation, related to questions of power, class, and modes of production. No texts exist in intellectual innocence. On the other hand, texts are also forms of cultural power, expressing and modifying the dominant ideologies through which we understand the world. This dialectical understanding of texts demands an interdisciplinary approach if they are to be properly understood: theology needs to be read alongside economics, politics, and social studies, as well as philosophy, with which it has traditionally been linked. The cultural situatedness of any text demands, both in its own time and in the time of its rereading, a radically interdisciplinary analysis.

The aim of this series is to provide such an analysis, culturally situating texts by Christian theologians and theological movements. Only by doing this, we believe, will people of the fourth, sixteenth, or nineteenth centuries be able to speak to those of the twenty-first. Only by doing this will we be able to understand how theologies are themselves cultural products—projects deeply resonant with their particular cultural contexts and yet nevertheless exceeding those contexts by being received into our own today. In doing this, the series should advance both our understanding of those theologies and our understanding of theology as a discipline. We also hope that it will contribute to the fast-developing interdisciplinary debates of the present.

F. D. Maurice and the Crisis
of Christian Authority

Jeremy Morris

OXFORD
UNIVERSITY PRESS

OXFORD

UNIVERSITY PRESS

Great Clarendon Street, Oxford OX2 6DP

Oxford University Press is a department of the University of Oxford.
It furthers the University's objective of excellence in research, scholarship,
and education by publishing worldwide in

Oxford New York

Auckland Cape Town Dar es Salaam Hong Kong Karachi Kuala Lumpur
Madrid Melbourne Mexico City Nairobi New Delhi Shanghai Taipei Toronto

With offices in

Argentina Austria Brazil Chile Czech Republic France Greece
Guatemala Hungary Italy Japan South Korea Poland Portugal
Singapore Switzerland Thailand Turkey Ukraine Vietnam

Published in the United States
by Oxford University Press Inc., New York

© Jeremy Morris 2005

British Library Cataloguing in Publication Data

Data available

Library of Congress Cataloging in Publication Data

Data available

Typeset by SPI Publisher Services, Pondicherry, India
Printed in Great Britain by
Biddles Ltd., King's Lynn

ISBN 978-0-19-926316-5 (Hbk.)
978-0-19-954531-5 (Pbk.)

1 3 5 7 9 10 8 6 4 2

Dedicated in gratitude to the memory of

Peter Hinchliff (1929–1995)

and

Colin Matthew (1941–1999)

Preface

My interest in F. D. Maurice was first aroused by reading Michael Ramsey on *The Gospel and the Catholic Church*. Over the nine years or so in which I have been working on this book, it has changed shape several times, beginning as a biography, changing into a monograph on ecclesiology, and ending up as an attempt to understand Maurice's theology, and particularly his treatment of the doctrine of the Church, from the perspective of the context in which it was produced. That evolution may help to explain some of the inevitable gaps in my approach. I had thought, once, to write something like a systematic critique of Maurice's entire theological project, but the sheer complexity and breadth of his work prevented that. Anyway, the few attempts that have been made to impose a systematic framework on his theology have not been very successful. Yet the theme of ecclesiology does provide a useful point of entry to the most significant aspects of his work, not least with reference to his impact on the development of Anglicanism. Maurice was passionately committed to the defence of his own adopted church, the Church of England, but in making that defence, he adumbrated principles that proved attractive to the new 'Anglicanism' of the growing, worldwide Anglican communion, as well as to many in the non-Anglican churches.

I am well aware that, in highlighting this theme, I am likely to disappoint some who might have hoped to see more than a passing reference to Maurice's eschatological theories, or to his reassessment of the doctrine of atonement. Likewise, those who are looking for a full critical biography will also be disappointed. Apart from a few brief forays into the archives, I have sought to concentrate on Maurice's published work. There is still a great deal to be written on Maurice's life, and on his situation in the literary and intellectual milieu of mid-Victorian Britain. I hope that much of what I say will be of some interest to others who might attempt such a task.

Even so, in order to understand Maurice's theology and ecclesiology in context, it has been necessary to follow a broadly chronological sequence, connecting major works to his intellectual development and his ministerial career. Biography, then, interweaves here with wider social and political events, and with the contours of Maurice's religious thought, and each throws light on the other. But it is generally with the published Maurice, and not the private Maurice, that I am concerned—the Maurice who was read, argued over, emulated, and rejected during and after his own lifetime.

Acknowledgements

Earlier drafts of some of the material for this book have appeared in article form. Chapter 2 draws briefly on 'Reconstructing the Reformation: F. D. Maurice, Luther, and Justification', in R. N. Swanson (ed.), *The Church Retrospective*, Studies in Church History, 33 (Woodbridge: Boydell, 1997) and on 'The Text as Sacrament: Victorian Broad Church Philology', in R. N. Swanson (ed.), *The Church and the Book*, Studies in Church History, 38 (Woodbridge: Boydell, 2004); Chapter 3 on 'Newman and Maurice on the Via Media of the Anglican Church: Contrasts and Affinities', *Anglican Theological Review*, 85 (2003); Chapter 4 on 'A "Fluffy-Minded Prayer Book Fundamentalist"? F. D. Maurice and the Anglican Liturgy', in R. N. Swanson (ed.), *Continuity and Change in Christian Worship*, Studies in Church History, 35 (Woodbridge: Boydell, 1999); and Chapter 6 on 'A Social Doctrine of the Trinity? A Reappraisal of F. D. Maurice on Eternal Life', *Anglican and Episcopal History*, 69 (2000). Acknowledgements are due to the publishers of all of these articles for copyright permission.

The personal and intellectual debts I have accumulated in the course of the research for this book are many. One stands out above all—to Dan Hardy, who rescued the project when it was in danger of becoming hopelessly over-ambitious, and helped me to see that a more modest proposal might have a better chance of actually being brought to completion. For his encouragement, his thoughtfulness, his sharp insight, and his breadth of knowledge, I am immensely grateful.

I should single out three others who have, over many years, been exceptionally supportive, and who have helped to shape my understanding of the nineteenth century. Two, alas, are dead, and I hope that this book can be at least a small way of marking how much I owe to them—Colin Matthew and Peter Hinchliff. This book is dedicated to their memory. The third is John Prest, whose patient exposition of the byways of British history enthused me so much when I was an undergraduate at Balliol, and who has remained a valued friend.

There is, inevitably, a long list of people whose views in one way or another have shaped what I have written here. They include Arthur Burns, Georgina Byrne, John Clarke, David Ford, Jim Garrard, Douglas Hedley, Brian Horne, Graham Howes, Paul Hullyer, Bill Jacob, Tim Jenkins, Frances Knight, Tim Larsen, Peter McEnhill, John Milbank, Edmund Newey, Peter Nockles, John Nurser, Simon Oliver, Catherine Pickstock, Alan Piggot, Ben Quash, Nick Sagovsky, Stephen Sykes,

William Taylor, David Thompson, Peter Waddell, Rex Walford, and Chris Williams. My thanks to them, and to anyone else whom I have failed to mention when I should have done so. Especial thanks must go to the editors of the series, Graham Ward, Serene Jones, and Tim Gorringe, to the editorial staff at Oxford University Press, and to the anonymous referees of the original typescript, which was happily quite different from what is presented here.

As always, my institutional debts are considerable too. The staff of the Cambridge University Library, the British Library, Lambeth Palace Library, and the library of King's College, London, have all been helpful at various times. For patience when my attention was elsewhere, and for much-valued friendship, I should also thank the people of St Mary's, Battersea, and Little St Mary's, Cambridge, the staff and students of Westcott House and of the Cambridge Theological Federation from my time on the staff at Westcott, and the Master and Fellows of Trinity Hall, and the community of the college chapel.

The greatest debt is the most personal—to my father David, to Isobel, William, and Ursula, who have had to put up with a preoccupied Daddy for far too long, and to Alex, my wife, a tower of strength.

Contents

CONTENTS

Introduction: The End of the Old Order

Frederick Denison Maurice (1805–72) was one of the foremost theologians of the modern Church of England. Through a series of bruising encounters with contemporary theologians he pioneered a creative response to the critical challenges of modernity, seeking to defend traditional Christian belief by a searching re-examination of biblical theology, and by a profound conviction of the integrity of Christian life and faith in time. This twofold task, paying attention in equal measure to contemporary criticism and to Christian orthodoxy, made Maurice peculiarly vulnerable to attack in his day as, alternately, too liberal and too conservative.[1] Yet his historical influence was immense: time after time his doctrinal conclusions foreshadowed later trends in modern theology.

The main focus of this book is Maurice's ecclesiology. In his attention to the doctrine of the Church, Maurice enunciated a series of critical principles that remain central to Anglican reflection in particular. He has been claimed as the theoretician of comprehensiveness, the inspiration for the Church of England's social witness, the founder of Christian Socialism, and the exponent of an ecumenical methodology which has encouraged *rapprochement* between Catholicism and Protestantism. He produced, albeit sketchily, a representative theory of ministry, in contrast to the hierarchical model supported by the Tractarians. He anticipated the baptismal ecclesiology

---

[1] The notorious assessments of two men who knew Maurice personally, Thomas Carlyle and John Stuart Mill, demonstrate the radical criticism of Maurice. Mill, for example, considered that Maurice's 'great powers of generalization, rare ingenuity and subtlety, and a wide perception of important and unobvious truths' served him 'not for putting something better into the place of the worthless heap of received opinions on the great subjects of thought, but for proving to his own mind that the Church of England had known everything from the first': J. S. Mill, *Autobiography*, ed. J. Stillinger (Oxford: Oxford University Press, 1969), 92. Carlyle, as quoted by his biographer, J. A. Froude, satirized Maurice thus:

> Thirty-nine English Articles,
> Ye wondrous little particles,
> Did God shape his universe really by you?
> In that case I swear it,
> And solemnly declare it,
> This logic of Maurice's is true.

(J. A. Froude, *Life of Carlyle: Carlyle's Life in London*, new edn. (London: Longmans, 1897), 41.)

embraced by some apologists for Anglicanism today.[2] And he supplied much of the theoretical undergirding for the 'Chicago–Lambeth Quadrilateral', the fourfold formula of Scripture, creeds, sacraments, and episcopacy which has guided Anglican approaches to inter-church relations over the last hundred years or more.[3] His influence came to stretch well beyond Anglicanism, as his work was read and absorbed by Free Churchmen and, in the twentieth century, by Roman Catholics too.

His influence in the formation of modern Anglican theology was decisive, and arguably greater than that of any other figure since Samuel Taylor Coleridge's death in 1834 and John Henry Newman's conversion to Roman Catholicism in 1845. Yet assessing Maurice's work and significance is not easy. His rhetorical and often cumbersome prose style is discouraging enough. His books are largely unobtainable now, his theological sympathies unfashionable. For one claimed by some to be the greatest theologian of his age, his name carries little weight with many modern Anglicans. He fails even to merit an entry in one recent dictionary of significant Anglican theologians.[4]

How, then, can the shape, influence, and significance of Maurice's theology be grasped today? It is not part of my purpose here to act directly as an apologist for Maurice's theology. His work does not necessarily provide the solution to contemporary Christian difficulties, though he remains fascinating as an instance of a theologian attempting to respond creatively to a wide sequence of issues problematic for modern theology. There are internal inconsistencies and areas of unexplored tension in his work, so that his doctrinal position often seems to fall apart under close critical analysis.

Nevertheless, these methodological weaknesses should not obscure the breadth of Maurice's theological imagination, and the fundamental consistency of his theological priorities. The source of his fascination for his contemporaries lay in his handling of ecclesiology in particular. But ecclesiology—perhaps more than any other—is a branch of Christian theology peculiarly vulnerable to the vicissitudes of context, and Maurice's ecclesiology cannot be detached from the various contextual challenges and influences upon it. This book seeks above all to make Maurice's thought on the nature and purpose of the Church accessible to the

---

[2] S. W. Sykes, 'Foundations of an Anglican Ecclesiology', in *Unashamed Anglicanism* (London: DLT, 1995), and P. Avis, *Anglicanism and the Christian Church: Theological Resources in Historical Perspective* (Edinburgh: T & T Clark, 1989).

[3] M. Woodhouse-Hawkins, 'Maurice, Huntington, and the Quadrilateral: An Exploration in Historical Theology', in J. Robert Wright (ed.), *Quadrilateral at One Hundred* (Oxford: Mowbray, 1988).

[4] A. E. McGrath (ed.), *The SPCK Handbook of Anglican Theologians* (London: SPCK, 1998).

modern reader, and to supply an interpretation and critique of it. But in order to present a coherent view of Maurice's thought, it is necessary to place his work in the complicated context of early nineteenth-century English Christianity. For Maurice's work was shaped above all by a prolonged crisis in the relationship of Church and State. The questions he sought to address concerned the authority of the Church and its place in society, detached as it increasingly was from the guiding philosophy and shape of State action and social welfare. Writing at a time when serious critical challenges to the dominance of the Christian tradition began to emerge in Western thought and politics, and were pursued in practical philosophies of action, Maurice sought to reverse the fundamental displacement of the Christian narrative from the centre of British life. That the reversal he sought has not in fact occurred, and that the displacement has, rather, deepened and intensified to an extent that Maurice could scarcely have imagined, should not prevent us from taking seriously the scale and nature of his response. This was a displacement that could not be unthought. Whilst many of Maurice's contemporaries assumed it could be, thinking that existing, conventional answers were sufficient to turn back the tide, he, in striking contrast, realized that the changing character and situation of the Church had to be understood, and that this required sympathetic, critical engagement with new ideas and changing institutions. For all its limitations, then, his vision of the role of the Church did consciously seek to rise to the challenges of his age.

These were immense. For the first time in Western history since the re-Christianization of Europe in the early Middle Ages, not just a particular interpretation of Christianity, but its very survival, was at issue. For long, Christians had been able to take for granted that their faith was the very basis of civilization. Now its relevance was at stake. New forms and principles of social organization were laying claim to social well-being, depicting Christianity itself as the obstacle to true social development. This was the fundamental problem that Maurice sought to confront. In order to understand the nature of his response, we must first grasp the source of the various crises facing the churches of Europe, and the Church of England in particular, and this forces us to look at the impact of war and revolution.

EUROPE IN CRISIS

In the history of modern Europe, the twenty-six years from 1789 to 1815 stand out as a period of seismic change. Within a mere generation, the stability and certainties of Europe's *ancien régime* were swept away in revolution, war, and social dislocation. The French Revolution, with its unprecedented attempt to reconstruct government and society according to a declared revolutionary ideology of liberty, equality, and fraternity, launched a chain reaction of conflict and upheaval across the continent, first through the missionary fervour of the revolutionary movement itself, and second through war and conquest. Whether one interprets the Napoleonic regime as a throw-back to Enlightened Despotism, or as the orderly continuation of the Revolution, Napoleon was a child of the Revolution. But the termination of his ambitions with defeat at Waterloo in June 1815 did not mark a return to the *status quo ante bellum*. The forces unleashed or stimulated by the Revolution—nationalism, democratic and egalitarian idealism, the transformation of the technology and techniques of war, amongst others—could not be suppressed. The possibility of revolution hung over Europe for most of the nineteenth century, surfacing again and again in particular movements or particular sequences of events. Not for nothing have historians of Europe often found it convenient to frame their narratives of the modern period with the designation 'Age of Revolution', taking events in France in 1789 as a defining point of reference.[5]

The non-specialist can enter into the study of this period only with some trepidation, for it has produced a vast secondary literature.[6] For many scholars, the Revolution and its consequences were to be celebrated as a vital, if bloody, stage in the evolution of modern democracy and the French Republic. Here, Marxist scholars have shared common ground with liberals and some conservatives. For others, it was neither distinctively 'modern', nor, at first, qualitatively different from other political crises of the eighteenth century.[7] But controversy is not restricted to events in France alone. If we turn our attention to British history, we get no nearer to a consensus on the character, direction, and values of British society as it faced the pressures generated by political change across the Channel and prolonged war. Here, too, the literature is immense, and complicated by the convergence of several sequences of events which historians have all too often treated as discrete, separable subjects of inquiry.

[5] W. H. Hutton may have begun this trend with *The Age of Revolution: 1648–1815* (London: Rivington, 1908), but the best-known examples are probably A. R. Vidler, *The Church in an Age of Revolution* (Harmondsworth: Penguin, 1961), and E. J. Hobsbawm, *The Age of Revolution* (London: Weidenfeld & Nicolson, 1962).

[6] A simple keyword search on 'French Revolution' in OLIS, the Bodleian Library's online catalogue, resulted in over 1,300 items, for example.

[7] For a brief guide to the main outlines of varying interpretations of the French Revolution, see W. Doyle, *Origins of the French Revolution*, 3rd edn. (Oxford: Oxford University Press, 1999).

Let me confine attention to just two of these. One is the political impact in Britain of the French Revolution and of the revolutionary wars that followed.[8] The *loci classici* for the ideological conflict that ensued are the Irish Whig Edmund Burke's *Reflections on the Revolution in France* (1790), a devastating indictment of the Revolution which, in the words of a modern French historian, 'provided the counter-revolution with its doctrine', and the English Radical Thomas Paine's response, *Rights of Man* (1791–2).[9] The sharpness of the pamphlet war that followed the appearance of the *Reflections* acutely symbolized the political polarization which the Revolution triggered in Britain. It has long been argued that the Revolution stimulated and encouraged movements for radical political reform which had already begun to make themselves heard in the second half of the eighteenth century. One of the most provocative modern studies along these lines is E. P. Thompson's *The Making of the English Working Class* (1963). This is a powerful reconstruction of the 'underground' world of radical artisans, writers, and revolutionaries whose enthusiasm for revolutionary principles survived government repression to emerge once again, after 1815, as a source of the development of working-class politics and consciousness. As Thompson says of the shoemakers, for example, '[t]hese artisans took the doctrines of Paine to their extreme—absolute democracy: root-and-branch opposition to monarchy and the aristocracy, to the State and to taxation'.[10] Just as revolution on the continent and war encouraged radicalism, however, it also solidified resistance to radicalism and to reform, pushing former political rivals together in reaction, and provoking the development of a culture of populist loyalism underrated by Thompson.[11] In sharp dissent from the school of Marxist historiography represented by Edward Thompson and Eric Hobsbawm, some English historians, most notably Jonathan Clark, have argued in favour of stability and social cohesion as marks of the British experience in this period.[12] To Clark, the defining moment, the end of Britain's *ancien régime*, did not come until the constitutional crisis that ended with parliamentary reform

[8] See C. Emsley, *British Society and the French Wars, 1793–1815* (London: Macmillan, 1979), and *idem* (ed.), *Britain and the French Revolution* (Harlow: Longman, 2000), and H. T. Dickinson (ed.), *Britain and the French Revolution 1789–1815* (London: Macmillan, 1989).

[9] J. Godechot, *The Counter-Revolution: Doctrine and Action 1789–1804* (London: Routledge, 1972), 66. Literature on the Burke–Paine exchange, and on other writers' responses to Burke, is also considerable: see M. Butler (ed.), *Burke, Paine, Godwin and the Revolution Controversy* (Cambridge: Cambridge University Press, 1984).

[10] E. P. Thompson, *The Making of the English Working Class*, 2nd edn. (Harmondsworth: Penguin, 1968), 172.

[11] See, e.g. H. T. Dickinson, 'Popular Conservatism and Militant Loyalism 1789–1815', in *idem* (ed.), *Britain and the French Revolution*.

[12] J. C. D. Clark, *English Society 1660–1832: Religion, Ideology and Politics during the Ancien Régime* (1985; 2nd edn., Cambridge: Cambridge University Press, 2000).

in 1832.[13] Clark rightly urges caution about the careless use of political terminology, such as 'class consciousness', 'liberal', 'conservative', 'radical', 'enlightenment', amongst others, which, read *into* the late eighteenth and early nineteenth centuries, betrays the teleological sympathies of modern political and historical discourse.[14] We can concede much to Clark's insistence that the period should be read on its own terms, with a proper emphasis on the significance of religion. Yet the fact remains that, by the beginning of the nineteenth century, powerful, if subterranean, movements of radical political reform were gaining ground in Britain. The Reform crisis, even interpreted as a predominantly conservative *coup*, fending off more radical reform by drawing the middle class into the constitution, nevertheless drew on—and for a time crystallized—long-developing traditions of political and social opposition. For these the French Revolution was surely a catalyst.[15]

But why was radical criticism of State, Church, and society attractive to so many in the early nineteenth century? Here we must turn to the second cluster of events. For a long time, historians regarded the years from around 1780 to the 1840s as marking the classic era of industrialization in Britain, the Industrial Revolution, in short. Here too revisionism has had its impact.[16] The conventional view was that, within two generations or so, British society passed from the pre-industrial, traditional world dominated by an agrarian population and life-style to an industrial, urban, factory-based society, with a nascent democracy to match. The transition, so it was argued, was marked by immense social and economic upheaval, with opportunities opening up for entrepreneurs and capitalists at the expense of the labouring poor.[17] Certainly that is how many writers and social commentators by the middle of the nineteenth century had come to view the recent past.[18] And modern historians have been able to

---

[13] The 2nd edn. of *English Society* is more cautious than the first in assigning decisive significance to the Reform crisis: 'What was lost in 1832 . . . was not "the old world" tout court, but the hegemonic status and the integrity of a certain body of ideas, beliefs, customs, and practices': ibid. 16.

[14] See in particular 'Keywords', ibid. 1–13.

[15] On the politics of the Reform crisis, see M. Brock, *The Great Reform Act* (London: Hutchinson, 1973), and also N. Gash, *Politics in the Age of Peel: A Study in the Technique of Parliamentary Representation, 1830–1850* (London: Longman, 1953).

[16] See especially M. J. Daunton, *Progress and Poverty: An Economic and Social History of Britain 1700–1850* (Oxford: Oxford University Press, 1995), ch. 5, 'Diversities of Industrialization', pp. 125–47.

[17] In addition to the school of Marxist historians represented by E. P. Thompson and others, see the earlier labour history of J. L. Hammond and B. Hammond, *The Town Labourer, 1760–1832* (London: Longman, 1917).

[18] On the formation of this view, see Raymond Williams in works such as *Culture and Society, 1780–1850* (London: Chatto, 1958), and *The Country and the City* (London: Chatto,

point to a series of local and national crises in the first half of the nineteenth century to bear this out, from the machine breaking of Luddism, through the Peterloo massacre and associated protests, to the Captain Swing riots of 1830 and the Chartist movement of 1838–48.[19] A furious debate has raged for three decades or more in modern British historiography over whether or not standards of living for the labouring poor rose or fell during the Industrial Revolution.[20] It has proved inconclusive, but there is still sufficient evidence at least of localized, temporary (but for all that, intense) social distress to make the point stand. The British constitution may have weathered the storms of the early nineteenth century well, but they were storms, nevertheless. They created a lasting impression of crisis and danger. The incidence of poverty and unemployment proved to be fertile both for religion and for political radicalism (and the two were by no means always separate). In the seventy years from 1801 to 1871, covering virtually the entire period of F. D. Maurice's life, the population of England, Scotland, and Wales more than doubled, from over 10.5 million to over 26 million.[21] Growth occurred mainly in the industrial towns and cities, fed by rural depopulation. In 1851, for the first time ever, more people were recorded as living in towns and cities than in the countryside. Whilst Bath recorded a relatively modest increase from 33,000 people in 1801 to 53,000 in 1861, Liverpool, by contrast, leapt from 82,000 to 472,000 in the same period. Living conditions in the new industrial cities became the preoccupation of parliamentarians and social commentators alike. Friedrich Engels, for example, the future collaborator of Karl Marx, produced what subsequently became (though not until the twentieth century) a famous survey of the conditions of the poor in Manchester in 1844, which broadened out into a wholesale critique of industrial capitalism.[22] The political ideals of the French Revolution fed into a stream of autonomous British radicalism.

1973). For an opposing reading, see M. J. Wiener, *English Culture and the Decline of the Industrial Spirit, 1850–1980* (Cambridge: Cambridge University Press, 1981).

[19] On these, for overall surveys see, e.g., M. I. Thomis, *The Luddites: Machine-Breaking in Regency England* (Newton Abbot: David & Charles, 1970); J. R. Dinwiddy, *From Luddism to the First Reform Bill* (Oxford: Blackwell, 1986); E. J. Hobsbawm and G. Rudé, *Captain Swing* (London: Lawrence & Wishart, 1969); R. Brown, *Chartism* (Cambridge: Cambridge University Press, 1998).

[20] A useful survey of earlier literature is A. J. Taylor (ed.), *The Standard of Living in Britain in the Industrial Revolution* (London: Methuen, 1975); see also Daunton, *Progress*, ch. 16, 'The Standard of Living and the Social History of Wages'.

[21] Population statistics here are derived from P. Mathias, *The First Industrial Nation: An Economic History of Britain 1700–1914* (1969; new edn., London: Methuen, 1983), 415–17.

[22] F. Engels, *The Condition of the Working Class in England in 1844* (London: Allen & Unwin, 1892; first published in German in 1845).

This world of political, social, economic, and (as we shall see) *religious* crisis formed the immediate context into which Frederick Denison Maurice was born near Lowestoft on 29 August 1805. Though he was given the first name 'John', this was rarely used by him later in life. By his family he was known usually as 'Frederick' or 'Fred', and more widely by the more formal initials and surname, 'F. D. Maurice'. The only surviving son of a Unitarian minister, Maurice's early years cannot but have been touched by aspects of the history of radicalism at the beginning of the nineteenth century. Maurice is usually appreciated from the standpoint of mid-Victorian stability and prosperity, dying as he did in 1872 when his career had reached an apogee with his recent appointment to a professorship at Cambridge. He would have been a good candidate for inclusion in Lytton Strachey's *Eminent Victorians*. His combination of moral earnestness, immense diligence, philanthropic and educational activity, and religious fervour would have placed him in good company with Thomas Arnold and General Gordon. The establishment of his reputation was greatly aided by his biography, which appeared in 1884. This succeeded triumphantly in showing the reading public much more of Maurice's engaging personality than they had ever been able to glean from his published writing.[23] The controversial episodes for which he is best known—Christian Socialism (1848–52), his dismissal from King's College, London, over his views on eternal punishment (1853), and his attack on Dean Mansel's understanding of revelation (1859)—all date from the middle years of the century. Yet his religious, political, and social views were largely formed before the accession of Queen Victoria, in years marked by a constant undercurrent of radical unrest and social upheaval. He came out of a tradition that, of all the various strands of religious belief in Britain, was most sympathetic to popular radicalism. Maurice's father Michael was a friend and, for a time, colleague of Joseph Priestley, the Unitarian minister whose chapel and house in Birmingham were destroyed by a 'Church and King' mob in 1791.[24] He joined the Peace Society, opposing the war with France and, according to his son's reminiscences later in life, supporting those 'who were persecuted by Mr. Pitt's Government and were suspected of French sympathies'.[25] His family evinced strong radical sympathies: 'Sir Francis Burdett was a great hero of my elder sisters. His going to

---

[23] On the reception of Sir Frederick Maurice's biography of his father, see T. Christensen, 'F. D. Maurice and the Contemporary Religious World', in G. J. Cuming (ed.), *Studies in Church History*, 3 (Leiden: Brill, 1966).

[24] F. Maurice, *The Life and Letters of Frederick Denison Maurice*, i (1884; 2nd edn., London: Macmillan, 1884), 6, 8.

[25] Ibid. 15.

the Tower and the watchword of his supporters took hold of my fancy.'[26] As late as 1823, as Michael Maurice's grandson records, he could affirm that 'The taking of the Bastille is still one of the *Dies Fasti* in my calendar'.[27]

Whilst F. D. Maurice was to turn away to some extent from this radical inheritance in embracing the Church of England, he remained sympathetic to some of his father's political and social views. His famous breadth of sympathy was undoubtedly influenced by his Unitarian upbringing, even if tracing particular affinities between Unitarian thought and his mature theology is not as straightforward as some scholars have assumed.[28] It would be straining a point to argue that the development of Maurice's thought can be approached only from the rather narrow perspective of the influences he inherited from his father and from the ferment of religious and political ideas of the revolutionary and Napoleonic wars. Nevertheless, in order to understand his theological formation, it is vital to grasp the nature of the challenge facing the Christian Church, and particularly the Church of England, in the first half of the nineteenth century. In order to carry this contextual description further, then, it is necessary to widen consideration of the impact of the French Revolution to include its effects on the Christian Church. In the next chapter we shall consider the particular nature of the crisis undergone by the Church of England in the first forty years or so of Maurice's life.

For Maurice's theology was contextual in two main senses. It explicitly addressed particular political, social, and ecclesiastical controversies of his day, aiming to provide a defence of the Church of England in a situation of great uncertainty and criticism. In this way, Maurice engaged directly with the various movements of social and religious criticism of his day. But his theology was also *broadly* contextual, reflecting (though not always consciously) deep-rooted fears faced by Christians. A discussion of the development of his theology in context must attend both to specific historical events, movements, and crises and to the general situation of Christian theology in a period of rapid change. Running like a thread through the period as a whole was the prospect of the destabilization of society through social and political revolution.

---

[26] Ibid. 16.

[27] Ibid. 9.

[28] Most notably D. Young, in *F. D. Maurice and Unitarianism* (Oxford: Clarendon Press, 1992); but also see D. Wigmore-Beddoes, *Yesterday's Radicals: A Study of the Affinity between Unitarianism and Broad Church Anglicanism in the Nineteenth Century* (Cambridge: James Clarke, 1971).

THE REVOLUTION AND THE CHURCH

In 1789–90, scarcely anyone could have predicted the catastrophic collapse of the French Church. As one historian has commented, 'only on the lunatic fringe of journalism had there been proposals to oust the established Church'.[29] Yet, within three years, the overthrow of the Church in France had taken place, 'one of the momentous events of modern history'.[30] Though members of the National Assembly were mostly reluctant Church reformers, the imposition of reform through the Civil Constitution of the Clergy and its associated oath late in 1791 divided the French Church.[31] War between France and its neighbours, and within France itself between the Revolutionary regime and opponents of the Revolution, turned loyalty to the Civil Constitution into a test of loyalty to the government. Persecution followed, especially under the Terror from late 1793. Somewhere between 30,000 and 40,000 clergy emigrated in these years. Up to 5,000 more may have been executed in Paris and the provinces. The worst incidents took place in areas of civil war: in November 1793, for example, 135 priests and monks were massacred at Lyon.[32] Just how frightening these events were to English observers—even 'enlightened' observers—can be gleaned from the description offered by Lady Sheffield, writing to her friend the sceptical historian Edward Gibbon in 1792 about the summary execution of the Archbishop of Arles and 120 Carmelite priests:

His appearance was so dignified and noble, that, during ten minutes, not one of these [revolutionary] wretches had courage to lift his hand against him: they upbraided each other with cowardice, and advanced; one look from this venerable man struck them with awe, and they retired. At last, one of the miscreants struck off the cap of the Archbishop with a pike; respect once violated, their fury returned, and another from behind cut him through the skull with a sabre. He raised his right hand to his eyes; with another stroke they cut off his hand. The Archbishop said, 'O! mon Dieu!' and raised the other . . . and then all pressed forward, and buried their pikes and poignards in the body.[33]

---

[29] J. McManners, *The French Revolution and the Church* (London: SPCK, 1969), 76.

[30] W. O. Chadwick, *The Popes and European Revolution* (Oxford: Clarendon Press, 1981), 445.

[31] The standard brief study of the subject until recently was McManners, *French Revolution*, but this has been superseded to some extent by the publication of M. Vovelle, *The Revolution against the Church: From Reason to the Supreme Being* (Cambridge: Polity, 1991), and by D. K. Van Kley, *The Religious Origins of the French Revolution: From Calvin to the Civil Constitution, 1560–1791* (New Haven: Yale University Press, 1996).

[32] Figures are from McManners, *French Revolution*, 106.

[33] Edward Gibbon, *Autobiography*, (Oxford: Oxford University Press, 1972), 297–8.

By late 1793 an active programme of 'de-Christianization' was under way in Paris and parts of the provinces, hand in hand in with the development of alternative revolutionary cults of Reason and of the Supreme Being.[34] By 1794, then, the Christian Church had been all but dismembered, reduced in parts of France to a persecuted, fragile minority. This situation was to prove unsustainable. The collapse of the Terror with the fall of Robespierre in July 1794 began the gradual reinstatement of the 'constitutional' Church, and under Napoleon a Concordat with the Papacy was signed in 1801 regularizing relations between the Papacy and the French Church, and thus reuniting the Church.

This brief narrative of events in France can give only a hint of the horror with which the fall of the Church was regarded throughout Europe, along with the fall of the monarchy in 1793 and the execution of the King and Queen and thousands of opponents of the Revolution. If the outcome of the revolutionary era was to demonstrate the remarkable persistence of popular Catholicism in parts of France, nevertheless the myth of the Church's indefectibility was severely shaken. Fuelled by the polemic of Burke and other critics of the Revolution, contemporaries assumed that hostility to organized religion was a direct outcome of revolutionary principles and ideology, and in turn of the trend of social and religious criticism articulated by the *philosophes*, the enlightened writers and artists of pre-Revolutionary France. Jean-Jacques Rousseau, for example, was held responsible for envisioning, in his *Du Contrat Social* (1757), a form of civil religion which would subserve the collective interests of the nation and which need not be identical by any means with orthodox Christianity.[35] Put that alongside his view that government is entitled to 'force' people to be free, and it seems as if Rousseau alone provided intellectual justification for the revolutionary assault on the Church.[36] The savagery of the attack on the Church at one level reinforced Protestant suspicion of Catholicism in Britain and elsewhere in Northern Europe, but at another level it overrode it. It seemed to suggest that *all* forms of Christian religion were ultimately dispensable to revolutionary ideology. Moreover, it confirmed Burke's warnings about the dire consequences of attempting to create government from first principles. Not only did it carry

---

[34] There is as yet no detailed monograph in English on this aspect, but see Vovelle, *Revolution against the Church*.

[35] On Rousseau's religious thought, in English, see R. Grimsley, *The Philosophy of Rousseau* (Oxford: Oxford University Press, 1973), ch. 6, 'Religion'; see also, in French, Y. Touchefeu, *Antiquité et le christianisme dans la pensée de Jean-Jacques Rousseau* (Oxford: Voltaire Foundation, 1999).

[36] J.-J. Rousseau, *The Social Contract* (Harmonsdworth: Penguin, 1968), 64.

implications for the fragility of Christian churches across Europe, but it also had wider implications for social order and stability.

The situation was particularly dire for established churches, allied as they were with the ruling monarchies and oligarchies against which revolutionary fervour was directed. The resolution of confessional conflict in the seventeenth century had depended, not on a modern concept of toleration (that is, toleration as effectively *indifference* to particular confessional viewpoints), but on the acknowledgement of limits to a State's power to impose particular religious opinions on all its citizens.[37] Yet this had not entailed any lessening of the force of public conviction about the intrinsic truth of particular confessional views, and about the right of states actively to encourage and defend that truth.[38] Across Europe, ruling regimes both supported and were supported by particular churches.[39] A challenge to the hegemony of particular governmental systems and élites on this basis could amount to a challenge to the truth of particular ecclesiastical systems. Correspondingly, criticism of established religion constituted a political threat. No absolute separation could be upheld between Church and State formally, despite attempts by some churchmen themselves to posit an alliance of the two as if they were equal but separate entities.[40] 'An alliance is between two things, that are in their natures distinct and independent', commented Burke, '[but] in a Christian commonwealth, the church and the state are one and the same thing, being different integral parts of the same whole'.[41]

Europe's established churches were inherently vulnerable to attack. The Reformation had destabilized Western Christendom. The medieval understanding of sovereignty, as expressed in papal documents and legal theory, asserted the coincidence of the temporal and spiritual powers under one overarching authority, the Papacy itself. As Innocent III put it bluntly in the twelfth century, 'the moon derives her light from the sun, and is in truth inferior to the sun . . . In the same way the royal power derives its dignity

---

[37] This was the essence of Burke's case against modification of the Act of Uniformity: 'it is not the rights of private conscience that are in question, but the propriety of the terms which are proposed by law as a title to public emoluments': E. Burke, *Speech on the Acts of Uniformity* (1772), in *Collected Works*, ed. F. H. Willis (Oxford: Oxford University Press, 1906), iii. 299. By the same token, Burke was in favour of specific acts of Dissenting relief.

[38] See Burke again: 'If you will have religion publicly practised and publicly taught, you must have a power to say what that religion will be which you will protect and encourage': ibid., 301.

[39] See W. R. Ward, *Christianity under the Ancien Régime, 1648–1789* (Cambridge: Cambridge University Press, 1999).

[40] Most notorious was William Warburton (1698–1779), author of *The Alliance between Church and State* (1736).

[41] Burke, *Speech on the Petition of the Unitarians* (1792), in *Collected Works*, iii., 319.

from the pontifical authority.'[42] By implication, political stability required religious uniformity. At the Reformation, this link was severed in Northern Europe, but in complex, differing ways in different countries. In England, Wales, and Ireland, for example, Henry VIII's repudiation of papal supremacy was achieved by the simple substitution of monarch for pope—the *royal* supremacy.[43] Religious uniformity was to be maintained by the imposition of one English liturgy. Catholicism, eventually, was persecuted and proscribed. In Germany, city-states reached accommodation with the new Reforming movements in religious settlements which, eventually, after years of internal conflict concluded at the Peace of Westphalia in 1648, recognized rival religious communities, Catholic and Protestant.[44] In France, the Catholic Church achieved some autonomy from Rome through the Gallican laws of 1682, but this was in turn secured by the savage repression of Protestant minorities and by the assertion of royal control over the Church.[45] This complexity and difference, on a long view, was inherently unstable. International conflict, mediated through religious conflict, could take on a savage dimension, as the seventeenth century had demonstrated. In the end, a measure of religious pluralism and toleration perhaps was inevitable. But, to last, it would require the dismembering and reform of long-established structures of ecclesiastical administration and law, and significant adjustments to the relationship of Church and State. Little of *that* had been carried through to a satisfactory conclusion by the end of the eighteenth century.

Furthermore, the established churches of Europe had preserved elements of medieval structure and organization that made them seem anachronistic and ill-equipped to adapt rapidly to social and political change. There were massive disparities in income, conditions, and career profile between high-born ecclesiastics and the far more numerous, poorer clergy. The situation of the Church of England will be examined in closer detail in the next chapter. Like its Anglican counterpart, the Catholic Church of France laboured under the burden of a medieval structure of law and administration closely bound up with the interests of the ruling élite. Moreover, in the absence of Reformation, the Church continued to hold

---

[42] H. Bettenson (ed.), *Documents of the Christian Church* (Oxford: Oxford University Press, 1950), 156.

[43] '[T]he king our sovereign lord, his heirs and successors, kings of this realm, shall be taken, accepted, and reputed the only supreme head in earth of the Church of England, called *Ecclesia Anglicana*': The Supremacy Act, 1534, in Bettenson (ed.), *Documents*, 319.

[44] See N. Hope, *German and Scandinavian Protestantism, 1700–1918* (Oxford: Oxford University Press, 1995); also, F. Eyck, *Religion and Politics in German History: From the Beginnings to the French Revolution* (Basingstoke: Macmillan, 1998).

[45] See McManners, *French Revolution*; also N. Ravitch, *The Catholic Church and the French Nation, 1589–1989* (London: Routledge, 1990).

largely untouched its medieval wealth and property. In some areas of the
country, such as Picardy and Cambresis, as much as a third of the land was
held by the Church.[46] The Church was uniquely exempt from ordinary
taxation. Yet its vast wealth was very unequally distributed. The junior
clergy felt increasingly resentful at the wealth of their ecclesiastical superiors in the years before the Revolution and despaired about their own
poverty. So a gap opened up between the junior clergy and their ecclesiastical seniors. Indeed, it was from the junior clergy in particular that
support for Church reform was to come at the beginning of the Revolution.[47] Even so, just as in England, there were countervailing trends,
including improvements in clerical education, episcopal efforts to reinvigorate dioceses, and a rise in Easter confessions and communions. Indeed, it
was even possible to describe the eighteenth century as something of a
'Golden Age' for the French Church, contrary to the popular stereotype of
widespread corruption and anticlericalism. Nevertheless, as McManners
somewhat histrionically puts it, 'this was the mellow autumn season
adorning the landscape with rich colours before the leaves began to fall
and winter came'.[48]

The Revolution in France amounted to something much more fundamental than an interruption in the settled pattern of French religious life.
It was an epoch-making event, which forced reform on the Church,
catastrophically attenuated its ministry for a time, and inscribed a permanent division for ever in French society between the Church and
Republicanism. Elsewhere in Europe, its effects were no less traumatic,
if less immediate. Established churches felt the shock of populist, radical
criticism. Religious Dissenters—especially in Britain—allied themselves
with political radicals. At stake was not only the nature of the relationship
between Church and State, but also the very character of society as it was
widely seen in *ancien régime* Europe. The problem that F. D. Maurice and
his Anglican contemporaries inherited, then, was one of startling and
fundamental significance, going to the heart of the received vision of
social life. It can be put at its sharpest in the following way. Could
Christianity serve any longer as the very fabric of values, relationships,
and commitments that sustained social life in Western Europe? Could
society, in turn, survive without the State sponsoring and supporting the
Church? Visions of human well-being radically different from those articulated by the established churches were being offered by the revolutionary

---

[46] Details here and in following paragraphs are from McManners, *French Revolution*.

[47] McManners describes this as a form of bourgeois resentment at aristocratic clergy:
Church and Society in Eighteenth-Century France, i: *The Clerical Establishment and its Social
Ramifications* (Oxford: Clarendon Press, 1998), 3.

[48] Ibid.

movements of the early nineteenth century. Their fulfilment depended on the utter transformation, if not the destruction, of the traditional churches. Radical political sympathies often ran hand in hand with religious faith, and many radicals were inspired by Christianity.[49] But for others the French Revolution symbolized human potential freed from religious faith altogether. This was indeed a crisis of authority for the Church.

THE CRISIS PROLONGED

With the triumph of reaction and the return of political stability to Europe in 1815, the prospects might have looked fair for what remained of the historic churches. But the genie could not be put back into the bottle. The revolutionary and Napoleonic wars had unleashed powerful political forces in Europe that made lasting religious settlement impossible. Growing democratic movements, nationalism, liberalism, and the early forms of socialism all raised difficult questions for the churches. Recurrent political crises, fuelled by social distress, marked the first half of the nineteenth century, culminating in 1848, the year of revolutions. This proved a period of decisive change for the Papacy, for example, which was forced progressively to abandon its territorial jurisdictions in Italy and which, under Pius IX, countered the dangers of nationalism and liberalism by a vigorous 'ultramontane' reassertion of its spiritual authority.[50] Catholic reaction was assisted by the emergence of a clutch of Catholic writers and theologians, many of them French, who strove to define anew the place of the Papacy in the modern, post-revolutionary world. Men such as De Maistre, Chateaubriand, Bonald, and Lamennais were, for all their differences, a sort of counterpart to the Anglican 'reaction', the Oxford Movement, with which F. D. Maurice was to show some limited sympathy.[51]

---

[49] One famous example was William Blake, who was strongly influenced by the 'subterranean', antinomian stream of English radical thought issuing from the Civil War and later transmitted through marginal religious groups such as the Muggletonians and Swedenborgians; see E. P. Thompson, *Witness against the Beast: William Blake and the Moral Law* (Cambridge: Cambridge University Press, 1993).

[50] See J. D. Holmes, *The Triumph of the Holy See: A Short History of the Papacy in the Nineteenth Century* (London: Burns & Oates, 1978), and F. J. Coppa, *The Modern Papacy since 1789* (London: Longman, 1998).

[51] Peter Nockles draws out some of these comparisons in ' "Church and King": Tractarian Politics Reappraised', in P. Vaiss (ed.), *From Oxford to the People: Reconsidering Newman and the Oxford Movement* (Leominster: Gracewing, 1996). See also A. R. Vidler, *Prophecy and Papacy: A Study of Lamennais, the Church, and the Revolution* (London: SCM, 1954); D. Klinck, *The French Counterrevolutionary Theorist, Louis de Bonald (1754–1840)* (New York: Lang, 1996);

At an imaginative level, the spectre of the French Revolution hung over British society throughout this period.[52] It was given powerful evocation in two popular works: Thomas Carlyle's *The French Revolution: A History*, which appeared in 1837, and Charles Dickens's *A Tale of Two Cities*, which was published in 1859 and drew directly on Carlyle's somewhat fictitious 'history'. Though it was based on a wide range of sources, Carlyle's eccentric prose and splendid imagination took wing, casting the events of 1789–96 in a lurid light. Here he is on the campaign of de-Christianization, for example: 'In all Towns and Townships as quick as the guillotine may go, so quick goes the axe and the wrench . . . . All highways jingle with metallic Priest-tackle, beaten broad . . . . Good Sainte Geneviève *Chasse* is let down: alas, to be burst open, this time, and burnt on the Place de Grève.'[53] The similarity of both Carlyle's and Dickens's visions to that of Burke is apparent. It sounded a cautionary note to an age that marked major steps towards parliamentary democracy. Something of that caution can be caught even in Tennyson's faith in social justice, fleetingly expressed in *In Memoriam*:

> And all is well, tho' faith and form
>   Be sunder'd in the night of fear;
> Well roars the storm to those that hear
>   A deeper voice across the storm
>
> Proclaiming social truth shall spread,
>   And justice, ev'n tho' thrice again
>   The red fool-fury of the Seine
> Should pile her barricades with dead.[54]

Another voice is that of Henry Wilson, contributor to the notorious Broad Church *Essays and Reviews* (1860), whose essay on 'the National Church' in that volume led to his arraignment before the Court of Arches for heresy. Wilson used the French Revolution as an instance of the way religion would naturally reappear if 'the human race, or a given people . . . were resolved into its elements, and all its social and religious institutions shattered to pieces'.[55] In Wilson and Tennyson, both alike in

---

R. A. Lebrun, *Throne and Altar: The Political and Religious Thought of Joseph de Maistre* (Ottawa: University of Ottawa Press, 1965).

[52] For a useful overview, see E. Royle, *Revolutionary Britannia? Reflections on the Threat of Revolution in Britain, 1789–1848* (Manchester: Manchester University Press, 2000).

[53] T. Carlyle, *The French Revolution: A History* (1837; London: Oxford University Press, 1907), ii. 355.

[54] A. Tennyson, *In Memoriam*, cxxvii, in J. D. Jump (ed.), *Alfred Tennyson: In Memoriam, Maud and Other Poems* (London: Dent, 1974), 148.

[55] H. B. Wilson, 'Séances historiques de Genève—the National Church', in B. Jowett *et al.*, *Essays and Reviews* (London: Parker, 1860), 170.

far from being reactionary apologists, we can catch a glimpse of the fear which revolution engendered in mid-Victorian Britain.

This fear was underscored by the persistence of outbreaks of mob violence and crowd action well into the late nineteenth century. At certain times, these could spring out of specific political grievances. Instances would be the Newport Rising of 1839, for example, or the Hyde Park riots in favour of reform of 1866.[56] Maurice's mother experienced an outbreak of local rioting in Southampton in 1830, under the 'Captain Swing' agitations, and wrote in graphic terms to her son about the threat.[57] And the largest and most ominous mass demonstration in London for a generation, the great Chartist demonstration on Kennington Common in April 1848, was a key event in Maurice's life, prompting Charles Kingsley to issue a placard urging restraint on workers which has commonly been taken as the start of the Christian Socialist movement. But such occasions were relatively rare, especially after the onset of mid-Victorian prosperity. Much more common were local outbreaks of violence, focused often around fairs (and their suppression), around the rupture of customary social relations, and around opposition to street preachers, temperance activists, and other middle-class critics of popular culture.[58] With local police forces either non-existent or, even towards the end of the century, small and thinly spread, it was difficult to contain a disturbance once it had begun. Victorian provincial life was surprisingly volatile.[59] There was a paradox about this violence. Threatening though it was, it was usually localized and contained, and reactive rather than progressive or revolutionary. Yet it was dangerous enough, and fuelled Victorian fears of the 'mob', and of the consequences of the breakdown of social order.

Against such a background, with the running awareness of poverty and despair in industrial Britain, and with the example of violent revolution on the continent at hand, it is no wonder that Victorian arguments about the role of the churches were closely bound up with arguments about order,

---

[56] See D. J. V. Jones, *The Last Rising: The Newport Chartist Insurrection of 1839* (Cardiff: University of Wales Press, 1999); J. Stevenson, *Popular Disturbances in England, 1700–1870* (London: Longman, 1979).

[57] Maurice, *Life*, i. 114–15.

[58] There are many local studies amplifying this picture; for general surveys, see Stevenson, *Popular Disturbances*; D. C. Richter, *Riotous Victorians* (London: Ohio University Press, 1981); on the customary background to community action, see R. W. Bushaway, *By Rite: Custom, Ceremony and Community in England 1700–1880* (London: Junction Books, 1982), and E. P. Thompson, *Customs in Common* (London: Merlin, 1991).

[59] One local illustration may suffice: twenty-two separate incidents of crowd disturbance have been identified in one metropolitan borough alone between 1865 and 1897: J. N. Morris, 'A Disappearing Crowd? Collective Action in Late Nineteenth-Century Croydon', *Southern History*, 11 (1989).

moral worth, and participation in political life. Behind the intense doctrinal controversies which fractured Victorian religious life lay profound anxieties about the status and security of religion and about social stability. This should not necessarily be seen in terms of simplistic arguments about religion as social control, a perspective fashionable for a time in the historiography of Victorian Britain.[60] To argue as much is to deny religious people genuine integrity and idealism, and to turn their beliefs into instruments for material ends. Nevertheless, the interests of social order were (and often are) served by religion, and there is a complex matrix of ideas and interests concerning the social body as a whole within which religious belief has to be located.[61]

To F. D. Maurice and his contemporaries Christian civilization teetered on the brink of collapse. It is all too easy, in retrospect, to see their fears as exaggerated. Historians now have come to see the mid-nineteenth century as a period of almost unprecedented Christianization in Britain, when Christians were more successful at building new churches and at filling them perhaps than at any time since the Middle Ages. The 'secularization' of British society in the nineteenth century can easily be overemphasized. Indeed, it may scarcely have happened at all.[62] Yet something decisive *was* happening to the political role and social status of religion, and this was to prove immensely significant for the future well-being of the mainstream churches. Christianity's pivotal place in the organization of British society, through a 'confessional' connection of Church and State, was threatened and then largely overthrown. Church men and women found themselves wondering what might be left of the national Church if the radical programme of reform were to find its way into the heart of government policy.

---

[60] The crudest instance is J. Hart, 'Religion as Social Control', in A. P. Donajgrodski (ed.), *Social Control in Nineteenth-Century Britain* (London: Croom Helm, 1977).

[61] For a subtle exploration of this matrix in terms of contemporary religion, see T. D. Jenkins, *Religion in Everyday English Life: An Ethnographic Approach* (Oxford: Berghahn, 1999).

[62] As Callum Brown has argued: see C. G. Brown, *The Death of Christian Britain* (Cambridge: Cambridge University Press, 2000).

1

The Demise of the Confessional State

THE CONFESSIONAL STATE

Maurice's decision to be baptized into the Church of England, and ultimately ordained into its ministry, was fraught with political implications. He was born into a religious tradition that did not enjoy legal toleration until he was 8 years old. It defined its very identity oppositionally, confronting what it took to be an oppressive State Church.[1] Dissenters were officially excluded from political office and from the ancient universities. They were subject to legal constraint, obliged to register their meeting-houses with a bishop or magistrate, and largely absent from the most privileged sections of society.[2] The church that Maurice joined as an adult, then, was not above political controversy, and his conversion was a political statement.

Historians disagree about the relevance of the term 'confessional State' to England at this time.[3] It should not be confused with the term 'confessional Church'. The Church of England did have its own doctrinal standards: namely, the Thirty-Nine Articles of Religion, the liturgy, the Ordinals, and the Homilies, though these last were not widely used by the early nineteenth century. But these were hardly a compact 'confessional' system of doctrine. The Articles especially aimed at preserving a certain comprehensiveness 'within the limits of a Christianity both Catholic and Reformed'.[4] Rather, the term 'confessional State' suggests an intrinsic link between Church and government. The reconstitution of the Church of England in the sixteenth century as a *national* Church had

---

[1] S. J. Brown, *The National Churches of England, Ireland and Scotland 1801–1846* (Oxford: Oxford University Press, 2001), 40–1.

[2] The incidence of these constraints had been substantially lightened, if not formally removed, over the years. See M. Watts, *The Dissenters, ii: The Expansion of Evangelical Nonconformity* (Oxford: Clarendon Press, 1995), 417–19.

[3] John Kent has recently denied its relevance to England, but his definition is an odd one—'one in which members of the state were automatically members of the Church, and vice versa'—which at a formal, constitutional level *would* seem to apply to the situation of England in the eighteenth century: J. H. S. Kent, *Wesley and the Wesleyans: Religion in Eighteenth-Century Britain* (Cambridge: Cambridge University Press, 2002), 3.

[4] O. O'Donovan, *On the 39 Articles: A Conversation with Tudor Christianity* (Oxford: Latimer House Publications, 1986), 12.

preserved the assumption that all English people, irrespective of their actual beliefs, were members of it. At the beginning of the nineteenth century, it was still the case that full inclusion within the body politic of England was possible only on the presumption that one could conform to the established Church.

The nature of the Church–State link had nevertheless changed over the centuries. The Elizabethan Act of Uniformity of 1559 had prescribed worship according to the *Book of Common Prayer* as the only permissible form in England, attaching penalties to failure to conform.[5] But the Civil War had led to the collapse of uniformity, in the face of widening Church divisions between 'Puritans' and moderates. The Restoration, with the 'great ejection' of some 2,000 Puritan clergy in 1662, finally forced Puritanism out of the Church of England.[6] The Toleration Act of 1689 recognized officially the existence of Dissent. Celebrated in the eighteenth century as an enlightened policy, toleration in practice was little more than a grudging concession to political necessity. By a series of measures, later labelled the 'Clarendon Code', the Restoration regime severely limited the capacity of Dissenters to hold public office.[7] The Tudor goal of uniformity had given way to a situation in which the legal and social hegemony of the Church of England was defended by discriminatory legislation. The English *ancien régime* preserved at its heart the assumption that the interests of Church and State were bound up together, but it had been forced to accept practically the beginning of religious pluralism.[8]

The arguments advanced by theologians for and against a particular pattern of Church–State relations had also changed over the centuries. Few in the sixteenth century publicly questioned the policy of religious uniformity. Rather, it was the content of uniformity that was controversial. Even Richard Hooker, the archetypal Anglican apologist for Establishment, actually devoted little space in his *Laws of Ecclesiastical Polity* to the principle of what was later called 'Establishment'. He assumed, with his medieval predecessors and with the Reformers, 'that church and commonwealth were two facets of a single entity . . . and that true religion was the foundation of the state'.[9] For Hooker and his opponents, 'pure and unstained religion ought to be the highest of all cares appertaining to

---

[5] G. R. Elton (ed.), *The Tudor Constitution*, 2nd edn. (Cambridge: Cambridge University Press, 1982), 410–13.

[6] On the ecclesiastical impact of the Restoration settlement, see J. Spurr, *The Restoration Church of England, 1646–1689* (New Haven and London: Yale University Press, 1991).

[7] Edited texts of the acts can be found in J. P. Kenyon (ed.), *The Stuart Constitution 1603–1688*, 2nd edn. (Cambridge: Cambridge University Press, 1986), 351–2, 356–9, 385–7.

[8] The situation in Scotland and Ireland was sufficiently different to merit consideration in its own right: see S. J. Brown, *National Churches*, 15–31.

[9] P. D. Avis, *Church, State and Establishment* (London: SPCK, 2001), 45–6.

public regiment'.[10] Only in the posthumously published, disputed eighth book of the *Laws* did Hooker examine explicitly the relationship of Church and State, and it is hard to dissociate this text's appearance finally in 1648 from the turmoil of civil war. Here lay 'the heart of Hooker's political philosophy', and it was one that assumed that there was no member of the English commonwealth 'who was not also a member of the Church of England'.[11]

Hooker's view remained dominant in the late seventeenth and eighteenth centuries, when, increasingly, the desirability of 'Establishment' (as it was now often called) was debated. A rival theory appeared in 1736 in William Warburton's *The Alliance of Church and State*.[12] Echoing Locke's contractualism, Warburton argued that Church and State were distinct if allied societies.[13] Actually, as R. W. Greaves observed, Warburton's theory presupposed more of a submission of Church to State than a strict alliance.[14] It had little influence directly on Anglican apologetic, and was avidly avoided by defenders of Establishment—Maurice included—in the next century. Its contractual arguments were to prove more popular with the radical opponents of Church and State than with most Anglican theorists.

This was clearer by the early nineteenth century, when arguments over the relationship of Church and State had become more polarized as a result of the French Revolution. Now, in the name of liberty of conscience, and with the example of France and the United States before them, critics of the Church of England questioned the need for any constitutional link at all. A more self-conscious strain of Anglican apologetic came into being. Following Burke, it was forced to defend the very principle of Establishment. Radical criticism of the confessional State engendered a sustained Anglican response, traceable in the 'classic' texts in defence of Establishment: Coleridge's *On the Constitution of the Church and State* (1830), Arnold's *Principles of Church Reform* (1833), Gladstone's *The State in its Relations with the Church* (1838), and Maurice's own *The Kingdom of Christ* (1838). Despite the idiosyncrasies of Maurice's work, his location within this new, self-conscious tradition was thoroughly 'of its age'.[15]

---

[10] R. Hooker, *The Laws of Ecclesiastical Polity*, ii, book 5.1 (London: Everyman, 1907), 12.

[11] P. Secor, *Richard Hooker, Prophet of Anglicanism* (Tunbridge Wells: Burns & Oates, 1999), 311.

[12] R. W. Greaves, 'The Working of the Alliance: A Comment on Warburton', in G. V. Bennett and J. D. Walsh (eds.), *Essays in Modern English Church History: In Memory of Norman Sykes* (London: A. & C. Black, 1966), 163–80; also S. Taylor, 'William Warburton and the Alliance of Church and State', *Journal of Ecclesiastical History*, 43 (1992), 271–86.

[13] Greaves, 'Working of the Alliance', 166.

[14] Ibid., 165.

[15] This is tacitly recognized in Alec Vidler's comparisons of Maurice and Gladstone on Church and State in A. R. Vidler, *The Orb and the Cross: A Normative Study in the Relations of Church and State with Reference to Gladstone's Early Writings* (London: SPCK, 1945), 31–2, 84–5.

We should be careful not to see this tradition of Establishment apologetic as automatically representative of a majority of Anglican opinion. Evangelicals were suspicious of the taint of 'worldliness' that Establishment could convey, and conscious also of convictions shared with Dissenting Evangelicals.[16] From the opposite end of the spectrum of Anglican opinion was to come the scepticism of Establishment, deepening into outright hostility in some cases, that marked the Oxford Movement.[17] Richard Hurrell Froude saw the effect of the legislative changes of 1828–32 on the Church of England as wholly regrettable. They had effaced 'in at least one branch of our Civil Legislature, that character which, according to our great Authorities, qualified it to be at the same time our Ecclesiastical Legislature'.[18] Defence of a modified Establishment became all but impossible for Froude, Keble, and Newman.[19]

Yet neither the Tractarian criticism of Establishment, nor the hankering of some 'Broad Churchmen' such as Thomas Arnold for an expanded (and ecclesiastically pluralist) national Church, for all their great influence, were to prove decisive for the Church of England's adaptation to the virtual collapse of the confessional State. Instead, what took place was a renewal of the Church from within, sponsored and supported at first by parliamentary legislation. Massive concessions to religious pluralism were made in the middle decades of the nineteenth century. Anglicans developed new arguments for the national role of the Church of England in the concept of 'comprehensiveness', which enabled a defence of the existing structure of the Church at the same time as proving flexible enough to accommodate internal division. Maurice's role in this shift was vital.

THE CRISIS FACING THE CHURCH OF ENGLAND

Why, though, did the need for a new kind of Anglican apologetic come about at all? As with the Catholic Church in France, the Church of

---

[16] On a pan-denominational 'Evangelical consensus' see, *inter alia*, M. A. Smith, *Religion in Industrial Society: Oldham and Saddleworth 1740–1865* (Oxford: Oxford University Press, 1994), 229–38. Smith expands here the observations of A. D. Gilbert, *Religion and Society in Industrial England: Church, Chapel and Social Change 1740–1914* (London: Longman, 1976), 51–3.

[17] On Tractarian views on Church and State, see P. B. Nockles, *The Oxford Movement in Context: Anglican High Churchmanship 1760–1857* (Cambridge: Cambridge University Press, 1994), 67–85.

[18] R. H. Froude, 'Remarks on State Interference in Matters Spiritual', in *Remains of the Late Reverend Richard Hurrell Froude*, Part 2 (London: Rivington, 1839), i. 185.

[19] It has even been argued that the Tractarians should be considered as political radicals: J. R. Griffin, 'John Keble, Radical', *Anglican Theological Review*, 59 (1971), and *idem*, 'The Radical Phase of the Oxford Movement', *Journal of Ecclesiastical History*, 27 (1976). This claim is dismissed at various points by Nockles, *Oxford Movement in Context*, including p. 78.

England was certainly vulnerable in the late eighteenth century.[20] There were massive disparities of income and wealth in the Church, with many clergy living in poverty. Private income and rising agricultural prosperity partly offset this, and there were significant, if limited, attempts to raise the incomes of the poorest clergy. But poverty reinforced the widespread practices of pluralism (the holding of two or more clerical offices simultaneously) and non-residence.[21] Diocesan organization and clerical discipline had become weak. Concerted efforts, from within the Church itself and from Parliament, were made in the early decades of the nineteenth century to remedy these defects, but their impact was limited, and they were to be engulfed by the constitutional crisis affecting Church and State alike at the end of the 1820s.[22] To these 'structural' weaknesses one could add the unpopularity of the tithe—the 'tax' due to clergy from the yield of agricultural land—and of the high proportion of clerical magistrates (as many as 40 per cent in some counties).[23] The Church appeared to many to be the weakest, most corrupt feature of the unreformed system of government. John Wade, a radical journalist, published a *Black Book* in 1820 that detailed the abuses of the Established Church, and sold over 14,000 copies. Described by E. P. Thompson as 'greatly superior to any other Radical investigation of the kind', the work nevertheless was factually inaccurate in many respects.[24] Yet its allegations resonated widely: an expanded version, the *Extraordinary Black Book*, published in 1831 at the height of agitation over reform, sold over 50,000 copies.[25]

---

[20] Amongst works devoted to the ecclesiastical crisis, the following are particularly important: O. J. Brose, *Church and Parliament: The Reshaping of the Church of England 1828–1860* (London: Oxford University Press, 1959); G. F. A. Best, *Temporal Pillars: Queen Anne's Bounty, the Ecclesiastical Commissioners and the Church of England* (Cambridge: Cambridge University Press, 1964); K. A. Thompson, *Bureaucracy and Church Reform: The Organizational Response of the Church of England to Social Change, 1800–1965* (Oxford: Clarendon Press, 1970); R. A. Burns, *The Diocesan Revival in the Church of England c.1800–1870* (Oxford: Oxford University Press, 1999); see also S. J. Brown, *National Churches*.

[21] The most detailed treatment of the condition of the Georgian Church of England to appear to date is in P. Virgin, *The Church in an Age of Negligence: Ecclesiastical Structure and Problems of Church Reform 1700–1840* (Cambridge: James Clarke, 1988); but this should be read in conjunction with the corrective offered by J. D. Walsh and S. Taylor, 'Introduction: The Church and Anglicanism in the "Long" Eighteenth Century', in J. D. Walsh, C. Haydon, and S. Taylor (eds.), *The Church of England c.1689–c.1833: From Toleration to Tractarianism* (Cambridge: Cambridge University Press, 1993), 1–64.

[22] See esp. Best, *Temporal Pillars*, 185–295, and Burns, *Diocesan Revival, passim*.

[23] On the tithe, see E. J. Evans, *The Contentious Tithe: The Tithe Problem and English Agriculture 1750–1850* (London: Routledge & Kegan Paul, 1976); on the clerical magistracy, S. J. Brown, *National Churches*, 10–11.

[24] E. P. Thompson, *Making of the English Working Class*, 846; S. J. Brown, *National Churches*, 170–1.

[25] S. J. Brown, *National Churches*, 171.

Wade's book, and radical literature like it, found a popular audience for a very simple reason: Dissent was expanding rapidly in the early nineteenth century. For reasons it is still difficult to analyse precisely, Dissenting churches were particularly adept at exploiting population increase, infused as they were by the growth of Evangelicalism and by the passing of Methodism outside the Church of England.[26] Wesleyan Methodist membership more than tripled between 1790 and 1815—quadrupled, if the breakaway Primitive Methodist connexion is included.[27] The older Dissenting traditions prospered, too, with the single exception of the Quakers, though membership numbers are hard to come by until the mid-nineteenth century.[28] Local patterns of Dissenting growth are complex.[29] In some places, Dissent (especially Methodism) flourished where Anglican church provision was strong, suggesting that Methodism in particular was a response to the perceived shortcomings of the Established Church. In other places, 'Old' Dissent—the Independents or Congregationalists, Presbyterians, Baptists, and Unitarians—thrived in the interstices between overstretched Anglican provision. Having languished at probably less than 10 per cent of the church-going population for most of the late seventeenth and eighteenth centuries, one estimate suggests that, for nearly 1,500 parishes in which a Dissenting presence could be traced in the late seventeenth century, by 1851 the proportion had risen to 60 per cent.[30] This growth was spectacular in the new industrial communities in particular. The religious settlement of England was unravelling, driven by the growth of religious pluralism.

Even so, the 'trigger' for constitutional change was a seemingly tangential one. It came from Ireland. Here, following savage repression of the rebellion of 1798, new urgency was given to attempts by the Anglican Established Church of Ireland to convert the Catholic population, through programmes of parish development and biblical education.[31] Yet the intended 'Second Reformation' of Ireland came to nothing. It merely intensified Catholic hostility to the Church of Ireland, a hostility exploited to the full by Daniel O'Connell and the Catholic Association in its campaign for the removal of Catholic disabilities. As David Hempton has written, 'Irish Protestantism . . . roused itself to vigorous activity at

---

[26] For a general account, see Watts, *Dissenters*, ii. 22–158.

[27] R. Currie, A. D. Gilbert, and L. Horsley, *Churches and Churchgoers: Patterns of Church Growth in the British Isles since 1700* (Oxford: Oxford University Press, 1977), 139–40.

[28] See the membership figures, ibid., 147–8.

[29] See in particular K. D. Snell and P. S. Ell, *Rival Jerusalems: The Geography of Victorian Religion* (Cambridge: Cambridge University Press, 2000), chs. 3, 'Old Dissent', and 4, 'The Geographies of New Dissent', pp. 93–172.

[30] Ibid. 265.

[31] See S. J. Brown, *National Churches*, 93–136.

precisely the time when Irish Catholics were no longer prepared to tolerate religious proselytism or ascendancy values.'[32] In the face of rising unrest, the government of the Duke of Wellington forced through Catholic Emancipation in 1829, with removal of the Test and Corporation Acts as a necessary prelude in 1828. These changes alone amounted to a significant modification of the prevailing relationship of Church and State. But worse was to come. They were the prelude, in effect, to a protracted constitutional struggle over parliamentary reform, in which the Church of England found itself under attack from Radicals and Dissenters. Its bishops' resistance to reform in the House of Lords identified it closely with a version of Establishment about to be overthrown for ever. At the height of the Reform crisis, severe rioting in October 1831 in Bristol led to the burning of the bishop's palace—an act of destruction that symbolized the imminent collapse of the Church of England.[33] John Wade warned the clergy that 'Your days are assuredly numbered; your lease is expired . . . A terrible storm is impending over the Church.'[34]

If the events of 1828–32 marked the end of one kind of political Anglicanism—the assumed, inherent superiority of a legally entrenched and privileged Church—its death was protracted and not conclusive. To the great surprise of many, the Church of England was to avoid the destruction feared in 1832 and to recover its vitality. It is surely significant that Maurice signalled his new-found Anglican identity almost at the point at which the threat to the Established Church was at its greatest. Yet the crisis in the Church, such as it was, was not rapidly resolved. If it signalled the end of the Anglican *ancien régime*, it was merely the beginning of a painful period of readjustment.

THE 'SECOND REFORMATION' OF THE CHURCH OF ENGLAND

Since Maurice was never a bishop or church statesman, little attention need be spent on the administrative reform of the Church of England. But an outline may be helpful at this point, if only to demonstrate the way in which the dramatic changes in the nature of Establishment impinged upon Maurice's work. Whilst the immediate crisis passed, criticism of Establishment continued at an unprecedented level of intensity. Anglicans could not but be aware of the persistent threat to their historic position of

[32] D. Hempton, *Religion and Political Culture in Britain and Ireland: From the Glorious Revolution to the Decline of Empire* (Cambridge: Cambridge University Press, 1996), 103.

[33] For other acts of hostility against the bishops, see S. J. Brown, *National Churches*, 175–6.

[34] Quoted, ibid. 176.

dominance. Despite the commonality of approach to religion exemplified in the success of Evangelical Anglicanism and Evangelical Dissent, the rise of Dissent only intensified sectarian competition. At the local level, this was concentrated particularly on education and church rates, but it included differences over culture and leisure, and especially drink.[35] Local communities became deeply divided, and in some places rival networks of Anglican and Dissenting businesses sprang up alongside church and chapel.[36] Alongside the national transformation of Church–State relationships ran a parallel transformation, under Nonconformist pressure, of the traditional relationship of the parish church to the local community.[37] In national politics too, the rise of Protestant Nonconformity as an electoral force presented a serious challenge to Anglican hegemony. By mid-century the Liberal Party was drawing much of its support from Nonconformity.[38] Militant Nonconformity had in view the disestablishment of the Church of England, pursued relentlessly, if ultimately with little success, by the Society for the Liberation of Religion from State Patronage and Control (or 'the Liberation Society'), founded by the Congregationalist anti-Establishment agitator Edward Miall in 1850.[39]

Militant Dissent—later to be labelled by its critics 'Political Nonconformity'[40]—was to enjoy a string of legislative victories in the late nineteenth century, including the final abolition of compulsory church rates in 1868, disestablishment of the Church of Ireland in 1869, and the creation of the basis of a national system of elementary education outside the control of the Church in 1870. These achievements, significantly carried by Gladstone's first great parliamentary majority (a majority dependent on Nonconformist support), removed some of the most obvious weaknesses or most objectionable features of the Anglican Establishment. But they had the corresponding—if paradoxical—effect of weakening arguments for the disestablishment of the Church of England itself.

---

[35] These local conflicts are explored acutely in W. R. Ward, *Religion and Society in England, 1790–1850* (London: Batsford, 1972).

[36] An interesting example is explored in B. H. Harrison and B. Trinder, *Drink and Sobriety in an Early Victorian County Town: Banbury 1730–1860*, English Historical Review Special Supplement, 4 (1969); further examples are in P. T. Phillips, *The Sectarian Spirit: Sectarianism, Society and Politics in Victorian Cotton Towns* (Toronto: University of Toronto Press, 1982).

[37] See, e.g., J. N. Morris, *Religion and Urban Change: Croydon, 1840–1914* (Woodbridge: Boydell, 1992), 105–27.

[38] See J. Vincent, *The Formation of the Liberal Party, 1857–1868* (London: Constable, 1966).

[39] D. M. Thompson, 'The Liberation Society 1844–1868', in P. Hollis (ed.), *Pressure from Without in Early Victorian England* (London: Edward Arnold, 1974), 210–36.

[40] See, e.g., the Congregationalist minister R. W. Dale's strictures in 1892, and an anonymous attack on 'Political Nonconformity' in 1909, both cited in D. M. Thompson (ed.), *Nonconformity in the Nineteenth Century* (London: Routledge & Kegan Paul, 1972), 236–7, 269–70.

By then the internal reform of the Church of England had proceeded apace. Here the most significant development by far was the establishment of a permanent Ecclesiastical Commission.[41] A succession of parliamentary acts in the 1830s and 1840s—the outcome of the Commission's programme to purge the Church of England of its worst abuses and to revitalize its organization—led to the gradual elimination of pluralism and non-residence, the augmentation of poor livings, the creation of new dioceses, and the reduction and reform of cathedral chapters.[42] Though fraught with political and theological controversy, the work of the Commission effectively transformed the national organization of the Church of England. Far from collapsing under the strain of internal corruption and external hostility, the Church of England had discovered a new vitality. It had undergone something like a 'Second Reformation', its most thorough-going reorganization since its 'First Reformation' of the sixteenth century. In succeeding decades, a national system of representative church government, including (eventually) lay representation came into being.[43] The Church's energy was apparent in the massive programme of church building under way across the country, financed mostly by local means and under the aegis of diocesan church building societies. Over 2,500 new Anglican churches were built in England and Wales between 1841 and 1875 alone.[44]

What is evident with hindsight was not evident to Maurice's contemporaries. The impact of administrative reform and renewed organizational energy were masked by the ferocity of Dissenting criticism and by the internal divisions of mid-Victorian Anglicanism. Change was, in any case, gradual, and always contested. If the Church of England had, by the 1840s, survived constitutional unsettlement, still its future was by no means assured. All through the mid-Victorian years, the impression of crisis persisted, despite the actual evidence of local growth.[45] 'Crisis' is a remarkably imprecise word, of course, and almost anything that challenged some or other element of the Anglican Establishment could reinforce the

---

[41] On this, Best, *Temporal Pillars*, remains the outstanding account.

[42] See ibid., 296–347 and also, more briefly, S. J. Brown, *National Churches*, 198–208.

[43] On the development of representative government in the Church of England, see again Burns, *Diocesan Revival*, 216–59; also M. J. D. Roberts, 'The Role of the Laity in the Church of England c.1850–1885' (D.Phil. thesis, Oxford University, 1974), and G. Byrne, 'Consulting the Faithful: The Role of the Laity in the Government of the Church of England 1861–1904' (M.Phil. thesis, Cambridge University, 1998).

[44] Gilbert, *Religion and Society*, 130.

[45] Hence the great difficulty historians have had in reaching a consensus on the strength and influence of Victorian Anglicanism: for a pessimistic assessment, see P. T. Marsh, *The Victorian Church in Decline: Archbishop Tait and the Church of England, 1868–1882* (London: Routledge & Kegan Paul, 1969).

sense that it was embattled. Radical criticism of its corruption and inefficiency in the 1820s and 1830s thus shaded almost imperceptibly into
criticism of its party divisions and of the theological unorthodoxy of
some of its members by the 1850s and 1860s. Maurice himself was to be
tainted by this means, even though his life's work was a defence of
Christian orthodoxy. The fragile confidence of the mid-Victorian Church
took a severe knock with the publication of the results of the 1851 national
religious census, which were claimed by some to demonstrate not only
that only 58 per cent of the population regularly attended church, but that
Anglicanism did not represent the majority of church-goers.[46] Thereafter,
no one could rely on arguments of numerical superiority.

Deeper issues were at stake anyway than those of ecclesiastical polity. If
the nineteenth century was in fact to prove remarkably religious—as
argued by a host of recent commentators[47]—nevertheless, the authority
of Christianity could no longer be taken for granted. Everywhere in
Europe it was open to challenge.

MAURICE AND THE TRANSFORMATION OF ANGLICANISM

The position of the Church of England in which Maurice died in 1872 was
thus very different from that into which he had been baptized in 1831. It
was a leaner, more dynamic, and certainly more efficient organization. Its
very survival no longer looked precarious. The provision of new churches
and church schools, the development of new evangelistic and pastoral
agencies, the reform of clerical discipline, the foundation of theological
colleges, and the development of a network of representative institutions
were all signs of the intensity with which the Church of England was
struggling to reassert its historic position of pre-eminence. Yet, for all that,
its survival had to be contended for, and its case made. Victorian Anglicanism, for all its energy, was the product not so much of one spasm of
reform, as of a running argument about the nature of a national Church.

To that argument, Maurice's contribution was formidable. His defence
of the Church of England, developed in the chilly years of the 1830s, was to
offer an attractive combination of breadth and distinctiveness to later
generations. Its distinctiveness was rooted in a description of intrinsic
features of the universal Church that could be traced in the Church of

[46] The best modern introduction to the census, and assessment of its results, is Snell and
Ell, *Rival Jerusalems*; see also, for a brief overview, B. I. Coleman, *The Church of England in the
Mid-Nineteenth Century: A Social Geography* (London: Historical Association, 1980).
[47] Above all see C. G. Brown, *Death of Christian Britain*.

England itself, reasserting the Church of England's catholicity and apostolicity no less forcefully than the Tractarians. Maurice produced an ecclesiology for Anglicans that preserved and valued historic continuities, and so defended its claim to be the Catholic Church *in* England. Yet its breadth was signalled in its ability to hold compatible what appeared to be competing doctrinal systems. The diversity of mid-nineteenth-century Anglicanism was transcended, in Maurice's view, by the fullness of the Church on which no one party had a purchase. Of course, the construction of a comprehensive ecclesiology for modern Anglicanism was not the achievement of one theoretician alone. Maurice shared and reflected the preoccupations of many of his contemporaries just as much as he moulded them. His work was often controversial, and he died something of an isolated and neglected figure. Yet his convictions touched influential voices of his own day, and generations after him.

Nor was his significance restricted to defence of the Church of England. The difficulties his church faced were symptomatic of the wider difficulties of Christianity in Europe. What Maurice proposed for Anglicanism could be applied—with some modification—to other churches too. Indeed, his attempt to find a constructive path through the apparently destructive implications of modern biblical criticism, and his emphasis on the social vocation of the Church, proved immensely attractive to many outside Anglicanism. Whilst pre-eminently a theologian of the Anglican way, he was also a figure of influence in non-Anglican Protestantism and Roman Catholicism.

Reading Maurice contextually requires attention to the period in which his views were formed, and this means the late 1820s through to the early 1840s. At the centre of his work in this period was a consideration of the role and nature of the Church. And this was—far from coincidentally—the period of greatest threat to the Church of England. From then on, the view of the Church which Maurice had reached by his late thirties remained largely unchanged to the end of his life. He continued to write on church matters from time to time, but the scope of his work expanded to include major themes of systematic theology—the nature of revelation, the justification of Trinitarian belief, the social character of redemption, amongst others. But he was always sensitive to currents of religious opinion, and the changing scope of his work paralleled the new challenges to theological orthodoxy that Christians were obliged to face as the century wore on. His work can and should be read in terms of a literary career spanning almost half a century, but to understand its character and shape, it is necessary first of all to understand its formation.

2

The Emergence of the Maurician Synthesis: A Coleridgean in Theology

For one who was to exert such a powerful influence on late Victorian Anglicanism, Maurice's background was surprisingly antithetic to the Church of England. The word 'conversion' inevitably springs to mind as a description of his move from Unitarianism to the Church of England, but can suggest too neat and transparent a process. He left no autobiographical account to match other famous conversions, such as the one Newman provided in his *Apologia Pro Vita Sua* (1864). The evidence of how he changed, and when and why, is incomplete. His intellectual formation was complex, given the range of views to which he was exposed. Unlike many converts, he continued to profess debts to the religious tradition he had left, even as he strongly criticized it. At the risk of minimizing the complexity of this story, it is possible to trace the outlines at least of a coherent interpretation of his development.

THE UNITARIAN BACKGROUND

Maurice's birth was into a household remote in almost every sense from the causes and places with which he was to be preoccupied for most of his life. The Suffolk coast was poor, and distant from London. His father, Michael Maurice, had been disinherited for his Unitarian views as a student at the Hoxton Dissenting Academy.[1] After a short time back at Hoxton as co-pastor to the most influential Unitarian of his generation, Joseph Priestley, Michael Maurice took up a small Dissenting congregation near Bungay in Suffolk in 1795, not long after Priestley had left Britain for America in disgust at the political reaction after the French Revolution. He supplemented his meagre stipend by taking in pupils, later moving to Normanstone, near Lowestoft.[2] The impression the sources convey is of a cautious, modest, but highly principled man. Seven years after John Frederick Denison was born on 29 August 1805, the fourth of six children,

---

[1] Young, *Maurice and Unitarianism*, 63.   [2] Ibid. 68.

the family moved to Frenchay, near Bristol, as their father feared his children 'having wrong views of their real situation, for their relatives of connection moved in higher stations than they were likely to fill'.[3] Michael Maurice was evidently aware of the limited possibilities open to the children of a Unitarian minister.

The Unitarian religious tradition was far from monochrome. There was little formal organization to bind the various congregations together. A number of different streams fed into what later became known as *the* Unitarian church, including certain of the Presbyterian congregations of England in the eighteenth century, the Old Connexion of General Baptists, and the Methodist Unitarians.[4] Since the basis on which these congregations existed was resistance to credal definition, it is almost impossible to describe common beliefs. Unitarians differed widely in religious conviction, from the materialism and extreme anti-Trinitarianism of Priestley himself, to the Arianism of the politically controversial Richard Price, and even to moderate Trinitarian belief. What they did hold in common were a suspicion of orthodox dogma, a valuing of religious freedom, and a strong conviction of the virtue of political and social reform. One of their most eminent twentieth-century historians was perhaps exaggerating only a little when he claimed that civil and religious liberty 'has always been one of the watchwords of Unitarians' and that it was 'natural that they should take the lead in all movements for religious freedom'.[5]

Despite their diversity, historians have been impressed by Unitarians' common debt to Enlightenment rationalism, and by their appeal to the educated. Described by Donald Davie as an 'enlightened intellectual minority', their strongest support lay amongst the middle class in the cities, including Manchester, Birmingham, Norwich, and London.[6] Recent accounts have stressed their debt to John Locke's materialist epistemology and to David Hartley's psychological determinism, but in this they have been unduly influenced by the prominence of Priestley and his intellectual successors.[7] Certainly Michael Maurice, despite his education at Hoxton Academy, did not share the sectarian stridency (as his son came to see it) represented by Thomas Belsham, the most prominent inheritor of

---

[3] Michael Maurice to Thomas Sanders, 14 Oct. 1824, cited ibid. 71.

[4] R. K. Webb, 'Quakers and Unitarians', in D. G. Paz (ed.), *Nineteenth-Century English Religious Traditions: Retrospect and Prospect* (Westport, Conn.: Greenwood Press, 1995), 105.

[5] R. V. Holt, *The Unitarian Contribution to Social Progress in England*, new edn. (London: The Lindsey Press, 1952), 17.

[6] D. Davie, *Essays in Dissent: Church, Chapel and the Unitarian Conspiracy* (Manchester: Carcanet, 1995), 55.

[7] Cf. K. Gleadle, *The Early English Feminists: Radical Unitarians and the Emergence of the Women's Rights Movement, 1831–51* (Basingstoke: St Martin's Press, 1995), and R. Watts, *Gender, Power and the Unitarians in England 1760–1860* (London: Longman, 1998).

Priestley's mantle. His attitude was influenced by the older strain of Presbyterianism rather than by the 'later Unitarian dogmatists'.[8] His theological position even in the 1790s was Arian.[9] Later in life he moved even further towards an orthodox position.[10] As Frederick himself was to remember, he baptized in the Trinitarian name, without necessarily endorsing formally the doctrine of the Trinity.[11]

It is difficult to discern what impact Michael Maurice's views had on his son's mature thought. Writing to his own son later in life, F. D. Maurice emphasized his father's reverence for the Bible, which he traced to the old 'Puritan' roots of Dissent.[12] He also pointed to the Unitarian desire for unity as a running theme of his own work.[13] Some scholars have tried to trace other themes of Maurice's theology to the permanent impress of Unitarianism, including the Fatherhood of God, a certain eschatological universalism, and criticism of penal substitutionary theories of atonement.[14] But if this has some plausibility, it also faces considerable difficulties. Maurice may have retained 'a deep thankfulness' for his Unitarian upbringing, but he was also sharply critical of it.[15] He could endorse the criticisms Gladstone made of Unitarianism in 1847, applying to it the Emperor Julian's observation on Christianity: 'I read, I understood, I condemned.'[16] He could write of Unitarians often plunging 'into a Pantheistic abyss'.[17] Simply because Unitarians endorsed principles also to be found in the work of the mature Maurice, it does not follow either that they were exclusively Unitarian or that Maurice could not have adopted them from other sources. The theme of the Fatherhood of God, for example, sits just as persuasively alongside Maurice's interest in Alexandrian Christology as it does his Unitarian heritage.[18]

---

[8]   Maurice, *Life*, i. 7.

[9]   D. Young, 'Rev. Michael Maurice, 1766–1855', *Transactions of the Unitarian Historical Society,* 19 (1989), 154. Young here is drawing on a letter from Priestley to Maurice, dated 25 Aug. 1792.

[10]   Ibid. 161.

[11]   Maurice, *Life*, i. 122: this did leave him open to the objection of Robert Hall that he must think he baptized in the name of 'an abstraction, a man and a metaphor': ibid. 123. On the avoidance of religious controversy, see ibid. 19.

[12]   Ibid. 19.

[13]   Ibid. 41; cf. also ibid. ii. 351; and also F. D. Maurice, *The Kingdom of Christ*, 2nd edn. (London: Rivington, 1842), i. 138–40.

[14]   Young, *Maurice and Unitarianism*, 195–273; Wigmore-Beddoes, *Yesterday's Radicals*, 90 f.

[15]   Young, *Maurice and Unitarianism*, 273.

[16]   Maurice, *Life*, i. 440.

[17]   Ibid. ii. 351.

[18]   Cf. P. Widdicombe, *The Fatherhood of God from Origen to Athanasius* (Oxford: Clarendon Press, 1994).

The connections may be plausible if uncertain theologically, but they are surely relevant politically. As we have seen, Unitarianism was instinctively in sympathy with political radicalism. Maurice's teenage idols were the radical politicians Henry Brougham, Francis Burdett, and Joseph Hume.[19] Later he distanced himself from radicalism, disavowing in particular the utilitarianism of Jeremy Bentham and James Mill. But it is hard to escape the conclusion that, growing up in full awareness of the struggle for constitutional reform gathering pace around him, he acquired an instinctive sympathy with popular movements that never disappeared altogether, surfacing in *The Kingdom of Christ* in his conviction that they represent something of the 'desire for catholicity', and later in his understanding of Christian Socialism.[20] His early religious reading included Daniel Neal's *History of the Puritans*.[21] At the age of 10, he was reading Edmund Calamy's *Abridgement of Baxter's History*, the great Dissenting account of the Puritan divines ejected from their livings in 1662 after the Restoration.[22] A certain emotional affinity with the Dissenting tradition remained with him, informing his sympathies with non-Anglican believers.

Maurice himself also ascribed significance to his family's abandonment of the Unitarian beliefs of his father. Opening up painful divisions within the family, first his sisters and then his mother began to embrace orthodox evangelical Christianity when Maurice was about 9 years old. The precise narrative of this change is complex.[23] By September 1821, when Maurice was 16, his mother had decided that she could no longer attend her husband's services or worship with him.[24] She and her daughters passed into Calvinism of various degrees, as did Maurice himself temporarily round about the same time.[25] By this means, a new set of influences was brought to bear on him, including the millennial theories of J. A. Stephenson, Anglican rector of Lympsham, with whom Maurice was later to live and serve for a time, and Thomas Erskine of Linlathen, the lay theologian of the Church of Scotland, whose *Brazen Serpent* (1831) was later to exert a profound influence on Maurice.[26] Erskine's influence was eventually to undermine Maurice's Calvinism, persuading him that God could not have

[19] Maurice, *Life*, i. 39.

[20] Maurice, *Kingdom of Christ*, 'Philosophical Movements' and 'Political Movements', i. 169–235.

[21] Maurice, *Life*, i. 19.

[22] Ibid. 37.

[23] Ibid. 11, 22, 25, 28; also F. M. McClain, *Maurice, Man and Moralist* (London: SPCK, 1972), 13–20.

[24] Maurice, *Life*, i. 42.

[25] Ibid. 43.

[26] Ibid. 28, 43, 108.

'destined' humanity to misery.[27] This was a view consonant with Maurice's later assurance that theology must start with love, and not sin. The bitterness of family division evidently underlined his later desire for unity.[28]

But his Calvinist period, in any event, cannot have lasted long. By 1823, he was expressing a desire to study at Cambridge, a decision his son was to describe as so unusual amongst his family's acquaintances that it made them suspicious.[29] It was a mark of the gulf opening up between Maurice and his father, for whom the Anglican dominance of Cambridge (reinforced by subscription to the Thirty-Nine Articles of Religion before graduating) had made attendance impossible.[30] Nevertheless, Cambridge could at least permit in theory greater latitude of belief than could Oxford, where subscription was required on matriculation—that is, before study even began. Perhaps the religious divisions in Maurice's family encouraged him to seek escape from the bitterness involved. By this time he had already begun to read widely in English literature, including the work of Coleridge.[31] At Cambridge, where Maurice began to study as a student of Trinity College in October 1823, Coleridge's influence amongst the circle of undergraduates with whom Maurice was to become friendly was paramount.[32] Maurice was one of the earliest members of the Cambridge Conversazione Society, or 'The Apostles', and described by many as its leading spirit.[33] Amongst its members, Coleridge himself was an invisible but omnipresent figure.[34] The shift in Maurice's views towards Coleridge was to represent the first of two vital stages in his theological evolution. The second was his decision to embrace the Church of England. These two changes were to take him a long way from his Unitarian inheritance.

EARLY WRITING

Whilst still an undergraduate, having transferred from Trinity College to Trinity Hall in 1825 to read law, Maurice began to write for the *Metropolitan Quarterly Magazine*, a Cambridge venture edited by Maurice himself and a friend.[35] For the next three and a half years, literary activity dominated his life. He moved to London in the summer of 1826 to begin working for the Bar, returning briefly to achieve a First Class degree

---

[27] Maurice, *Life*, i. 43.   [28] Ibid. ii. 351.   [29] Ibid. i. 49.   [30] Ibid. 175.
[31] 'I had read Coleridge before I came up': ibid. 176.   [32] Ibid. 45.   [33] Ibid. 56.
[34] Cf. P. Allen, *The Cambridge Apostles: The Early Years* (Cambridge: Cambridge University Press, 1978), 56–76; also W. C. Lubenow, *The Cambridge Apostles, 1820–1914: Liberalism, Imagination, and Friendship in British Intellectual and Professional Life* (Cambridge: Cambridge University Press, 1998).
[35] Maurice, *Life*, i. 61.

in Civil Law, but refusing the subscription that would enable him to take his degree; at this stage his religious views had not decisively settled on the Church of England.[36] In London, however, his time was occupied chiefly with writing for, and then editing, the *Athenaeum* and the *London Literary Chronicle*. In these years Cambridge friends such as John Sterling and Julius Hare brought him into contact with the London literary scene, though he was always somewhat shy.[37] This was very much a progressive milieu. He was involved in a debating society formed by J. S. Mill and J. A. Roebuck, both of them to become linchpins of mid-Victorian progressive opinion. Indeed, to Mill, the advent of 'the Coleridgians, in the persons of Maurice and Sterling' in 1828 was the saving of the society, as 'a second Liberal and even Radical party, on totally different grounds from Benthamism and vehemently opposed to it'.[38]

The articles Maurice produced in these years provide the first clear indication of the intellectual change he underwent in his movement from Unitarianism to the Church of England. They reflected two main areas of interest: the literary culture of the day (especially the impact of the English Romantic writers) and political controversy. Mill's identification of the 'Coleridgean' Maurice as 'Liberal and even Radical', though somewhat anachronistic (since 'Liberal' was rarely used in this sense in the 1820s), neatly captures the spirit of Maurice's journalism, with its antagonism to utilitarianism and materialism, its appeal to spiritual principles, and yet its espousal of progressive causes. But there is, all the same, a discernible shift in tone and scope from 1825 to 1829. The articles for the *Metropolitan Quarterly Magazine* include gossipy, jejune comment on literary rivals. A series of articles called 'The Age of Folly' poked fun at the utilitarians and their ilk.[39] 'The New School of Cockneyism' extended this attack to *Blackwood's Magazine*, whilst paying backhanded compliments to the 'old school' of Hazlitt and Leigh Hunt.[40] These articles echoed the political language of the age, highlighting the 'Jacobinism' of these writers in a way that suggested some sympathy with it.[41] A review (not certainly by Maurice) of Mignet's *Histoire de la Révolution Française* could commend the Revolution as 'a mighty drama', with its subject 'the struggle between feudalism and equality of rights'.[42] Maurice himself contributed two articles to the progressive *Westminster Review* in 1827–8, signalling again where his political sympathies lay.[43] But the articles written for the

---

[36] Ibid. 71.   [37] Ibid. 76.   [38] Mill, *Autobiography*, 77.

[39] F. D. Maurice, 'The Age of Folly', *Metropolitan Quarterly Magazine*, nos. 1–4 (1825–6).

[40] Maurice, 'The New School of Cockneyism', ibid. nos. 1 and 3.

[41] Cf. ibid., no. 1, p. 35.   [42] ibid., no. 2, p. 411.

[43] F. D. Maurice, 'Montgomery's "Pelican Island" ', *Westminster Review*, 8 (1827), and 'Theobald Wolf Tone's Memoirs', ibid., 9 (1828).

Athenaeum in 1828–9 reflect a different spirit. They comprise a series of separate essays on leading literary figures, and point to support for liberal causes. But the ironic, rather flippant comments on the contemporary literary world have largely gone. At the same time the articles exemplify a growing metaphysical leaven, as if—approaching his mid-twenties—Maurice began to place his literary and political enthusiasms in a new religious and philosophical context.

Many of the enthusiasms one might expect of a sympathizer with the growing tide of popular reformism are there. Maurice continued to welcome the 'shattering of thrones, the convulsions of governments, the earthquake shocks of universal opinion' that marked the end of the previous century.[44] He criticized the reactionary views of Robert Southey, though in a spirit the mature Maurice could hardly have endorsed: 'He is, indeed, a mournful example of the ruin which may be wrought upon the fairest minds, by attaching an universal feeling to particular institutions, and by professing to find all truth in the creed of one establishment'.[45] He commended Henry Brougham's 'unvarying and admirable' opposition to Catholic disabilities, but criticized his approach to parliamentary reform as relying too much on the aristocracy and not enough on the people.[46]

Yet other emphases are apparent too. There was, surpisingly, little criticism of Wordsworth, who is praised for his willingness to discern in ordinary human beings 'that true catholic faith in our nature'. The poet, Maurice claimed, teaches us to search for that on which human beings agree: namely, the source of universal harmony in all who 'are in communion with the divine nature'—a significant first use by him of the term 'communion'.[47] Even in his piece on Southey, the breadth of the poet's sense of fraternal sympathy is approved: 'this feeling of brotherhood with all mankind . . . teaches him to see in God an essential love breathing into all men a capacity for higher than earthly things'.[48] Great writers are symptoms of 'mighty principles of moral advancement' that 'live eternally in the hearts of the people'.[49] Coleridge's influence is marked. Reviewing Julius and Augustus Hare's *Guesses at Truth*, for example, he observes that they are 'profound admirers of Mr. Coleridge; in which last respect . . . we

---

[44] F. D. Maurice, 'Sketches of Contemporary Authors, no. 1', *The Athenaeum*, 16 Jan. 1828.

[45] F. D. Maurice, 'Sketches of Contemporary Authors, no. 3. Mr Southey', ibid., 29 Jan. 1828.

[46] F. D. Maurice, 'Sketches of Contemporary Authors, no. 7. Mr Brougham', ibid., 29 Feb. 1828.

[47] F. D. Maurice, 'Sketches of Contemporary Authors, no. 5. Mr Wordsworth', ibid., 19 Feb. 1828.

[48] Maurice, 'Southey'.

[49] Maurice, 'Sketches, no. 1'.

avow ourselves of their opinion'.[50] Even as the Anglican settlement began its period of acute instability, without seeming to abandon altogether the reformist views of the Establishment's critics, Maurice's own political and religious inclinations were beginning to turn in the same direction as those of his mentor Coleridge.

THE INFLUENCE OF COLERIDGE

When and where did Maurice come under the spell of Coleridge? He claimed, as we have seen, to have 'read Coleridge' before going up to Cambridge in 1823. Certainly his reading would have included Coleridge's poetry, but what else? He later claimed to have defended Coleridge's metaphysics in a debating society at Cambridge that presumably was 'the Apostles'.[51] It is unlikely that he had read the *Aids to Reflection* before this discussion, as it was published only in 1825. Possibly he had read the *Biographia Literaria* (1817), the periodical *The Friend* (1809), or *The Statesman's Manual* (1818). By the late 1830s, he had read not only these works, but also the *Aids* and *On the Constitution of the Church and State* (1830), as all were mentioned in the second edition of *The Kingdom of Christ* (1842).[52] But the general effect of his study at Cambridge cannot be ignored too. Here, he encountered Julius Hare as one of his tutors. Hare also exercised a profound and directly personal influence on Maurice, partly through his close teaching of the text of Plato's *Gorgias*.[53] Maurice was to be regarded as a Platonist, and the extent to which that designation was appropriate is a question to which we shall have to return. But Hare was also an enthusiastic follower of Coleridge, and his reading of the Platonic tradition was unquestionably mediated through Coleridge. He attended some of Coleridge's London lectures in 1817–18, acted as a supplier of German books to Coleridge, and by the early 1820s was attending Coleridge's Thursday soirées at Dr Gilman's house in Highgate.[54] Moreover, the general milieu of Cambridge, too, was one much more receptive to the philosophical interests of Coleridge, Hare, and others than was Oxford.

Accordingly, it is impossible to do anything other than shadow Maurice's own suggestion that, by the time he was an undergraduate at

---

[50] F. D. Maurice, 'Review of A. and J. C. Hare's, *Guesses at Truth*', *The Athenaeum*, 13 Aug. 1828.

[51] Maurice, *Life*, i. 178.

[52] Maurice, *Kingdom of Christ*, vol. i, pp. xi–xviii.

[53] Maurice, *Life*, i. 54.

[54] N. M. Distad, *Guessing at Truth: The Life of Julius Charles Hare*, (Shepherdstown, W. Va.: Patmos Press, 1979), 39.

Cambridge, he was already in some sense a Coleridgean. Apart from brief references in letters in his son's biographical memoir, two main sources can flesh out the lines of influence. One is the specific references made in his published works to his reading of Coleridge. The most important of these are the dedication to the second edition of *The Kingdom of Christ* (1842), some five pages on Coleridge in his *Moral and Metaphysical Philosophy*, Part iv: *Modern Philosophy* (1862), and Maurice's anonymous introduction to Julius Hare's posthumously published *Charges* (1856).[55] The other is a series of five unpublished letters written by Maurice to Coleridge's daughter Sara in 1843.[56]

Of these, the clearest by far is the 'Dedication' to *The Kingdom of Christ*, addressed to Coleridge's son Derwent.[57] It is a description of the insights Maurice had drawn from Coleridge's works, prompted by critics' views that the first edition had demonstrated the pervasive influence of Coleridge.[58] From the *Friend*, he drew the conclusion that inquiry into the nature of society was necessarily incomplete and provisional, and that this was tantamount to a methodological principle of liberty, freeing him to search for truth and insight in the works of those who differed greatly from Coleridge himself.[59] From the *Aids to Reflection* he drew the distinction between fixed, eternal truth and 'that which is factitious and accidental'—that is between the truth of the reason, and the truths of the understanding.[60] And from *On the Constitution of the Church and State*, he took the principle of 'the opposition and necessary harmony of Law and Religion', which formed the basis of his own theory of the relation between Church and State in *The Kingdom of Christ*.[61]

At the risk of truncating or oversimplifying the pattern of influence, three main areas can be identified. First, Coleridge pointed to a renewed metaphysical approach to religion that located the apprehension of religious truth in the universal experience of humankind, rather than in the

---

[55] The relevant pages in the *Moral and Metaphysical Philosophy*, ii (1862; new edn., London: Macmillan, 2 vols., 1873) are ii. 668–72.

[56] Frank McClain used this correspondence extensively in 'Maurice and Sara Coleridge: Baptism and Human Nature', *Anglican Theological Review*, 54 (1972). The letters themselves are kept at King's College, London.

[57] Derwent was by then Principal of St Mark's Training College for teachers in Chelsea, to which Samuel Clark—friend and correspondent of Maurice—subsequently went as Vice-Principal: Samuel Clark, *Memorials from Journals and Letters*, ed. E. J. H. Clark (London: Macmillan 1878), p. x.

[58] A careful reading of the relevant passage in the 'Dedication' suggests that Maurice himself found it difficult to deny the claim, without going on, as he does, to specify debts and areas of disagreement: Maurice, *Kingdom of Christ*, vol. i, p. xi.

[59] Ibid., pp. xiii–xvii.

[60] Ibid., pp. xvii–xx.

[61] Ibid., pp. xx–xxi.

deductive power of the individual consciousness. This depended on an assumption of a unity of knowledge and moral excellence, 'latent', as Fenton Hort was to put it, 'throughout Coleridge's philosophy'.[62] In turn, it illuminated the ontological hierarchy of creation: the visible world 'was most thoroughly substantial to him, *because* he believed it to be sustained by an unseen world'.[63] Material reality, then, could not be understood correctly as an aggregation of individual entities, but as a symbolic, sacramental system. In the first 'Lay Sermon' in *The Statesman's Manual*, Coleridge famously characterized the role of the symbol as 'the translucence of the eternal through and in the temporal', and added that it 'always partakes of the reality which it renders intelligible'.[64] No human creed or formula could completely capture the truth of faith. Religious language, then, for Coleridge could not achieve analytical precision: rather, in the significant phrase of John Coulson, it realized intuition according to a 'fiduciary use'.[65] This ontological transfiguration of language and symbol was entirely characteristic of Maurice's mature work. By implication, for Maurice and Coleridge alike, the supposition of significant elements of political radicalism, including utilitarianism, that social life could be satisfactorily reordered according to a rational, human blueprint was morally and spiritually deficient.

Second, Coleridge, like Maurice after him, accused the dominant empirical tradition in English philosophy—the tradition of Locke and Hume—of contracting 'reason' to the point where it became merely a calculating faculty. Conceiving of the mind in this way was itself symptomatic of the atomizing individualism that Coleridge saw as typical of the utilitarians, and he included the leading Anglican apologist of his day, William Paley, in this.[66] Instead, he reached back through the Enlightenment to resuscitate the view of 'reason' held by the Cambridge Platonists of the seventeenth century—including Ralph Cudworth and Henry More—and by Robert Leighton, the Scottish archbishop. In doing so, he adopted the distinction between 'reason' and 'understanding' traceable

[62] F. J. A. Hort, 'Coleridge', in *Cambridge Essays* (London: Parker, 1856), 324.

[63] Ibid. 334.

[64] Quoted in J. R. Barth, *Coleridge and Christian Doctrine*, new edn. (New York: Fordham University Press, 1987), 23.

[65] J. Coulson, *Newman and the Common Tradition: A Study in the Language of Church and Society* (Oxford: Clarendon Press, 1970), 26. Stephen Prickett's criticism of Coulson's interpretation of Coleridge does not affect this observation: S. Prickett, *Romanticism and Religion: The Tradition of Coleridge and Wordsworth in the Victorian Church* (Cambridge: Cambridge University Press, 1976), 10.

[66] D. Hedley, *Samuel Taylor Coleridge's* Aids to Reflection: *A Romantic Philosophy of Religion* (Cambridge: Cambridge University Press, 2000), 156–8.

through Kant back to ancient philosophy.[67] *Aids to Reflection* is the text in which this is developed decisively.[68] It is the understanding that, for Coleridge, corresponds to Enlightenment 'reason', as a faculty for organizing sense impression. If that alone is taken to be the summit of human capability, it leads to 'a shallow humanism that sees the good life as attainable through prudence and self-sufficiency'.[69] 'Reason', by contrast, for Coleridge was, in effect, a spiritual capacity, reflecting the indwelling image of God, and therefore a conclusion from the Christian doctrine of creation. He quoted with approval Henry More: '[The] light within me, that is, my Reason and Conscience, does assure me that the Ancient and Apostolic Faith . . . is solid and true.'[70] For Coleridge, faith subsisted in the synthesis of reason and the individual will, a conception that reunited the Catholic idea of faith as intellectual assent to divine revelation and the post-Reformation Protestant tendency to see faith as an act of will.[71] Once again, the unity of knowledge and moral value is striking. For Coleridge, '[t]he renewal of the human will is seen as the heart of genuine wisdom'.[72] The high estimate in which Coleridge, like Hare and Maurice after him, held Martin Luther is explicable in the light of this conception of faith.[73]

Maurice again largely followed Coleridge's concepts of reason, understanding, and faith, though in his hands the terminology was somewhat different. He distinguished the apprehension of theological truth from the construction of human 'systems' of thought that, based on 'opinion' or 'notions' alone (truths of the understanding), can only distort the reality they claim to represent. Coleridge himself used the term 'notions' in precisely the same sense.[74] Some caution has to be exercised here, since the pejorative use of the word 'system' to denote the speculative

---

[67] Barth points out that in Plato the distinction runs between *nous* and *dianoia*; in Aquinas it has become that between *ratio* and *intellectus*: J. R. Barth, *Coleridge*, 17.

[68] Cf. Hedley, *Coleridge's Aids*, 258–60.

[69] Ibid. 9.

[70] S. T. Coleridge, *Aids to Reflection*, new edn. (New York: Chelsea Publishing House, 1983), 94–5.

[71] J. R. Barth, *Coleridge*, 30, 32.

[72] Hedley, *Coleridge's Aids*, 15.

[73] Cf. L. O. Frappell, 'Coleridge and the "Coleridgeans" on Luther', *Journal of Religious History*, 7 (1973): for Coleridge, 'Luther's heroism lay in his readiness to employ all his faculties, of reason, emotion and imagination, in an integrated search for the truth': ibid. 315. Cf. also J. I. Lethaby, ' "A Less Perfect Reflection": Perceptions of Luther in the Nineteenth-Century Church of England' (Ph.D. thesis, Cambridge University, 2001); and J. N. Morris, 'Reconstructing the Reformation: F. D. Maurice, Luther, and Justification', in R. N. Swanson (ed.), *The Church Retrospective*, Studies in Church History, 33 (Woodbridge: Boydell, 1997).

[74] 'Notions of the Understanding that have been generalized from *Conceptions*; which conceptions again, are themselves generalized from objects of sense': Coleridge, *Aids to Reflection*, cited in Hedley, *Coleridge's Aids*, 195.

construction of simplified theological *schemata* unrelated to the complexity of faith was common enough.[75] Nevertheless, the debt to Coleridge on this point is inescapable. It gave Maurice an epistemological principle with a double edge. It enabled him, on the one hand, to articulate a position in which a theology of participation in God, undoubtedly reached in part through a reading of the Greek Fathers, was combined with a philosophy of mind which described how spiritual knowledge, or knowledge of 'man' as 'spiritual being', or of 'man as man', was possible.[76] But it also enabled him to synthesize other theological positions, through the examination of the process of systematization whereby genuine spiritual and theological insight, through the perversity of the human mind, could be simplified, unbalanced, and distorted in the practice of religion. This is ultimately the source of the plasticity of Maurice's historical explanations: he aimed to encompass the production of genuine insight with its embedding in accretions of human error.[77] To do this, he used a dialectical methodology, accompanied at times by a dialogical form. His characteristic intellectual milieu was not systematic exposition as such, but an exploratory pattern of argument, in which contrasting positions were probed again and again to discover their hidden presuppositions; truth was pursued spirally. His concern was to identify the point at which theology overreached itself, so that the exposure of its limitations opened up the prospect of other perceptions or other dimensions of truth. This had serious implications for the charge that Maurice encouraged a systematic *theory* of 'comprehensiveness', as we shall see later.

Finally, there is a much more specific area of influence: namely, the theory which Coleridge adumbrated in *On the Constitution of the Church and State* (1830). This will be examined in greater detail in Chapter 4. But Maurice was at pains to point out, even as he acknowledged how closely he followed Coleridge on this, that Coleridge himself had not worked out a systematic ecclesiology. Coleridge never explicitly addressed the question of the Church itself as a universal society, or, as Maurice puts it, 'the

---

[75] Newman, for example, also used 'system' sometimes in this way: see, e.g., 'Faith and Obedience', in *Parochial and Plain Sermons* (1836; new edn., London: Longman, 1891), iii. 96: 'I wish from my heart that [people] could be persuaded to read Scripture with their own eyes, and take it in a plain and natural way, instead of perplexing themselves with their human systems.'

[76] The phrase 'man as man', frequently used by Maurice, may again have a Coleridgean antecedent: Richard Holmes cites notes for lectures Coleridge delivered at the Surrey Institution in 1812/13 in which it appears to function in precisely the same way as in Maurice: Holmes, *Coleridge: Darker Reflections* (London: HarperCollins, 1998), 320.

[77] On the influence of this method of argument on Coleridge, Shelley, Wordsworth, and Maurice, see D. Newsome, *Two Classes of Men: Platonism and English Romantic Thought* (London: Murray, 1974).

question whether there be a Universal Society for man as man'.[78] Touching on specific issues such as baptism, the eucharist, the orders of ministry, and the Scriptures, Maurice recognized significant divergence from what he took to be Coleridge's own views.[79] Now Coleridge's essay was no more than a sketch, or outline of a theory of Church–State relations, drawing on his conception of the ends of both. At work in it was his notion of an idea, as 'that conception of a thing, which is not abstracted from any particular state, form, or mode, in which the thing may happen to exist at this or that time; nor yet generalized from any number or succession of such forms or modes; but which is given by the knowledge of its *ultimate aim*'.[80] For Maurice, adapting Coleridge's view, the Church, founded on the relationship of God with his creatures, functioned as a teleological principle, that was inseparable from history and yet identifiable within it.

Yet, as already implied, Maurice could not have derived his ecclesiology as such from Coleridge. This is surely the explanation of the otherwise puzzling contrary accounts he gave. On the one hand, as we have seen, there is direct evidence of extensive influence. Maurice's basic philosophy, including his ontological assumptions, his epistemology, and his understanding of human capacities, was profoundly indebted to Coleridge. Possibly the influence was so pervasive that the mature Maurice took it for granted. On the other hand, he did also deny influence, and this seems to have encompassed principally Coleridge's theology.[81] He also came to the view that Coleridge had too little regard for facts.[82] Even here, there are grounds for some disquiet. The unpublished correspondence with Sara Coleridge in 1843 mostly reinforces the position I have outlined: namely, a positive philosophical influence, a more muted response from Maurice theologically, but it does contain a number of hints that a more specifically theological influence was indeed at work.[83] Moreover, some recent

---

[78] Maurice, *Kingdom of Christ*, vol. i, p. xxiii.   [79] Ibid., pp. xxviii–xxix.

[80] S. T. Coleridge, *On the Constitution of the Church and State*, new edn. (London: Everyman, 1972), 4.

[81] Distad claims a letter of Maurice's written in 1855 to an unknown correspondent denies the theological influence of Coleridge: Distad, *Guessing at Truth*, 39. This letter is now in the University of Kansas Library, and does not at all support Distad's construction of it. What it does signal is Maurice's admission that he had not read Coleridge's *Confessions of an Enquiring Spirit* for many years, and recalled that though an 'important counteraction' to some current views on inspiration, it was 'not an adequate explanation of the subject': Special Collection MS P21D:1. I am grateful to the staff of the University of Kansas Library for copying this letter to me.

[82] 'Coleridge belonged to another generation than ours—one of which the business was to indicate the preciousness of truths as distinct from facts': Maurice, in a letter to Edmund Strachey, c.1838; cf. Maurice, *Life*, i. 251.

[83] For example, Maurice seemed to acknowledge with approval that Coleridge suggested that sacraments were 'the transcendental language, bringing out truths full orbed of which in our [notions?] & systems we can but exhibit one side': F. D. Maurice to Sara Coleridge, 1 Mar. 1844: King's College London College Archives, ref. GB 0100 KCLCA K/PP83.

work on Coleridge has tended to reassert his theological orthodoxy, and above all the Trinitarian character of his work.[84] Maurice himself—as a letter to his friend R. C. Trench in 1834 demonstrated—was well aware of this: 'The day before his death Coleridge spoke . . . of the Trinity, ending with, "Remember, that is the foundation of all my philosophy" '.[85]

Drawing these threads together, it is possible to trace a picture of Maurice's development that at least fits the facts as we have them. By his early twenties, Maurice had already come under the literary influence of Coleridge. He was known as a 'Coleridgean', and that identity was reinforced by his study at Cambridge, his growing friendship with Julius Hare, John Sterling, and other 'Coleridgeans', and his sympathy with Platonism. Under these combined influences, Maurice became a liberal or progressive literary Romantic, participating actively in London literary society, and mixing with those of similar political sympathies. But his trajectory was one taking him in the late 1820s ever closer to orthodox Anglicanism. Here the influence of Coleridge continued, but much reduced. In Maurice's own mind, it seems, the fixing of his basic intellectual understanding was such that it enabled him to free himself from the attribution of a strong theological and even personal debt. His literary and theological activity in his mature years was, strikingly, *not* to be dominated by preoccupation with Coleridge. He came to see himself in quite other terms than that of a 'Coleridgean'. Instead, what came decisively to the fore were the theology, the liturgical inheritance, and indeed the life of the Church of England. In this time of intense ecclesial conflict, Coleridge may have provided a working methodology, but the application and development of it were very much the results of Maurice's conversion.

EUSTACE CONWAY

The most startling document that illustrates the shift in Maurice's views in the late 1820s is his one novel, *Eustace Conway* (1834), written between 1828 and 1830. Few scholars have paid much attention to it, but it is vital evidence of Maurice's conversion. Writing it was, as one scholar has recognized, a major instrument in helping Maurice to clarify his views.[86] It was begun in late 1828, at a time when Maurice was struggling

---

[84] '[The] speculative or philosophical doctrine of the Trinity is the central idea, or better the hidden agenda, in *Aids to Reflection*': Hedley, *Coleridge's Aids*, 8.

[85] Quoted by C. R. Sanders, *Coleridge and the Broad Church Movement* (Durham, NC: Duke University Press, 1942), 192.

[86] C. Want, 'Frederick Denison Maurice and *Eustace Conway*', *Anglican Theological Review*, 54 (1972), 331.

financially through the failure of the *Athenaeum*, and through his uncertainty over his future career and views.[87] He finally abandoned literary work and left London in 1829 to nurse his dying sister Emma and concentrate on the novel.[88] In the course of this year, his resolution to seek ordination in the Church of England began to take shape. The draft of the novel was finished after he had begun a second spell at university, this time at Oxford, where he went in December.[89]

Eustace Conway is a somewhat stylized and overdramatized novel of ideas. It is littered with a 'bewildering and sometimes deadening' number of subplots, and the sheer complexity of the novel makes it at once hard to summarize neatly and yet easy to discount largely for the purposes of the analysis here.[90] But the main outline of the book is straightforward enough. It traces its eponymous hero's intellectual development, from political radicalism and sympathy with the utilitarians, through outright atheism (and an unspecified experiment in crime) to a mystical religious and philosophical position that Maurice calls 'Spiritualism', and then on to orthodox Christian belief at the end of the book. Three figures—the first two of them villains—personify contrasting positions: Marmaduke Humbold, philosophical utilitarianism; an emigré German, Kreutzner, transcendental mysticism, or 'Spiritualism'; and finally Wilmot, Anglican orthodoxy.

Maurice's aim appears to be to 'test' ideas or values adopted by various characters in the novel through examining their consequences in particular, imagined situations. For almost one-third of the novel, the central theme is Eustace Conway's determination to adopt a position of consistent political radicalism. Conway's favourite reading at this stage is James Mill's *Essay on Government*, with its 'immediate application to the present state of things'.[91] Yet, filled with self-disgust at being taken in by a selfish woman on whom he had a crush, his Benthamism is overcome by 'impulses of a deeper mood'.[92]

A similar pattern of enthusiasm followed by disappointment dominates the second volume, with Conway following Kreutzner's assertion that God has his chosen engine 'in our wills, finds his choicest service in our freedom, and exerts his mightiest power in drawing our souls into accordance with the harmony which breathes through this, and his innumerable other worlds'.[93] Conway abandons his recent atheism through it, but in turn has to abandon Kreutzner's position, as he realizes the futility of its excessive optimism. The whole of the third volume, apart from the continuation of the convoluted action of the plot, is devoted to the further

---

[87] Maurice, *Life*, i. 90.   [88] Ibid. 98–9.   [89] Ibid. 104.

[90] Want, 'Maurice and *Eustace Conway*', 334.

[91] F. D. Maurice, *Eustace Conway; or, the Brother and Sister* (London: Bentley, 1834), i. 85.

[92] Ibid. 228.   [93] Ibid. ii. 172.

transition Conway must make from the Spiritualism of Kreutzner to full Christian orthodoxy. Wilmot criticizes Kreutzner's creed for its exclusive attention to the cultivation of human faculties, and so its failure to acknowledge the limitation of human capacity: 'There is a self-sufficiency, an impertinence in these appeals to experience, which I cannot away with. They profess to prove every thing, and in reality prove nothing.'[94] Wilmot urges on Conway belief, not in orthodox doctrines, but in a living God, 'the God of Revelation'.[95] And Wilmot proceeds to explain how he himself encountered this God in the Bible, where he found that 'man is indeed dealt with as man'.[96] The Bible shows the law which connects human beings to God: 'I had discovered that the relation between me and my Maker, in virtue of which alone I was a man, had been severed. I saw, and when I reflected upon its nature, felt, that I had lost my capacity for the relation.'[97] At the end of the novel, as the narrator indicates, Eustace has realized what he has been resisting, and has finally begun to embrace orthodox Christian belief:

Some men think it an act of great moral daring, to proclaim their doubts, whether an Aristocracy is not mischievous, and a Church establishment abominable. Eustace Conway endured many a fierce conflict, before he could find courage to acknowledge that either was necessary. . . . He had run the gauntlet of opinions— he had acknowledged Society as God, with the Utilitarians—he had acknowledged Self as God with the Spiritualists—he now confessed that He is God whose praise is in the Churches.[98]

What is telling about this novel is its twofold relationship to Maurice's conversion. At points obviously autobiographical, it schematizes elements of Maurice's own passage from radicalism through to Anglican orthodoxy. But we should note that it does this through engaging points of view that Maurice himself did not ever hold—utilitarianism, atheism, and 'Spiritualism'.[99] It is as if Maurice was testing alternate philosophical and political standpoints through the medium of their imagined impact on real people, and finding them wanting. The main lines of his metaphysical philosophy were, as we have seen, laid down *before* he began the novel, through his education at Cambridge and his absorption of the influence of Coleridge.[100] Thus, the real point of the novel was not to display his own progress from within, but rather to explore and confirm the theological position to which he was already tending. And this reinforces the second

---

[94] F. D. Maurice, *Eustace Conway; or, the Brother and Sister* (London: Bentley, 1834), iii. p. 55.

[95] Ibid. 106.   [96] Ibid. 112.   [97] Ibid. 115.   [98] Ibid. 270–2.

[99] Significantly, this is a trajectory much closer to that of Coleridge than of Maurice himself.

[100] This is a point overlooked by Want, 'Maurice and *Eustace Conway*'.

aspect of its relationship to Maurice's conversion. The real significance of
the novel lies, then, in the historical context of its writing—the fact that
Maurice could contemplate embracing Anglican orthodoxy precisely at
the time when the Church of England's weakness was most exposed to
public criticism.

MAURICE AND PLATONISM

At this point, it is necessary to consider briefly whether or not the end
result of this process of intellectual development was to mark Maurice as a
Platonist, as sometimes alleged. The sharpest modern exponent of this
view was Torben Christensen, who described Maurice as a Platonist who
subsumed Christian doctrine under a rigid metaphysical framework.[101]
Christensen claimed that, for Maurice, 'the truth of an idea establishes the
historical validity of its outward embodiment'.[102] Christensen's critique,
implying that Maurice reinterpreted the data of Revelation and assimilated
it to a pre-existent ontological hierarchy, or spiritual 'order' in creation,
echoed some of Maurice's most strident nineteenth-century critics, foremost amongst whom were James Rigg and Robert Candlish.[103]

Yet this perspective is intrinsically unpersuasive, when account is taken
of Maurice's preoccupation with divine action in history.[104] Platonism of
the kind that Christensen considered Maurice to represent could not
attribute final significance to the events of history, but only to its underlying principles. On this view, material reality is a cipher. By contrast, to
Maurice the events of history were precious and unique as the field within
which God was at work. God's action in history was an extension, or a
continuation, of his creative power. His providence in history was con-
tinuous: 'The acts of God are the true commentaries on his Word. For he
is with us to interpret both.'[105] History itself was a key to understanding
God's purposes. It was an anticipation of that which is to come, albeit an
imperfect one. Maurice claimed to have learnt from his reading of Joseph

---

[101] T. Christensen, *The Divine Order: A Study of F. D. Maurice's Theology* (Leiden: Brill, 1973).

[102] Ibid. 157.

[103] J. H. Rigg, *Modern Anglican Theology* (London: Heylin, 1857); R. S. Candlish, *Examination of Mr. Maurice's Theological Essays* (London: Nisbet, 1854).

[104] A. M. Allchin's riposte, reviewing Christensen's book when it first appeared in English,
remains pertinent: 'There is also the question . . . of the strongly historical and biographical
nature of much of Maurice's writing. This . . . seems scarcely compatible with the work of
one who does not take history seriously': A. M. Allchin, 'F. D. Maurice as Theologian',
Theology, 76 (1973), 517.

[105] F. D. Maurice, *The Gospel of the Kingdom of Heaven* (1864; new edn., Macmillan, London:
1893), 368.

Butler 'to look upon the future world not as generically unlike the present, but as the unfolding and developing of that which is imperfect and seminal here'.[106]

Maurice's basic understanding of history in this respect did not depart significantly from the doctrine of many of the early Christian writers. Like Augustine, for example, he retained a semblance of Platonic ontology, which was nevertheless relativized by his determination to follow the biblical account of the economy of salvation. Whilst it is true that he had recourse to the idea of a 'divine order' underlying the temporal order, and that he saw this as instantiated in certain key forms of human organization, at the same time he never absolutized particular moments, aspects, or events in history outside the economy of salvation. Moreover, as we shall see later in his treatment of Revelation, even the events of sacred history were more than mere archetypes: they were effective as events *in* history. Just as for Augustine, then, so for Maurice there were, by implication, two different kinds of historical event: those subsumed under the economy of salvation, and narrated in the Scriptures, and those 'outside' it. Yet *all* historical events had their place in God's providence, and indicated its nature. His theology of communion, a theme central to his mature theology, also reflected this position, and here he was surely right to draw on Augustine's account of his conversion to support his argument that, despite the constraints of history, what was given to the believer in faith transcended those limits.[107]

Maurice did tend to emphasize the language of ecstatic possession in faith, so that the communion of human beings with God was described sometimes in terms which could be taken to reduce or minimize the impact of fallen humanity and its subjection to the conditions of temporality, and so in turn the hubris of human complacency. He also tended to oversimplify the operation of providence in history, especially given his schematic attention to the significance of family and nation as basic forms of human organization. This was especially the case in his treatment of national identity, as we shall see in Chapter 4. Yet, paradoxically, he downplayed the role of God's special providence in history outside the events of the economy of salvation. This is clear again and again from his treatment of miracles. Even when he accepted entirely the historicity of reported miracles, as in the biblical accounts, he emphasized their continuity with nature, rather than any exceptional, interruptive character. One example will have to suffice here. Discussing the earthquake in Acts 16

---

[106] Maurice, *The Word 'Eternal' and the Punishment of the Wicked: A Letter to the Rev. Dr. Jelf Canon of Christ Church and Principal of King's College* (Cambridge: Macmillan, 1853) 18.

[107] Maurice, *What is Revelation?*, (London: Macmillan, 1859), 137–8.

which freed Paul and Silas from gaol, Maurice effectively assimilated the
miracle to the moral interpretation of all earthquakes, at the same time
as acknowledging divine action in it: 'I think the earthquake was
appointed by God, as every earthquake is appointed by God. . . . I delight
to believe . . . that because it proceeds from God there are moral
purposes in it, and in every earthquake.'[108]

There were also, certainly, important elements of an ontological structure in Maurice's theology as a whole that would support the designation
'Platonist'. His multi-layered view of reality, his sense of material things as
inherently sacramental, his language of 'divine order', his assumption that
certain forms of social organization were the outworking of that divine
order, and his constant recourse to the idea that the eternal world was
'manifested' in various ways in the created world, all pointed towards this
conclusion. Yet his deployment of these concepts was not systematized in
the way Christensen has suggested. Moreover, there were important signs
of positive dissent from Plato's doctrines, and from the doctrines of later
Platonism, throughout Maurice's work.[109] Above all, his metaphysical
framework was always at the service of the biblical narrative of creation
and redemption. Like Augustine before him, Maurice's account of divine
providence in history was a markedly personal one, driven by a conception
of God as creator *ex nihilo* (unlike the myth of creation described in the
Timaeus) and by a profound conviction of God as personal being. This
basic revision of Platonic ontology alone, in its reference to the outworking of God's providence through historical events, determined that
Maurice's understanding of history could not be explicated chiefly in
terms of static, immutable 'Forms' in the mind of God.

The complexity of this question is further illustrated by Maurice's
conception of language, a subject that merits a chapter in its own right
but which can be noted here only in passing.[110] Maurice shared with
others eventually described as Broad Churchmen a conviction that philology was a kindred discipline to theology. They saw literature itself as

---

[108] Maurice, *The Acts of the Apostles: A Course of Sermons* (London: Macmillan, 1894), 263.

[109] A few examples of Maurice's revision of commonly held 'Platonic' positions: his
rejection of the notion of the inferiority and discardability of material things, in *The Kingdom
of Christ*, 1st edn., (London: Darton & Clark, 1838), iii. 22; his criticism of the 'earthly demons'
of Neoplatonism in *Prophets and Kings of the Old Testament* (1853; 3rd edn., London: Macmillan, 1871), 324; and perhaps most significantly his denial that Plato's doctrine of the immortality of the human soul, as laid out in the *Phaedo*, can be identified with the 'eternal life' of the
New Testament, in 'Dr. Lushington, Mr. Heath, and the Thirty-Nine Articles', *Macmillan's
Magazine*, 5 (1862), 154.

[110] But see, for a fuller account, J. N. Morris, 'The Text as Sacrament: Victorian Broad
Church Philology', in R. N. Swanson (ed.), *The Church and the Book*, Studies in Church
History, 38 (Woodbridge: Boydell, 2004).

sacred and inspired work, with the Bible as its apex.[111] Through the study of language, the product of a God-given capacity for communication, human beings could discern something of the depth, the ontological relatedness, of God's creation. Maurice's friend Richard Trench, a pioneer of philological study, asserted that language was a 'witness for great moral truths', since God himself had imprinted the seal of truth on it, so that men are 'continually uttering deeper things than they know'.[112] For Maurice, words had a 'living, germinating power', a view shared of course with (and influenced by) Coleridge.[113] Close analysis of a word such as 'right' could uncover a hierarchy of meaning that disclosed an implicit ordering of value in the world, from 'right' as opposed to 'left' to 'right' as opposed to 'wrong'.[114] Yet, again with Coleridge and with Trench, Arnold, Hare, and others, this was not, for Maurice, an abstract conception of language. Rather, it presupposed that language itself was a product of history, and had to be analysed historically. Broad Churchmen accordingly made an original and important contribution to the development of the historical study of language in Britain.[115] Language, in essence, for Maurice and these writers, was sacramental. Careful study of it could penetrate the surface of material reality to apprehend the metaphysical structure of the world. Yet this was always, intrinsically, a historical task. It required attention to the dense texture of human history, with a readiness to grasp the complex, multi-layered nature of historical process. Here too, then, 'Platonism' was scarcely an adequate designation of Maurice's position, since his metaphysical convictions required precisely an understanding of the historical formation of human society that is absent from conventional views of what constitutes Platonism.

TOWARDS ANGLICAN ORTHODOXY

How and when did Maurice finally conform? Maurice was formally baptized into the Church of England on 29 March 1831, with Thomas Acland

---

[111] Compare Gladstone's conviction that Homer was a parallel, if inferior, 'revelation' to the Bible: H. C. G. Matthew, *Gladstone 1809–1874* (Oxford: Clarendon Press, 1986), 153.

[112] R. C. Trench, *On the Study of Words* (1851; new edn. London: Parker, 1855), 10.

[113] F. D. Maurice, 'On Words', in *The Friendship of Books* (London: Macmillan, 1893), 40. Though published posthumously in this volume, the lecture 'On Words' was actually delivered at Guy's Hospital *c.*1838.

[114] Ibid. 42–5.

[115] H. Aarsleff, *The Study of Language in England 1780–1860* (1967; new edn., Westport, Conn.: Greenwood Press, 1978), 191–2, 214–41. See also the work of another disciple of Maurice, the philologist F. W. Farrar, esp. *Chapters on Language* (London: Longman, 1865), and *The History of Interpretation* (London: Macmillan, 1886).

(High Churchman and friend of Gladstone) and William Jacobson (his tutor at Exeter College and later bishop of Chester) acting as the sponsors required by the Prayer Book.[116] This was not, officially, a *re*-baptism—at least, there are no signs that it was such. But the *Life* makes it clear that his father's practice as a Unitarian was to baptize in the Trinitarian name, and that Maurice's decision was therefore a painful one for him.[117] Maurice himself regarded his father's practice as reflecting 'a very sacred meaning'.[118] But it is difficult to avoid the conclusion that, despite all his later generous words towards Unitarians, at this stage of his life he saw baptism as a sharp dividing line between the Church and his Dissenting background. It followed that the position of Christian orthodoxy was one capable of definite, clear, and authoritative articulation. A later Presbyterian admirer of Maurice was to be scathing about the incident: if it was his father's imperfect faith that made his first baptism insufficient, 'was the rite only efficacious in the Church of England? But what was this but to fall into the worst error he [Maurice] attributed to Dr Pusey and the Tractarians?'[119]

Something of the Anglican orthodoxy Maurice was to embrace would have been imbibed in his formal education, through which he would have encountered some of the foundational texts of early nineteenth-century Anglican orthodoxy. At Cambridge, for example, he studied Paley's and Butler's works, albeit with the acknowledgement that these furnished 'the evidences of Christianity' and were thus a general introductory study rather than a means of indoctrination.[120] At Oxford, he became a member of Exeter College, and thus had to subscribe to the Thirty-Nine Articles in order to be matriculated.[121] There he would have had to demonstrate knowledge of Butler again, and of the Thirty-Nine Articles and the Gospels in Greek, as compulsory conditions of qualification for the BA.[122] Butler in particular remained an abiding interest, throughout his life.[123]

---

[116] Maurice, *Life*, i. 123.   [117] Ibid. 122.   [118] Ibid. 123.

[119] J. R. Tulloch, *Movements of Religious Thought in Britain during the Nineteenth Century* (1885; new edn., Leicester: Leicester University Press, 1971), 265.

[120] Maurice, *Life*, i. 48.

[121] Maurice's reasons for preferring Oxford to Cambridge are not specified in the *Life*; there was evidently strong encouragement from William Jacobson, but this has to be weighed against the attempt of Julius Hare to persuade him otherwise: ibid. 99–101. It is at least conceivable (but cannot be put more strongly than that) that Oxford's stronger reputation as a bastion of Anglican High Churchmanship drew him there.

[122] M. G. Brock and M. C. Curthoys (eds.), *The History of the University of Oxford*, vi: *Nineteenth-Century Oxford, Part 1* (Oxford: Clarendon Press, 1997), 10.

[123] The more substantial references are in Maurice, *Theological Essays* (Cambridge: Macmillan, 1853), 218–35; idem, *What is Revelation?*, 441–5; and idem, *Moral and Metaphysical Philosophy*, ii. 459–68.

The five years from Maurice's move to Oxford, where he eventually took a second-class degree in *Literis Humanioribus* in 1832, to his ordination as deacon in January 1834, were evidently of the utmost significance in forming Maurice's lasting ecclesial affiliation and, to an extent, his ecclesiological position. But his son's treatment of this period in the *Life* is far from satisfactory. Little is said there about his Oxford studies, apart from some general comments to the effect that he found the university's religious life somewhat 'barren'.[124] It is extremely difficult, then, to prove that it exercised any lasting influence on his intellectual formation. But there are a number of considerations that make this likely. First is the fact that the Thirty-Nine Articles came to occupy such a prominent place in his defence of Anglicanism; he subscribed to them on matriculation in December 1829, studied them as part of the mandatory theological element of the BA, subscribed to them again on ordination in 1834, and defended subscription in a pamphlet of 1835.[125] Second is the presumption that he would have known of Oxford's reputation as a bastion of High Church orthodoxy.[126] Third is scattered evidence of his theological interests and acquaintances, from hearing Keble and Newman preach, to discussing theological and other matters with Gladstone, Thomas Acland, and others.[127] Finally, there is the general consideration that, far from lingering in the torpidity which Newman himself claimed as typical of the university before Keble's clarion call in 1833, the 'Oxford Movement' to all intents and purposes had actually begun in 1829, with the hostile reaction of the university to Peel's enactment of Catholic Emancipation.[128] Put together, all these considerations point to a chronology of conformity in Maurice's case, and to his Oxford years as to an extent decisive in this, which cannot finally be established conclusively stage by stage.

Theological influences other than that of Coleridge had a role to play in Maurice's theological formation. One of these was the eschatological

---

[124] Maurice, *Life*, i. 103.

[125] F. D. Maurice, *Subscription no Bondage, or the Practical Advantages Afforded by the Thirty-Nine Articles as Guides in all the Branches of Academical Education* (Oxford: Parker, 1835).

[126] 'In religious questions Oxford stood not for discussion and free thought, but for unquestioning acceptance of the Church of England's doctrine'; Brock and Curthoys (eds.), *Nineteenth-Century Oxford*, 11. Brock points out that, in the early years of the nineteenth century, the university's regulations regarding conformity had actually been tightened up considerably.

[127] See, e.g., Maurice, *Life*, i. 108–9, 115, 118; later in life, Maurice wrote that he had heard sermons at the university church—presumably preached by its then vicar, Newman—which 'chilled my heart', but there is nothing in the *Life* from his Oxford period to support this: Maurice, *What is Revelation?*, 262.

[128] See esp. P. B. Nockles, ' "Lost Causes and . . . Impossible Loyalties": The Oxford Movement and the University', in Brock and Curthoys (eds.), *Nineteenth-Century Oxford*, 196–267, esp. 199–206.

theory of Joseph Adam Stephenson, Maurice's first incumbent, under whom he worked and studied at Lympsham in Somerset in 1833. Frank McClain has argued persuasively that Stephenson's influence on Maurice was just as significant as Maurice's on Stephenson, and that, in particular, Maurice learned from Stephenson to regard the kingdom of Christ as 'already and quite literally established'.[129] The emphasis Maurice came to place (for example, in *The Kingdom of Christ*) on an existing spiritual society, conceived as an existing kingdom with Christ as its head, accordingly was probably derived from a theological influence different in kind from that which he had encountered hitherto. Nevertheless, *pace* McClain, this should be seen as a natural development, rather than a radical break in Maurice's theology: though the idea of an existing kingdom was capable of millenarian application, as was the case for Stephenson himself, for Maurice it was placed in a firmly Augustinian framework, as referring to the revelation of the order to which history is tending, and to which the Church, in its mixture of human and divine elements, imperfectly conforms on earth.

Another influence was that of Thomas Erskine, the Scottish lay theologian, whose work Maurice first encountered through a friend of one of his cousins.[130] According to his son, the substantial contact, however, came through his Oxford friend, James Bruce (later earl of Elgin).[131] Erskine's *The Brazen Serpent* (1831) was to prove particularly fruitful for Maurice, with its criticism of the way in which the common religion of Scotland had turned the doctrines of atonement, justification by faith, and predestination into propositions in which belief was necessary, a form of 'religion of works'.[132] Erskine, much as Maurice was to do, criticized the covert atheism of such a view, contrasting it with the living faith brought through the death and resurrection of Christ, the 'head of our nature'.[133] Erskine's argument, and even his language, in places is extraordinarily close to Maurice's mature position: '[Christ] was indeed the head of every man, and therefore when he died, he died for every man.'[134] Maurice wrote of Erskine, after reading *The Brazen Serpent*, that 'I am certain a light has fallen through him on the Scriptures, which I hope I shall never lose'.[135] How much of Maurice's mature theological position can be attributed to the influence of Stephenson and Erskine, however, is

---

[129] McClain, *Maurice*, 54.   [130] Maurice, *Life*, i. 43.   [131] Ibid. 108.

[132] Cf. O. J. Brose, *Frederick Denison Maurice: Rebellious Conformist* (Athens, Oh.: Ohio University Press, 1971), 45 f.

[133] T. Erskine, *The Brazen Serpent, or Life coming through Death* (1831; 3rd edn., Edinburgh: David Douglas, 1879), 39.

[134] Ibid. 42.

[135] Maurice, *Life*, i. 121.

extremely uncertain. A correspondence of ideas is not the same thing as a definite influence. That there was some affinity between them is evident, and that Maurice expressed interest and gratitude for their work is significant as far as it goes. But we should not lose sight of the fact that the general shape of Maurice's emergent theology in the late 1820s, dominated as it was by Coleridge's speculative metaphysics, became wedded to the doctrine, devotion, and institutions of the Church of England. This is arguably a much more convincing starting-point for a consideration of his theology as a whole.

In all this, the decision to seek ordination came gradually. Early in 1829, as he was beginning to think about returning to Cambridge for further study, his mind was still far from made up about the possibility of becoming a clergyman, about which (as he wrote to his father) he had been thinking only for the last three months.[136] After he began at Oxford, late in the same year, he wrote to Julius Hare that he was still unable to consider ordination. Maurice was fully aware of the predicament of the Church of England: 'At present the difficulties which surround a clergyman seem to me so overwhelming, that, even with a strong impression of the grandeur of the office . . . I almost shrink from the thought of encountering them'.[137] Throughout 1831, at the height of the controversy over parliamentary reform, when criticism of the Established Church was more bitter than ever before, arguments within his family set the scene for what his son called the confirmation of 'the more definite form' his convictions had been taking for some years.[138] By 1832, a letter to Acland indicated that key elements of his mature ecclesiological convictions, including the link between Protestantism and nationality, had been formed.[139] The same letter also showed how far he had travelled from his early radical sympathies. Though still critical of Toryism, and supportive of some consequences of the French Revolution, Maurice implicitly marked out his own position over and against Toryism (of the kind represented by David Hume), liberalism, and radicalism.[140] By 1833, working under Stephenson at Lympsham, he was perhaps increasingly influenced by Stephenson's own growing tendencies towards a form of Anglican High Churchmanship: '[Stephenson] attached increasing importance to the apostolic derivation of bishops, and the ordination of ministers,

---

[136] Ibid. 93.   [137] Ibid. 103.   [138] Ibid. 126.

[139] 'I endeavour to prove that Protestantism is not predicable of a Church . . . I endeavour to prove that Protestantism is predicable of a nation': ibid. 141. The letter in question contains a summary of a much longer manuscript that unfortunately seems no longer to exist.

[140] 'The Toryism of Hume and his disciples shown [in the missing manuscript] to be the mother of Liberalism. All who bring back that form of Toryism denounced as secret abettors of Radicalism and infidelity': ibid. 142.

and whatever else concerns the constitution of the church, as one body, existing from age to age.'[141] There he finally decided to seek ordination, accepting the offer of a title at Bubbenhall, near Leamington, in the diocese of Lichfield.[142] This was no pragmatic or lukewarm step. The accumulated force of growing conviction can be inferred from his full awareness of the catastrophic situation in which the national Church seemed to find itself in the wake of the Reform crisis. Only when we place Maurice's decision—the culmination of years of soul searching—in the context of the troubled history of the Church of England in this period, can we see just how clearly and firmly he must have held to his new-found Anglican convictions. To his father he denied that he was seeking 'a bed of down'; instead, of the Church whose ministry he was joining he could admit '[that] as an establishment it will be overturned, I know not how soon, I am nearly convinced; yet I would rather be a member of it now than in the days of its greatest prosperity'.[143]

---

[141] This quotation is from Maurice's memoir of Stephenson, written in 1838: ibid. 151.

[142] Maurice's ordination documents have survived in the archives of King's College, London. They confirm that he was ordained deacon on 26 Jan. 1834, and priested a year later on 18 Jan. 1835, on both occasions by the bishop of Lichfield and Coventry, Henry Ryder, in Eccleshall parish church: King's College, London: Relton Library, Box 5037-M4-R.

[143] Maurice, *Life*, i. 153.

3

The Catholicity of Protestantism: Redescribing the Church

THE RISE OF PARTY CONFLICT IN THE CHURCH OF ENGLAND

The four years from Maurice's ordination in January 1834 to the appearance of the first edition of *The Kingdom of Christ* in 1838 were momentous ones, both for the national Church and for Maurice himself. The Church of England, like the newly reformed House of Commons, managed to ride the storm of radical expectation and then disappointment that followed the passage of the Great Reform Act. It was not dissolved or disestablished. Grey's Whig-Liberal government proved to be short-lived and internally divided, collapsing late in 1834 after sponsoring several reforming measures of lasting significance, including the Factory Act of 1833, a reform of the Poor Law in 1834, and reform of the municipal corporations.[1] Far-reaching as these measures were, they did not represent the passage to democracy for which many supporters of parliamentary reform had hoped. Reform of the Poor Law was a case in point: it ushered in the dreaded 'union workhouses', hated and feared by the poor of Victorian England, and satirized so fiercely by Dickens and others. Amongst this raft of legislation was the Irish Church Temporalities Act of 1833, a measure designed both to draw the sting of Catholic dissatisfaction with the Anglican Establishment in Ireland, and to increase the efficiency of the Establishment itself. But this Act was to provoke concerted opposition from within the Church of England.

Maurice was welcomed and celebrated by many of those who most fiercely resented the radical threat to the Church. But, by 1837–8, he had distanced himself from the emergent Oxford Movement, and marked out a distinctive position. It was not that the basis of his theological convictions changed fundamentally in these years. The formative period of his life, at least in relation to the development of his theology, was largely

[1] A. Briggs, *The Age of Improvement 1783–1867*, new edn. (London: Longman, 1979), 268–85, remains an illuminating account of the difficulties and achievements of the Whig government.

complete by the time of his ordination. Those who later claimed to discern
no significant change in Maurice's views from then until his death were
largely correct.[2] But it was one of the paradoxes of Maurice's position that
a firm, even dogmatic adhesion to traditional Anglican doctrine was allied
to a theological method that permitted him to register sharp disagreement
with many of those who claimed precisely to be defending the historic
identity of the Church of England.[3] In these years, Maurice came to
recognize that there were indeed many different forms of 'Anglican orthodoxy', and his own was not at all identical to that of many of his Oxford
contemporaries.[4] Where Tractarianism sought to bolster the national
Church by a vigorous reassertion of its presumed apostolic authority,
contrasting it sharply with all other shades of Protestantism as well as
(more ambiguously) Roman Catholicism, Maurice offered an interpretation of its history that sought to include within it positive if separated and
apparently competing traditions.

A critical appreciation of *The Kingdom of Christ* must be central to any
attempt to understand the shape of Maurice's ecclesiology and his view of
Anglicanism, since it is by far his most substantial work on the Christian
Church. It forms the main focus of this chapter. But its writing must be
read against the background of widening 'party' divisions within the
Church of England. Maurice was eventually (and reluctantly) to be identified with one specific group, the so-called Broad Church. But if, in the
early 1830s, he inclined in fact towards the Tractarians, he did so without
any intention of signalling 'party' affiliation. Discussion both of his position at this time and of the wider, internal complexity of Anglicanism has
been impeded by the unfortunate tendency of many historians to read
back into the early nineteenth century 'party' labels that were crystallized
only as a result of Tractarianism, and not as a pre-condition of it.[5] Thus,

---

[2] Tulloch, *Movements of Religious Thought*, 283.

[3] See ibid. 276: 'He was the most positive if not the most definite of thinkers . . . .
Maurice's theology was therefore profoundly dogmatic.' In the twentieth century, Gabriel
Hebert similarly characterized Maurice's work, if perhaps also idealizing it: 'there never was a
theologian more radically opposed to the spirit of Liberal theology, or a more thorough
dogmatist'; yet Maurice 'saw through' the assumption that faith could be identified with
'correct beliefs': A. G. Hebert, *Liturgy and Society: The Function of the Church in the Modern
World* (London: Faber, 1935), 108.

[4] See Pietro Corsi's warning against the assumption of a 'phantasmic entity called "Anglican orthodoxy" ' in this period: P. Corsi, *Science and Religion: Baden Powell and the Anglican
Debate, 1800–1860* (Cambridge: Cambridge University Press, 1988), p. viii. If I have sometimes
disregarded this warning, it is only to point to the contrast between Maurice's Dissenting
background and the congeries of Anglican teaching to which he 'converted'. The point about
the pluralism of Anglican belief is incontestable.

[5] For clarification of the changing terminology of church party in the early nineteenth
century, Nockles, *Oxford Movement*, 25–43, is essential.

talk of distinct 'Evangelical' and 'High Church' parties in the early nineteenth century is strictly anachronistic. 'Low Church' at this stage did not designate Evangelicalism, but the Latitudinarianism of eighteenth-century divines such as Benjamin Hoadly.[6] Evangelicals often held what later came to be regarded as 'High' views. As Peter Nockles has argued, '[T]he anti-Low Church credentials of Evangelicals prior to 1833 primarily rested on their relatively high views of apostolical authority and order.'[7] Nor was the term 'orthodox', often preferred by those who chose to distinguish themselves from Evangelicals, itself without ambiguity.[8]

It was Tractarianism that provoked the solidification of the language of party into the tripartite division of 'High', 'Broad', and 'Low' that had come to be familiar by the third quarter of the nineteenth century. Appalled at the abandonment of central elements of the Anglican constitution, and in particular by the Whig government's interference in the Irish Church in 1833, Newman, Keble, and Hurrell Froude all sought to buttress the Anglican *via media* by emphasizing the intrinsic spiritual authority of the Church apart from the State, criticizing the opportunism of Whigs and Tories alike. Tractarianism, in origin, was thus at once seemingly progressive in politics and reactive in ecclesiology. Its core doctrine was the apostolic succession of the ordained ministry. Newman famously asserted, in the first of the *Tracts for the Times*, 'I fear we have neglected the real ground on which our authority is built,—OUR APOSTOLICAL DESCENT'.[9] For the Tractarians, the constitutional crisis of 1828–32 served only to confirm the fact that the final security for the Church lay in its historical fidelity to Christ's commission, guaranteed by the external sign of the succession of bishops. Though it later became a movement of theological, sacramental, and liturgical renewal, Tractarianism's presenting cause was the collapse of the confessional State. Yet its solution to the crisis over the Church's national authority, its connection of sacramental validity to apostolic succession, was rejected by many who regarded themselves as High Churchmen, and above all by Evangelicals.[10] It led to growing tensions within the Church of England.

The increasing isolation of the Tractarians was first marked by their opposition to the appointment of the 'Whig' theologian R. D. Hampden as

---

[6] See F. W. Cornish, *The English Church in the Nineteenth Century* (London: Macmillan, 1910), i. 6.

[7] Nockles, *Oxford Movement*, 150. See also P. Toon, *Evangelical Theology, 1833–1856: A Response to Tractarianism* (London: Marshall, Morgan & Scott, 1979), 184–6.

[8] On this, see Nockles, *Oxford Movement*, 30.

[9] J. H. Newman, 'On the Ministerial Commission', cited in J. R. Moore (ed.), *Religion in Victorian Britain*, iii: *Sources* (Manchester: Manchester University Press, 1988), 9.

[10] Nockles, *Oxford Movement*, 152.

Regius Professor of Divinity at Oxford in 1836.[11] Their stridency created
resentment amongst Hampden's friends and allies at Oxford, and in
particular the 'Noetic' school of Oriel College, with which Newman
himself had once been briefly associated.[12] The widely respected Thomas
Arnold, for example, weighed in on Hampden's side with a vitriolic article
in *The Edinburgh Review*, entitled 'The Oxford Malignants', that also served
to damage his own reputation.[13] The Hampden affair symbolized the
disenchantment of many moderate Anglicans with the Tractarians. Opposition amongst Evangelicals was sparked particularly by the publication
of Hurrell Froude's literary *Remains* in 1838–9, with its sarcastic references
to the sixteenth-century Reformers. Here, commented Chadwick, 'the
repudiation of Protestants appeared before the public in a new and shocking light'.[14] Suspicious that new elements of Tractarian piety, such as
reverence for the saints, the use of auricular confession, and a eucharistic
theology of real presence, signalled a covert 'Romanizing' trend, Evangelicals became bitter opponents. The effect of this intensifying strife was to
mark the emergence of a 'central' strand in Anglicanism, self-consciously
concerned either to reject decisively what was thought to be the sectarianism of Evangelicalism and Tractarianism, or to mediate between distinct parties in the hope of articulating an inclusive vision of Anglican
theology. What came to be called the 'Broad Church', a term made
famous by William Conybeare in an article in the *Edinburgh Review* in
1853, was a response to the Tractarian attempt to reconceive the Church
of England's Catholic heritage.[15] It also sought to underline the validity of
the national Church, to make its social authority dependent on its ability
to register and contain widening doctrinal disagreement.

[11] For an influential account of the Hampden affair sympathetic to the Tractarian view, see
R. W. Church, *The Oxford Movement: Twelve Years 1833–45* (1891; new edn., Chicago: University
of Chicago Press, 1970), 113–24.

[12] On the influence of the 'Noetic' school, see D. Forbes, *The Liberal Anglican Idea of History*
(Cambridge: Cambridge University Press, 1952); Corsi, *Science and Religion*, 83–149; R. Brent,
Liberal Anglican Politics: Whiggery, Religion, and Reform, 1830–1841 (Oxford: Clarendon Press,
1987).

[13] 'The offence caused by it, even amongst his friends, was very great': A. P. Stanley, *The
Life and Correspondence of Thomas Arnold* (London: Fellowes, 1844), ii. 9.

[14] W. O. Chadwick, *The Victorian Church*, i (London: A. & C. Black, 1966), 175.

[15] See the note inserted by Maurice's son into the *Life*, ii. 607, in which reference is made to
Stanley's original article of 1850, and to Conybeare's. Maurice, his son says, 'always com-
plained that Mr. Conybeare had "bestowed" the title of "the Broad Church" '. There is a
modern, critical edition of the three variants through which Conybeare's essay passed, edited
by R. A. Burns: W. J. Conybeare, 'Church Parties', in S. Taylor, *From Cranmer to Davidson:
A Church of England Miscellany*, Church of England Record Society (Woodbridge: Boydell Press,
1999), 215–385.

In the emergence of the 'Broad Church' synthesis, Maurice was a pivotal influence, if a semi-detached one. In *The Kingdom of Christ*, he was to articulate an ecclesiology that shared many characteristics with the work of Thomas Arnold, Arthur Stanley, Richard Whately, and others, and yet which also represented a different strand of thinking from theirs, almost a different pedigree. In their way of thinking about the Church, consistent with the Noetic concentration on the establishment of 'rules or guides to induction', a distinction could be made between the particular doctrines of the Church of England and the social function of the national Church.[16] If doctrine was not, as such, relativized, still the implication was that the Church's utility rested, not on particular expressions of truth, secured through authoritative trad-ition—the Tractarian position—but on its capacity to accept the doctrinal pluralism of the English people. Arnold's position echoed Coleridge's distinc-tion between the Christian Church and the national Church. But, for Maur-ice, this distinction was not to be used as a way of loosening the national Church's doctrinal authority. He upheld a 'High Church' conception of order and doctrine, insisting, for example, on episcopacy and on an ordered liturgical life as essential features of the universal Church, at the same time as attempting to prize apart these institutional aspects of the Church, or 'signs', from particular theological lines of interpretation. In these years in the 1830s, his blending of High Church doctrine and the 'Broad Church' principle of comprehensiveness came to fruition.

We can trace this trajectory through his troubled relationship with Tractarianism. Oxford friends were central to this, including Thomas Acland, later a Liberal politician and ally of Gladstone. Acland, with his Tractarian connections in mind, encouraged Maurice to write a defence of the requirement to subscribe to the Thirty-Nine Articles of Religion on matriculation at Oxford.[17] Written against the background of a proposal to abolish subscription, Maurice's pamphlet *Subscription no Bondage* was published early in 1835. He denied that imposition of the Articles marked a test of Church membership, since that was defined rather by communion with the Church. Instead, they were a 'security for the good faith of Churchmen'.[18] At Oxford they were 'conditions of thought', outlining on what basis the university's education would stand.[19] Education under these conditions, grounded also on baptism, with its admission into the 'universal constitution for man as man' (that is, the Catholic Church), would help a man to rise 'to a feeling of personal distinctness which he can never get in any other way, and which is so essential to his being, that all moral or spiritual cultivation without it is impossible'.[20]

[16] Brent, *Liberal Anglican Politics*, 161.   [17] Maurice, *Life*, i. 168–9.
[18] Maurice, *Subscription no Bondage*, 12.   [19] Ibid. 12–13.   [20] Ibid. 45–6.

This was surely a forced interpretation of the role of the Articles, and one not readily accepted by either side of the debate on subscription. Both Arnold and Stanley, who supported the inclusion of Dissenters in the university, plainly considered subscription an unnecessary bar.[21] Opponents of the proposed change also considered subscription a matter of submission, but one they approved of.[22] Even so, Maurice's defence of the Articles struck a chord with the Tractarians, and for a few months he was favoured as a potential ally. He was included amongst a list of guests at E. B. Pusey's theological club in Oxford.[23] He was even canvassed by the Troctarians as a possible candidate for the Chair of Political Economy at Oxford.[24]

But Maurice's disillusionment with the Tractarians was rapid. It came with the publication of Pusey's views on baptism in the summer of 1835. Maurice himself later described how he had read Pusey's *Tract* (presumably number 67, the first of a trilogy) while on his way to attend a meeting of the Clapham Sect, and had been overcome with horror at what he was reading.[25] As his son recounted, 'at last he sat down on a gate . . . and made up his mind that it represented the parting point between him and the Oxford school'.[26] The main aim of the tract was to reassert the consistency of the doctrine of baptismal regeneration with Scripture. Maurice can hardly have dissented from this.[27] But he may have misinterpreted or misunderstood the main drift of the tract. As Pusey's biographer Liddon pointed out, he seems to have taken Pusey's point to be the denial of the universality of the gift of the Incarnation. He assumed Pusey's argument implied that regeneration depended entirely on the faith of the believer, and effected a change of nature in the believer. This, however, is not what Pusey actually says. Pusey meant only to reassert the objectiveness of the sacrament itself.[28] Maurice also regretted the extremity of

---

[21] Stanley, *Life of Arnold*, i. 386–7; R. E. Prothero, *Life and Correspondence of Dean Stanley* (1893; new edn., London: Nelson, 1909), 82–3. Interestingly, here Stanley simply included Maurice's name amongst the 'party' of Newman, Moberly, Keble, and Pusey.

[22] 'Thus the Tractarians rested their defence of subscription on the grounds that religion was to be approached with a submission of the understanding': Nockles, *Oxford Movement*, 222.

[23] J. H. Newman, *Letters and Diaries of John Henry Newman*, v, ed. T. Gornall (Oxford: Clarendon Press, 1981), 161.

[24] Maurice, *Life*, i. 209–10, 213.

[25] Ibid. 186, 237.

[26] Ibid. 186.

[27] Maurice was quoted by his amanuensis, Edward Strachey, as saying 'Dr Pusey sets out a most important truth with regard to Baptism—a truth utterly neglected and denied by the Evangelical party': ibid. 205–6. See H. P. Liddon, *Life of Pusey*, i (London: Longman, 1893), 343–58.

[28] Ibid. 350.

Pusey's language on post-baptismal sin, but in this reaction he was not alone: even High Church allies of Pusey were uncomfortable.[29]

Once he had rejected Tractarianism, his view of it did not change substantially. Retrospectively, we can discern two distinct phases in the development of his reactions to the dominant schools within the Church of England at that time, Evangelicalism and Tractarianism. His attitude to Evangelicalism was sealed by his theological formation through reading Coleridge, Erskine, McLeod Campbell, and others and his friendships with Julius Hare and John Sterling, and was largely in place by the early 1830s, if not then as stridently expressed as were to be his views on Tractarianism. His youthful rejection of a narrow, populist Calvinism made him suspicious of common Evangelical interpretations of atonement and election.[30] He warmly endorsed, however, the Evangelical sense of the living power of Scripture, and its Christological personalism, its vivid sense of the immediacy of the presence of Christ to the believer. But he believed that Evangelicalism did not pay sufficient attention to the institutional means by which the experiential core of Evangelical belief could be sustained in practice and in time, and this meant that its theology was essentially exclusive, since it depended on correct belief.[31] Correspondingly, he endorsed the High Church attention to church order. For a time, his newfound confidence in the historic formularies of the Church of England, following his two years in Oxford, allowed him to assume some point of agreement with the new movement of 'High Church' revival under way in Oxford. However, the break with Tractarianism came when he suspected Newman, Pusey, and their followers of using the ordinances of the Church, such as the sacraments, and the order of ministry as a means of exclusion, distinguishing 'correct' belief again from 'incorrect'.[32]

The double movement of affirmation and repudiation implied in this attitude to both groups is a vital key to understanding Maurice's ambiguous position within Anglicanism. It found clear expression in a formula to which he returned again and again, exemplified in his short pamphlet, *Reasons for Not Joining a Party in the Church* (1841). Published in the wake of the furore over Newman's *Tract 90*, with its suggestion that the Thirty-Nine Articles could be held consistently with the full range of Roman doctrine, this was a direct challenge to W. F. Hook's claim that the time had come for men to take sides in the Church.[33] Maurice suggested, with many of the 'old' High Church, 'that the words *Party* and *Church* are

---

[29] D. Forrester, *Young Doctor Pusey: A Study in Development* (London: Mowbray, 1989), 189–90.
[30] Maurice, *Life*, i. 43. [31] Ibid. ii. 234. [32] Ibid. i. 236.
[33] W. F. Hook, *A Letter to the Rt. Rev. the Lord Bishop of Ripon, on the State of Parties in the Church of England* (London: Rivington, 1841).

essentially hostile to each other'.[34] As Hook himself doubtless would have done, he recognized the 'deep value and meaning of Protestant principles'.[35] But he acknowledged that these principles, whilst affirming the faith of the individual, required the corresponding affirmation of truths about 'the constitution of society, and the being of God'.[36] Neither Protestantism nor Catholicism could satisfactorily exist without the other.

In summary, in an over-schematized way, Maurice took the truth of Evangelicalism to be concerned essentially with personal faith, and thus as inward and experiential, and the truth of Tractarianism with corporate faith, the faith of the Church, and thus as external and institutional. This was hardly a satisfactory account of doctrinal division in the Church of England. Maurice's repudiation of party left him with little scope to acknowledge, on the one hand, the readiness of many Evangelicals to uphold the institutional forms of the Church of England, and on the other, the integrity and inner strength of conviction of many of the Tractarians. Personally, of course, Maurice could often refer approvingly to the character and faith of those with whom he disagreed. He could perhaps have argued legitimately, too, that this attempt to hold on to both sets of values did no more than reflect an older view of the position of the Church of England precisely at risk from the intensity of party conflict.[37] But the repudiation of party simply could not prevent the perception that he, and others like him, actually represented a third party, a 'no party' party, as he was all too well aware.[38] Nevertheless, it is at least a clue to the almost inevitable identification of Maurice eventually with the Broad Church, as a middle way between Evangelicalism and Tractarianism, that he attempted to defend simultaneously a High Church ecclesiology along with a Protestant theology of salvation. What was at stake for Maurice was the national character of the Church of England. The exclusiveness of both extreme parties was endangering the breadth of the Church, making it vulnerable to criticism both from Dissent and from Roman Catholicism. This was no way to defend the authority of the Church of England, and its historic mission, at a time when its very existence appeared to be under threat. What Maurice was seeking was a vision of the Church of England that could transcend the particularities of competing church parties. It was

---

[34] F. D. Maurice, *Reasons for Not Joining a Party in the Church: A Letter to the Ven. Samuel Wilberforce* (London: Rivington, 1841), 7.

[35] Ibid. 13.

[36] Ibid. 14.

[37] A point he made implicitly against Hook: ibid. 8–9.

[38] 'I knew also that I was in danger of attaching myself to a party which should inscribe "No Party" on its flag': but this was a retrospective view: Maurice, *Life*, i. 239.

this motive above all that was to influence the writing of his most important work.

THE FIRST EDITION OF *THE KINGDOM OF CHRIST*

The Kingdom of Christ, Maurice's first major theological work, was composed originally as twelve letters to a young Quaker, Samuel Clark, who was in the process of conforming to the Church of England.[39] But Clark's friendship was never much more than a catalyst for the book. Rather, its aim was to amplify the different conception of the Catholic Church that Maurice had come to hold from that advanced by the Tractarians. The original letters were addressed to Quakers, but written 'really concerning ourselves more than them'.[40] Prompted by a controversy within Quakerism over the rise of Evangelical beliefs, Maurice in effect used a defence of the older Quaker doctrine of the 'inner light' to mark his criticism of Pusey's view of baptism:

Reflecting much on this controversy and connecting it with what was passing in the English Church, it seemed to me that the old Quakers were affirming a most grand and fundamental truth; but that it had become narrow and contradictory, because they had no ordinance which embodied it and made it universal; that we, on the other hand, forgetting their Quaker principles . . . necessarily made baptism a mere ceremony or a charm. The two being united expressed to me the reconciliation of the High Church baptismal regeneration with the Evangelical demands for personal faith.[41]

Maurice's objection to Pusey's theory centred on the implication that sacramental grace changed the *nature* of the believer from a condition of sin to a condition of grace. In effect, he implied, Pusey undermined God's providence by presenting creation as utterly separated from God. Human beings were lost unless saved out of their condition of sin by the application of baptismal grace. This was a doctrine of salvation by baptism. For Maurice, taking his cue from the universality of the reconciliation effected by the Incarnation, such a view was tantamount to a denial of the goodness of creation. Maurice's alternative ecclesiology aimed to derive the Church's instrumentality in mediating salvation to human beings in history from the kingdom already initiated in the life, death, and resurrection of Christ. It was a fundamental axiom of Maurice that God had created human beings for communion with each other and with himself.

---

[39] See Clark, *Memorials from Journals and Letters*, esp. 23, 41, 48, 64, 67.
[40] Maurice, *Life,* i. 237.   [41] Ibid. 237.

This relationship constituted the primary truth of theology, under which all other doctrines stood.[42]

Appointed as chaplain to Guy's Hospital in London in mid-1835, Maurice did not begin writing what was to become *The Kingdom of Christ* until August 1836 at the earliest.[43] The moderate High Churchman Walter Hook informed Newman in December 1835 that Maurice had told an 'evangelical' meeting near Coventry that he would 'answer' Pusey on baptism.[44] In the course of writing, however, the original focus of the work slipped. What began as polemic broadened into a treatise of much wider scope. *The Kingdom of Christ* was to appear in three forms. The first was as the twelve letters on baptism, written in late 1836 and 1837.[45] These were subsequently gathered together in three volumes and published as one work by Darton and Clark, Clark's employer, in 1838. This first edition had little impact, apart from offending Maurice's erstwhile friends at Oxford.[46] He decided to recast it completely. The revised edition, published in 1842, subsumed its treatment of baptism under a central section of the book that dealt with the six 'signs' of the Catholic Church. It brought to the fore the theme of the Catholicity of the Church that had been latent in the original (and retained) title: *The Kingdom of Christ, or Hints to a Quaker Respecting the Principles, Constitution and Ordinances of the Catholic Church*. Maurice never revised the work again, and so it is the second edition that has served as the basis of all subsequent reprintings and that came to be known and read by subsequent generations. For that reason, for most of this chapter it is the second edition to which I shall refer. Nevertheless, at certain points Maurice's formulation of his views is clearer in the first edition than in the second, so reference will be made to the first edition whenever necessary. By reconstructing his work, and pushing the controversy over Pusey's views on

[42] 'I was sent into the world that I might persuade men to recognise Christ as the centre of their fellowship with each other, that so they might be united in their families, their countries, and as men, not in schools and factions': ibid. 240.

[43] Cf. a letter from E. Strachey, dated 18 Aug. 1836: 'Maurice is going to write a series of Letters on Baptism': Maurice, *Life*, i. 202.

[44] Newman, *Letters*, v. 181; Newman replied, 'I am annoyed but not surprised about Maurice. He will hardly go the lengths you report. He has corresponded with Pusey, I believe.' If Maurice did indeed write to Pusey, the letter has not apparently survived.

[45] Edward Strachey wrote in December 1836 that Maurice had 'given up his Letters on Baptism, and is writing others on Quakerism at the urgent request of Mr Clark'; this somewhat misleading description may at least point to Maurice's apparent confusion about the aim of the letters, as well as their date of composition: Maurice, *Life*, i. 212.

[46] With typical modesty, he referred to its 'many minor but serious mistakes': Maurice, *Kingdom of Christ*, vol. i, p. v. Newman confided to Keble in February 1837 that Maurice had published a 'rambling theory' of baptism, a reference to the first two letters: *Letters and Diaries of John Henry Newman*, vi, ed. G. Tracey (Oxford: Clarendon Press, 1984), 27–8.

baptism firmly into the background, he hoped to describe a vision of the Catholicity of the Church of England that transcended internal division.

CATHOLICITY AND HISTORY

The Kingdom of Christ is a long and complex work that defies easy classification. In order to apprehend its central arguments, it will, I think, help the reader if I spend a little time considering the general perspective on history that Maurice brought to bear on his subject-matter. This is because, at the heart of the work, is a methodology of historical exposition and theological retrieval in which a particular reading of Church history is used to identify permanent features of the Christian Church. Maurice's conception of religious truth as embedded in language, and of language itself as shaped through history, implied not only that history itself could be read as an unfolding record of God's interaction with his creation, but that the truth of history could be reached only *through* history, since God revealed himself not otherwise than in the events of history. 'I know well the double danger of giving a mere dry summary of events, or of going into endless disquisitions,' he acknowledged, '[but] I do think both may be avoided if we seriously believe that our business is to study our records earnestly and devoutly; because they *have* a meaning in them which we may be helped to draw out; not because we must put a meaning into them.'[47] This was no less true of the history of the Church.

It is scarcely surprising that history should have been a dominant theme of Maurice's theology. The nineteenth century was a period in which historical approaches to theology came to the fore. As a professional academic discipline, history came into its own in Maurice's lifetime, with the first steps towards the foundation of departments of history at the old and new universities, and the award of history degrees.[48] The development of a tradition of historical writing, based on an assumption of objectivity and supported by systematic methodological rigour in the use of sources, was pioneered by historians who included friends and acquaintances of Maurice himself, such as J. R. Green and J. R. Seeley.[49] History was

[47] F. D. Maurice, *Queen's College, London: Its Objects and Method: A Lecture Delivered in the Hanover Square Rooms* (London: Rivington, 1848), 25.

[48] See P. Slee, *Learning and a Liberal Education: The Study of Modern History in the Universities of Oxford, Cambridge and Manchester, 1800–1914* (Manchester: Manchester University Press, 1986).

[49] On the development of Victorian historiography in general, see J. W. Burrow, *A Liberal Descent: Victorian Historians and the English Past* (Cambridge: Cambridge University Press, 1983); A. D. Cullen, *The Victorian Mirror of History* (London: Yale University Press, 1985); R. Jann, *The Art and Science of Victorian History* (Columbus, Oh.: Ohio State University Press,

political and religious fuel: from Dissenting historians with an interest in overturning Establishment versions of national history to agnostic historians with an interest in decrying the influence of all the churches, the continuing political, social, and religious relevance of history was evident. Nor was the Church of England itself immune from the general enthusiasm for, and faith in, the potential of historical understanding. Tractarians, Evangelicals, and Broad Churchmen alike appealed to competing versions of history to support their doctrinal positions.

Maurice can be located broadly within the school of historical thinking labelled 'Liberal Anglican'. In a famous essay, Duncan Forbes saw the Liberal Anglican school as sharing the Romantic reaction against the optimism, utilitarianism, and individualism of the eighteenth century, articulating this particularly through the concept of the personality of nations, with the corollary that history is cyclical: nations, or civilizations, proceed through stages of infancy, maturity, and decline.[50] Thomas Arnold, for example, conceived 'the social progress of states' as an understanding of history from 'inside' a nation, with its history the result of an internal class struggle.[51] But Arnold and his peers always saw history as governed by the outworking of God's providence. Julius Hare claimed that 'Only through Christianity has a nation ever risen again' and that 'the Church of God alone . . . is indestructible'.[52] History as a whole was not a record of *equivalent* civilizations, but the outworking of an implicitly ordered or hierarchical understanding of human sociality. For Maurice, as for Arnold, all the 'facts' of nature, civilization, politics, economics, and religion were intimately related, and common language and practice, as much as the language and practice of élites, formed the material of history. Thus, when Maurice touched on various approaches to writing English history, he acknowledged the worth of the broadest possible interpretation of 'Popular History': it would include the Poor Law, agrarian revolts, municipal government, education, domestic life, ballads, plays, and pictures, amongst other things.[53]

Yet Maurice's understanding of history cannot be squeezed tightly into the strait-jacket of Forbes's 'Liberal Anglican' idea. Though also emphasizing national culture and identity, the theory of national personality, and

---

1985); C. Parker, *The English Historical Tradition since 1850* (Edinburgh: John Donald, 1990); A. Brundage, *The People's Historian: John Richard Green and the Writing of History in Victorian England* (Westport, Conn.: Greenwood Press, 1994).

[50] Forbes, *The Liberal Anglican Idea of History*.

[51] Ibid. 20–9.

[52] J. C. Hare, *The Mission of the Comforter* (1846), cited in Forbes, *Liberal Anglican Idea of History*, 56.

[53] F. D. Maurice, 'English History', in *Friendship of Books*, 157–8.

its concomitant, the cyclical rise and fall of states, was not generally central to his view of history. Significantly, it was clearest precisely in that one series of lectures in which he shadowed Arnold closely, the *Lectures on the Religion of Rome*.[54] There was an implicit linearity in Maurice's understanding of the history of the Church. The assumption that there is a divine goodness to be sought out in all the vicissitudes of human history became a methodological assumption when it was used as a way of tracing particular ideas through history as evidence of God's providence.

The first edition of *The Kingdom of Christ* contained a chapter in which he set out a general framework for the interpretation of Church history. This chapter was not included in the second edition. It is, however, an indispensable summary of his position. The Catholicity of the Church was embedded in the changing circumstances of human history: 'our principles have this test of soundness and permanence, that they are implied in the thoughts and feelings of men, and cannot without an effort . . . be contemplated apart from them'.[55] Such a view forced one to conceive of Catholicity *through* history, and not apart from it. There were particular signs or ordinances of the visible Church through which the universal (the Catholic) society could be identified:

Now it has been my object to shew [*sic*], that a body constituted by Baptism, upheld and united by the Eucharist, instructed by the written Word, preserved alive in each age by a succession of ministers, expressing its united will in acts of worship, does embody that principle, for which your Society [the Society of Friends] is the witness . . . does fulfil the idea of a Church Catholic.[56]

As an embodied 'fellowship', the institutions and ordinances of the Church were the means both of constituting the fellowship and of transmitting its blessings to succeeding generations. The historian could demonstrate 'how a body thus constituted may be the divine means of declaring to all men their relationship to God; and of putting them into the condition of realising it'.[57] This hermeneutic of Catholicity could be traced through the main events in the history of the Western Church, as tension mounted between its external order and its internal, spiritual being. Even the Reformation showed the same fatal flaw in divided Christendom, as sects multiplied, and Christianity came to be thought of

---

[54] F. D. Maurice, *Lectures on the Religion of Rome*, in *Learning and Working* (Cambridge: Macmillan, 1855), 207.

[55] *The Kingdom of Christ*, 1st edn., ii. 262. All subsequent references to the 1st edn. are signified simply by the insertion of the words '1st edn.'; otherwise all references are to Macmillan's 4th edn., published in 1891, which in turn replicated the revised, 2nd edn. of 1842.

[56] *The Kingdom of Christ*, 1st edn., ii. 266.

[57] Ibid. 296.

as residing exclusively in one or other of the two great systems of doctrine, Catholicism and Protestantism.[58]

The history of Christendom was a fragmented one, a descent into rigidified theological 'systems' and sects, within which, nevertheless, the Catholicity of the Church could still be found, albeit dispersed. Maurice's providential reading of the Church's history directed him towards a theological rehabilitation of the idea of Christian unity. His hermeneutic of Catholicity, applied in such a way as to demonstrate the persistence of the Church in all sects which professed the Triune name despite the increasing fragmentation and sectarianism of Western Christendom, enabled him to reconceive the unity of the Christian Church beyond the exclusive ecclesiological emphases of the Catholicism and Protestantism of his day.

THE KINGDOM OF CHRIST 1: CATHOLICITY THROUGH HISTORY

Late in 1841, as public controversy over the Oxford Movement was at its height, Maurice was revising *The Kingdom of Christ*.[59] He had good reason to emphasize that his position was different from that of the Tractarians. Though the first edition had attracted few reviews, two had not distinguished his argument sufficiently from the Oxford Movement. The *Christian Remembrancer*, a High Church periodical, had simply glossed long quotations from the book with extravagant praise.[60] To make matters worse, the pro-Dissenting *Eclectic Review* had entirely misread Maurice's purpose as 'to philosophize Puseyism into a transcendental theology'.[61] It assumed, astonishingly, that Maurice was writing in defence of Roman Catholicism: 'He further describes the church of England as a branch of the universal church, that is, of the church of Rome.'[62] Maurice's views were perhaps open to some misinterpretation. Even as he sought to clarify the grounds of his disagreement with Pusey, he refused to align himself with those seeking to drive the Tractarians out of Oxford. He argued against Lord Ashley's attempt to suppress Tractarianism in Oxford by

---

[58] *The Kingdom of Christ*, 1st edn., ii. 338.

[59] Maurice, *Life*, i. 304, 325–6.

[60] *The Christian Remembrancer*, 22 (1840), 132. Christensen erroneously placed this review in the January edition; in fact it appeared in March: Christensen, 'F. D. Maurice and the Contemporary Religious World', 72.

[61] *The Eclectic Review*, Feb. 1840, 151.

[62] Ibid. 156.

legislative means.[63] Later still, he argued against the condemnation of W. G. Ward (as an Anglican) over his publication of the strongly pro-Roman *Ideal of a Christian Church* (1844).[64] Making few explicit references to controversy, Maurice carefully stepped round the Tractarian–Evangelical disputes, presenting his work as if it transcended internal division in the Church. Yet it was, through and through, a work of careful, distinctive positioning. Writing to R. C. Trench in December 1841, Maurice admitted that he was trying to impede conversions to Rome, by bringing out that 'the highest form of Catholicism (not of Anglicanism) [was] the direct opposite of Popery . . . and . . . that Popery is not the excess of everything good, but simply the denial of it'.[65]

In its revised form, *The Kingdom of Christ* was less diffuse. Its argument was presented more systematically and more sharply, with more extended treatment of its central motifs. Maurice's famous prolixity did not altogether desert him. But there is a greater clarity and coherence about the book's central purpose, which is to trace the lineaments of the Catholicity of the Christian Church, both in history and in the contemporary Church of England. As he searched through the history and constitution of different branches of the Church, as well as different movements in history formally outside the Church, Maurice used this principle to identify particular features that pointed to the existence of the 'spiritual society', or Catholic Church:

[T]here rose up before me the idea of a CHURCH UNIVERSAL, not built upon human inventions or human faith, but upon the very nature of God himself, and upon the union which He has formed with his creatures: a Church revealed to man as a fixed and eternal reality by means which infinite wisdom had itself devised. The tokens and witnesses of such a Church, it seemed to me, must be Divine, but the feeling of its necessity, apprehensions of the different sides and aspects of it, must, if it be a reality, be found in all the different schemes which express human thought and feeling.[66]

To Maurice, the question whether such a 'Universal Society' really existed was one of the most important subjects of his day.[67] And through it, the whole of human history opened up for inquiry: 'all thoughts,

---

[63] See F. D. Maurice, *On Right and Wrong Methods of Supporting Protestantism: A Letter to Lord Ashley* (London: Parker, 1843). This pamphlet attracted the approbation of the Tractarian *British Critic* in Oct. 1843: p. 519.

[64] See F. D. Maurice, *The New Statute and Mr. Ward: A Letter to a Non-Resident Member of Convocation* (Oxford: Parker, 1845); also *idem, Thoughts on the Rule of Conscientious Subscription, or the Purpose of the Thirty-Nine Articles, and our Present Perils from the Romish System in a Second Letter to a Non-Resident Member of Convocation,* (Oxford: Parker, 1845).

[65] Maurice, *Life,* i. 321.

[66] Maurice, *Kingdom of Christ,* vol. i. p. xxviii.

[67] Ibid., p. xxiv.

schemes, systems, speculations, may contribute their quota to some one which shall be larger and deeper than any one of them'.[68] This search for a larger and deeper reality is itself a search for the knowledge of God without which 'all pursuit of Unity . . . is the pursuit of a phantom'.[69] This is true also of parties within the Church, and of the place of the creeds of the Church: Coleridge, Maurice affirmed, had taught us to see that religious truth cannot be the result of human inquiry, but the presupposition of it.[70] By this means, Maurice tacitly acknowledged that his work was not an attempt to demonstrate the compatibility of the idea of the Christian Church with a scheme of human reason, but rather an attempt to explore what the Catholicity of the Christian Church might be, given that it exists. The method was reflexive: Catholicity is the presupposition of the work, but also its constitutive content. Maurice traced through the history of the Church that which he had already announced as existing for all time.

If Catholicity represents the dominant theme of the work, an important subsidiary one is that of nationality. Maurice's providential view of history predisposed him to see the emergence of distinct national identities as an essential aspect of God's purposes for the world. Influenced by the general nineteenth-century sympathy for nationalism, he absolutized what was a particular historical development.[71] Two elements of his theory of nationality are particularly relevant. The first is his view that, far from representing one amongst a number of possible forms of social organization, nations are an intrinsic part of the kingdom of God. They are, in his words, along with the family, 'lower and subordinate parts' of the 'spiritual constitution'.[72] The second is that the concept of the nation is inherently Protestant: in asserting its autonomy, it must perforce repudiate the transnational pretensions of the Papacy.[73]

As a result, throughout *The Kingdom of Christ* Maurice assumes that the Catholic Church is not a totalizing or all-encompassing institution that should absorb other forms of social organization. It was, for Maurice, the highest part of the spiritual constitution, having a specific role that could legitimately be defended against others if they sought to intrude on it. But

---

[68] Maurice, *Kingdom of Christ*, vol. i. p. xxiv.   [69] Ibid., p. xxiv.   [70] Ibid., p. xxv.

[71] As I have argued with regard to his understanding of Luther; see Morris, 'Reconstructing the Reformation'.

[72] Maurice, *Life*, i. 306

[73] See especially F. D. Maurice, *Three Letters to the Rev. W. Palmer* (London: Rivington, 1842), and also Maurice, *Life*, i. 141. This is not an *exclusive* definition of Protestantism; elsewhere, Maurice seems to lay the emphasis on the assertion of the individual elements of faith as the hallmark of Protestantism: see, e.g., Maurice, *On Right and Wrong Methods of Supporting Protestantism*.

it could not obliterate the lower and subordinate institutions of nation and family. The relevance of Maurice's use of the term 'constitution' is noteworthy, signifying an order of government of the universe. He envisaged a theory of constitutional balance in which Church, nation, and family mutually reinforced and stabilized each other.[74] Furthermore, in circumscribing the role of all three institutions in this way, Maurice was actually making provision for the exercise of that characteristic nineteenth-century ideal, freedom—something his critics have usually overlooked. In the first edition, he even suggested that the medieval conflicts between civil and ecclesiastical authorities had the effect of erecting the Church into a bulwark against civil tyranny.[75] What emerged from this was an attempt to acknowledge the complex and pluriform character of existing, historical societies, and to articulate a providential reading of this very pluriformity. National, social, political, and other movements retained significance within a wider providential framework.

Since Maurice's abiding assumption included the *existing* Catholicity of Christian churches, his presentation of the history of this *idea* of the Catholic Church was undertaken from within the Church itself, and amounted to an examination of separated Christian churches. So his 'history' (though it is needless to point out that this is not a work of ecclesiastical history, but an ecclesiology built around a historical teleology) was written inside out. Rather than begin with the united Church, he began instead with diversity and schism, and traced the presence within them of elements of the Catholicity of the Church. This constituted the first part of the revised edition. Having laid out these 'hints' of the Catholic Church, only then did he proceed to expound what it is, how it might be identified in history, and how it is actually found in his own Church—the subject of the second and third parts, to be examined in the two following sections.

Yet Maurice's approach in the first part changed subtly half-way through. Three relatively short chapters addressed major branches of Protestant Christianity; the Quakers, the 'Pure Protestants' (the Lutheran and Reformed traditions), and, controversially, the Unitarians. His approach to each of these in turn was strikingly similar. The dominant, positive principles were stated first, objections to them countered, and then their distortion or abandonment in historical development described. In the much longer, fourth chapter, however, Maurice used a very wide canvass indeed, surveying historically a vast range of religious, philosophical,

---

[74] On the contrasts between Maurice's theory of differentiated roles for Church and State and Gladstone's confessional theory of the State, see Vidler, *The Orb and the Cross*, 31–2.

[75] Maurice, *Kingdom of Christ*, 1st edn., i. 326.

political, and social movements in the West since the Reformation, and making little attempt to work through positive principles and their corruption into 'notions' or 'systems' systematically. Instead, in this fourth chapter, his method was one of retrieval, directed towards tracing the desire for a 'spiritual society' through all these various, mutually critical or contradictory movements.

But this schema left a difficulty. It would be tempting to assume that the first three chapters simply covered the Protestantism that is 'within' the Catholic Church, and the fourth chapter movements outside it. But that cannot be the case, for two reasons. First, the section on 'Religious movements' in the fourth chapter includes coverage of Methodism and Irvingism (the Catholic Apostolic Church founded by Edward Irving), which both retained many, if not all, of the 'signs' of the Catholic Church that Maurice went on to elaborate in the second part of the book. Second, the inclusion of the Quakers and, above all, the Unitarians in the first three chapters suggested that some other underlying, operative principle in fact was at work here, rather than the simple assumption that these were 'parts' of the Catholic Church. What that principle might be, if it was anything other than a historical observation about the actual character of Protestant bodies, was not clear.[76] The status of Unitarianism in particular was left uncertain in Maurice's text. At this point in the text, the reader could be forgiven for supposing that its 'Pure Protestantism' did indeed mark its presence within the wider Catholic Church. Later, however, Maurice proceeded to elaborate a theory of the 'signs' of the Catholic Church that included the Catholic creeds, and thus implicitly ruled out Unitarianism as a religious body. Moreover, to confuse matters further, the positive principles were not drawn together into a systematic ecclesiology, but left undeveloped as fragmented, piecemeal elements. The inference was that Catholic Christianity contained within itself a series of positive principles as definite truths that could be asserted of the Gospel of Jesus Christ. But no attempt was made here, finally, to define those principles comprehensively. Nor was any attempt made to define 'Catholicity', or at least to produce a systematic concept that could clarify the underlying basis on which Maurice's selection of historical data rested.

This proved a significant weakness of Maurice's theory, rendering the exact status, or relationship to the Catholic Church, of a whole range of movements of opinion somewhat unclear. Yet it arose from his determination to reason inductively. The historical nature of Maurice's argument

---

[76] Maurice's selective choice of the major strands of Protestantism reflected a view of Protestantism scarcely satisfactory even from the point of view of English Dissent—consider the almost complete absence of discussion of the Baptists, for example.

implied that the positive principles themselves promoted partiality and distortion in history, because they could not be encountered other than in the very complexity of real human relations. Maurice did not present an ideal view of the Church on one side of the argument, contrasted with a real view of the Church's history on the other. The 'idea' of the Catholic Church he traced could exist only in its actual history. The Catholicity of Protestantism was thus discernible, according to Maurice, in the very character of the different sects or churches.

Maurice's treatment of 'Pure Protestantism' will serve as a suitable illustration. Having described the four 'positive principles' of 'Pure Protestantism', as justification through faith, election, the sole authority of Scripture, and the principle of nationality, he devoted considerable space to disabling common objections to the first three.[77] So, for example, to the claim that Luther's theology of justification by faith confused the subjective crisis of personal conversion with the universal condition of the justified was opposed the view that the one thing Luther meant to avoid was the implication that human feeling was itself any basis for justification.[78] On the contrary, Luther's understanding made the work of justification entirely that of God alone. Far from being a description of an internal crisis or self-conversion, it was an abandonment of self in openness to God. For the Lutheran, 'union with another [i.e. God] is his law; separation from him his transgression'.[79] The point of parrying objections in each of the first three chapters was simple: it rejected the sectarian dismissal of the founding principles of these three subsections of Protestantism, and so left them in place as truths of Catholic Christianity.

But the principles were embedded in history. Each had a specific tendency that had led to the emergence of 'systems' based on it. An overemphasis on election (the second positive principle) had led, in Calvinism, to the rejection of traditional church order, and especially episcopacy.[80] The exclusive concentration on *sola scriptura* had led—for example, in the hands of Zwingli—to a disparagement of the creeds, the sacraments, and the authority of the Fathers of the Church.[81] In Lutheranism, Luther's own high regard for the creeds and sacraments was gradually abandoned, as the doctrine of justification was turned into a conviction that the *feeling* of justification was a credible test for its presence. And in reaction to that subjective turn, Lutheranism recovered, but then absolutized its regard for its founding confessions, and so it came to be seen that 'believing these confessions must mean believing justification'.[82] What had begun, for Luther, as 'living acts of faith and devotion'

---

[77] *Kingdom of Christ*, i. 65–74.   [78] Ibid. 85–6.   [79] Ibid. 88.
[80] Ibid. 109.   [81] Ibid. 110–11.   [82] Ibid. 115–16.

had come to be articulated as 'very precise and accurate expressions' of 'definitions and propositions'.[83] Thus, 'Pure Protestantism' was encompassed in an analytical movement from its founding principles through to the growth and development of these distinctive theological insights in the very different histories of the branches of Protestantism in existence in Maurice's day.[84] Maurice explicated the relationship of principles to systems through a historical method that contrasted aspects of the spiritual truth given to human beings (the truth found out by 'reason') with the ensnaring of truth in the provisional, partial, intellectual constructions of the human understanding.

There is an incompleteness about Maurice's exposition here, as already acknowledged. Looking forward, briefly, to the world of modern ecumenical theology, it would seem natural to conclude that Maurice envisioned the rehabilitation of all of these positive principles into a richer and more comprehensive idea of the Catholic Church, and that such an idea was at best only partially present even in his own Church. But that remains an inference from these chapters, and not an explicit conclusion.

Having placed the search for the 'principles' of the Catholic Church in the foreground in the first three chapters, Maurice's focus shifted in the final chapter of Part 1 to a search, not so much for specific principles (though some emerged), but for the fragmented *presence* of Catholicity in various movements, including those which had little to do ostensibly with the Christian Church. However much it differed in scope from the first three, this fourth chapter was consistent in its assumption that there is truth in various movements of thought within Protestantism, and that this truth itself must be consistent with the Catholicity of the Church. So Maurice was able to claim that the creation of a distinctive machinery of organization by Methodism was itself an indication of a Catholic feeling (the dependence of voluntary combination on 'some higher and more universal relation') in 'the very heart' of Protestantism.[85] Kant's reaction against the empiricist tradition was taken to be evidence itself of the demand for 'something Catholic . . . as the very groundwork of faith', because it overthrew the view that individual experience alone can establish the truth of religion.[86] Even the French Revolution, despite the professed atheism of many of its protagonists, in its very search for a

---

[83] *Kingdom of Christ*, i.116–17.

[84] Significantly, Maurice did not discuss Zwinglianism at any length, simply because it 'was not able to work out a system or church for itself': it was not necessary for his teleological view of the development of Protestant principles, since it disappeared in the sixteenth century: ibid., 130.

[85] Ibid. 157.

[86] Ibid. 194.

'universal polity', demonstrated the persistence of the idea that there is a universal, spiritual society for all human beings.[87] At this point, the reader could well feel that Maurice's method had become absurdly over-extended. Almost anything, any group, movement, or association in human affairs, could be ransacked for principles or features that were supposed to point to deeper truth. The pliability of Maurice's method becomes transparent here, and it is perhaps understandable that he failed to develop this chapter as an integral part of his argument. Yet the main point was clear enough. All these movements were 'hints' that there is a Catholic Church that is the basic truth of all human association, and therefore the key to resolving the social, political, and religious divisions of the nineteenth century. What that Church might be, and how it might be identified in practice, is the subject of Part 2.

THE KINGDOM OF CHRIST 2: THE 'SIGNS' OF THE CATHOLIC CHURCH

The title of Part 2 is 'Of the Catholic Church and the Romish System'. Its main purpose was to identify the institutional features of Catholicity. No systematic view was presented of the Roman Catholic Church, which was dealt with mainly in relation to its failure to preserve adequately the six 'signs' of Catholicity that Maurice enumerated. The question at issue for Maurice was only 'Why is the Romish Church not *the* Catholic Church in England?'

A first chapter of 'Recapitulation' reinforced the impression that the principles identified in relation to Quakerism, 'Pure Protestantism', and Unitarianism in Part 1 were to be regarded as complementary aspects of the truth of the Catholic Church. Maurice admitted, for example, that the Lutheran view of justification (and especially the *anti*-individualism implied in its emphasis on God's initiative) was necessary as a complement to the Quaker doctrine of the indwelling Word.[88] The desire for a universal society evident in the political movements of the eighteenth and early nineteenth centuries must be complemented by the acknowledgement of a 'spiritual' society.[89] In a short but pregnant passage, Maurice rolled up the conclusions of Part 1 with the suggestion that the kingdom of God, or spiritual society (and so by implication the Catholic Church), is itself a determining fact of human being: 'the spiritual and universal society must

---

[87] Ibid. 206–18.   [88] Ibid. 244.
[89] 'It is equally impossible for men to be content with a spiritual society which is not universal, and with a universal society which is not spiritual': ibid. 251.

be involved in the very idea of our human constitution, say rather, must be that constitution, by virtue of which we realise that there is a humanity'.[90]

In a short second chapter on 'Indications of a Spiritual Constitution', Maurice suggested briefly two dimensions of the kingdom of Christ that find embodiment in actual human societies, the family and the nation. As we have seen already, for Maurice these are subordinate elements of the spiritual society. This was the first explicit enunciation in Maurice's published work of themes to which he was to return again and again. The element of nationality and its bearing on the Church received further consideration later in *The Kingdom of Christ*; the family did not.[91] There is, then, a certain lack of balance in the discussion. Here, all that was suggested was that the family is a microcosm of the relations of mutual dependence which characterize the kingdom of God as a whole, and the primary form in which the perception of 'spiritual things' is mediated to human beings.[92] Family and nation are interdependent. Following Coleridge's 'opposition and necessary harmony of Law and Religion', however, family, nation, and, by implication, Church, are not *absolutely* harmonious. There is evidence in history that the principles of family life may be in conflict with national polity (Maurice here referred to Sparta, Athens, and Rome), even though at the same time the civil law both defines responsibilities (thus apparently encroaching on relations) and resists actions that erode human community.[93] The nation, like the family, Maurice concluded, thus had the characteristics of a spiritual constitution, inasmuch as it was founded on interdependence.[94] But both family and nation were limited elements, and gave way in time to the desire for something 'more comprehensive'.[95] In summary, in this chapter, vital elements of the overall framework of the 'spiritual constitution', the kingdom of God, were sketched.

This bare framework of family, nation, and Church was given more substance in the succeeding chapter on 'The Scriptural View of this Constitution'. Though short, this was arguably the central axis of the whole book. It contained a summary view of the biblical basis of the Church, providing a necessary grounding of ecclesiology in the mission, words, and life of Jesus himself, and in the inspired witness to him.[96]

---

[90] 'It is equally impossible for men to be content with a spiritual society which is not universal, and with a universal society which is not spiritual': ibid. 252.

[91] Maurice did finally make good this neglect in *Social Morality* (London: Macmillan, 1869).

[92] Maurice, *Kingdom of Christ*, i. 261, 264.

[93] Ibid. 267–8.

[94] Ibid. 268.

[95] Ibid. 269.

[96] Maurice's desire to ground his ecclesiology explicitly in Scripture surely reflected an implicit ordering of the sources of Christian doctrine which, however mediated through the

Maurice disavowed a systematic intention in this. Indeed, in a comment that fittingly illustrated his own practice, he suggested that system and method were by their very nature opposites.[97] Again, a Coleridgean perspective was present: 'system' denotes the construction of a rigid, simplified intellectual framework which cannot do justice to the complexity of reality ('that which is most opposed to life, freedom, variety'), whereas 'method' suggests the presence of a principle of interpretation which will bring to the surface the inner harmony of the text. Thus, reading the Bible as a collection of disparate texts would not yield a completely self-consistent doctrinal system. But it could be read for its underlying principles.

Yet here Maurice did not gather and survey biblical references to the Church, nor expound critically foundational events such as Pentecost, but instead traced the emergence of the Church through the history of the Jewish people. Family, nation, and Church were linked in a historical argument that threw a light on his understanding of their respective roles in the spiritual constitution. Family and nation were particularly germane to the history recorded in the Old Testament. The covenant between God and Israel was, said Maurice, a fundamental idea of the Bible.[98] But it was a covenant with, in the first instance, a family, with Abraham at its head.[99] Scripture described the establishment of a nation through this family in the Exodus story. The laws that had reflected the human relations of the family became the laws of a whole people, a nation.[100] The idea of the kingdom of God emerged out of the progressive transposition of human relations through the family, and the nation, to the revelation of the very basis of society in human dependence on God. This universal truth, expressed in the Church, was at once the result of a historical process and the revelation of the 'root' of Jewish history.[101] But it was in the life and ministry of Jesus that it was, finally, expressed. The proclamation of the kingdom of God is, Maurice said, the central idea of the Gospels.[102] As an internal kingdom, it was permanently true, through the incarnation of Christ: 'a communion had been opened

---

Church's tradition, did give priority to Scripture, and is in line with his avowed 'Protestantism'. Contrast the lack of explicit attention to the scriptural foundations of ecclesiology in, e.g., William Palmer's *Treatise on the Church of Christ* (London: Rivington, 1838), Gladstone's *The State in its Relations with the Church* (1838), W. G. Ward's *Ideal of a Christian Church* (London: Toovey, 1844), and J. H. Newman's *Essay on the Development of Christian Doctrine* (1845), ed. J. Cameron (Harmondsworth: Penguin, 1974).

[97] Maurice, *Kingdom of Christ*, i. 272–3.   [98] Ibid. 273.   [99] Ibid. 274.
[100] Ibid. 276–8.   [101] Ibid. 295.   [102] Ibid. 286.

between the visible and the invisible world'.[103] Externally, the universal
society was established through Christ's life, death, and resurrection.[104]
The whole story of Scripture culminates in the emergence of the Church:
'every step of the story . . . [leads us] to notice the Church as the child
which the Jewish polity had been carrying in its womb'.[105]

There are two questions raised by this exposition, neither of which is
answered directly. The first is simply: What is the relation between the
internal and external aspects of the universal kingdom? In describing the
Church as the root of Jewish history, Maurice suggested that it always
existed as an idea in the providence of God. But in identifying its foundation in the historical Jesus, Maurice implied that it had a definite beginning
in history. Maurice did not mean, *contra* 'Platonizing' readings, to suggest
that the temporal event of the Church was somehow less important than
its eternal existence. The meaning, Maurice says, 'must be embodied in
acts'.[106] The Church was established on 'the accomplishment' of the union
of heaven and earth in Jesus.[107] Yet, as an eternal idea, an aspect of God's
providence, it was also always present. The Church is both eternally true
and existent, since all creation is an unfolding unity of creative, providential design, and also a specificity of human relations. It is itself, essentially, a
continuation of the intersection of human and divine in the Incarnation
itself.[108]

Yet, further, what is the relation between the Church and the universal,
spiritual society? No definitive answer can be given on the basis of
Maurice's text. His talk of the Church as the 'highest part' of the spiritual
constitution, and of the family and nation as lower parts, suggests a
hierarchy of separate, but related, elements of social organization within
the one spiritual polity. But Maurice also used the terms 'spiritual' or
'universal' society and 'Church' interchangeably at times. Thus he could
write, 'we must not forget that while this universal society, according to
the historical conception of it, grew out of the Jewish family and nation, it
is, according to the theological conception of it, the root of both'.[109] It
would seem that the Church cannot be both a part of the spiritual
constitution, alongside other parts, and yet also identical with it. Yet,

---

[103] Maurice, *Kingdom of Christ*, i. 292.   [104] Ibid. 293.   [105] Ibid.
[106] Ibid. 292.   [107] Ibid. 293.

[108] This is far from an original note in Anglicanism, though it is a characteristic one for the
'revival' of incarnational theology in the nineteenth century. Much later, Charles Gore, for
example, was to use even more explicit language than Maurice in this respect: 'The Church is
the body of Christ. It is the extension and perpetuation of the Incarnation in the world. It is
this, because it embodies the same principle, and lives by the same life': C. Gore, *The
Incarnation of the Son of God* (1891; new edn., London: Murray, 1922), 219.

[109] Maurice, *Kingdom of Christ*, i. 295.

whilst this issue was never faced explicitly, it can perhaps be hypothesized from Maurice's account, on the one hand, that the actual families, nations, and the Church of history are the temporal instantiation of the kingdom of God, the 'spiritual constitution', but that, on the other hand, only the Church really identifies itself consciously and completely with the providential purposes of God. In language that Maurice himself did not use, we might say that the Church is both 'already' and 'not yet', perfect and yet provisional. It is complete in itself, and as such a revelation of the final purpose or end of history, and yet also itself on the way towards that end.

All the more significant, then, are the marks by which the Church is known in history. Maurice proceeded to examine these in his influential discussion of the six 'signs' of the Catholic Church in the fourth chapter of Part 2. Interestingly, we should note in passing that, at the very beginning of the chapter, he used the word 'locality' in place of 'nationality', a substitution rich in interpretative possibilities.[110] But there is one other comment worth noting here. Maurice said that the existence of definite, distinctive 'signs' was essential to the Church's universality: if it lost its distinctness, 'it loses its meaning, loses . . . its universality'.[111] In other words, it ceased to be the Church if these external 'signs' were compromised. That this was so was an indication that Maurice's ecclesiology, for all its blurred edges and paradoxes, inhabited the same sacramental understanding of reality as that of his contemporaries in High Church Anglicanism. It provided, at this stage, an important indication that the ecumenical sympathy of Part 1 of *The Kingdom of Christ* did not involve simply an exaggerated or exclusive emphasis on the invisibility of the Catholic Church.

Maurice may have been drawing deliberately on a tradition already extant within Anglicanism: namely, the identification of the external 'notes' or signs by which particular churches could be considered truly part of the Catholic Church. This was a tradition with roots in Patristic history, but which became especially important in the aftermath of the Reformation. Thus, for example, in his *Apology of the Church of England* (1562), Bishop John Jewel in the sixteenth century had already laid down a defence of the Church of England's Catholicity against the Roman Church, emphasizing a common inheritance of faith in the Catholic creeds, and a common possession, *inter alia*, of the threefold orders of ministry, the sacraments of baptism and eucharist, and canonical

---

[110] Hence the Romantic nationalism of aspects of Maurice's writing on ecclesiology could in theory be purged to make way for the modern recognition, in ecumenical dialogue, of the importance of local ecclesial diversity.

[111] Maurice, *Kingdom of Christ*, i. 301.

Scriptures.[112] But Jewel did not isolate these as defining 'notes' of the Church's Catholicity. Richard Field did, however, in his *Of the Church* (1606), in which faith, sacraments, and orders of ministry were claimed to 'perpetually distinguish the true Catholic Church from all other societies of men'.[113] Field's development of the idea was followed by other Anglican writers, mainly from the High Church school. Later in the nineteenth century, the four 'notes' of creeds, baptism and eucharist, threefold ministry, and Scripture were to be taken as defining the basis of possible Church reunion for Anglicans, and formalized in the Chicago–Lambeth Quadrilateral.[114] Maurice's formulation of the six 'signs' of the Catholic Church in *The Kingdom of Christ* has been widely taken as directly influential in the emergence of the Quadrilateral.[115] That this long history of the idea of the 'notes' of the Church is somewhere in the background seems likely, but again it cannot be proved.[116]

Thus, with little theoretical preparation or explanation, Maurice plunged into a detailed analysis of the six 'signs' of the Catholic Church. Each of these merits detailed discussion, but exposition here will have to be succinct. The six 'signs' can be divided notionally into three groups; but in order to do this, I shall revert to the order of exposition followed largely in the first edition. This is because, in the second edition, it is difficult to discern a specific rationale in the order chosen. Here, I class together the two dominical sacraments of baptism and eucharist, as in the first edition. A second group consists of Scripture and the creeds, though in the first

---

[112] See J. E. Booty (ed.), *John Jewel's Apology of the Church of England* (London: SPCK, 1963), 22–30; but see also W. M. Southgate, *John Jewel and the Problem of Doctrinal Authority* (Cambridge, Mass.: Harvard University Press, 1963), ch. 12, 'The Church', for a clear exposition of the reasons why Jewel's defence of the Catholicity of the Church of England does not erect these features of common inheritance into a theory of the *essential* character of the Church; for Jewel, the Catholic Church subsists in the entire body of the faithful in doctrine, without regard for institutional form.

[113] Cited in P. E. More and F. L. Cross (eds.), *Anglicanism* (London: SPCK, 1935, 45); there is a brief discussion in H. R. McAdoo, *The Spirit of Anglicanism: A Survey of Anglican Theological Method in the Seventeenth Century* (London: A. & C. Black, 1965), 373–5.

[114] Adopted by the Lambeth Conference in 1888 for all the Anglican churches; for a full text, see G. R. Evans and J. R. Wright (eds.), *The Anglican Tradition: A Handbook of Sources* (London: SPCK, 1991), 354–5.

[115] See, e.g., Woodhouse-Hawkins, 'Maurice, Huntington, and the Quadrilateral'.

[116] Identification of 'notes' of the Church in the way outlined in this paragraph should not be confused with the tradition of the four 'marks' or 'notes' of the Church derived from the Nicene Creed as One, Holy, Catholic and Apostolic, though it was often subsumed under this. Though William Palmer, in his *Treatise on the Church*, based the first part of his work on the Unity, Sanctity, Catholicity, and Apostolicity of the Church, and discussed the ancient tradition of these four 'notes', he was not averse to describing the historic succession of the ministry as a 'note' of the Church, under the heading of 'The Church Apostolical': ibid. i. 143. Maurice did not go so far as to unchurch non-episcopal churches.

edition the latter were subsumed under liturgical forms. Finally, Maurice's treatment of the historic ministry and liturgical order can, to an extent, be taken together.

There are a few clues here to a general theory of sacraments. Perhaps following Augustine, he acknowledged a very broad view of sacred signs, according to which almost anything in God's creation, by virtue of its createdness, points to its maker.[117] Yet there were specific sacraments, which had a 'pure untroubled element, which has no significancy [*sic*], except as the organ through which the voice of God speaks to man, and through which he may answer: "Thy servant heareth" '.[118] Baptism and eucharist were ordained to carry a special meaning over and above their natural signification of washing and eating, and both signified and effected a beginning or real change of some kind. So Maurice could speak of baptism as 'obtaining a blessing', and as 'the admission of men into [the everlasting kingdom] at the first'.[119] He could speak of the eucharist as a means through which believers 'really receive . . . all the spiritual blessings', including 'that strength and renewal by which [the individual spirit is] enabled to do its appointed work'.[120] But he could also stress that the sacrament does not initiate the spiritual reality itself, but symbolizes and translates its eternal reality into temporal terms.[121] Baptism was the final step in the 'gradual discovery' of the divine, Trinitarian unity that lies at the heart of all unity between men and women.[122] As the first edition put it even more succinctly, baptism is 'the sacrament of constant union'.[123] And the eucharist, too, signified a permanent presence, localized and received precisely because it is an omnipresence of God.[124] Elsewhere, Maurice described it as 'the Sacrament of [Christ's] continual presence with His universal family'.[125]

---

[117] 'No doubt the world is full of sacraments . . . all have a holy sacramental meaning, and should be viewed as such by us': Maurice, *Kingdom of Christ*, ii. 87. Compare Augustine, as cited in H. Bettenson, *The Later Christian Fathers* (Oxford: Oxford University Press, 1970), 244.

[118] Maurice, *Kingdom of Christ*, ii. 87.

[119] Ibid. i. 306–7.

[120] Ibid. ii. 63.

[121] Whilst in the 1st edn. of *The Kingdom of Christ*, Maurice openly criticized the High Church view of baptism as an event which marks an entrance into a new relationship (needless to say, it is the idea of a *new* relationship with which he had difficulty, rather than the idea of 'event'), by the revision of the 2nd edn. all direct references to the 'High Church' view had disappeared: Maurice, *Kingdom of Christ*, 1st edn., i. 96–111.

[122] Maurice, *Kingdom of Christ*, i. 329.

[123] Ibid., 1st edn., i. 96.

[124] Maurice, *Kingdom of Christ*, ii. 81.

[125] F. D. Maurice, *The Prayer-Book Considered Especially in Reference to the Romish System: Nineteen Sermons* (1849), with *The Lord's Prayer* (London: Macmillan, 1880), 230–1.

In summary, Maurice implied a threefold theory of sacraments, unrelated explicitly to the traditional, Catholic theory of sacramental composition, but consistent with it. In every sacrament there was an 'ordinance', or specific provision ordained by God (in effect this includes 'matter' and 'form'), a temporal action in the life of the believer effected by the sacrament (here 'intention' is relevant in the form of faith as a receiving power), and a permanent and eternal union between God and human beings, established in Christ, which ultimately drove the operation of the sacrament itself.[126]

So baptism both began the believer's life in the kingdom *and* instantiated for the believer a union with God already true through the reconciling life and ministry of Jesus Christ. Baptism, for Maurice, was egalitarian, in that it dispensed with the idea of all spiritual gradations between human beings.[127] All human beings had a spiritual 'eye', which could be closed by self-will, or opened through 'baptismal fellowship'.[128]

Asserting the centrality of the eucharist in Christian worship, Maurice's position bore some comparison to that of his High Church contemporaries.[129] He presented an objective view of sacramental presence, but one located primarily in the gathered community of the Church, rather than in the consecrated elements as such.[130] Nevertheless, consecration was necessary to 'divert' the elements from their ordinary use as bread and wine, in order that they might become 'purely sacramental'; celebration by an ordained minister was necessary for this.[131] Here, again, Maurice's language was suggestive, but insufficiently precise. 'Diversion from ordinary use' could imply the total annihilation of the substance of bread and wine,

---

[126] In a very suggestive letter to Sara Coleridge, Maurice hinted at a conception of sacraments as a divine language expressing the fullness of truths which human language could articulate but partially: 'The deepest conviction in my mind . . . is that there is some organ for the higher spiritual realities and apprehensions answering the purpose which verbal forms and propositions answer for the facts of the understanding. Such an organ tho' [illegible] of all seems to be to him [i.e. Coleridge] provided for us in *Sacraments*. These, I look upon as the transcendent language, bringing out truths full orbed of which in our [illegible] & systems we can exhibit but one side or [illegible].' Letter dated 1 Mar. 1843, King's College, London, Archives, Relton Library, Box 5037–M4–R.

[127] This is vividly echoed in the description of Maurice's disciple, the Christian Socialist priest Stewart Headlam, of baptism as 'the great sacrament of equality': S. D. Headlam, *Christian Socialism: A Lecture* (London: Fabian Society, 1892), 7.

[128] Maurice, *Kingdom of Christ*, i. 327.

[129] Ibid. ii. 57–8. In addition to High Churchmen, there were also Evangelicals contending *re* the importance of the eucharist: see C. J. Cocksworth, *Evangelical Eucharistic Thought in the Church of England* (Cambridge: Cambridge University Press, 1993), 72–7.

[130] Hence his combination of a view of faith as a receptive power with criticism of the Lutheran doctrine of 'real presence' for over-individualizing presence: Maurice, *Kingdom of Christ*, ii. 84–6.

[131] Ibid. 87, 106.

but it is unlikely, *prima facie*, that Maurice would have endorsed such a view.[132] Later in the book, he suggested that the Anglican liturgy implies no change as such in the elements, but does imply a doctrine of real presence.[133]

There are similar ambiguities in his view of eucharistic sacrifice. The participation of the faithful in the eucharist was participation in the completed sacrifice of Christ.[134] Every eucharist was derivatively sacrificial: Christ's own sacrifice has formed the Church as one body, by reconciling humankind to God.[135] But Maurice's primary aim in his treatment of the eucharist as 'sign' of the Catholic Church was not to produce a new theory of the sacrament, but to emphasize God's prior initiative in it:

I have maintained that because the sacrifice had once for all accomplished the object of bringing our race, constituted and redeemed in Christ, into a state of acceptance and union with God, *therefore* it was most fitting that there should be an act whereby we are admitted into the blessings thus claimed and secured to us.[136]

The relationship between baptism and eucharist was left undefined. Recent attempts to harness Maurice to a baptismal ecclesiology, in which the Church is, in effect, coterminous with the community of the baptized, press Maurice further than his own writing will go.[137] As we have seen already, it is by no means certain that Maurice's treatment of the 'principles' of the Catholic Church in Part 1 would allow him unreservedly to apply the term 'Catholic Church' even to all Christian communities using Trinitarian baptism. In describing baptism and eucharist as 'signs' of the Catholic Church, Maurice was committing himself to a position in which they were taken almost to be *necessary* signs. But he presented no theory of impaired communion between churches, nor did he explain how the

---

[132] The 2nd edn. of *The Kingdom of Christ* was completed before the issues of eucharistic presence and sacrifice had become highly controverted in High Church circles: Pusey's sermon *The Holy Eucharist a Comfort to the Penitent* was not preached until May 1843, Robert Wilberforce's *The Doctrine of the Holy Eucharist* was published in 1854, and John Keble's treatise *On Eucharistical Adoration* was published in 1857. Controversy over eucharistic theology was mainly a feature of Tractarianism post-1845.

[133] Maurice, *Kingdom of Christ*, ii. 369. Inasmuch as this seems to connote a notion of real, objective, but spiritual (as opposed to trans- or con-substantial) presence, it may be compatible with certain strands of Anglican eucharistic theology from the seventeenth century: see, e.g., H. R. McAdoo and K. Stevenson, *The Mystery of the Eucharist in the Anglican Tradition* (Norwich: Canterbury Press, 1995), esp. chs. 1–4. Maurice's treatment is hardly clear enough to assert this with any certainty, but it is at least likely that he would have favoured McAdoo and Stevenson's appropriation of the notion of *mystery* as the primary context in which eucharistic presence is to be conceived.

[134] Maurice, *Kingdom of Christ*, ii. 63.

[135] Ibid. 70.

[136] Ibid. 74.

[137] See Avis, *Anglicanism and the Christian Church*, 260–70.

Catholic Church might survive without its 'signs'. Thus it is not possible to go further simply than to say that *both* sacraments are intrinsic elements of the Catholicity of the Church of Christ, as it exists in the world.

Scripture and creeds form, for our purposes, the second group of 'signs', and can be dealt with together. Both are sources of doctrinal authority, and interdependent. The Nicene and Apostles' creeds have a common relation to baptism, in that the central fact they present, 'a condescension of God to man', is also 'the primary postulate' of the spiritual constitution as signified by baptism.[138] But Maurice described them as complementary presentations of the knowledge of God: the Apostles' Creed declared the 'distinct personality' of Father, Son, and Spirit, whereas the Nicene Creed demonstrated the relations within the Godhead.[139] In this doctrinal role, they were witnesses to the principles encountered in the Bible, and they were required to check misinterpretations of the Bible.[140] As Maurice said, 'the creed is a document which has served as a protection to the meaning of the Scriptures against the tendency which the Church doctors in different ages have exhibited to disturb and mangle them'.[141] Thus, the creeds are a sign of the Church's Catholicity precisely because they are a statement of the central truths of the Christian faith.

Scripture, to Maurice, had a self-authenticating quality. The possibility of the canon was the same as the possibility of Scripture itself.[142] The very existence of such a witness to the truth of the Christian faith as that presented in Scripture was also—on the presupposition of the truth of the revelation—a guarantee of its ultimate consistency. The Scriptures for this very reason were to be taken 'for granted', rather than grounded upon some ulterior principle such as primitive antiquity.[143] This did not rule out critical inquiry, but it did reflect a critique of rationalist criticism that used a general principle of reason to assess the truth of Scripture. The ideas of Scripture could not be separated from the events to which it witnessed; otherwise 'living ideas [are turned] into mere notions and apprehensions of our mind'.[144] This was a defence of the historicity of Christian revelation: the events are intrinsic to the truth to which they point. What is true of the relation between Scripture and the events it describes is also true, by implication, of the relation between Scripture as sign and the Catholic Church itself. Thus, Church and Bible are interdependent.[145]

The third, and final, group of 'signs' consisted of the ministry of the Church, and fixed forms of worship, or liturgy. Both derived their

---

[138] Maurice, *Kingdom of Christ*, ii. 8.   [139] Ibid. 9–10.   [140] Ibid. 13–14.
[141] Ibid. 21.   [142] Ibid. 180.   [143] Ibid. 188.   [144] Ibid. 192.
[145] Ibid. 214.

authority as signs specifically from the persistence of the Church through time. Maurice's view of the institution of the threefold ministry in its basic elements was again broadly High Church, though most of his comments were confined to episcopacy. Episcopacy was the 'root' of all forms of ministry; found also in the East, it was universal in the West until the sixteenth century, and still existed in many of the churches of the Reformation, as well as the Roman Catholic Church.[146] Grounded in Christ's calling of the apostles, episcopacy was one of the 'appointed and indispensable signs' of the spiritual and universal society.[147] It perpetuated that office, apostleship, by which the Church was constituted at its foundation.[148] So ordination was a warrant of continual inspiration, in contrast to the 'occasional' inspiration of the Old Testament prophets.[149] A fixed liturgical tradition was a sign that 'in the deepest and most practical sense there is a community which the distinction of tongues and the succession of ages cannot break'.[150] Thus liturgy, like the ministry, both symbolized and guaranteed the historical existence of the Catholic Church. It was not merely an aggregate of prayers of individuals, but the prayer of the body of the Church as a whole.[151]

In both instances there were significant variations from conventional High Church views. In relation to ministry, Maurice departed from a monarchical model of episcopacy. The ministry of the ordained mediated Christ to the people, but representatively and not vicariously. It was a representative role, because it demonstrated a real union between God and human beings, whereas the vicarious role (which Maurice assumed to be true of Roman Catholic theology of ministry) presumed the presence of a veil separating men and women from God.[152] Furthermore, as Maurice argued, 'according to the representative doctrine all ministers exhibit Christ in that office to which they are called', and so the whole body of bishops, and each bishop in his own jurisdiction, 'present him to men as the bishop or overseer of the Church'.[153] Since this representative doctrine was expounded in critical response to Roman Catholic teaching, it was not fully developed here. Its implications for an Anglican theology of Church order, and also for *lay* vocations, were profound, however. In relation to liturgy, Maurice claimed that the Catholicity of the Church was served, not by absolute uniformity, but by local diversity. Locality and persistence in time were complementary elements of the function of liturgy as a 'sign' of Catholicity.[154]

---

146 Ibid. 110–13.   147 Ibid. 120.   148 Ibid. 149.   149 Ibid. 133.
150 Ibid. 29.   151 Ibid.   152 Ibid. 171–2.   153 Ibid. 175.
154 Ibid. 28.

Thus, in relation to each of the six 'signs' of the Catholic Church, Maurice presented a wide-ranging but condensed and partial exposition of significant ecclesiological themes. Section by section, Maurice addressed one further question. What are we to make of the claim to Catholicity of a Church which still possessed all of the six signs intact, just like the Church of England, yet which also possessed a near-universal presence in the world, such as the Roman Catholic Church? *The Kingdom of Christ's* aim of demonstrating how all that is positive in the separated branches of the Christian Church is preserved intact in the Church of England assumed Anglicanism as its very starting-point. It did not set out to prove from first principles that the Church of England uniquely conformed to the true biblical doctrine of the Church. To do that would have required a fundamental theology of faith and the Church, a 'system' of the kind Maurice abjured. Even so, he appeared to assume that if the Church of England was not uniquely the Catholic Church, nevertheless the Catholicity of the Church subsisted in the Church of England more completely than it did in other churches of the realm.

Why was this so? Why was it not possible simply to substitute Roman Catholicism for Anglicanism in Maurice's argument? Maurice offered two reasons. First, though the Roman Catholic Church had preserved the outward form of the signs of Catholicity, it had perverted their inner meaning. The Roman Church had individualized the sacraments of baptism and eucharist, turning them from corporate acts that derived their efficacy from Christ's continual union with his Church into events which were effective in themselves. The sacramental theology of *opus operatum* had led, in the case of baptism, to a view of the sacrament as the personal acquisition of purity, rather than the renunciation of personal worth.[155] The Roman view of the eucharist assumed a repeated sacrifice, by which the priest pleaded for admission into the presence of God, and did not claim the privilege of admission for the gathered people.[156] Here, Maurice was evidently recycling contemporary misconceptions about Roman Catholicism. Like many of the Anglican intelligentsia, he was reasonably well-travelled in Europe, but he rarely drew anything from his exposure to continental Catholicism other than the conviction that his own prejudices about popular Catholicism were correct.[157] He was able to call 'Popery' 'not the excess of everything good, but simply the denial of it'.[158] He may have confused 'popular Romanism' with the official theology of the

---

[155] Maurice, *Kingdom of Christ*, ii. 337–9.   [156] Ibid. ii. 101–6.

[157] Prothero, for example, has an account of Maurice and Stanley on holiday together on the continent in 1840; Maurice, Stanley said, 'is a most enthusiastic traveller': Prothero, *Life . . . of Stanley*, 138.

[158] Maurice, *Life*, i. 321.

Roman Catholic Church, as Newman was later to admit he himself had done.

But his chief objection centred on the connected issues of authority and nationality.[159] He rejected outright the suggestion that there could be any visible substitute on earth for Christ's headship of the Church. Elsewhere, he wrote that the doctrine of a visible centre was 'a monstrous practical heresy'.[160] The pretension of the Papacy to universal dominion confused the signs of the Church with the ecclesiastical arrangements that had been put in place to secure them, and so the 'Divine origin and constitution of the Church' was obscured.[161] It was perhaps an implication of Maurice's emphasis on the kingdom of Christ that he should also have had a corresponding emphasis on Christ's kingship, and that his view of any form of universal primacy should be one in which authority was consensual rather than hierarchical.[162] But this was strengthened by his view of nationality. The Reformation's reassertion of the rights of national sovereigns over the territorial jurisdiction of the Papacy had, for Maurice, divine warrant.

By the end of this chapter on the 'signs', Maurice had sketched the main outlines of his account of Catholicity. He had identified three dimensions of the Catholic Church as extrapolations from Scripture, doctrine, and history: namely, its principles, signs, and constitution. The 'principles' of the Catholic Church were presented only as 'hints', not as a comprehensive view. But implied in his approach was the belief that Christian doctrine is complex and multi-faceted, striving to capture comprehensively the mystical reality it expresses, but in most historical circumstances doing so at best partially. Sectarianism masked the presence within separated churches of aspects, or 'principles', of the one greater truth for which the Catholic Church stood. But the Catholic Church itself was part of a 'spiritual constitution', an ordering of the universe by God: there was a convergent trajectory in history in the created desire of human beings for the spiritual society and the Catholicity of the Christian Church itself. The Church prefigured creation in union with its creator, and as such was the 'spiritual constitution' in its highest state on earth, but it was also one part,

---

[159] 'A body acknowledging itself connected with the Church in all previous ages by the bond of sacraments, of creeds, of worship, of ministerial succession, has the prima facie marks of Catholicity . . . If the Romish body say that it stands in certain notions about sacraments and about orders, and not in its sacraments and in the orders themselves, that declaration is a practical renunciation of its claims to be a Church': Maurice, *Kingdom of Christ*, ii. 374.

[160] Maurice, *Life*, i. 326.

[161] Maurice, *Kingdom of Christ*, ii. 322.

[162] See Maurice, *Gospel of the Kingdom of Heaven*, *passim*, for exposition of the theme of Christ's kingship.

albeit the highest, alongside other elements of social organization: namely, the family and the nation. Despite its history of change, disunity, and conflict, it was indefectible, its persistence protected by material signs or ordinances in history.

THE KINGDOM OF CHRIST 3: THE NATIONAL CHURCH

By the time Maurice got to the point in *The Kingdom of Christ* at which he wanted to discuss the relationship between the Church and the nation—in the final chapter of Part 2—his overall position had already been sketched sufficiently to make his task little more than one of clarification. The same is also true of the whole of Part 3, which in the second edition consisted of two short chapters on the Church of England. The final chapter of Part 2, 'The Church and the Nation', contained a brief summary of Maurice's position. His conception of the nation as a subordinate element of the spiritual constitution had two competing implications. The nation was a permanent, divinely ordained mode of organization. Undoubtedly he over-simplified his description of different national cultures, and over-idealized 'Englishness' in particular. But his argument did nevertheless contain an implicit check to this. As a *subordinate* element in the spiritual constitution, the nation, with all the authority which flows from national self-determination, was open to challenge by the Church, should it exceed its natural responsibilities.

   Even so, the language of divine national vocation was stronger than that used in the first edition of the book. Maurice baldly reasserted the biblical root of the 'Divine principles' of national society.[163] Just as the Old Testament was fulfilled in the New, so the kingdom of Christ, the universal society, did not supersede nations, but was instead the 'quickening spirit' of them.[164] Imperial Rome had set itself up illegitimately as a universal dominion.[165] Remarkably, Maurice judged the Constantinian settlement a failure, attempting to graft the universal spiritual society on to a pretended temporal one. Thus all attempts to suppress national society or autonomy were doomed. The argument was circular: Maurice simply assumed those very 'national principles' whose force or existence he concluded from his consideration of history. The whole history of modern Europe demonstrated the necessary interaction of Church and nation:

As before, a spiritual element was proved to be necessary to uphold a legal society, so now, a legal element, a body expressing the sacredness and majesty of law, is

---

[163] Maurice, *Kingdom of Christ*, ii. 235.   [164] Ibid. 240.   [165] Ibid. 241.

shewn to be necessary in order to fulfil the objects for which the spiritual and universal society exists.[166]

So national society and the Church were harmonious and in creative tension: 'God's gracious purposes' are that 'these two powers must be meant continually to act and react upon each other, and to learn better, by each new error they commit, their distinct functions, their perfect harmony'.[167]

In the remainder of the chapter, Maurice considers in turn a series of objections to his theory. Against those who would separate Church and nation absolutely on the grounds that the State is secular, he reaffirmed the spiritual character of the nation.[168] Against the 'Patricians' (an unusual designation which seems to indicate a desire to return to the universal government and order of the Church in its early centuries), Maurice proposed a distinction between ordinances and ceremonies: national churches did not contradict the existence of a universal Church, but possessed their own characteristic forms of ceremony within the ordinances, principles, and constitution of the Catholic Church.[169] Possibly this was yet another barb against the Tractarians, with their insistence on the ancient *regulum fidei*. Since the Reformation, Maurice argued, it had been evident to 'thinking persons' that there were 'two principles struggling in Christendom for supremacy': one, in Protestantism, resisting the spiritual power's claim to extra-national dominion, and the other, in Catholicism, resisting particular states' efforts to divide their subjects from the Church.[170] It may be the will of God in the modern era, Maurice suggested, to reconcile these elements—a hint of Maurice's own ambition in *The Kingdom of Christ*.[171]

It was in the final, short Part 3 of the work that the implications of Maurice's ecclesiological theory for the Church of England in particular were spelt out. The two chapters of this part of the book constituted a short *summa* of Maurice's entire method. There were four basic steps in the argument.

First, Maurice posed the question, 'Are these principles applicable to our circumstances as Englishmen?'[172] He denied that he was seeking to establish the inherent superiority of the English Church.[173] His concern, instead, was to demonstrate that national society and the universal society, or Church, could not be separated from each other, but must work in conjunction, so that 'that form of character which is intended for each nation' might be developed through the 'spiritual body' within it.[174] The

---

[166] Ibid. 246.   [167] Ibid. 247.   [168] Ibid. 297.
[169] Ibid. 321–2.   [170] Ibid. 327.   [171] Ibid. 328.
[172] Ibid. 361.   [173] Ibid.   [174] Ibid. 362.

Catholicity of the Church could not be deduced simply from accumulating the opinions of individual Anglican divines.[175] Through the medium of the liturgy, as the primary vehicle of the national identity of the Church, Maurice re-examined briefly his six 'signs' of Catholicity, affirming their continued presence within the Church of England. In essence, they constituted the basis of the Church of England's claim to Catholicity.[176]

The second step of his argument involved a historical assessment of the vicissitudes of the Church of England since the Reformation. This assumed a claim of historical continuity: a body 'acknowledging itself connected with the Church in all previous ages by the bond of sacraments, of creeds, of worship, of ministerial succession, has the *prima facie* marks of Catholicity'.[177] The Roman Catholic Church could not claim this, because it had corrupted the signs of Catholicity into 'notions', a form of anti-Catholicism.[178] But the Church of England did not seek to systematize itself. Its Articles did not begin, as was the case with Calvinism, from a conviction of human sinfulness which then became the basis of a theological system, but from a restatement of the 'Catholic foundation' of the Trinity, the Incarnation, the being of God, the Scriptures, and the creeds.[179]

All of the positive principles which Maurice had detected in Quakerism, Lutheranism, Calvinism, and Unitarianism were present, he claimed, 'in the forms of our English Church'.[180] But their corruption of these principles into 'systems' was deliberately rejected. And the principles themselves were combined with a conjunction of religious and civil authority. Both the sense of religious autonomy and the idea of civil responsibility were present at the inception of the Reformation in England.[181] Thus, as the act of a sovereign, rather than an outcome of changing belief as such,

---

[175] Maurice, *Kingdom of Christ*, ii. 363. Maurice is here indirectly criticizing the Tractarian practice of constructing *catenae* of authorities in support of a particular doctrinal position, which is then claimed to represent that view of the Church as a whole.

[176] From a perspective of Reformation scholarship, some aspects of Maurice's treatment of the six 'signs' in relation to the *Book of Common Prayer* are more persuasive than others. His conception of the liturgy as embodying Scripture, and of the creeds as 'acts of allegiance', 'preparations for prayer', and 'steps to communion', for example (Maurice, *Kingdom of Christ*, ii. 365, 373), is convincing enough, but it is less certain that his understanding of the notion of real presence in the eucharist is entirely consonant with the eucharistic theology at least of the first and second Prayer Books. On this last point, see D. MacCulloch, *Thomas Cranmer: A Life* (New Haven and London: Yale University Press, 1996), *passim*, but esp. ch. 9, 'Welcoming King Josiah: 1546–9'.

[177] Maurice., *Kingdom of Christ*, ii. 374.

[178] Ibid. 374.

[179] Ibid. 377.

[180] Ibid. 379.

[181] Ibid. 383.

the Reformation represented a reassertion of the nationality of the English Church.[182] But the Church of England was far from perfect. Despite the preservation of the essential form of the Church of England at the Restoration, the conflicts of the seventeenth century resulted in a narrowed conception of the Church, a conception initially projected through the attempted persecution of Dissenting minorities.[183] Then the increasing materialism of the eighteenth century took hold: the idea of the union of Church and State was reduced to an arrangement held together by 'some material outward terms of agreement'.[184] In this adverse historical judgement on the Church of England of an earlier age, Maurice was very much a child of his time.[185]

The third stage in his argument presented the three modern reactions to the eighteenth-century Church: the Liberal, Evangelical, and Catholic 'systems'.[186] Consistently with his method in the work as a whole, each of these positions was no sooner outlined than its essential principle was affirmed at the same time as its embodiment in an intellectual system was rejected. Thus the appeal of the 'Liberal' to the Church's adaptability in every age, its 'expansive power' was acknowledged, and yet the Liberal system's rejection of historic formularies was itself criticized.[187] The Evangelical's reassertion of faith in a real relationship between God and human beings was affirmed, at the same time as the Evangelical system's rejection of the location of this real relationship within the Church itself was rejected.[188] The Catholic's defence of the authority and spiritual power of the Church was confirmed, at the same time as the Catholic system's tendency to turn Church doctrine into a mediatorial or vicarial system was rejected.[189] All of these systems, Maurice argued, subverted each other, because their very tendency towards systematization undermined their own central principles.[190] But each of them also bore witness to 'the existence of a Divine Order'.[191] And what Maurice saw as a 'natural' English antipathy to system building limited the power, and so the defects, of each of these systems: 'in England we have a clearer witness

---

[182] Ibid. [183] Ibid. 386–7. [184] Ibid. 388. [185] Ibid. 397.

[186] In the context of the emergent language of church party, Maurice's assumption that these three represent contemporary Anglicanism comprehensively is significant. See, on the language of church party generally, Burns's introduction to Conybeare's 'Church Parties', 215–58. Maurice's tripartite discussion of Anglicanism in the 1842 edition of *The Kingdom of Christ* has been overlooked on p. 234 of Burns's essay, where Maurice appears as a proponent of a two-party division.

[187] Maurice, *Kingdom of Christ*, ii. 402–3.

[188] Ibid. 403–4.

[189] Ibid. 405–7.

[190] Ibid. 408.

[191] Ibid. 409.

than there is anywhere of our right to . . . emancipation' from these systems.[192]

The scene was set for the final, fourth step of Maurice's argument in relation to the contemporary Church of England. His dialectical examination of the principles and defects of each of the dominant party views within the Church of England had led to a vigorous reassertion of the comprehensive Catholicity of the Church. The regeneration of the English Church, Maurice asserted, would depend upon a reaffirmation of the principles each of these parties already held: 'they are the sap which is to invigorate and restore the oak trunk which has been standing for so many ages on our soil'.[193] But to do so, churchmen had to disavow party divisions. The political character of Englishmen practically obliged them to take up party organization when they had adopted particular principles.[194] At the risk of false accusations of eclecticism or syncretism, churchmen had to seek to reaffirm together the distinct principles of each 'school' of Anglicanism.[195] Maurice did not actually use the word 'comprehensive' here, but the implication of his argument was that the ecclesiology of the Church of England stood or fell by its comprehensive affirmation of its central principles, principles that by implication were also those of the Catholic Church as a whole.

Thus, Maurice's great survey of the ecclesiology of the Church of England drew to a close with a process of historical retrieval. Unlike the retrieval advocated by the Tractarians, however, his did not involve so much a return to a distant past, as the discernment and reassertion of principles that had always lain close to the heart of the Church of England. If the result of Maurice's argument was indeed a series of 'hints' about the principles, ordinances, and constitution of the Catholic Church, there were numerous *lacunae* and much imprecision in its presentation. It represented an unusual and possibly unique attempt to perceive the lineaments of the Catholicity of the whole Church in the particular history of one part of it. The complexity of the task that Maurice had set himself derived from his twofold aim to identify and uphold the Catholicity of the Church of England, and to affirm the Catholicity of separated portions of the Christian Church. Simultaneously, Maurice aimed to be a good Anglican and a good ecumenist. At points, the connection between these two goals simply proved unsustainable. He could present a coherent description of the external marks of Catholicity, the six 'signs', with the implication that failure to retain one or more of these marks impaired Catholicity, but without articulating any obvious connection to the 'principles' he had

---

[192] Maurice, *Kingdom of Christ*, ii. 410.   [193] Ibid. 411.
[194] Ibid. 413.   [195] Ibid. 412.

identified in the opening chapters of the book. He assumed intrinsically the truth of the Anglican position, and was obliged correspondingly to present the Roman position as formally correct in its possession of the 'signs', but internally corrupt. He read into the position of the national Church elements of national culture and character that were seemingly absolutized, against the grain of his own historical methodology. For much of the book, the concern to expound an ecclesiology that was true to the Church of England yet also ecumenically sensitive could be sustained only at the most general level of description.

THE JERUSALEM BISHOPRIC

The Kingdom of Christ remained Maurice's most sustained treatment of ecclesiology. Yet its status as an Anglican 'classic' was essentially the work of the twentieth century, not the nineteenth. Though Charles Kingsley called it, on Maurice's death, 'the ablest "Apology" for the Catholic faith which England has seen for more than two hundred years', this was the biased view of a disciple.[196] Maurice's obituaries, and the reviews of his son's *Life*, downplayed the work, or ignored it altogether. The radical *Westminster Review*, for example, asserted in 1884 that Maurice was 'most generally known only by his "Moral and Metaphysical Philosophy" '.[197] Certainly it was that work, the *Moral and Metaphysical Philosophy*, that was influential for many late nineteenth-century Anglicans, such as J. R. Illingworth.[198] But *The Kingdom of Christ* was to outlast Maurice's other works, above all because it encapsulated his view of the Christian Church. In time, its argument about Catholicity inhering in Church institutions and yet reflecting wider human aspirations was to be seen as central to the 'Mauricean' perspective. Just how adaptable to particular circumstances his theory was can be seen from his *Three Letters to the Rev. W. Palmer*, written in the heat of the dispute over the Jerusalem bishopric.

The proposal to establish a joint Anglican and Lutheran bishopric in Jerusalem in 1841 had its origin in British and German policy in the Middle East.[199] An initiative of the Prussian diplomat Chevalier Bunsen, friend and admirer of Maurice, it involved the alternating appointment of

[196] C. Kingsley, 'Frederick Denison Maurice: In memoriam', *Macmillan's Magazine*, 26 (1872), 84.

[197] *Westminster Review*, 122 (July and October 1884), 288.

[198] A. L. Illingworth, *The Life and Work of John Richardson Illingworth* (London: Murray, 1917), 244.

[199] 'The powers were manoeuvring for the loot which lay about as Turkey collapsed': Chadwick, *Victorian Church*, i. 189.

Anglican and Lutheran bishops, with shared jurisdiction over each other's admittedly small congregations in the Middle East.[200] But it provoked Tractarian outrage on two counts: first, because it appeared to treat German Lutheran churches as equivalents to the Church of England despite their loss of apostolic succession, and second, because it looked like an Erastian 'interference' in Church affairs.

Maurice's response to pamphlets of the Tractarian theologian William Palmer attacking the scheme was issued in a composite work, *Three Letters to the Rev. W. Palmer* (1842).[201] These letters constituted his most substantial contribution to Anglican ecclesiology apart from *The Kingdom of Christ*, and have attracted varying degrees of appreciation and opprobrium accordingly. They were met by hostile replies from Palmer himself, Pusey, and James Hope, amongst others.[202] But arguably they were more in tune with traditional High Church Anglicanism than was Tractarian criticism of the scheme, and more in line with actual Anglican practice in the late seventeenth and eighteenth centuries.[203] Norman Sykes, for example, saw Maurice as upholding and restating the Caroline position on episcopacy in his letters against Palmer, and even Peter Nockles has acknowledged that Maurice's arguments were 'in accord' with those of traditional High Church ecclesiology, even though his view of Catholicity was 'altogether more nebulous'.[204]

In fact, Maurice's position in these letters represented no more than a clarification of the argument of *The Kingdom of Christ*, with an endorsement of the scheme's approach to Church unity, and an interesting early use of the language of communion for a description of inter-church relations. The Catholicity of the Church could be identified through the

[200] The standard account of the proposal is R. W. Greaves, 'The Jerusalem Bishopric, 1841', *English Historical Review,* 64 (1949), but there is useful material too in Nockles, *Oxford Movement,* 157–64. Evidence of Bunsen's meetings with, and admiration for, Maurice can be gleaned from F. Bunsen, *A Memoir of Baron Bunsen* (London: Longmans, Green, 1868), *passim.*

[201] This was William Palmer of Magdalen College, Oxford, and not William Palmer of Worcester College, author of the *Treatise on the Church* (1838).

[202] See W. Palmer, *Aids to Reflection on the Seemingly Double Character of the Established Church, with Reference to the Foundation of a 'Protestant bishopric' at Jerusalem* (Oxford: Parker, 1841); E. B. Pusey, *A Letter to his Grace the Archbishop of Canterbury on Some Circumstances Connected with the Present Crisis in the English Church* (London: Parker, 1842); J. R. Hope, *The Bishopric of the United Church of England and Ireland at Jerusalem* (London: Stewart, 1841).

[203] See especially two articles by J. E. Pinnington: 'Anglican Openness to Foreign Protestant Churches in the Eighteenth Century: A Gloss on the Old Priest and New Presbyter Thesis of Norman Sykes', *Anglican Theological Review,* 51 (1969), and 'Church Principles and the Early Years of the Church Missionary Society: The Problem of the German Missionaries', *Journal of Theological Studies,* 20 (1969).

[204] N. Sykes, *Old Priest and New Presbyter: The Anglican Attitude to Episcopacy, Presbyterianism and Papacy since the Reformation* (Cambridge: Cambridge University Press, 1956), 213; Nockles, *Oxford Movement,* 164.

presence within it of external signs and articulated principles. These were not themselves *guarantors* of Catholicity, but necessary, historical expressions of the authority that proceeded from the presence of Christ himself within his Church. Palmer, Maurice alleged, displayed an 'utterly negative' view of his own Church, claiming that the Establishment's 'Protestant' character would lead many to leave her.[205] Since the centre of the Church was Christ, to retain people in the Church of England, they had to have this centre exhibited to them.[206] Such a thing was impossible in the Roman Church, because the Papacy had set aside the reality of the Incarnation by asserting its own visible headship, 'outraging and insulting' the communion of the visible and invisible worlds.[207]

The terms 'Catholic' and 'Protestant' were complementary and not contradictory. The Church was 'most Catholic when most Protestant'; Catholicity inhered in those churches separated by national as opposed to dogmatic differences.[208] Drawing on his understanding of the spiritual constitution, Maurice could describe nations as wholly Protestant; 'the universal body sinks into a contradiction, when it refuses to recognise the personality of each body [or national Church]'.[209] Thus unity required proper recognition of national distinctions:

> The strongest desire I am conscious of, is that of bringing all men to the feeling that there can be but one Church,— though that Church may exist in a number of different nations—though it may be quite right that in some subordinate particulars it should be modified by the character of those nations—though it is, I believe, actually demanded by its constitution, that it should recognise and sustain the distinct government of each of those nations.[210]

The universality of the Church demanded that particular churches seek to 'enter into communion with all', without sacrificing the principles on which communion must rest.[211] In theory this could include a relation of communion with the bishop of Rome, but only if that did not compromise the national principle of the Church of England.[212] Thus, almost incidentally, Maurice introduced into his argument the relatively novel language of 'communion' as a way of describing relations between churches.

These two basic steps in his argument—Catholicity inhering in the Church by virtue of its one centre, Christ, and the complementarity of

---

[205] Maurice, *Three Letters to the Rev. W. Palmer*, 1.   [206] Ibid. 7.

[207] Ibid. 10.   [208] Ibid. 16.

[209] Ibid. 19. Maurice's argument bears close comparison with Bunsen's own view, which cast the scheme's leading idea as 'that true catholicity supposes, as collateral principle, the acknowledgment of a national independence': Bunsen, *Memoir*, i. 611, cited in Greaves, 'Jerusalem Bishopric', 343.

[210] Maurice, *Three Letters to the Rev. W. Palmer*, 52.

[211] Ibid. 25.

[212] Ibid. 26.

Catholicity and 'Protestantism' as a recognition of national identity—
provided the essential backdrop to his endorsement of the proposal to
establish the Jerusalem bishopric. Maurice rejected *tout court* the 'Eastern
position' that there could be no Church without bishops, on the grounds
that, manifestly, churches of this kind did exist; episcopacy, then, in
language Maurice did not use, was not of the *esse* of the Church.[213]
Bishops were, however, a desirable—indeed, providential—means of ordering and uniting the Church, signifying by their appointment that
Christ's Church was a constitution for all.[214] The scheme was an admirable attempt by the Prussian government to seek communion with the
English Church by an 'act of homage' to episcopacy.[215] At first glance, this
looks inconsistent with Maurice's conviction that episcopacy was one of
the six 'signs' of the spiritual constitution. But the implication is surely that
'sign' fell somewhere between possibility and necessity. Modern Anglican
ecumenical theology has taken a similar line, with its suggestion that the
historic succession of ministers is a sign but not a guarantee of the
Church's apostolicity.[216] Ambiguities inevitably remain.[217]

Maurice's arguments notwithstanding, the Jerusalem bishopric as conceived in 1841 was tainted by the intensity of controversy surrounding it,
and the joint scheme lasted only forty years.[218] But Maurice's discussion of
it presented a significant model for future ecumenical method. Acknowledgement of local diversity, the extension of episcopacy by voluntary
agreement, the language of relations of communion, the aim of establishing a relation of communion without producing compromise formulae or
institutional bonds of organic unity—although not original and not by any
means restricted to Maurice alone—nevertheless the forcefulness of his
presentation of these principles anticipated much modern ecumenical
method. It represented a direct, practical application of his dynamic
conception of Catholicity as a vocation for all churches that would take
account of their distinctive histories. It also marked out an alternative
ecumenical route for Anglicanism from the mechanistic, Arnoldian conception of extending Church polity to incorporate Dissenting churches.

---

[213] Maurice, *Three Letters to the Rev. W. Palmer*, 57.   [214] Ibid. 53, 55.   [215] Ibid. 38.

[216] For the fullest exposition of the Church of England's position to date, see House
of Bishops, *Apostolicity and Succession* (London: General Synod of the Church of England,
1994), 21–6.

[217] Compare the use made of this position in the Porvoo agreement, which established
relations of full communion between the Anglican churches of Britain and Ireland and the
Baltic and Scandinavian Lutheran churches, with the more muted language of the Anglican–
Roman Catholic conversations: *Together in Mission and Ministry: The Porvoo Common Statement*
(London: Church House Publishing, 1993), 26–9; ARCIC-II, *Church as Communion* (London:
Catholic Truth Society/Church House Publishing, 1991), 22–3.

[218] Greaves, 'Jerusalem Bishopric', 352.

If the scheme for a Jerusalem bishopric was the most direct contemporary issue to which Maurice's ecclesiological theory was applied, nevertheless his life's work remained influenced by the perspective he had mapped out in *The Kingdom of Christ*. Yet, from the mid-1840s, his writing appeared to change direction, turning increasingly away from explicit preoccupation with ecclesiology to wider issues of social action, public morality, and biblical interpretation. In part, this may have reflected the loss of momentum and heat in High Church circles that followed Newman's conversion to Roman Catholicism in 1845. By the mid-1840s, too, it was evident that the immediate crisis of the Church of England had passed: its survival was assured, and reform of its order and organization was well under way. Perhaps, too, Maurice felt that he had little further to say beyond what he had already written on the Church. In a broader sense the question of what the Church is remained at the very centre of his work. Much of what he wrote subsequently is unintelligible without this acknowledgement. The defence and, above all, the thriving of the Church of England was an overriding, permanent concern of his. As a theologian, preacher, and educator, his work continued to be suffused with the reading of Catholicity he had developed in the crisis years of the 1830s.

4

Church and Nation

Maurice's understanding of the nation as one of the three forms of social life providentially ordained as part of the spiritual constitution implied that the Christian Church was intrinsically related to national identity and character. A church truly possessed of Catholicity could be the church of the nation. Maurice himself did not much like the word 'Established', and claimed to prefer 'English' in its place.[1] But this depended on a particular reading of history. Only by tracing historically the lineaments of Catholicity in the Church of England could its identity as *the* Catholic Church in England be proved. By this means, Maurice sought to justify the State's recognition of the Church of England against a rising tide of radical and Dissenting criticism.

A reader encountering Maurice's work for the first time today is likely to be struck by the way in which much of his language reflects a preoccupation with order and harmony. He wrote constantly of the 'divine order', for example, and used language such as 'ordinance' and 'spiritual constitution'. In doing so, he appeared to describe and sanctify a particular polity as an absolute, eternal pattern of human organization. Disorder was an affront to God: Christianity had inherited from Judaism the notion that God was the king of the nation, and so the very ground of its order.[2] In the post-revolutionary world that was the nineteenth century, like many of his contemporaries, he sought not merely a satisfactory account of the theology of the Church of England, but a revival of its perceived role as the fulcrum around which social harmony and peace could be re-established. For Maurice, what one scholar has called 'the Victorian quest for a source of authority in political and social affairs' was to be fulfilled above all in a greater realization of the national role of the Church of England.[3] Maurice's use of the language of order, ordinance, and constitution was integral, then, to his theological vision, and it cannot in turn be reduced to a narrowly reactionary agenda. It reflected deep unease about the absence of social cohesion in Britain, and a conviction that the source of true

[1] Maurice, *Life*, i. 255.
[2] F. D. Maurice, *The Patriarchs and Lawgivers of the Old Testament* (London: Parker, 1851; 2nd edn., Macmillan, 1855), 218.
[3] H. S. Jones, *Victorian Political Thought* (Basingstoke: Macmillan, 2000), 26.

unity—and so of true participation in society—would be found in the Christian Church.

It is no accident that Maurice's revision of *The Kingdom of Christ* occurred not only at a time when controversy over Tractarianism was reaching its peak, but when English society was troubled once again by social unrest, and in particular by Chartism. In 1839–40 he edited the *Educational Magazine,* and one of his leading articles made precisely this connection. Commenting on Carlyle's pamphlet on Chartism, he admitted that 'Churchmen have no reason to expect any great favour at his [Carlyle's] hands', and yet, 'however much he may abuse Churchmen, he will be better able than most men to make us feel our need of a Church'.[4] Characteristically, Maurice managed to turn even Carlyle's *French Revolution* to his own advantage, claiming that there Carlyle had 'borne more unconscious testimonies to the worth of a constitution, not based on human ordinances and conventions, but upon a divine order'.[5] But Maurice and Carlyle were at one in this. The reader who struggled through to the end of Carlyle's tortured, angry polemic about the 'condition of England' encountered a remarkable endorsement of the principle of national religious education, and a conviction that the chief obstacle to this lay in the faithlessness and division of Christians themelves: 'To "teach" religion, the first thing needful, and also the last and the only thing, is finding of a man who *has* religion.'[6]

Both Maurice and Carlyle, the one an English convert to the Established Church, the other a Scottish free-thinker, considered social disorder at root a moral and religious problem. To study Maurice's ecclesiology in all its breadth is to move from his doctrine of the Church, with its understanding of Catholicity identified historically, to his description of the national and social purposes fulfilled by the Church. The context and shape of his defence of Church–State relations is the subject specifically of this chapter. Attention here will be paid to Maurice's concept of 'comprehensiveness', and its function in justifying the legally protected position of the Church of England. In the next chapter, our attention will spread more widely still, to discern the way in which the theory of *The Kingdom of Christ* found application in the movement that came to be called 'Christian Socialism'. But first it is necessary to consider in more detail the current of criticism faced by the Established Church in Maurice's lifetime.

---

[4] Quoted in Maurice, *Life,* i. 278–9.   [5] Ibid. 279.

[6] T. Carlyle, 'Chartism', in *Selected Essays* (London: Dent, 1915), 232; italics original.

THE ATTACK ON THE ESTABLISHMENT

The context of Church–State relations changed subtly in the mid-nineteenth century. The crisis of 1828–32 in Britain was of unusual intensity. The interlocking nature of arguments about constitutional, ecclesiastical, and social reform reflected the fact that what was at issue was the character of the English constitution and religious settlement. Yet, paradoxically, this concealed significant differences among critics of Establishment, since Dissenters and atheist radicals alike could combine to attack the evidently corrupt nature of the Church of England. The radical journalist John Wade's assault on the inefficiency and inequality of the Church of England attracted the support of many Dissenters. Yet, behind Wade's work stood that of the atheist Jeremy Bentham, whose *Church-of-Englandism and its Catechism Examined* (1818) had argued, not just for the disestablishment of the Church of England, but its complete dissolution.[7] This was hardly an argument many Dissenters could support in the long run.

But by the time Maurice revised *The Kingdom of Christ*, the work of the new Ecclesiastical Commission was well under way. The breadth and thoroughness of church reform was to undermine fatally arguments against 'old corruption'. Moreover, the constitutional changes of 1828–32 had removed some of the most pressing grievances of Dissenters and Roman Catholics. They had also begun a process of recurrent parliamentary reform that, whilst largely unforeseen and unplanned, was never again to carry the same severe implications for the Established Church as had seemed to confront it in 1831 and 1832. Wade ran his Church and State arguments again late in the 1840s, claiming that monopoly, disavowed in commerce, 'continues rampant in religion', but he failed to carry anything like the conviction he had done in 1831.[8]

Yet, if the Church of England, seized by the spirit of efficiency and mission epitomized by the energetic Bishop Blomfield of London, now began to demonstrate a quite unexpected vitality, the argument about Establishment was carried to a new level.[9] A more militant form of Dissent emerged, under the leadership of the Congregationalist Edward Miall. Chastising Dissenters for their cautiousness, Miall urged on them 'a final grapple with ecclesiastical tyranny', arguing that 'THE ENTIRE

---

[7] S. J. Brown, *National Churches*, 169–70.

[8] J. Wade, *Unreformed Abuses in Church and State: With a Preliminary Tractate on the Continental Revolutions* (London: Effingham Wilson, 1849), 191.

[9] On the sources of the mid-century Anglican revival, see esp. Burns, *Diocesan Revival in the Church of England*, esp. ch. 10, 'Conclusion: Contextualizing the Diocesan Revival', pp. 260–75.

SEPARATION OF CHURCH AND STATE is really [our] object'.[10] The Church of England's very success in reforming itself, and its renewed commitment to church building, merely served to stimulate Dissenting opposition. The case which Dissenters made for disestablishment now hinged on an appeal to freedom of conscience. The very existence of a State Church implied an unequal treatment of different religious groups in the State. As Miall later argued, 'It shows you a nation sharply divided by law in regard to their religion into two great sections—the one privileged, the other tolerated.'[11] Militant Dissent, organized through the Liberation Society, would not be satisfied by the removal of specific, pressing 'grievances', but only by the abolition of the Church–State link altogether.[12]

Militant Nonconformity's commitment to freedom from ecclesiastical tyranny, its emphasis on the formation of moral character, and its support for a non-interventionist approach to the State produced a powerful political ideology.[13] Opposition to Establishment was thus carried into government through the electoral success of Gladstone's Liberal party. Its high point was reached towards the end of Maurice's life, with Gladstone's 1868 administration, the passage of Irish Church disestablishment in 1869, and the abolition of University tests in 1871. Hostility to Establishment was orchestrated powerfully at local level, too, with opposition to compulsory church rates (finally abolished by Gladstone in 1868) and to Anglican church schools.

Maurice's published reflections on the nature of Church–State relations do not fit neatly into the conventional narrative. He wrote almost nothing, for example, on the Gorham judgement, the decision of the Judicial Committee of the Privy Council concerning an Exeter clergyman's repudiation of the doctrine of baptismal regeneration, a decision that traumatized High Churchmen with its seeming implication that a secular court could adjudicate on the doctrine of the Church of England, and prompted his friend Henry Manning's conversion to Roman Catholicism.[14] But he did write substantially on the issue of subscription, on national and religious education, and on the Irish Church. The question of Establishment, and the 'nationality' of the Church of England,

---

[10] E. Miall, *The Nonconformist's Sketch Book* (1842), quoted in D. M. Thompson, *Nonconformity in the Nineteenth Century*, 107.

[11] Speech in the House of Commons, cited ibid. 188.

[12] D. M. Thompson, 'The Liberation Society 1844–1868'.

[13] See S. Koss, *Nonconformity in Modern British Politics* (London: Batsford, 1975); also D. W. Bebbington, *The Nonconformist Conscience: Chapel and Politics, 1870–1914* (London: Allen & Unwin, 1982).

[14] The conventional account remains J. C. S. Nias, *Gorham and the Bishop of Exeter* (London: SPCK, 1951).

remained a central preoccupation. It is impossible to understand the
nature of the case he made for the Church of England as an answer
to the divisions and uncertainties of his age without attending to this
perspective.

NATIONALITY AND HISTORY

In Part 2 of *The Kingdom of Christ* Maurice had emphasized the divinely
ordained character of national organization and government. National
society was distinct from, yet complementary to, the universal society,
or Church: '[The] law protests against the selfish, individual principle, and
raises a standard against it . . . [and] the Gospel comes to exterminate that
same selfish principle out of the mind and heart of the man.'[15] All God's
dispensations, including nations, aimed to 'restore the Divine image in
man'.[16] Church property was historically distinct from national property,
only in order 'by different arrangements to make it available for the
education of the nation from age to age'.[17] But this was little more than
an amplification of Coleridge on Church and State. Coleridge had distinguished between the *Propriety*, or property held by landed interests, and
the *Nationality*, or land held in trust for the whole nation, as complementary constituent factors of the commonwealth, 'opposite, but correspondent and reciprocally supporting, counterweights'.[18] Coleridge saw the
national Church as the third great estate of a nation, the first being the
landowners, who provided for 'permanency', and the second the mer-
chants, manufacturers, and artisans, who provided 'progressiveness' and
'personal freedom'. It was the third estate that Coleridge most admired, as
an order aiming 'to preserve the stores, to guard the treasures, of past
civilization, and thus to bind the present with the past' and in short 'to
secure and improve that civilization, without which the nation could be
neither permanent nor progressive'.[19]

In distinguishing between the Christian Church and the national
Church, Coleridge identified the 'clerisy' with the whole of the cultivated,
professional élite, and not just the clergy of the Church of England.[20]
Maurice concurred that Coleridge's theory did not provide sufficient
specificity for an Anglican argument.[21] But the relevant chapter title in
Coleridge's work was actually headed 'Of the Church of England, or

---

[15] Maurice, *Kingdom of Christ*, ii. 274.   [16] Ibid. 277.   [17] Ibid. 289.
[18] Coleridge, *On the Constitution of the Church and State*, 26.   [19] Ibid. 34.
[20] Ibid. 44.   [21] Maurice, *Kingdom of Christ*, vol. i, pp. xx–xxi, xxiii.

National Clergy, according to the Constitution'.[22] Coleridge had not sought to construct a systematic theory of Establishment, drawing on the traditional *loci* of Christian theology, namely the biblical texts and Church tradition, but rather synthesized an account of history. He read the general purpose of Establishment into the specific role of the Church of England in the nation's history. As for Maurice, it did not make sense to justify Establishment abstractly. Coleridge accounted for the role of the national Church according to a threefold concept of order ('permanency'), freedom, and human flourishing ('civilization'), and implied that this structure, a notional constitutional balance, could be detected in England's history.[23] In his usual piecemeal way, he had sketched out one solution to the problem of ecclesial authority in a time of anti-Establishment rhetoric. Maurice applied Coleridge's argument more thoroughly, yet more rigidly, than ever his intellectual mentor had done. The tripartite 'spiritual constitution' of family, nation, and Church, with its understanding of interlocking, mutually reinforcing and yet distinct functions, runs like a *leitmotif* through his work.

The crucible of Coleridge's theory was the crisis of the confessional State. He aimed to clarify the *Idea* of the national Church, in order to strengthen appreciation of it. His development of the idea of 'nationality', 'a rhetorical move of great importance for Victorian political thought', may have begun well before then, probably in the early 1810s.[24] But there is little sign of its imprint in Maurice's early journalism. It was surely the successive events of 1828–32, combined with the impact on Maurice of reading Coleridge's treatise when it appeared in 1830, that crystallized the theory that appeared in *The Kingdom of Christ*. The earliest trace of it is an undated letter probably contemporary with the siege of Antwerp by French forces allied to the English in late 1832.[25] Maurice there suggested that the Church as such could not be Protestant, but Catholic, since Protestantism was *'predicable* of a *nation'*, by which he seems to have meant that Protestantism entailed a protest against the trans-national authority of the Papacy, and subsisted therefore in nationhood: 'A nation exists in the acknowledging of the Righteous God', and protested against all attempts to suppress its independence under God.[26] Every nation

---

[22] Coleridge, *Church and State*, 33.

[23] For a brief contemporary application of Coleridge's concept, see T. D. Jenkins, 'Church and Intellectuals, Nation and State', *Theology*, 98 (1996), 452–6.

[24] H. S. Jones, *Victorian Political Thought*, 22.

[25] Maurice, *Life*, i. 240. The letter contains a summary of a lost manuscript that would appear to have opposed the English policy of assisting the French to resist the king of the Netherlands' attempt to suppress a Catholic uprising.

[26] Ibid. 241; italics original.

aligned to the Papacy 'must be a God-denying nation, because the Pope *to the nation is God*'.[27]

One of the most fruitful of Maurice's applications of the concept of nationality was in the field of educational theory.[28] In *Politics for the People* (1848), for example, his vocational and spiritual concept of education was described in such a way as to suggest that it could uncover, beneath surface inequalities, 'the real secret of equality' in a nation, the knowledge of our 'common relation' to God.[29] The secret of education for Maurice was its potential to bring us out of narrowness and self-preoccupation.[30] Church education promoted anti-sectarianism, inside as well as outside the Church.[31] Maurice warned that '[i]f we determine that we will call ourselves teachers of the whole nation when we are not, we do but destroy the possibility of our ever becoming such'.[32] Education would encourage the sense of belonging 'to a people', possessing an inheritance from the past as well as prospects for the future.[33] And so Maurice not only supported extensive Church action in education, but the emergence of a State-sponsored system, making due allowance for a central, national role for the Church of England.[34]

But Maurice's understanding of nationality was also capable of wider application, locating the national Church in the context of a providential reading of history. Its roots lay in his specific view of the place of nations in the 'divine order'. History, for Maurice, bore witness to 'that order which man has been continually violating'.[35] In the 'original divine order' of the world, the 'dispersion' and 'distinctions' of the nations were 'the fulfilment of God's designs for the race which He had made after His own likeness'.[36] The New Testament showed the completion or fulfilment of that which had been partially effected in the Old. The one presented the history of 'a peculiar Nation', the other 'a universal Church unfolding itself out of that

---

[27] Ibid. 242.

[28] Maurice's educational theory and practice is worth a study in its own right: see, e.g., P. W. Jackson, 'F. D. Maurice's Educational Theory: A Philosophical Examination' (Ph.D. thesis, King's College, London, 1983).

[29] *Politics for the People*, 6 (3 June 1848), 100.

[30] F. D. Maurice, 'The Government Scheme of Education', *English Journal of Education*, NS 1 (1847), 208.

[31] Ibid. 207.

[32] F. D. Maurice, *The Education Question in 1847: A Letter Addressed to the Editor of the English Journal of Education* (London: Bell, 1847), 15.

[33] F.D. Maurice, *The Workman and the Franchise: Chapters from English History on the Representation and Education of the People* (London: Strahan, 1866), 204.

[34] Maurice, 'Government Scheme', 205.

[35] F. D. Maurice, *Sermons on the Sabbath-Day* (London: Macmillan, 1853), 123.

[36] Maurice, *Patriarchs*, 79.

nation'.[37] God, then, had been using nation and Church 'for His purposes,—has been claiming each for a distinct part of His kingdom'.[38] The same principle applied to English history. God had taught England's rulers 'that it is our vocation to resist every power, papal, imperial, democratic, which strives to destroy the peculiarities of race, family, individual,—and to construct a society which shall be an artificial corporation, not a living body'.[39] The nation was a theological fact, a providential reality. Remarkably, Maurice could claim that 'there is an immortality for a nation, and that when one of its citizens separates his interests from its interests he loses the practical sense of his immortality, because he loses the sense of his relation to the righteous and everlasting God'.[40] All this implied that the separation of Church and State, advocated by Miall and the Liberation Society, would entail the separation 'of all that is meant to be united and harmonious in our hearts', and would enable the triumph of indifference. Nation and Church would practically cease, as 'each will succeed in robbing us of the other'.[41]

Maurice's endorsement of the principle of a national Church was common enough amongst Anglicans. But the practical usefulness of his theory was weakened in two ways. First, it operated at an abstract, generalized level, and offered no precise guide to the acceptance or rejection of particular legislative arrangements. Despite his defence of the royal supremacy, of the existing state of Church–State relations, and of the role of the Church in national education, Maurice could offer little concrete advice in controversies over the precise nature of Establishment. In fact, on a number of specific issues, Maurice endorsed changes that might have seemed to undermine his theory, such as the admission of Dissenters to the ancient universities. Though the possibility that his defence of Establishment might be able to accommodate specific concessions is an attractive one, his theory could not itself determine what concessions would be acceptable and what unacceptable.

This pointed to a second, related weakness. The providential argument in support of nationality did not adduce detailed criteria by which particular historical features of the history of nation and Church could be assessed. This did not prevent Maurice himself from making sharp judgements about particular events and individuals. But in order to reach those judgements, he had to bring to bear additional principles that the argument from nationality could not itself supply. So he could claim, like a true admirer of Edmund Burke, that the 'Glorious Revolution' of 1688

---

[37] Ibid. 257.   [38] Ibid. 272.   [39] Ibid.
[40] F. D. Maurice, *The Ground and Object of Hope for Mankind* (London: Macmillan, 1868), 46.
[41] Maurice, *Patriarchs*, 273.

demonstrated that God was an 'actual King over kings', and that order was preserved by the enshrining of this principle in legal acts.[42] But, without a detailed examination of the rhetoric and motives of the protagonists of the Revolution, it is not clear at all why the event had to be interpreted in this way. Was it to suggest that *all* rebellion against a reigning monarch demonstrated that God was 'an actual King over kings'? And if not, then why was the principle true in this case when presumably it was not in Monmouth's rebellion of 1685? The very pliability of Maurice's argument, given the generalized character of the description of the 'divine order' he offered, militated against the historical method he claimed to follow.

Thus the attractiveness of the argument from nationality masked a certain plasticity, that made its connection with practical proposals by no means straightforward. This criticism by no means emptied Maurice's theory of value, however. Though it constituted a novel development of Coleridge's view of the relations of Church and State, Maurice's understanding of nationality and the national Church, whilst broadly supporting the Anglican settlement in England, was not obviously intended to defend one particular set of legal or constitutional arrangements as such. Instead, behind his defence of Establishment lay a broader goal of articulating a vision of the Church of England as the Church *for* England. The concept of nationality was intrinsic to Maurice's vision, but his chief preoccupation was with the Church itself, rather than with the constitutional arrangement of Establishment. It was the crisis of the *Church* that drove his search for a new way of conceiving of the Church of England.

Nevertheless, from a modern perspective an additional weakness of Maurice's theory is evident. The very centrality of the concept of nationality in his work points to the presence of general nineteenth-century convictions about the force and distinctiveness of national character and identity, influenced by Romanticism, that were to lose their appeal later in the twentieth century. Maurice, like many of his era, appeared to suppose that nationality was a relatively unproblematic concept.[43] Even as he shared the Liberal Anglican view of historical change, nevertheless he tended to absolutize particular features of national development as if they were abiding, permanent expressions of national character. The very title of the relevant section of *The Kingdom of Christ* said as much: 'What is the form of character which belongs especially to Englishmen? To

---

[42] F. D. Maurice, 'Politics Ancient and Modern, II: Do Kings Reign by the Grace of God?', *Tracts for Priests and People*, 10 (London: Macmillan, 1862), 40.

[43] But for a telling examination of the relationship of Christianity to nationalism in this period, see J. Wolffe, *God and Greater Britain: Religion and National Life in Britain and Ireland, 1843–1945* (London: Routledge, 1994).

what kind of depravation is it liable?'[44] Lurking behind his ecclesiological theory, one suspects, was always an assumption that there was a natural and inevitable 'fit' between Anglican ideas, institutions, and practices, and Englishness. Maurice did not subject this assumption to critical examination.

ARGUMENTS ON CHURCH AND STATE

Where should we place Maurice's argument in relation to other theoretical perspectives on Church and State? The most direct comparison is with the theory advanced by W. E. Gladstone in two books, *The State in its Relations with the Church* (1838) and *Church Principles considered in their Results* (1840). Gladstone also made the concept of nationality ('religious nationality', in his words) central to his argument. Influenced by the Aristotelianism he had imbibed at Oxford, Gladstone used the principle as a way of describing the appropriate form of national religion for each nation—Anglicanism for England, but Islam for Islamic nations, a diversity of religious groups for the United States, and so on.[45] But focusing on the State rather than the Church in the earlier of the two books, Gladstone argued for the near identity of Church and State. The State had a 'moral personality' (the Arnoldian overtones are striking) that obliged it to seek to recognize and support the highest form of truth:

[As] the nation fulfils the great conditions of a person . . . it has that kind of clear, large, and conscious responsibility which can alone be met by its specifically professing a religion, and offering, through its organ the State, that worship which shall publicly sanction its acts.[46]

This, allied with his principle of nationality, made Gladstone strongly opposed to any further dilution of Establishment. He was, after all, famously called by Macaulay 'the rising hope of those stern and unbending Tories'.[47] Like his Tractarian friends, he rested the authority of the Church of England absolutely on the principle of apostolic succession. 'Faced with a choice', Colin Matthew has commented, 'Gladstone always put Anglican apostolical purity first'.[48] Gladstone too owed something to Coleridge. He had read *On the Constitution of the Church and State* carefully in 1837, and commented approvingly in his copy that 'We do not claim to

---

[44] Maurice, *Kingdom of Christ*, ii. 389.   [45] Matthew, *Gladstone 1809–1874*, 64.

[46] Gladstone, *The State in its Relations with the Church*, 4th edn., i. 105.

[47] T. B. Macaulay, 'Gladstone on Church and State', in *Critical and Historical Essays*, new edn. (London: Longman, 1850), 457.

[48] Matthew, *Gladstone 1809–1874*, 40.

be the Universal Church of the whole earth—but we claim to be the Church of this realm corresponding in all material laws with that model which was established and intended to be universal'.[49] But in spirit his defence of Establishment was a curious fusion of High Church Toryism and Coleridge. Its dependence on 'apostolical purity' made it, in the context of division over Tractarianism, unlikely to recommend itself widely. From the view of the State, it looked unrealistically static and incapable of adapting to suit changing circumstances. Gladstone never abandoned the theory formally, but he was forced to acknowledge its practical unworkability.[50]

Gladstone's high view of the State in fact aroused some Tractarian suspicion of latent Erastianism. More typical of Tractarian attitudes to the State was John Keble. His sermon on 'National Apostasy' in 1833 set the tone of resentment and rebellion with which the Tractarians were to greet anything that smacked of State interference in the affairs of the Church. On this he never wavered. He did not oppose Establishment in principle. He commended it as 'a great temporal blessing, in the hands of Him who knows whether we shall improve or abuse it'.[51] But his approval was conditional. The Church's authority was independent of the State, rooted in its apostolic commission, and not to be set aside in order to convenience State policy. The principle of nationality featured little in this. Keble's pastoral letters, written in the wake of the Gorham judgement of 1850, called on the Church to recover its self-government, such as its ability to declare its own doctrine, to issue its own canons, and to nominate its own bishops. If these liberties were incompatible with Establishment, Keble argued, then 'speedy measures' should be put in place to end the State connection.[52]

One radical defence of Establishment can be discounted briefly as having had almost no impact on Maurice's views. The Scottish theologian Thomas Chalmers in 1833 published a remarkably popular series of lectures entitled *Church Establishments Defended.* Originating in part in Chalmers's Glasgow ministry, in which he championed the systematic extension of the parish system, with church building, as a solution to the problems of urban deprivation, these placed the defence of the national religious establishments of Britain on a utilitarian basis.[53] This was

---

[49] Cited, Matthew, *Gladstone 1809–1874,* 39.

[50] This is explored illuminatingly, ibid. 59–73; see also P. Butler, *Gladstone: Church, State and Tractarianism: A Study of his Religious Ideas and Attitudes 1809–59* (Oxford: Clarendon Press, 1982), *passim.*

[51] J. Keble, *Difficulties in the Relations between Church and State* (Oxford: Parker, 1877), p. xv.

[52] Ibid. 25.

[53] See the summary account in S. J. Brown, *National Churches,* 79–82.

attractive at first to many, including Gladstone.[54] But Maurice never paid it serious attention. He criticized Chalmers's argument for appealing to self-interest, and for assuming that the fundamental basis of human social life was sinfulness.[55]

The significance of Tractarian suspicion of Establishment is often underestimated. When most members of the Church of England were busy attempting to shore up the Church–State link, the Oxford Movement pioneered a vision of the Church's authority that could countenance separation from the State. This was to prove very important to modern Anglicanism, as it evolved from State Church to worldwide communion.[56] But Maurice's ecclesiology also served this changing context well, since it was more open to the possibility of ecumenical encounter, and more capable of accommodating the internal diversity of Anglicanism. Even in Gladstone's lifetime his view of the moral personality of the State later had to be balanced with a proportionate stress on freedom of conscience.[57] And there lay the rub. The dissolution of elements of the 'confessional State' in 1828–32 occurred because of the growth of religious and political pluralism. But that process was hardly arrested or contained by reform. As the nineteenth century wore on, Anglicans witnessed, not a gradual return to their pre-reform dominance, but increasing evidence of religious and political differentiation, including the rise of Roman Catholicism in Britain, the vitality of Nonconformity (especially in Wales), the appearance of a small but vociferous 'secularist' movement, new forms of social organization such as trade unions and co-operative societies, new educational institutions, to name but a few. This served only to underline the process whereby institutions of the State were gradually uncoupled from the influence of the Church.

A use of the principle of nationality comparable to that of Gladstone, but with strikingly different prescriptive consequences, was made by Thomas Arnold in his *Principles of Church Reform* (1833). Here again, the affinities with Maurice's theory are evident. Arnold's main aim was to accommodate religious pluralism. His perception of the basic problem was sharp enough:

---

[54] Ibid. 195, 317–20.

[55] Chalmers, Maurice claimed, held 'that as men are fallen creatures, religion must be distasteful to them; that there will be no natural demand for it, therefore that it must be recommended by all external aids and influences. No doctrine could be so much in harmony with a theology which was built upon the acknowledgement of sin': Maurice, *Life*, ii. 182–3.

[56] W. L. Sachs, *The Transformation of Anglicanism: From State Church to Global Communion* (Cambridge: Cambridge University Press, 1993); W. M. Jacob, *The Making of the Anglican Church Worldwide* (London: SPCK, 1997).

[57] P. Butler, *Gladstone*, 41–2.

[There is] nothing more reasonable than that national education should be in accordance with the national religion . . . But the Established Church is only the religion of a part of the nation, and there is the whole difficulty. The Reformers, or rather their successors in Elizabeth's time, wished to root out Dissent by the strong hand. This was wicked, as I think, as well as foolish: but then, if we do not root out Dissent, and so keep the Establishment co-extensive with the nation, we must extend the Establishment, or else in the end there will and ought to be no Establishment at all, which I consider as one of the greatest evils.[58]

Like Gladstone, Arnold assumed a near identity of Church and State: 'The State in a Christian country is the Church, and therefore has much to do with religion.'[59] Yet his disagreement with the position Gladstone was to adopt was evident too: 'The Church, as such, has no divinely appointed government.'[60] Unlike Gladstone and Maurice, who both, in their different ways, sought to root the authority of the national Church in ecclesiological principles that were 'divinely appointed', Arnold's starting-point was the recognition of a social fact, the existence of a national Church spread through every part of the country.[61] To this he added the common Reformation argument about unity on fundamentals of belief. The national Church should be extended to comprehend within it those Protestant Dissenters who shared this common basis of belief: 'Nothing, as it seems to me, can save the Church, but an union with the Dissenters.'[62] Despite the evident attraction of the proposal to some, it was, however, easy to see it as indifferent to ecclesiological principle. This combined with Arnold's well-known hostility to High Churchmanship, fatally compromised what was otherwise a novel solution to the crisis of Establishment. Moreover, Arnold almost certainly misread or misunderstood Dissenting hostility to the national Church. Though a sense of exclusion typified some Nonconformist attitudes, Dissenters' suspicion of State action in the religious sphere had stronger and more positive grounds, arising in part from the conviction, shared with theorists of political economy, for example, that centralized institutions of government might actually inhibit the formation of moral character.[63]

---

[58] Stanley, *Life of Arnold*, ii. 16.

[59] T. Arnold, *Fragments on Church and State: Written in 1827–1840 and Published as Appendices to the First Edition of the Fragment on the Church* (London: Fellowes, 1845), 17.

[60] Ibid.

[61] Here Arnold too was indebted to Coleridge: he considered the setting aside of 'property' for public use as the basis of the national organization of the Established Church: Arnold, *Principles of Church Reform*, 93–7.

[62] Stanley, *Life of Arnold*, i. 348.

[63] See H. S. Jones, *Victorian Political Thought*, 35–40; also B. Hilton, *Age of Atonement: The Influence of Evangelicalism on Social and Economic Thought, 1785–1865* (Oxford: Clarendon Press, 1988).

The immediate context of Arnold's proposal was the Reform crisis. But his case for an expansion of the Establishment became a permanent feature of Victorian debate. The Broad Churchman Henry Wilson restated Arnold's argument in a new form in *Essays and Reviews* (1860). The early Church had been 'multitudinist', Wilson argued, basing its identity on moral behaviour and not on common creeds.[64] But this had been obscured over the ages by credal correctness. To recover its national appeal, the Established Church had to rediscover its 'multitudinist' character, requiring much greater freedom to interpret Scripture than was currently possible.[65] In short, 'if the national Church is to . . . correspond ultimately to the national character, the freedom of opinion which belongs to the English citizen should be conceded to the English Churchman'.[66] Wilson's proposal fared no better than Arnold's in practice: under suspicion of universalism, his essay was one of those from the volume arraigned before the Court of Arches for heresy.[67] The irony of the Arnoldian perspective was that it aimed at including in the national Church Protestant Nonconformists whose own theology would not permit them to accept the derogation of doctrine that the Broad Church seemed to be advocating.[68]

It was perhaps Maurice's sensitivity to this that led him away from the Broad Church argument of encompassing Dissent by extending Establishment. The ecclesiology he had advanced in *The Kingdom of Christ* attempted to honour the positive truths of the various branches of Dissent, and yet to defend the Catholicity of the Established Church. For Maurice, as for Gladstone, the historic structures of Anglicanism were not arrangements of convenience, but carriers of theological truth. Divinely appointed means of grace, they were in the broadest sense 'sacramental'. It was this, incidentally, that made Maurice such an attractive figure to Michael Ramsey in the twentieth century: 'Here is a theologian whose emphasis upon Church order springs directly from his sense of the Gospel of God.'[69] So Maurice's defence of the Church–State link could not be aligned with the Broad Church tradition of Arnold and his followers. Despite some commonality of approach, it was sufficiently distinctive to

---

[64] H. B. Wilson, 'Séance historiques de Genève—the National Church', in V. Shea and W. Whitla, (eds.), *Essays and Reviews: The 1860 Text and its Reading* (Charlottesville, Va.: University Press of Virginia, 2000), 282.

[65] Ibid. 291–2.

[66] Ibid. 294.

[67] See I. Ellis, *Seven against Christ: A Study of* Essays and Reviews (Leiden: Brill, 1980); see also Shea and Whitla (eds.), *Essays and Reviews*, 689–731.

[68] See the comments of the Methodist theologian Joshua Rigg in *A Comparative View of Church Organizations* (1887); 2nd edn. (London: Charles Kelly, 1891), 67–84.

[69] A. M. Ramsey, *The Gospel and the Catholic Church* (London: Longman, 1936), p. 214.

constitute a different theory altogether. Maurice cut between the High Tory argument of Gladstone and the Broad Church: though agreeing with the principle of nationality, loosely stated, from the one he dissented on the duties of the State and on the source of Church authority, and from the other on the adequacy and theological weight of the historic formularies and institutions of Anglicanism. How could he at once defend the existing institutions of the Church of England and argue as he did for a recovery of the breadth and inclusiveness of the national Church?

THE COMPREHENSIVENESS OF THE NATIONAL CHURCH

Comprehensiveness was not explicitly enunciated as one of the principles of the Catholic Church in *The Kingdom of Christ*. It was hinted at in Maurice's treatment of party division within the Church of England, where his analysis proceeded using essentially the same historical and dialectical method applied to the main branches of Protestantism in the first part of the book. The positive principles of Evangelicals, Liberals, and High Churchmen were affirmed, but in systematized form were found to lead to distortion or error. So, Maurice claimed, we can see that 'there is a divine harmony, of which the living principle in each of these systems forms one note'.[70] The principle of comprehensiveness, by inference, safeguarded this divine harmony of true doctrine in the Church's actual, historical existence.

The principle had a double application. First, it related to the interior reality of the Church, expressing the comprehensiveness of the Church's faith. The complementarity of positive principles subserved this comprehensiveness of faith, as did attention to the practice of faith in worship, prayer, and moral living. When Maurice wrote of the unity of faith, he had in mind the enacting of theology in practice. Social division was the consequence of a failure to realize the internal communion of the Church, which 'has not believed that . . . the law of Love, the polity of members united in one Head, or brethren confessing a common Father, is a real one'.[71] Maurice's understanding of the relationship between theology and faith (individual and corporate) was not so very far from some current

---

[70] Maurice, *Kingdom of Christ*, ii. 401.

[71] Maurice, *The Prayer-Book*, 341.

[72] As spelled out in Vladimir Lossky, *The Mystical Theology of the Eastern Church* (1957; new edn., London: J. Clarke, 1991), 7–22; but see also the cautious words of Denys Turner, *The Darkness of God: Negativity in Christian Mysticism* (Cambridge: Cambridge University Press, 1995), 1–8.

applications of the term 'mystical'.[72] He sought to express at one and the same time the *unfathomability* of the gift of God in Jesus Christ, with its breadth and depth beyond all human systems of thought, and its nearness to human life, through an incarnation of divinity in the life, words, and deeds of Christ himself.[73] For Maurice, faith oriented us practically to God: faith 'took hold' of our existence, and 'should be the act of the man himself, of that which is most truly, radically human in him . . . in direct contact with that which is most living and most substantial'.[74] The comprehensiveness of the faith was to be found in lives of complete fidelity to God's will.

But, second, 'comprehensiveness' was also an external principle. It referred to the breadth of principles, formularies, and ordinances of the Church, which aimed to permit the inclusion of different theological systems within one polity. But this exterior, institutional dimension of comprehensiveness operated within clearly defined boundaries. So Maurice both acknowledged broad institutional parameters in, for example, his writing on the Church of England, and articulated an understanding of the institutional life of the Church as a striving towards the inner unity of faith that was already its privileged possession. The comprehensiveness of the institutional parameters was not static: they were safeguards for an inner dynamic of development towards unity. It was in this sense, as an awareness of the dynamic nature of faith and of the Church, that Maurice later wrote of his whole life as a 'desire for Unity'.[75]

The comprehensiveness of the Church was not *identical* to its Catholicity, but in its double aspect it operated as a condition for Catholicity. Its persistence in the history of the Church of England pointed to the Church's national permanence, and its relationship with the abiding form of the nation. Here, Maurice's ecclesiological theory was far removed from the Tractarian tendency to emphasize the essential character of one external definition of the Church: namely, the apostolic succession, in order to secure its internal fidelity. For Maurice, no less an emphasis on

---

[73] Maurice distinguishes practically between two different kinds of 'mysticism'. One, which he does call 'mysticism', amounts to the suppression of individual feeling, in the interests of cultivating a special, personal sense of individual attainment; this Maurice criticizes by contrast with Catholicism, which, he says, 'begins with God and terminates in God', whereas mysticism (in this sense) 'begins with God and terminates in the individual': Maurice, *Kingdom of Christ*, 1st edn., ii. 248. The second meaning, under the name 'mystic', Maurice does not disavow: this amounts to a desire for a personal presence of God, with the recognition that this experience is a life-changing one: Maurice, *What is Revelation?*, 247–9.

[74] Maurice, *What is Revelation*, 258–9.

[75] 'The desire for Unity has haunted me all my life through; I have never been able to substitute any desire for that, or to accept any of the different schemes for satisfying it which men have desired': Maurice, *Life*, i. 41.

the interrelationship of external and internal characters of the Church depended on adherence to a wide range of institutional signs, no one of which was absolutely privileged over the others.[76]

Use of the term 'comprehensiveness' came to be seen as characteristic especially of the Broad Church. This was never a coherent, compact body of theological opinion, however. Though displaying some common tendencies in theology, 'Broad Church' was a description reached almost by subtraction, taking away from traditional Anglicanism the distinctive emphases of Evangelicalism and Tractarianism. Thus, it could include clergy who combined a traditional allegiance to the principle of Establishment with a conservative attitude to liturgy and doctrine, and with a horror of factionalism.[77] But it could also include those of a progressive or radical cast of mind. It could include Archbishops Tait and Frederick Temple, who would certainly fit the former description, but it could also include Benjamin Jowett and J. W. Colenso, who would be closer to the latter.

At least three different senses of comprehensiveness can be identified amongst theologians and church leaders of the Broad Church.[78] The first is the sense in which the term was used, for example, by W. J. E. Conybeare in relation to the 'anti-theoretical' Broad Church in his famous article on church parties.[79] The English Church was 'comprehensive' because it contained latitude of theological opinion, anchored by a core of common doctrine defined by the formularies.[80] Conybeare suggested that the 'doctrines taught by this party are the same in which both High and Low Church are agreed'.[81] So this idea of comprehensiveness depended upon the assumption of the Protestant idea of fundamentals of faith.[82] The Church of England insisted on this Catholic core of

---

[76] For a survey, still useful in essentials, of the High Church emphasis on apostolic succession, see A. B. Webster, 'Church Order and Re-Union in the Nineteenth Century', in K. M. Carey (ed.), *The Historic Episcopate in the Fullness of the Church* (Westminster: Dacre Press, 1954), in addition to the extensive work of P. B. Nockles, cited elsewhere.

[77] See R. A. Burns, 'Introduction' to Conybeare, 'Church Parties', 239–45.

[78] In his seminal essay, Conybeare recognized only two—those appearing here as the first and second versions. See ibid. 240. In, so it seems, subsuming Maurice under the 'theoretical' school, and so associating him implicitly with Stanley, Conybeare was actually doing considerable disservice to Maurice. Maurice's son and biographer records his father's dissatisfaction with Conybeare's 'narrowing' of his and Julius Hare's position, but seems not to have appreciated the basis of that dissatisfaction: Maurice, *Life*, ii. 607.

[79] Conybeare, 'Church Parties', 345.

[80] Ibid. 341.

[81] Ibid. 341.

[82] On the tradition of 'fundamentals' in Anglicanism, see S. W. Sykes, 'The Fundamentals of Christianity', in *Unashamed Anglicanism*, 64–80; for a critical survey of its use, see Y. M. J. Congar, *Diversity and Communion* (London: SCM, 1984), 107–25.

doctrine, but comprehended diversity of opinion on other matters. The Church's relationship with the State, on this view, was a subsidiary question, important only inasmuch as it was through the mechanisms of Establishment that the comprehensiveness of the Church was protected. This view was widespread, though not ubiquitous. Arguably, it permeated the attitude of Brooke Foss Westcott to the Church of England, for example.[83] It was also the view of Archibald Tait, of whom Peter Hinchliff has written: 'He was determined to preserve the comprehensive character of the Established Church . . . But he also insisted that clergymen should stay within the limits of the range of opinion which was permitted in the Church of England.'[84] Frederick Temple also adhered to this policy as Archbishop of Canterbury.[85] Whilst supporting some liberty of theological inquiry, it need not imply expansion of the doctrinal limits of Anglicanism.

The second, Arnoldian version of comprehensiveness, on the other hand, positively advocated just such an expansion. Conybeare called it 'theoretical'.[86] Comprehensiveness here denoted the inclusion of widely differing, even contradictory, Church polities under one ecclesial umbrella. Arnold's disciple and biographer, Arthur Stanley, consistently advocated the abolition of University tests throughout his life. That Stanley always had something of *this* sense of comprehensiveness in view was acknowledged by his own biographer, who wrote that he desired 'to stretch the borders of the Church to its widest possible limits . . . that it might more worthily sustain its national character'.[87] Stanley faced difficulties over admitting a Unitarian minister to communion at Westminster Abbey, and argued against the disestablishment of the Church of Ireland on the grounds that there should be a policy of concurrent endowment of Roman Catholic, Anglican, and Dissenting churches in Ireland.[88] The

[83] See, e.g., B. F. Westcott, 'The Position and Call of the English Church', in *Lessons from Work* (London: Macmillan, 1901).

[84] P. B. Hinchliff, *Frederick Temple, Archbishop of Canterbury: A Life* (Oxford: Clarendon Press, 1998), 53. That Tait was not inclined to expand the limits of the Church of England to draw into it Nonconformists is emphasized by P. T. Marsh: 'Tait's desire for amity with the Nonconformists was, in fact, rather shallow . . . . His nearest approximation to reunion was to make the Church of England more attractive to Nonconformists in the hope that some would join it': *Victorian Church in Decline*, 247.

[85] Hinchliff, *Frederick Temple*, 137.

[86] Conybeare, 'Church Parties', 345.

[87] Prothero, *Life of Stanley*, 398–9. For an interesting, if rather strained, exploration of the suggestion that Stanley in particular, as a Broad Churchman, provided a model for modern inter-faith dialogue, see H. W. French, 'The Victorian Broad Church, Seedbed of Twentieth-Century Religious Pluralism and Implicit Religion: An Historical Perspective', *Implicit Religion*, 1 (1998), 55–67.

[88] Prothero, *Life of Stanley*, 383–5, 407.

Arnoldian view was also held by Stanley's close friend Benjamin Jowett, Master of Balliol College, Oxford.[89]

But there was a third form of the argument. Here, comprehensiveness was defined with reference to society at large. Some Broad Church Anglicans thought the Church should aim to encompass the whole of society, irrespective of belief as such. William Fremantle, for example, in his *The World as the Subject of Redemption* (1885), drew his definition of the Church so widely that it encompassed all circles of human activity. Fremantle traced the genesis of his ideas in Hooker, Coleridge, and, significantly, Arnold.[90] Here, comprehensiveness was really a missionary term. It sought to reaffirm the national mission of the Church of England by emphasizing the breadth of its social responsibility. At its worst it represented a *reductio ad absurdum* of the Anglican claim of nationality, illustrated in the extraordinarily literal sense in which Samuel Barnett, for example, took his parish-wide responsibilities at St Jude's, Whitechapel. Barnett employed 'chuckers-in' to round up passers-by for the services, and went round his parish in disguise 'to find out what parishioners really thought about the church and parish machinery'.[91]

These three versions of comprehensiveness were not incompatible, and in the hands of some churchmen shaded into each other. When Stanley used the word 'comprehensive' in relation to the Church of England, usually all three versions were present at once.[92] Maurice held the third, but in a limited way through a recognition of the practical constraints on the Church's efforts to live up to its national responsibility. Of the other two versions, it is absolutely clear that he did not hold anything other than the first. He is, admittedly, sometimes represented as holding something like the second.[93] But he specifically repudiated Arnold's position,

[89] On Arnold's influence on Jowett, see P. B. Hinchliff, *Benjamin Jowett and the Christian Religion* (Oxford: Clarendon Press, 1987), 48–9. Hinchliff, however, says little explicitly about Jowett's view of the comprehensiveness of the Church of England, though it is evident that, in relation to Balliol at least, Jowett was antipathetic to religious tests: p. 44.

[90] On Fremantle, see P. T. Phillips, 'The Concept of a National Church in Late Nineteenth-Century England and America', *Journal of Religious History*, 14 (1986).

[91] L. E. Nettleship, 'William Fremantle, Samuel Barnett and the Broad Church Origins of Toynbee Hall', *Journal of Ecclesiastical History*, 33 (1982), 566.

[92] See particularly A. P. Stanley, *Essays Chiefly on Questions of Church and State* (London: Murray, 1870).

[93] It is possible to read Stephen Sykes's understanding of Maurice in that light: cf. 'the failure to be frank about the issues between the parties in the Church of England has led to an ultimately illusory self-projection as a Church without any specific doctrinal or confessional position': S. W. Sykes, *The Integrity of Anglicanism* (London: Mowbray, 1978), 19. For a clearly erroneous association of Maurice with this position, see R. Rouse and S. C. Neill (eds.), *A History of the Ecumenical Movement 1517–1948* (London: SPCK, 1954), 274.

claiming that the Church of England was already more comprehensive than Arnold's scheme could ever make it.[94] He questioned the value of ecumenical schemes that might achieve church unity at the cost of compromising or conceding points disputed over many centuries.[95]

For Maurice to have suggested that the doctrinal limits of the national Church had to be expanded to include other denominations would have fatally undermined his argument that the history of the Church had providentially guided it into the position in which it expressed both Catholic and Protestant principles in their fullness. To him, the Broad Church desire to expand or modify the dogmatic profession of the Church was dominated by a spirit of contemporary rationalism. In abandoning the Articles, he alleged, the Broad Church merely abandoned any chance of escaping from the 'narrow dimensions' of sectarian positions: 'I cannot find that the Broad Church has any such message. All I hear from it is a cry to leave the sixteenth century and believe in the nineteenth.'[96]

In practice, the connection of interior and exterior comprehensiveness was far from obvious. Ordinances require concrete historical expression in order to be effective. Yet as such they may be the product of particular circumstances, and reflect particular values and opinions. Were the Catholic creeds, for example, enduring and unchangeable expressions of the faith of the Christian world, or were they the result of sheer historical contingency? Unless Maurice could demonstrate that the Anglican formularies were *actually* comprehensive, his theory would remain, in Newman's memorable words about the *via media*, a 'paper theory'.

In *Subscription no Bondage*, Maurice had implied that the formularies were already all that his theory required. His letters and papers of the 1840s reflected that position.[97] But it was to be tested by the controversy over his view of eternal punishment in his *Theological Essays* (1853) that led to his dismissal from King's College in 1853. Just what his defence might be had been indicated years before. In an earlier publication, *The New Statute and Mr Ward* (1845), Maurice had taken the seventh of the Thirty-Nine Articles as an instance of the comprehensiveness of the formularies. Its reference to 'eternal life' he accepted in 'the very strictest sense', meaning by that not what the Reformers themselves in all probability signified, but what Maurice took to be Jesus's meaning in the 'Farewell' discourse in John 17: 3: 'And this *is* life eternal, that they might know thee the only true

---

[94] Maurice, *Subscription no Bondage*, 117.   [95] Maurice, *Ground and Object of Hope*, 75.
[96] F. D. Maurice, 'The Thirty-Nine Articles and the Broad Church', *The Spectator*, 2 Apr. 1870, p. 435.
[97] See, e.g., Maurice's letter of 14 Mar. 1849 to R. W. Jelf, his Principal at King's College, London: Maurice, *Life*, i. 524.

God, and Jesus Christ, whom thou hast sent.'[98] The Reformers, Maurice admitted, would have meant 'future state', precisely the interpretation he denied.[99] But then the Articles did not prescribe any one interpretation offered by a council or doctor of the Church.[100]

But his defence was beside the point. The relevance of the Articles was never put to the test. King's College, for all its Anglican origins and connections, was a private corporation, and could take its own view of whom it wished to employ, and on what basis it chose to employ them. It could, without challenge, appropriate to itself its own conception of Anglican orthodoxy, and insist on that as its basis of teaching.[101] Its ruling council made no explicit reference to the formularies in the resolutions it passed at a special meeting on 27 October 1853, asserting merely the 'dangerous tendency' of Maurice's teaching.[102] So, in an institution explicitly founded to support the principles of the Established Church, the claimed comprehensiveness of the Anglican formularies proved to be a fiction.

It is hard to avoid the conclusion that this must have confirmed decisively a suspicion Maurice had entertained for some years, that the comprehensiveness of the formularies was undermined practically by party spirit. His view of subscription had evidently been changing even before the controversy over the *Essays*. At the beginning of 1853, months before the *Theological Essays* appeared, he had refused republication of *Subscription no Bondage* unless he was permitted to add a statement withdrawing his support for continuing subscription at the ancient universities.[103] He now claimed that subscription should not be enforced at the universities, not because education ought to be conceived on a non-confessional basis (Maurice always held the reverse in principle), but because in practice the Articles were not received as conditions of education, but were twisted into 'a different sense, which is dangerous to honesty', from that which Maurice himself had proposed.[104] In essence, the Articles were being used as vehicles of a partisan view of faith.

The basis on which he now advocated change was significant. Comprehensiveness could be used as a principle for reform. In a rapidly changing context, with continuing Nonconformist pressure on Establishment, increasing division over biblical interpretation, and protracted party conflict

[98] Maurice, *New Statute and Mr Ward*, 20.

[99] Maurice, *New Statute and Mr Ward*, 21.   [100] Ibid. 20.

[101] For the foundation and ethos of King's College in the mid-nineteenth century, see D. A. Dowland, *Nineteenth-Century Anglican Theological Training: The Redbrick Challenge* (Oxford: Clarendon Press, 1997), 35–63.

[102] Maurice, *Life*, ii. 191.

[103] For whatever reason, the pamphlet did not reappear: ibid. 154–5.

[104] Ibid. 154.

in the Church, to have any chance of success, Maurice's concept of comprehensiveness had to demonstrate a capacity to adapt to change. However comprehensive in spirit, if the formularies were not used in that spirit, then the interior sense of the comprehensiveness of faith could become a justification for changing them.

A PRINCIPLE OF REFORM: THE CASE OF THE LITURGY

A significant instance of the adaptability of comprehensiveness was Maurice's view of the liturgy. Usually conservative in his attitude to liturgical revision, one recent commentator has even called him a 'Prayer-Book fundamentalist'.[105] He used the plain text of the Prayer Book, resisting the suggestion that the language of the sixteenth century should be jettisoned in the nineteenth: 'Old charters have always been the barriers against prerogative, the grand helps to the assertion of eternal principles.'[106] And yet he has been seen as the fountainhead of the Anglican equivalent of the Liturgical Movement, with all the implications that follow for the architecture and texts of modern Anglican worship.[107] Though this view is exaggerated, his approach to liturgical revision was not as hostile or as rigid as was once supposed. Through the principle of comprehensiveness he helped to lay down one of the central axioms that has guided Anglican liturgical revision.

In *The Prayer-Book Considered Especially in Reference to the Romish System* (1849), Maurice described the liturgy as a barrier against sectarianism: 'I am sure it may be the instrument of raising us out of our selfishness and divisions.'[108] He attacked the idea, common in the battles between Tractarians and Evangelicals, that the Anglican formularies were a compromise, in which the Articles stood on the Evangelical side, and the Prayer Book on the Tractarian side. The Prayer Book itself was a witness against the sin

---

[105] S. W. Gilley, 'The Ecclesiology of the Oxford Movement', in P. Vaiss (ed.), *From Oxford to the People* (Leominster: Gracewing, 1996), 69.

[106] Maurice, 'Dr. Lushington, Mr. Heath and the Thirty-Nine Articles', 156.

[107] See especially Hebert, *Liturgy and Society*; D. Gray, *Earth and Altar: The Evolution of the Parish Communion in the Church of England to 1945* (Norwich: Canterbury Press, 1986); J. Fenwick and B. Spinks, *Worship in Transition: The Twentieth-Century Liturgical Movement* (Edinburgh: T & T Clark, 1995). As Christopher Irvine has said of Gabriel Hebert, 'he takes the thought of F. D. Maurice as the framework for his own arguments, and sets out to explain the view that the Church was both a human and divine institution, given, as it were, to make tangible in the world, the catholicity of God's dealings with humanity': *Worship, Church and Society* (Norwich: Canterbury Press, 1993), 60.

[108] Maurice, *The Prayer-Book*, p. xvi.

of exclusiveness.[109] Here, and elsewhere, he showed no interest in the burgeoning study of liturgical history, well under way by mid-century in the hands of High Church scholars such as William Palmer and J. M. Neale. The *Book of Common Prayer* was a unified whole, the living voice of the Church. Its purpose was to express the inclusivity of the economy of salvation, and this always determined the sense in which he read particular passages.

The function of the Absolution, for example, was to stand for the principle that 'God has redeemed men in His Son, and has claimed them for His own by His Spirit', against 'a multitude of notions coming forth from opposite quarters . . . which slander the character of God and war against the freedom of man'.[110] Use of the Apostles' Creed was

a continual protection against traditions, that when they try to force themselves upon us, we can always put this forward as a declaration . . . that it is the Eternal Name into which we are baptized, and in which the whole Church and each member of the Church stands.[111]

The service for infant baptism demonstrated that the proper principle of English society was that all human society rests on its divine birth in redemption, and not on its natural birth.[112] The service should liberate us from partisan struggles over baptismal regeneration: it was a 'witness that man is not his own saviour by his faith or by his works'.[113]

Maurice treated the liturgy as one for the whole nation: it was a symbol of the universal yet national character of the Church. Time and again he placed liturgical texts within an overarching framework that drew explicitly on his primary theological assumptions. Giving due weight to the notion of inclusivity, Maurice was freed by his apparent indifference to questions of scholarly accuracy to accommodate the idea of particular changes designed to overcome practical sectarianism. He condemned the so-called State services, which commemorated the death of Charles I, the birth and restoration of Charles II, and the saving of Parliament from the Gunpowder Plot, had remained annexed to the Prayer Book, and were finally abolished in 1859.[114] They had done more harm than good, obscuring the fact that God was 'the real King of the Nation'.[115] They breathed 'the excitement and revenge of a triumphant party'.[116]

[109] Ibid., pp. xiii, 13.

[110] Maurice, *The Prayer-Book*, 43.   [111] Ibid. 147.

[112] F. D. Maurice, *The Church a Family: Twelve Sermons on the Occasional Services of the Prayer-Book* (London: Parker, 1850), 28–9.

[113] Ibid. 32.

[114] R. C. D. Jasper, *The Development of the Anglican Liturgy 1662–1980* (London: SPCK, 1989), 48.

[115] Maurice, *The Prayer-Book*, 158.

[116] Ibid. 159.

He also, eventually, changed his mind on the liturgical use of the Athanasian Creed, which the rubric of the Prayer Book prescribed in place of the Apostles' Creed at Morning Prayer on certain festivals. For most of his life, Maurice was an ardent defender of the Creed, and of its use. Here he was on the same side as his High Church detractors, such as Liddon and Pusey.[117] Objections to the Creed fastened mainly on its damnatory clauses, and were mounted by those, such as A. P. Stanley, who on many other issues were Maurice's allies.[118] But when the issue was raised again by the Ritual Commission in 1870, Maurice gave cautious approval to the idea that it should be banished from public services.[119] He recognized that his claim that the damnatory clauses expressed what *he* understood as 'eternal', and not what virtually everyone else understood, was no longer sustainable, in the face of the fierceness of controversy.[120] The only way, he concluded, to avoid the opposing parties' interpretations was to remove the creed from use. Once again, then, a proposal for change was adopted on the basis of the principle of inclusion, excluding what he took to be narrow and distorted interpretations.

The most striking instance of Maurice embracing the possibility of change in the Anglican formularies came towards the end of an article written in 1860 on Prayer Book revision, mooted by the Evangelical peer Lord Ebury.[121] Maurice objected strongly to revision, believing that it could only contract the inclusive character of the liturgy.[122] But there was a twist in his argument. Revision would require an amendment to the Act of Uniformity, whereas the Act should not be amended, but abolished.[123] He acknowledged that his providential reading of the history of the Church could lead him to defend the Act, but 'Divine Wisdom' behind the passage of the Act in 1662 was not sufficient reason to keep it on the statute book in 1862.[124] Mere amendment would probably lead to more restrictive legislation, not less.[125] Maurice scarcely began to work through what the implications of repeal would have been. This startling proposal to remove the sanction of law from the Church's use of the liturgy could

[117] J. O. Johnston, *Life and Letters of Henry Parry Liddon* (London: Longman, 1905), 156–66.
[118] Prothero, *Life of Stanley*, 385–90.
[119] F. D. Maurice, 'A Few More Words on the Athanasian Creed', *Contemporary Review*, 15 (1870), 479–94; see also Maurice, *Life*, ii, 618–19.
[120] Maurice, 'A Few More Words', 489–93.
[121] Ebury's proposals are discussed briefly in R. C. D. Jasper, *Prayer Book Revision in England 1800–1900* (London: SPCK, 1954), 63–7.
[122] F. D. Maurice, 'On the Revision of the Prayer-Book and the Act of Uniformity', *Macmillan's Magazine*, 1 (1860), 425.
[123] Ibid. 427.
[124] Ibid.
[125] Ibid. 428.

surely have led to outright liturgical anarchy. It would at least, as Maurice recognized, have placed an even heavier burden of responsibility on the bishops than they already carried for ensuring that the worship of local churches was kept within the canonical limits of the Church.[126]

So, then, in a number of specific instances Maurice was prepared to countenance change in the liturgy of the Church, and in the overall pattern and use of the formularies that underpinned the liturgy, in a way that carried serious implications for worship. If he resisted the need for textual amendment as such, he was pushed, slowly but surely, towards supporting practical reforms that, in the long run, were part of a process of increasing liturgical diversity in the Church of England. His underlying aims were invariably couched in terms of an appeal to comprehensiveness, depicting party strife in the Church as necessarily divisive. Behind this lay his assumption that religious truth was a complex, multi-faceted but integrated whole that could scarcely be exemplified by one group or party alone in the Church. But the very ubiquity of party division forced him back, step by step, it seemed. Comprehensiveness was a useful way of *describing* the national ambition of the Church of England. But was it anything more than that? Could it, for example, provide a coherent rationale for another Anglican church facing an altogether more severe and immediate challenge to its Established status?

MAURICE AND THE DISESTABLISHMENT OF THE CHURCH OF IRELAND

For most of Maurice's lifetime, there were two national Anglican Establishments in Britain, not one. The Church of Ireland, a Protestant episcopal church like the Church of England, was united to its sister church by the Act of Union in 1801. But arguments made in favour of Establishment in England and Wales would be severely tested in the case of the Church of Ireland. By the early 1860s the episcopal establishment in Ireland was in trouble. The Irish census of 1861, which, for the first time, counted denominational affiliation, shocked supporters of the Irish Church by showing that only 12 per cent of the population were members of it.[127] Claiming to have a national, parochial ministry, its support was thin and varied regionally. Its greatest strength was in the north, reaching 37 per cent of the population in Fermanagh, but in the south it dwindled to

---

[126] F. D. Maurice, 'On the Revision of the Prayer-Book and the Act of Uniformity', *Macmillan's Magazine*, 1 (1860), 428.

[127] E. Brynn, *The Church of Ireland in the Age of Catholic Emancipation* (New York and London: Garland, 1982), 451.

5.3 per cent in Munster and even 4.2 per cent in Connaught, and was completely overshadowed by Roman Catholicism.[128] It was a church particularly of the land-owning and professional classes. Some 50 per cent of Irish landowners were Irish Episcopalian, but the proportion of land they held was much higher than that.[129] Ironically, sustained efforts to reform the Irish Church had begun to pay off by the 1860s.[130] The number of benefices and churches had increased, and, on the eve of disestablishment, the Irish Church was probably 'more efficient in providing religious services to its constituency . . . than at any time during the preceding century'.[131] But it was resented as the church of the English ascendancy. In the face of rising nationalism and revived, ultramontane Catholicism, it was politically beleaguered.

The prospect of disestablishment of the Irish Church thus appealed to Protestant Nonconformists and Roman Catholics alike. The attraction of disestablishment to Gladstone's Liberal Party, with its broad range of support embracing Protestant Nonconformists and Irish Catholics as well as many Anglicans, was evident. It was a policy that could help to unite the party, propel it back into office, and also (in conjunction with land reform) make a major step towards the pacification of Ireland. Gladstone himself had come to realize the inapplicability of his own vaunted principle of 'religious nationality' to the Church of Ireland: 'If an established church could not represent "religious nationality", he favoured the opposite extreme of voluntaryism.'[132] Opponents of disestablishment were, naturally, the Irish clergy themselves, many Conservatives, and many other English Anglicans. Maurice's friend Richard Trench was archbishop of Dublin from 1863, and, according to one historian, entirely unsuited to task of guiding the Irish Church through this troubled time. He was 'saintly, uncompromising, gentle', when the Church needed a 'rugged, truculent negotiator'.[133] Trench's policy was absolute resistance.

Maurice's response at first glance once again looked remarkably similar to Gladstone's. His most substantial comments were in a series of eight articles for *The Daily News*, a Liberal newspaper. His starting-point, with Gladstone, was the observation that the 'national' argument used in relation to the Church of England could not work in the case of the

[128] R. B. McDowell, *The Church of Ireland 1869–1969* (London: Routledge & Kegan Paul, 1975), 3.

[129] Ibid.

[130] On the attempts to reinvigorate the Irish establishment in the early nineteenth century, see Brynn, *Church of Ireland*, but also S. J. Brown, *National Churches*, 93–167.

[131] D. H. Akenson, *The Church of Ireland: Ecclesiastical Reform and Revolution 1800–1885* (New Haven and London: Yale University Press, 1971), 218.

[132] Matthew, *Gladstone 1809–1874*, 193.

[133] Akenson, *Church of Ireland*, 238.

Church of Ireland: there, the 'Established Church' was not the 'national Church'.[134] Blithely ignoring the sensitivities of those native Irish men and women who might well have considered themselves Anglican by conviction, Maurice described the Irish Church as an attempt to extend the English royal supremacy overseas. By ignoring popular resistance, the application of force to support the Established Church in Ireland had turned a Protestant church into a sort of internal contradiction.[135] Whereas Protestantism was a witness for the 'sacredness of national life', in Ireland it had become the very opposite.[136]

These modern Protestants are not supporting the Church, but their party; they are not supporting the Church, for they have never conceived the possibility of such a church as Christ established—a church not for one race but for all races.[137]

Yet Maurice backed away from endorsing whole-heartedly the 'voluntarist' argument of Gladstone. He too rejected concurrent endowment, the favoured solution of some Anglicans: the endowment of Roman Catholicism would be a 'wild Erastian dream'.[138] But he seemed genuinely to believe that disestablishment would produce a revivified Irish *Anglican* Church, and that the State's educational role in particular would be enhanced, not diminished.[139] The terms in which Maurice outlined this suggestion are frankly mystifying—'If the State is able to cultivate in [the Irish people] the sense of law and justice, there will be a union of Church and State, such as there has not been yet'—until one remembers his conception of Roman Catholicism as a corruption of the 'spiritual society'.[140] He seemed to think that disestablishment would automatically free the Church of Ireland to assume a true nationality. It seems not to have occurred to him seriously that in fact Roman Catholicism throughout much of Ireland had become so closely identified with nationalism that it was inconceivable that the church of the gentry could supplant it.

But then the situation of the Irish Church did expose the weaknesses of Maurice's argument on Church and State. The sheer inability of the Church of Ireland to function as a truly national Church set one half of Maurice's argument, nationality as the basis of establishment, against the other half, namely the possession of the ordinances, principles, and 'signs'

---

[134] F. D. Maurice, 'The Irish Church Establishment', *Contemporary Review*, 7 (1868), 55.
[135] F. D. Maurice, 'On Church and State, I', *The Daily News*, 14 Aug. 1868.
[136] F. D. Maurice, 'The Dean of Cork and the Irish Establishment', *Contemporary Review*, 7 (1868), 587.
[137] F. D. Maurice, 'On Church and State, III', *The Daily News*, 22 Aug. 1868.
[138] Maurice, 'Church and State, I'.
[139] F. D. Maurice, Review of 'A Few Words on Irish Church Questions' by W. G. Clark, *Cambridge University Gazette*, no. 3 (11 Nov. 1868).
[140] Ibid.

of the Catholic Church. By the latter set of criteria, the Church of Ireland should presumably have been regarded as the closest to the universal Church of all the churches in Ireland. Yet Maurice's own interpretation of Irish history assumed that it had functioned in the opposite way. It had abandoned its comprehensive, 'national' vocation and become sectarian. In all this, Maurice was hinting at something like a third church for Ireland, a church that could have all the institutional features of the Church of Ireland, and yet transcend the sectarian identities of Irish politics and religion. But this was not an obvious deduction from Maurice's original formulation of his theory in *The Kingdom of Christ*. There, Maurice had described the nation as a subordinate part of the 'spiritual constitution'. Here, the inability of the Irish Church to function as a true national Church had broken the link between nationality and Catholicity. The principle of nationality had become practically the determining factor in Maurice's understanding of the Irish Church, and its possession of the principles, ordinances, and 'signs' of the Catholic Church had receded into the background.

Maurice might have responded that production of a *theory* of Church and State was never his intention. In the case of Ireland, as in England, his aim was to interpret the history of the Church as he found it. Even so, he had insisted that 'a union of Church and State [is] implied in the existence of each, and [is] necessary for the protection of moral freedom'.[141] The experience of the Irish Church, however, suggested that such a view did not have universal applicability. Furthermore, his analysis produced no clear, guiding principles for definite action, beyond support for disestablishment. He disavowed the intention of producing his own 'plan'.[142] He said little about the question of disendowment, and on that question his own words could have been turned against his support for Gladstone: 'Take away the Church from the State, and the State is no longer a guardian of common interests. It is always tempted to prefer individual interests to them; at last to contemplate no interests but these.'[143] *The Daily News* found his argument bewildering.[144] Perhaps his analysis of the failure of the Irish Church to be a truly 'national' Church could be applied with some force to the Church of England too.

---

[141] Maurice, 'Church and State, I'.

[142] Maurice, 'Irish Church Establishment', 63.

[143] F. D. Maurice, 'Church and State, IV', *The Daily News*, 27 Aug. 1868.

[144] Editorial, *The Daily News*, 28 Sept. 1868: '[W]e sincerely regret our inability to comprehend distinctly the conclusions at which he ultimately arrives.'

COMPREHENSIVENESS—A MEANS TO UNITY

The Church of England suffered a setback itself in mid-century. In 1851 the only official national census of church-going in England and Wales was undertaken, and its results were published in 1854. It came as a shock to Anglicans to discover that, according to the summary report, not only did some five and a quarter million people who should have been able to attend church not do so, but Anglican attendances were exceeded by the total number of Dissenting and Roman Catholic attendances combined.[145] This arguably made the position of the national Church much more tenuous than had long been assumed. The figures were open to challenge, and have triggered a long and complicated debate amongst historians.[146] These were, after all, figures of attendance, and the totals included various estimates and depended on certain presuppositions. When numbers of places of worship, numbers of sittings, schools, and Sunday scholars, along with baptisms, weddings, and funerals, were taken into account, the position of the Established Church looked more secure. There were, however, significant local variations in the patterns of denominational strength. Already it was clear that Anglicanism had long been losing ground to Dissent in Wales.[147] This trend was to set the background for the long haul to Welsh disestablishment, achieved eventually in 1914. In England and Wales together, though, the census results gave a fillip to Nonconformist militancy, and it is hardly surprising that the experiment was never repeated.

No wonder, then, that there was such sensitivity to the question of the disestablishment of the Irish Church. Not only were the churches of Ireland, England, and Wales notionally joined by the Act of Union, but arguments about the numerical weakness of Anglicanism in Ireland could be applied, perhaps by anticipation, to the changing situation in England and Wales. Yet Maurice took little account of this. His basic argument in favour of the Church–State link remained unchanged after its formulation in *The Kingdom of Christ*. His language about the roles of the nation and Church was remarkably consistent from then until the publication of *Social Morality* in 1869. He practically assumed the force of the case for identifying the national Church in England with the Anglican Church, and for the corresponding link between the nation and its Church. Failing to give substance adequately to his understanding of national culture and identity,

---

[145] For basic figures based on the published report, see Chadwick, *Victorian Church*, i. 365–7.

[146] See esp. Snell and Ell, *Rival Jerusalems*, 1–53.

[147] For an overview of select Welsh counties, see ibid. 201–9.

it is difficult to see how his argument could have provided more than a general description of an idealized relationship.

For this reason, the influence of Maurice's view never extended much beyond the membership of the Church of England itself. It could not take note sufficiently of the deepening religious pluralism of English and Welsh society. But it did, through the principle of comprehensiveness, provide an encouraging and even persuasive case for Anglicans to take seriously their own perception of their national responsibilities. Yet even here some ambiguities remained. In presuming a close fit between the external, institutional framework of the Church and its interior comprehensiveness of faith, Maurice seemed to imply that particular institutional arrangements could be characterized as ideal. Yet he never quite said this. This pointed to a more general epistemological difficulty. He appeared to suggest that truth is accessible to human beings in such a way that it can be practically apprehended apart from the particular limitations of finite human minds, a position apparently implied by his antagonism to the language of 'system'.[148] Here, the difficulty was compounded by the fact that the language of ecclesial necessity and validity was largely foreign to him. He did not directly pose the question, for example, of how, *and under what conditions and in what forms*, episcopacy was absolutely necessary for the Church to be the Church. His defence of comprehensiveness was mounted at the general level. It was enough, he seemed to be implying, to see these specific ordinances in place, in order to assume that there, behind all limited or partial human systems of belief, was present the Church of Christ.

Maurice failed to consider the epistemological difficulties of his theory largely because he offered it, not so much as an analysis of knowledge in the context of ecclesial practice, as a commentary on devotional practice. Here, his theory of comprehensiveness had remarkably full implications. The unity of the Christian Church was not grounded in cognitive identity, but in common participation in the divine reality of Christ himself. This was structured in history through the faith, life, and institutions of the Church. But this meant that what it was to be a Christian actually entailed a reversal of much conventional language of faith. Human beings did not reach out from their own subjectivity to lay claim on the object of faith, but were always presented with an 'already' of faith, a givenness of Christ in history through the Church, that preceded the faith of the person. To put it more crudely, what the Church was, was always bigger, deeper, and

---

[148] As is suggested in H. Cunliffe-Jones, 'A New Assessment of F. D. Maurice's "The Kingdom of Christ" ', *Church Quarterly*, 4 (1971).

more comprehensive than any one believer, or group of believers, could possible conceive.

Undoubtedly, there was a certain covert theme of indefectibility at work in Maurice's notion of the comprehensiveness of the national Church. Maurice would probably have agreed with the idea of the Church itself as a sacrament.[149] There was a constant dialectical contrast in his work between the distortion, corruption, and even betrayal of elements of the Church by its own members and the comprehensive vocation of the Church, which he saw implicitly as never entirely subverted by these means. So he contrasted the narrowness and special pleading of the religious world with the fact that, through its establishment, the Church of England had been 'set in high places, and has a voice to reach all classes of society . . . to tell all by words and acts, that they are members of one body'.[150] Those selfsame sectarian members of church parties were also, on another view, unconscious witnesses to the inclusiveness of the Gospel.

It was also a consequence of Maurice's view of the sacramentality of the ordinances of the Church that considerable latitude of individual belief could coexist with full observation of the discipline of the Church.[151] Orthodoxy, in the conventional, narrow sense of adherence to a series of dogmatic propositions, was not the central aspect of his idea of what it meant to be a member of the Church. It would be more accurate to say that his primary emphasis was on *orthopraxis*—hence his claim that the faith of the poor, the simple, and the uneducated was resistant to the distortions of theological systems.[152] But hence also his conviction that propositional tests of belief would contract the breadth and depth of the Gospel. The Articles, by contrast, were an 'invaluable charter', protecting the Church against ecclesiastical tyranny (he meant mainly the Papacy) and 'the systems of the present day'.[153]

Nevertheless, Maurice's principle of 'comprehensiveness' was in theory a dynamic one. The power of historical adaptation was the corollary of the divine nature of the Church, and not the contradiction of it: 'it [i.e. the

---

[149] So much is implied, for instance, in the Catholic theologian B. C. Butler's appreciation of Maurice in *The Idea of the Church* (London: DLT, 1962), 31–5; on this very extensive idea in modern (especially Roman Catholic) ecclesiology, see, e.g., Walter Kasper's chapter on 'The Church as a Universal Sacrament of Salvation' in *Theology and Church* (London: SCM, 1989).

[150] Maurice, *Patriarchs*, pp. xxii–xxiii.

[151] This was echoed in his friend and disciple J. M. Ludlow's defence of dissent 'within' the Church: see his, 'Dissent from, and Dissent in the Church', in *Dissent and the Church*, Tracts for Priests and People, 9 (London: Macmillan, 1861).

[152] Both the significance of *orthopraxis* and the idea of the faith of the poor are present, for example, in Maurice's defence of infant baptism: 'Christ has preached at the fonts, when we have been darkening counsel in pulpits': *Gospel of the Kingdom of Heaven*, 282–3.

[153] Maurice, *Life*, i. 399.

Church] could not have been divine if it had not been capable of adaptation to new exigencies'.[154] Furthermore, as Richard Norris has pointed out, Maurice was not opposed to the modern idea of systematic theology, but to the substitution of human interpretation for the mystery of God himself.[155] However inadequate his hermeneutic might appear from a late twentieth-century standpoint, Maurice's aim was far from eirenic: 'in his estimation opposing systems cannot be reconciled and different principles do not need to be reconciled'.[156]

Thus Maurice was not a defender of theological latitude as such. His idea of comprehensiveness did not contend that all dogma is proximate at best. It derived instead from a conviction that the fullness of the Church was indeed embedded in human society, if often obscured practically, and that it was possible to identify the 'signs' of Catholicity by a close analysis of the history of particular churches. It was an assumption of his ecclesiology that some churches more perfectly embodied the Church than others, that the Church of England did so in particular, and indeed that the many parties of the Church of England themselves varied in the extent to which they actually realized the truth they sought to articulate. His ecclesiology was vulnerable on all these points, but it was indeed comprehensive in the sense that his vision of the Church of Christ was itself a comprehensive vision, inclusive of all redeemed humanity.

Comprehensiveness was a means to an end. Whilst securing institutional protection for the existing elements of Catholic Christianity within the national Church, it subserved the wholeness of the Church. It was, then, ultimately an eschatological principle. The presence of different, albeit fragmented elements of Catholicity, even in the form of the principles of different party systems that were subject to distortion in history, did signify the continuing importance and power of the universal Church. Maurice's strong conviction that this was true above all of the Church of England drove his perception of the Church's national vocation. Comprehensiveness was itself a condition of further growth towards unity, but it also represented an active principle in relation to the Church's situation in human society, the next major theme to which we must turn.

---

[154] Maurice, *Acts*, 78.

[155] R. Norris, 'Maurice on Theology', in F. McClain, R. Norris, and J. Orens, *F. D. Maurice: A Study* (Cambridge, Mass.: Cowley, 1982), 19. It is precisely on this point—the necessity of theology's assumption that it is God himself whom believers apprehend in faith—that Ellen Flesseman-Van Leer perceived a common theological starting-point for Maurice and Barth: *Grace Abounding: A Comparison of F. D. Maurice and Karl Barth* (London: King's College, 1968), 2–3.

[156] Norris, 'Maurice on Theology', 17.

5

The Church in Society

For ten years after the publication of *The Kingdom of Christ* in 1838, Maurice's writing settled into a steady pattern. His quarrel with the Tractarians was behind him. His reputation in the Church at large was a growing one. His controversial pamphlets, such as those on church party division and on the Jerusalem bishopric, brought his name before the reading public. Wider recognition followed, with his appointment in 1845 as Boyle lecturer.[1] Published as *The Religions of the World and their Relations to Christianity* (1847), his lectures were a pioneering attempt to interpret the major world religions as carriers (albeit flawed ones) of spiritual wisdom, according to a hierarchy of truth and value that placed Christianity unquestionably at the summit.[2] He was appointed Warburton lecturer, too, by the archbishop of Canterbury, delivering his lectures on the Epistle to the Hebrews.[3] In these years, he was also working steadily on the first volume of what he was to regard as his most substantial work, his two-volume *Moral and Metaphysical Philosophy*, a survey of Western philosophy and theology that originated in an article for the Coleridge-inspired *Encyclopaedia Metropolitana*, in 1835.[4] It was this, rather than *The Kingdom of Christ*, that was to be held up as Maurice's most significant work at his death, though its reputation has not been sustained.[5]

---

[1] Maurice, *Life*, i. 416.

[2] Space does not permit detailed consideration here of Maurice's contribution to comparative religion, but it has recently received attention in K. Cracknell, *Justice, Courtesy and Love: Theologians and Missionaries Encountering World Religions 1816–1914* (London: Epworth Press, 1995), 35–60.

[3] Maurice, *Life*, i. 418. His son later speculated that the Boyle and Warburton appointments were made in appreciation of his defence of the Jerusalem bishopric scheme: Maurice, *Life*, i. 521.

[4] Ibid. 185. On the background to Coleridge's involvement, see R. Holmes, *Coleridge: Darker Reflections*, 446, 451, 461–2. Holmes implies that the *Encyclopaedia* was abandoned in 1818, a year after it began, but in fact it was continued in supplementary volumes until 1845: see R. L. Collison, *Encyclopaedias: Their History Throughout the Ages* (New York: Hafner, 1964), 178–9.

[5] See the anonymous review of Maurice's *Life* in the *Westminster Review*, 122 (1884), 288: 'Maurice is most generally known only by his "Moral and Metaphysical Philosophy".' The most extravagant assessment was that of J. M. Ludlow, who claimed that it was one of the half-dozen literary works of its age that would survive to the thirtieth century: Ludlow,

These were years of settlement, too, in Maurice's ministry and personal life. In 1840 he was appointed to the professorship of English literature at the recently founded King's College, London, a position he held simultaneously with his chaplaincy at Guy's.[6] When a theological department was formed at King's in 1846, Maurice was the natural choice as one of the professors of theology. This obliged him to give up Guy's, but later that year he was appointed as chaplain of Lincoln's Inn, a post he could hold concurrently with that at King's.[7] Here he was to remain for fourteen years. As his preaching gained in fame, he gathered a congregation of disciples and followers that was to include many kindred spirits in Christian Socialism. Thomas Hughes, the author of *Tom Brown's Schooldays*, was to claim that 'the daily attendance at chapel began to increase', and that when Maurice preached on Sunday afternoons, young men came 'by the hundreds . . . because they feel that he has got something to tell them which they want to know'.[8]

Domestic happiness accompanied his professional success at first. Maurice married Anna Barton, sister of the wife of his friend John Sterling, in 1837.[9] His sons Frederick and Edmund were born in 1841 and 1843.[10] But then came tragedy, in a form familiar enough to the Victorians. Late in 1844 Anna fell ill with tuberculosis, and died in March the following year.[11] Alone, Maurice wrestled to bring up his two sons and to attend to his increasing professional responsibilities. As we should bear in mind in considering Maurice's role in the Christian Socialist movement, he occupied the role and status of a busy professional man and gentleman. With his appointment to Lincoln's Inn, he moved to 21 Queen Square, Bloomsbury, in a terrace of substantial Queen Anne houses. There were servants to look after the most pressing domestic chores, servants who are shadowy figures, featuring scarcely at all in the published correspondence.[12] Maurice was not wealthy, but there is little sign of actual hardship in his biography. Despite his eldest son's impression of isolation, Maurice possessed an extensive network of social, literary, and ecclesiastical contacts, including John Stuart Mill, Thomas Carlyle, Alfred Tennyson, Henry

'Some of the Christian Socialists of 1848 and the Following Years I', *The Economic Review*, 3 (1893), 491.

[6] Maurice, *Life*, i. 283.

[7] Ibid. 426.

[8] Ibid. 428–9.

[9] Ibid. 234.

[10] The most illuminating treatment of Maurice's family life is that in McClain, *Maurice*, 94–118.

[11] Maurice, *Life*, i. 403–10.

[12] One brief reference, for example, is to his wife's maid sitting near him on his deathbed: ibid. ii. 641.

Manning, and Samuel Wilberforce. His friendship with the Hares was further sealed in 1849, when he married Georgiana Hare, sister of Julius.[13] Though Georgiana was to suffer for years from illness, she certainly brought renewed companionship and domestic stability.

Had Maurice himself died late in 1847, his career retrospectively would have looked like a steady crescendo of recognition and success. What later generations were to regard as his most important work of theology had been published, and the main lines of his thought had been laid down in what was already a large body of work. He appeared as an original, yet largely conservative, defender of the Anglican settlement. Yet his career was about to enter its most turbulent period. Three public controversies, differing widely in scope and character, were to mark this middle period of his life, beginning with the movement called Christian Socialism, which ran from 1848 to approximately 1854, continuing through his dismissal from King's College for alleged heterodoxy in 1853, and on to his quarrel with Henry Mansel in 1859–60 over the doctrine of Revelation. The lasting effect of all three of these controversies was to radicalize Maurice's subsequent reputation. In this chapter, we are concerned mainly with Maurice's Christian Socialism, and then with the social implications of Maurice's view of the Church more widely.

Yet there are ambiguities in all this, and it is as well to note them now. Maurice's reputation as a founder of Christian Socialism is well documented.[14] His legacy and inspiration for later generations of Socialist Christians seem unquestionable. After the collapse of the first Christian Socialist movement, perhaps his most immediate impact was on the second generation of Christian Socialists, who included moderates such as Brooke Foss Westcott and Henry Scott Holland, and more radical figures such as

---

[13] Maurice, *Life*, ii. 552.

[14] The most recent contributions to this very extensive literature include C. Bryant, *Possible Dreams: A Personal History of British Christian Socialists* (London: Hodder & Stoughton, 1996), and A. Wilkinson, *Christian Socialism: From Scott Holland to Tony Blair* (London: SCM, 1998), but older and generally more detailed accounts include C. E. Raven, *Christian Socialism 1848–54* (1920; new edn., London: Frank Cass, 1968); T. Christensen, *The Origins and History of Christian Socialism 1848–1854* (Aarhus: Universitetsforlaget, 1962); P. D'A. Jones, *The Christian Socialist Revival 1877–1914: Religion, Class and Social Conscience in Late Victorian England* (Princeton: Princeton University Press, 1968); and E. R. Norman, *The Victorian Christian Socialists* (Cambridge: Cambridge University Press, 1987). Two supplementary accounts of interest are P. T. Phillips, *A Kingdom on Earth: Anglo-American Social Christianity 1880–1940* (University Park, Pa.: Penn State University Press, 1996), and J. Pinnington, *Kingdom and Commonwealth: The Christian Social Union and its Legacy to Radical Social Thought in the Church of England* (Croydon: Jubilee Group, 1997); this last item deserves a much wider readership than it currently commands.

Thomas Hancock and Stewart Headlam.[15] Through the Christian Social Union, Maurice's social thinking has become part of the stock-in-trade of modern Anglican social theology.[16] But it has always been difficult to square this with his own political opinions, which oscillated between a romantic Toryism and a Gladstonian Liberalism. He was scathing about Chartism's 'unrighteous pretensions', at the same time as acknowledging that it made 'righteous demands', and he never regarded democratic assemblies and representative systems of government with much favour.[17] Most of his friendships suggested an inclination towards political Liberalism.[18] But colleagues and friends such as J. M. Ludlow found him at times exasperatingly impractical in his approach to party politics.[19]

The impossibility of placing Maurice squarely in the political controversies of his day has left his modern interpreters with a difficulty. Was he a Socialist or not? Some have found it impossible to acknowledge that he was so in any meaningful sense. For Edward Norman, Maurice 'emptied "Socialism" of its political content'; his real adhesion to Christian Socialism was 'slight'.[20] Labour historians have often ignored Maurice and the Christian Socialist movement altogether.[21] An implicit assumption of many of these writers is that true Socialism is defined by reference to economic policy, with collective control over the means of production as the basis of political life for Socialist societies. By this standard of economic foundationalism, Maurice's Christian Socialism looks thin indeed. Others, even acknowledging an ethical Socialism, have been chary of Maurice's

---

[15] On Westcott and Holland, see, *inter alia*, the books of Jones, Wilkinson, and Pinnington cited above. On Hancock and Headlam together, see A. M. Allchin, *The Spirit and the Word* (London: Faith Press, 1963). Headlam's regard for Maurice especially was of the highest; his biographer says that he was 'the great influence in Headlam's life', and quotes a passage from Headlam's lecture on 'Maurice and Kingsley' to the Fabian Society which illustrates just how Headlam read him: '[The most important part of his teaching] was the Fatherhood of God, with, as its corollary, the eternal Sonship of Christ and consequently the Brotherhood of Man': F. G. Bettany, *Stewart Headlam: A Biography* (London: Murray, 1926), 19–20.

[16] See the brief tribute to Maurice in Ronald Preston, *Religion and the Persistence of Capitalism* (London: SCM, 1979), pp. vii–viii.

[17] Maurice, *Life*, i. 278; there are numerous references possible for his unflattering comments on mass democracy, including a letter to J. M. Ludlow in December 1848, in which he called the sovereignty of the people 'in any sense or form . . . as at once the silliest and most blasphemous of all contradictions': ibid. 485. For a more nuanced view, see Maurice, *The Workman and the Franchise*.

[18] This would be true, for example, of Julius Hare, Charles Kingsley, Lord Tennyson, John Stuart Mill, amongst others.

[19] J. M. Ludlow, *The Autobiography of a Christian Socialist*, ed. A. D. Murray (London: Frank Cass, 1981), 157, 227.

[20] Norman, *Victorian Christian Socialists*, 32.

[21] G. D. H. Cole, for example, made only the briefest of passing references to the Christian Socialism of 1848–54 in his popular classic *British Working Class Politics 1832–1914* (London: Labour Book Service, 1941).

apparent sacralizing of existing political arrangements through his concept of the divine order. Maurice's influence, says Rowan Williams, was characterized by 'benevolent paternalism': 'There can be no denying [his] stature as a theologian and teacher, but it is important not to be blind to the manifold weaknesses of his political thinking.'[22] Others still have played down the significance of Christian Socialism in Maurice's life as a whole. Vidler noted that it was no more than an 'incidental aspect' of his thought, a judgement echoed by Edward Norman.[23]

Yet assessments like this miss the mark. They reflect too ready a concern to fix the thought of a mid-nineteenth-century figure by later arguments over Socialism. The atheist Socialism of Marx and Engels was almost entirely absent from the early movements of British and French Socialist thought with which Maurice and his companions were familiar. It was not at all evident to them that Socialism, in the sense they took the term, which was quite different from the dominant usage of later generations, was antithetical to Christianity. Nor was it at all evident that it was antithetical to the dominant political philosophies of mid-Victorian Britain. Conservatives and Liberals alike might, at this period, call themselves Socialist in some sense, though the term was always contentious. Conservatives such as Benjamin Disraeli shared with political radicals criticism of the industrial bourgeoisie. One of Maurice's sympathizers in Christian Socialism was Cuthbert Ellison, a fringe member of the Tory-Radical 'Young England' group with which Disraeli was also associated.[24] Liberals saw the extension of permissive social legislation (legislation, that is, that put the responsibility for initiating action into the hands of local authorities) as the chief means by which the working class could be advanced.[25] Of the leading Christian Socialists, Ludlow was the one best informed about Socialist theory. His models were French ones: namely, the theories of Philippe Buchez, Louis Blanc, and Felicité de Lamennais, in which the search for a solution to social conflict, including the encouragement of workers' associations, also entailed sensitivity to religion.[26] These French

[22] R. D. Williams, 'Liberation Theology and the Anglican Tradition', in R. D. Williams, and D. Nicholls, *Politics and Theological Identity* (London: Jubilee Group, 1984), 19.

[23] A. R. Vidler, *The Theology of F. D. Maurice* (London: SCM, 1947), 11; Norman, *Victorian Christian Socialists*, 14.

[24] Raven, *Christian Socialism*, 124. On 'Young England', see P. Smith, *The Young England Movement* (High Wycombe: University Microfilms, 1971), and also J. Morrow (ed.), *Young England: The New Generation*: (London: Leicester University Press, 1999).

[25] See J. M. Prest, *Liberty and Locality: Parliament, Permissive Legislation, and Ratepayers' Democracies in the Mid-Nineteenth Century* (Oxford: Clarendon Press, 1990).

[26] On Ludlow's interest in French Socialism, see Ludlow, *Autobiography*, 112–13, 172–5; also N. C. Masterman, *John Malcolm Ludlow: The Builder of Christian Socialism* (Cambridge: Cambridge University Press, 1963), 87–92.

theorists knew or cared little for British political economy. It was Marx who fused political economy with German philosophy and French Socialism, according to Engels, and in 1848 the influence of Marx's Socialism lay mostly in the future.[27]

The source of Maurice's interest in what came to be called 'Christian Socialism' lay instead in his continuing preoccupation with the social role of the Christian Church. It was never anything other than a direct application of his ecclesiological convictions. Hence his reluctance to be drawn into practical politics. It was one thing to articulate a vision of Catholicity inhering in the separated portions of the Christian Church, but another to explore the implications of this vision for society as a whole. It followed from his adumbration of ecclesial comprehensiveness as the principle of the national Church that the mission of the Church also had to be embodied socially. It had to be enacted in a specific historical and social context. As well as internal church conflict, the evidence of continuing, deep-seated popular resentment of the Church of England and all that it stood for demanded a defence of the social relevance of his ecclesiology too.

Tracing the causes of a movement of opinion is difficult. Personalities have their bearing, as do events. Without Ludlow, without Charles Kingsley, and without many of the other contingent causes of Christian Socialism, it is unlikely that Maurice would have become involved in practical schemes of action. Yet the overriding stimulus for his involvement was his realization that the national vocation of the Church of England was at stake. What happened at this juncture to provoke that realization?

SOCIAL CRISIS AND THE 'YEAR OF REVOLUTIONS'

After the constitutional changes of 1828–32, the sense of challenge and threat never departed altogether from mid-Victorian Anglicanism. Yet the Reform crisis had complicated roots, including the emergence of awareness of the appalling social costs of industrialization and working-class aspirations for democracy. These sensitivities only intensified in the years after the Great Reform Act. Chartism, the movement associated with demands for the 'People's Charter' (six points of parliamentary reform that included universal male suffrage, annual elections, and the secret ballot) peaked in the years 1839–42, drawing strength particularly in the industrial north of England, in South Wales, and in London.[28] The 1840s

---

[27] D. McLellan, *The Thought of Karl Marx*, 2nd edn. (London: Macmillan, 1980), 15.

[28] For a classic narrative, see M. Hovell, *The Chartist Movement* (1918; new edn., Manchester: Manchester University Press, 1966). Hovell entitled his 18th chapter 'The Decline of Chartism 1842–53'. For a more recent discussion, see R. Brown, *Chartism*.

were a decade in which industrial conflict and the development of workers' organizations have led some historians to conclude that Britain at last
saw the emergence of a distinct working-class consciousness.[29] There was
exceptional immiseration, yet unparalleled technological and economic
growth.[30] The railways, the telegraph, mass consumer production, and
gas lighting represented progress. Yet, as Hobsbawm comments, 'How
was one to find quantitative expression for the fact . . . that the Industrial
Revolution created the ugliest world in which man has ever lived, as the
grim and stinking, fog-bound back streets of Manchester already tes-
tified?'[31] It was Manchester that Friedrich Engels described in his shocking
survey of working-class living, *The Condition of the Working Class in England*
(1845). These were the 'Hungry Forties', made notorious above all by
novelists who sought to expose the unacceptable conditions of the poor,
including Mrs Gaskell in *Mary Barton* (1848), for example, Benjamin
Disraeli in *Coningsby* (1844) and *Sybil, or The Two Nations* (1845), Charles
Dickens in *Hard Times* (1854), and even Charles Kingsley himself in *Yeast*
(1848) and *Alton Locke* (1850).[32]

Of how much of this was Maurice aware? Presumably he read news-
papers and periodicals, and participated to that extent in the new media
world of his age. His acquaintance with Carlyle, and his appreciation of
Carlyle's essay on Chartism strengthen that supposition. One scholar has
argued that Maurice showed little concern at all for the poor and for those
outside the Church.[33] But this is a tendentious comment that shows little
appreciation of the comprehensive spirit of his conception of the national
Church, and anyway neglects significant evidence of his willingness to
support literary and educational work.[34] His advocacy of an extensive
programme of religious education, to be supported by the State, has to
be seen in this light.[35] Though it hardly sprang from a concern for the
working class, his establishment of Queen's College as an educational

---

[29] Two classic modern discussions straddling this controversy are J. Foster, *Class Struggle
and the Industrial Revolution: Early Industrial Capitalism in Three English Towns* (London:
Weidenfeld & Nicolson, 1974), and P. Joyce, *Work, Society and Politics: The Culture of the
Factory in Later Victorian England* (Brighton: Harvester, 1980); see also *idem, Visions of the
People: Industrial England and the Question of Class 1848–1914* (Cambridge: Cambridge Univer-
sity Press, 1991).

[30] See Hobsbawm, *Age of Revolution*, 359–71.

[31] Ibid. 360.

[32] On the background and nature of much of this literature, see K. Tillotson, *Novels of the
Eighteen-Forties*, (1954; new edn., Oxford: Clarendon Press, 1983).

[33] Christensen, *Christian Socialism*, 29–33.

[34] On this, I am at one with P. R. Allen, 'F. D. Maurice and J. M. Ludlow: A Reassessment of
the Leaders of Victorian Christian Socialism', *Victorian Studies*, 11 (1968), 461–82.

[35] F. D. Maurice, *Has the Church, or the State, the Power to Educate the Nation?* (London:
Rivington, 1839).

institution for women (mainly governesses) in 1847–8 is also evidence of extra-ecclesial concern.[36] Even so, his main interests in these years were his writing, his ministry, and his family, and much of the contemporary anxiety about the condition of England passed him by.

But that changed in 1848. Across Europe, economic scarcity and harvest failure destabilized society just at the time when there were signs that the post-Napoleonic autocracies were failing politically. As Hobsbawm has commented: 'Rarely has revolution been more universally predicted . . . An entire continent waited, ready by now to pass the news of revolution almost instantly from city to city by means of the electric telegraph.'[37] Revolution, after all, in this 'most revolutionary half-century', was the preoccupation of aristocrat, bourgeois, worker, and peasant alike, whether from fear or from hope.[38] When it happened, it was a confusing mixture of mass uprisings, bourgeois *coups*, parliamentarianism, and nationalism. Risings in Prussia and other German states, in Austria, Hungary, and Italy, were all ultimately suppressed with some bloodshed.[39] But it was events in France that most affected Britain, as in 1789 and 1830. The overthrow of the constitutional monarchy of Louis Philippe was followed by an attempt to create workers' associations in Paris and other major cities, and by the creation of the Second Republic. In Britain, Chartist leaders thought their moment had come. There were connections between Chartist leaders and French radicals, and on both sides with German workers' leaders (including Engels, who wrote for the Chartist *Northern Star*).[40] Disturbances all over the country in March 1848 followed the news of Louis Philippe's flight. In early April, a Chartist Convention in London called for a National Assembly.[41] The Chartists' programme was to be presented to Parliament on 10 April, accompanied by a huge petition which, the Convention claimed, had been signed by six million people (the actual figure proved to be less than two million).[42] A mass demonstration in support was planned.

By early April, then, the threat of revolution hung over Britain. Born of the horror of revolution in Europe, awareness of the miserable living conditions of the poor, and experience of occasional outbursts of popular violence, the 'social fear' that haunted the Victorian imagination flared

---

[36] Maurice, *Life*, i. 455–6; see also R. G. Grylls, *Queen's College, 1848–1948: Founded by F. D. Maurice* (London: Routledge, 1948).

[37] Hobsbawm, *Age of Revolution*, 370–1.

[38] Ibid. 359.

[39] For a brief summary, see P. Jones, *The 1848 Revolutions* (London: Longman, 1991).

[40] Hovell, *Chartist Movement*, 285–6.

[41] Ibid. 289.

[42] Ibid. 292.

into life. Church leaders had more reason to fear than most. Radical hostility to the Church of England was unabated. By now, some labour organizations and groups were also openly atheist. Robert Owen, early advocate of co-operation and Socialism, had been notoriously anti-religious.[43] The atheist turn of Socialism was signalled in that classic text of Communist literature, *The Communist Manifesto*, which acknowledged and criticized Christian forms of Socialism. In setting out to define just what true socialism might mean, it was necessary for Marx and Engels to reject false Socialisms. Their words on that score were sobering reading for Christian Socialists. Marx's general position on religion had already been marked out in his *Introduction to a Contribution to a Critique of Hegel's Philosophy of Right*: religion was 'the self-consciousness and self-esteem of man who has either not yet won through to himself or has already lost himself again'.[44] It was 'the sigh of the oppressed creature . . . the *opium* of the people'.[45] But it was an inverted consciousness. The abolition of religion would be the abolition of an '*illusory* happiness of the people' and thereby 'the demand for their *real* happiness'.[46] Now, in 1848, Marx and Engels together dismissed religious practice, even when it sought egalitarian ends. Institutional Christianity was the product of a feudal era. Its Socialism, such as it was, was reactionary: 'Nothing is easier than to give Christian asceticism a socialist tinge. Has not Christianity declaimed against private property, against marriage, against the state?'[47] But, chillingly, they went on: 'Has it not preached in the place of these, charity and poverty, celibacy and mortification of the flesh, monastic life and Mother Church? Christian socialism is but the holy water with which the priest consecrates the heart-burnings of the aristocrat.'[48]

Maurice probably never read Marx or Engels. They were marginal figures on the English working-class scene. We can be confident, likewise, that Marx never read anything by Maurice. Marx's words dismissing Christian Socialism were written months before the English movement got going, and two years before Maurice adopted the term 'Christian Socialism'.[49] But Maurice shared with Marx and Engels, and all of the

[43] See R. Owen, *Book of the New Moral World* (London: Wilson, 1836).

[44] Karl Marx, *Early Writings*, ed. L. Colletti (Harmondsworth: Penguin, 1975), 244.

[45] Ibid.; editor's italics.

[46] Ibid.; editor's italics.

[47] Karl Marx, *The Revolutions of 1848*, ed. D. Fernbach (Harmondsworth: Penguin, 1973), 89.

[48] Ibid. 89.

[49] The *Communist Manifesto* was written in London (in German) in January 1848: *Revolutions of 1848*, 62. The term 'Christian Socialism' was actually adopted by Maurice early in 1850, as a title for a series of tracts to 'commit us at once to the conflict we must engage in sooner or later with the unsocial Christians and the unchristian Socialists': Maurice, *Life*, ii. 35.

Socialist pioneers, a concern to improve the conditions of the poor. Clergy were at the forefront of Victorian society's well-intended but often ineffectual attempts to eradicate poverty.[50] Sympathy for the plight of the poor was hardly controversial. To Marx and Engels, the chaos of revolution represented the only serious hope for dismantling social injustice. To Maurice and his friends, revolution would itself produce further violence and oppression. If, superficially, Maurice agreed that the social upheavals of the age demonstrated the bankruptcy of contemporary Christianity, his prescription could not have been more different from Marx's communism. To Maurice, the Church was not a reflection or articulation of social injustice, but the antidote to it. Injustice was proportionate to the Church's historic inability to effect the comprehensiveness of its vocation. Maurice's view was virtually an inversion of Marx's. Social change was dependent on Christian mission in the fullest sense. Christianity was the true revolutionary ideology. This perspective ran through his theology, and was never abandoned even after he lost interest in the immediate, practical schemes of Christian Socialism. As he was to put it years later,

A Baptism of the Spirit and of fire is needed, as much for the physical as for the moral regeneration of the earth and of man . . . . In daring to say we have a Gospel to the poor, we affirm that there is nothing in His creation so low but He designs to raise it.[51]

1848 was a challenge to the authenticity of that vision.

CHRISTIAN SOCIALISM

In a study principally of Maurice's theology, there is no space for a detailed analysis of Christian Socialism itself, especially given the welter of books already available. Instead, I shall present an outline only, in order to contextualize the theological dimension of Maurice's Christian Socialist sympathies. Hardly a coherent movement at first, Christian Socialism was an unfolding chain of responses that never worked itself into a programme as such. The initial impulse was not Maurice's alone. Two newly formed friendships were the catalyst for the fresh direction taken by his thinking. First was John Malcolm Ludlow (1821–1911), a barrister who had met

---

[50] On this, see G. Kitson Clark, *Churchmen and the Condition of England, 1832–1885* (London: Methuen, 1973), and also K. S. Inglis, *Churches and the Working Classes in Victorian England* (London: Routledge & Kegan Paul, 1963).

[51] F. D. Maurice, 'On Preaching to the Poor', *Sermons Preached in Lincoln's Inn Chapel*, (1856–9; new edn., London: Smith Elder, 1860), ii. 314–15.

Maurice at Lincoln's Inn, and mentioned previously.[52] Writing from personal experience of the revolutionary situation in Paris, Ludlow realized
the significance of the new Socialist ideas. Adopting French Socialism's
idealism, he nevertheless feared its secular implications.[53] Socialism, he
wrote to Maurice, 'must be Christianised or it would shake Christianity to
its foundation'.[54] Maurice was at first cautious ('I see my way dimly'), but
soon he was circulating Ludlow's letter to others, and acknowledging to
Ludlow himself that 'the necessity of an English theological reformation,
as the means of averting an English political revolution and of bringing
what is good in foreign revolutions to know itself, has been more and
more pressing on my mind'.[55] This was late in March 1848, whilst fears
about popular unrest and the revival of Chartism were growing. The
second person was Charles Kingsley (1819–75), vicar of Eversley in Hamp-
shire, who had met Maurice in 1844 and had already come to regard him as
his theological mentor.[56] Ludlow—intense, withdrawn, careful, and yet
most democratic in sympathies—and Kingsley—energetic, exuberant,
incautious, yet conservative—together forged a friendship with Maurice
that lay at the centre of Christian Socialism.[57] Kingsley came up to London
for the day of the great Chartist meeting, and produced placards (printed
as leaflets) which were circulated amongst the crowds two days later.[58] But
Ludlow began to think more constructively about engaging with the
situation of the poor.

At the risk of imposing too neat an interpretation on Christian Socialism, I would suggest that there were three distinct phases of activity. The
first lasted from 1848 until late 1850. It was marked by a flurry of
educational and literary activity. *Politics for the People* was a short-lived,
cheap weekly newspaper begun by Maurice and others at the beginning of
May 1848. Aimed at the labouring classes, its articles touched on questions

---

[52] Ludlow, *Autobiography*, 101.   [53] Ibid. 112.   [54] Maurice, *Life*, i. 458.
[55] Ibid. 459.   [56] Ibid. 371–6.
[57] The standard life of Kingsley is that edited by his wife: F. E. Kingsley, *Charles Kingsley: His
Letters and Memories of his Life* (1877; new edn., London: Macmillan, 1899). There are modern
studies, including S. Chitty, *The Beast and the Monk: A Life of Charles Kingsley* (London: Hodder
& Stoughton, 1974); B. Colloms, *Charles Kingsley: The Lion of Eversley* (London: Constable,
1975); S. K. Sharma, *Charles Kingsley and the Victorian Compromise* (New Delhi: Vani Prakashan,
1989). None of these represents a satisfactory account of Kingsley's religious thought, though
for some useful material see Lethaby, ' "A Less Perfect Reflection" ', 183–200.
[58] Maurice, *Life*, i. 460–1. Kingsley's letters to his wife convey his excitement: '[11 April]
The events of a week have been crowded into a few hours. I was up till 4 this morning, writing
placards under Maurice's auspices . . . Pray, pray help us. Maurice has taken me into counsel,
and we are to have meetings for prayer and study, when I come up to London, and we are to
bring out a new set of "Tracts for the Times", addressed to the higher orders . . . . A glorious
future is opening. Both Maurice and L[udlow] seem to have driven away all my doubts and
sorrows, and I see the blue sky again and my Father's face!': Kingsley, *Charles Kingsley*, 62–3.

such as parliamentary reform, the relation of capital to labour, and schemes for the unemployed.[59] But, with poor circulation, it scarcely lasted two months. It was nearly two years before another attempt to reach a wide readership was tried, this time with *Tracts on Christian Socialism*, followed shortly by *Tracts by Christian Socialists*. Again, neither series proved commercially viable.[60] But at the heart of the movement in these years were seemingly minor, practical ventures. Weekly Bible classes, usually held in Maurice's house, sprang out of regular meetings of sympathizers originally concerned with the management of *Politics for the People*.[61] Maurice presided. Though without a fixed agenda, discussion invariably reached the point at which Maurice's own view was sought out.[62] These meetings were an exercise in applied exegesis, with the biblical text used as the means through which contemporary social, political, and ecclesiastical difficulties could be explored. Ludlow subsequently regarded them as the 'very backbone of the Christian Socialist movement'.[63] Not only was the movement essentially a theological one, with its main preoccupation not primarily the reorganization of society, but rather the renewal of the Church's social mission, but it depended on a small and fairly tightly knit body of supporters. Around the trio of Maurice, Ludlow, and Kingsley there gathered enthusiasts and professionals, including some famous and not-so-famous Victorian names, such as Thomas Hughes, the novelist, Edward Vansittart Neale, the pioneer of co-operative societies, and the scientist Charles Mansfield, amongst many others. The weekly Bible class was perhaps the major means (aside from his preaching and writing, that is) by which Maurice's influence was dispersed to the inner circle of his followers.[64]

There were other projects, too. One was the formation of a night school for men in what Ludlow called 'a black spot . . . within a stone's throw' of Maurice's house.[65] The school in Little Ormond Yard began in July 1848, with the leasing of a house and the hiring of a housekeeper and a teacher.[66] Shortly after it was begun, a 'ragged school' was formed there for children. According to Ludlow, Hughes took a particular interest in the

---

[59] As Maurice's 'Prospectus' instanced in the first issue: *Politics for the People*, no. 1 (6 May 1848), 1.

[60] See Christensen, *Christian Socialism*, 134–42.

[61] Maurice, *Life*, i. 481, 487.

[62] Ibid. 488–93; the account is that of Charles Mansfield, writing to Ludlow.

[63] J. M. Ludlow, 'Some of the Christian Socialists of 1848', 493.

[64] Raven called the meetings 'the sacrament, the effective symbol of [the Christian Socialists'] unity, the means whereby they received their inspiration': Raven, *Christian Socialism*, 134.

[65] Ludlow, *Autobiography*, 135.

[66] Maurice, *Life*, i. 482.

Little Ormond Street school.[67] It lasted at least a year, with Maurice a benign if rather aloof supporter.[68] Eventually it was taken over by the local parish clergy. Another project pursued by Mansfield, Kingsley, and Ludlow was the formation of a national health league, prompted by visiting the squalid condition of parts of Bermondsey during the cholera epidemic of 1849.[69] Here the stimulus was Henry Mayhew's account of the appalling sanitary conditions of parts of London.[70] Mayhew's famous letters on the labouring poor, published in the *Morning Chronicle* from October 1849 to December 1850, intensified public concern about public health and poverty.[71] Yet the health league itself came to nothing, checked by Maurice's reluctance to get drawn into the creation of a separate national organization. It was better far, in his view, to concentrate attention on local, neighbourhood schemes.[72]

The piecemeal nature of these initiatives is evident. There was no obvious relationship between the short-lived attempts at reaching the reading public through tracts and journals and the other schemes propounded by various members of the group, except that established through friendship, the Bible classes, and a great deal of idealism. Maurice provided a theological rationale, but even then not all shared his particular commitments. Neale in particular was not a believer.[73] Moreover, this effort was paternalist. It was provision *for* the working class, and persuasion *of* them by educated social superiors. There was little to separate the group from any other group of middle-class do-gooders. Their specific local projects looked like the philanthropic pursuits of churches up and down the poorer parts of Britain.

But the disparate and personalized nature of the group's activities did at least open up contacts with workers and political activists. Ludlow made contact with Walter Cooper, a tailor and Chartist.[74] Kingsley made the acquaintance of another Chartist, Thomas Cooper, like his namesake at

---

[67] J. M. Ludlow, 'Thomas Hughes and Septimus Hansard', *The Economic Review*, 6 (1896), 298; see also Ludlow, *Autobiography*, 135–7.

[68] Maurice, *Life*, i. 548.

[69] Raven, *Christian Socialism*, 147.

[70] Ludlow, *Autobiography*, 154.

[71] The articles formed part of the basis of Mayhew's famous *London Labour and the London Poor* (1861); for a selection of the original articles, see E. P. Thompson and E. Yeo (eds.), *The Unknown Mayhew* (Harmondsworth: Penguin, 1973).

[72] See Christensen's account of the failure of the scheme, in *Christian Socialism*, 120–4. The key source for Maurice's views is a letter to Ludlow in Maurice, *Life*, ii. 23–7. As I shall argue below, Christensen somewhat underestimates the force of Maurice's commitment to local endeavour.

[73] Ludlow, *Autobiography*, 163.

[74] Ibid. 144–6.

this time an atheist, but later to return to orthodox Christianity.[75] In time, joint meetings were organized between the Christian Socialists and workers' representatives, and held from March 1849 at a nearby public house.[76] The effect was to crystallize the Christian Socialists' effort in a new direction. This was the formation of workers' associations, co-operative agencies defined by trade, and committed to distributing profit and ownership proportionately amongst the participating workers. Here too Ludlow's role was decisive. He took as his model the workers' associations he had observed in France during his visits from 1848 to 1850.[77] Again stimulated by Mayhew's accounts of the fragility of London employment, as well as by personal contacts, Ludlow and others oversaw the creation of specific workers' associations. Whether he realized it at first or not, Ludlow had hit upon a form of activity that chimed in with Maurice's theology of communion. The theme of co-operation became for Maurice a practical embodiment of his basic theological principles and, to the surprise of his younger followers, he 'entered heartily' into the scheme.[78] Indeed, the name 'Christian Socialist', now adopted (early in 1850) for a series of tracts, actually sprang out of this particular proposal.[79] It is strictly applicable, then, only from this, the second stage of the movement.

A Council of Promoters of the scheme was formed, under Maurice's presidency; offices were leased, at first in Oxford Street and then in Charlotte Street; and a Central Board of management was formed.[80] In turn, separate workers' associations were formed, under the overall supervision of the Central Board. The first of these was the Working Tailors' Association, formed in February 1850.[81] A further seven associations were formed soon afterwards, including shoemakers, builders, printers, bakers, and needlewomen.[82] A journal was founded in November 1850 to promote the philosophy and organization of co-operation, *The Christian Socialist*, shortly rechristened *The Journal of Association*, and printed, appropriately, by the Working Printers' Association from their premises in a court off Fleet Street.[83] A 'Hall of Association' was built in 1852 for the

[75] See 'Thomas Cooper (1805–92), Chartist, Lecturer and Author', in J. Bellamy and J. Saville (eds.), *Dictionary of Labour Biography*, ix (Basingstoke: Macmillan, 1993), 52–5.

[76] Ludlow, *Autobiography*, 146.

[77] Ludlow's autobiography is a vital source here: ibid. 165–78.

[78] Maurice, *Life*, ii. 31.

[79] Ibid. 35.

[80] For a clear, basic narrative, see Raven, *Christian Socialism*, 184–224; see also Christensen, *Christian Socialism*, 124–33, 142–51.

[81] Christensen, *Christian Socialism*, 132.

[82] Raven, *Christian Socialism*, 189.

[83] Ibid. 195. On the controversy between Maurice and Ludlow over the title of the journal, see Christensen, *Christian Socialism*, 209–15.

umbrella organization, the Society for Promoting Working Men's Associations (SPWMA), in Castle Street by the North London Working Builders (another one of the associations).[84] The SPWMA and the London associations demonstrated, according to one historian, a 'definitely missionary character', sending delegates and activists on proselytizing tours of northern England, and encouraging the affiliation of other co-operative organizations.[85] In this, Neale was especially instrumental.[86] But once again success was short-lived. The SPWMA was beset by internal struggles over strategy and control, by disastrous mismanagement of funds, and by the inability of the member associations to function at a satisfactory rate of profit. Nearly all of the associations foundered in the mid-1850s, as did the SPWMA itself. There were lasting results, nevertheless. A few associations survived, impetus had been given to the co-operative movement more widely, and some individuals, including Neale and Ludlow, remained personally committed to the cause.[87] Yet Ludlow himself, Kingsley, and Maurice were convinced that workers were not yet sufficiently well-educated to manage independent business institutions on their own.[88] Ludlow evidently regarded the failure of the associations, and the abandonment of them by Maurice in particular, as the end of Christian Socialism.[89]

Yet, arguably, there was a third stage. This was the creation of the Working Men's College. It was this that absorbed Maurice's energies increasingly in the mid-1850s, diverting his attention from association. Founded in 1854, it was the offshoot of the meetings between Chartists, workers, and the Christian Socialists.[90] Directly, however, it was prompted by Maurice's dismissal from his chair at King's College in 1853, in a controversy we shall examine in the next chapter. At a public meeting held in the Hall of Association in December 1853, a speaker in support of Maurice proposed the idea that he might become professor of a 'Working Man's College'.[91] At the prompting of the SPWMA in January 1854, Maurice proceeded to draw up a scheme. Premises of a failed association (rented by Maurice himself) were retained in Red Lion Square, and the

---

[84] J. F. C. Harrison, *A History of the Working Men's College, 1854–1954* (London: Routledge & Kegan Paul, 1954), 16.

[85] Raven, *Christian Socialism*, 215.

[86] See P. N. Backstrom, *Christian Socialism and Co-operation in Victorian England: Edward Vansittart Neale and the Co-operative Movement* (London: Croom Helm, 1974).

[87] J. M. Ludlow and L. Jones, *The Progress of the Working Class 1832–1867* (London: Alexander Strahan, 1867), 142.

[88] Harrison, *Working Men's College*, 15; Raven, *Christian Socialism*, 315.

[89] Ludlow, *Autobiography*, 263–4.

[90] The standard history is Harrison, *Working Men's College*.

[91] Maurice, *Life*, ii. 221.

college began there shortly afterwards with a series of day and evening classes on various subjects.[92] The college drew a wide variety of teachers, including some well-known figures such as D. G. Rossetti, John Ruskin, Fitzjames Stephen, and Frederic Harrison, along with Maurice, Kingsley, Ludlow, Hughes, and other of the Christian Socialists.[93] Detached in time somewhat from the ideals of its founders, it nevertheless proved a success in the long run, establishing itself as a permanent and, as I write, still surviving institution.

By the mid-1850s, Christian Socialism as a distinct movement was at an end. For all its retrospective significance, its practical achievements were limited to the creation of the Working Men's College and a minor contribution to the history of the co-operative movement in Britain. Its publications achieved some notoriety, not least because of a hostile review by J. W. Croker of some of Maurice's and Kingsley's work in a *Quarterly Review* article headed 'Revolutionary Literature'.[94] This in turn raised difficulties for Maurice at King's College, an ominous sign, bearing in mind the controversy that was to break on him in 1853.[95] Without a doubt the movement had inspired a number of men who carried something of its idealism into a variety of other spheres of work. Given the failure of most of its ventures, however, what role should we accord it in the development of Maurice's theology? His involvement was paradoxical. It was central, and inspirational, according to all of the participants who subsequently wrote about the movement. Yet he was marginal to many of the practical schemes, and a check or brake on his more enthusiastic followers. This ambiguity has made assessment of the place of Christian Socialism in Maurice's intellectual development peculiarly difficult. There is a case for seeing his involvement as a logical extension of his theological commitments, however, and one that inevitably led him to a degree of suspicion about practical schemes that might imply the creation of distinct 'party' spirit.[96] A closer look at Maurice's theological rationale for the movement demonstrates just how well it fitted his wider theological and ecclesiological arguments, yet also helps us to understand its limitations.

As Maurice's published sermons on the Lord's Prayer indicate, early in 1848 he was already seeking to discern what the implications of the developing European crisis might be for his theological position. Almost

---

[92] Ibid. 233.

[93] See Ludlow, *Autobiography*, 266–77.

[94] [J. W. Croker] Anonymous, 'Revolutionary Literature', *Quarterly Review*, 89 (1850–1).

[95] Maurice, *Life*, ii. 78–86.

[96] Christensen is surely correct to emphasize Maurice's conviction that Ludlow's more doctrinaire, economic Socialism could lead to a new form of sectarianism: Christensen, *Christian Socialism*, 214–15.

from the opening page he emphasized how social division inhibits true worship of God, since it reflects self-preoccupation: 'How can we look round upon the people whom we habitually feel to be separated from us by almost impassable barriers . . . and then teach ourselves to think that in the very highest exercise of our lives these are associated with us?'[97] This was to repeat the position he had already established earlier. His interpretation of church division depended on the assumption that there was an inner, existing unity in human society resting on the unity of God: 'this idea of the unity of God must in some way or other be the ground of all unity among men'.[98] Notwithstanding Ludlow's and others' exasperation with Maurice's impracticality, his Christian Socialism was simply another presentation of his thinking on the Church. His writing in this first period of Christian Socialism was not extensive, at least in comparison with other periods of his life, but what there was reflected again and again *existing* theological insights. In the 'Prospectus' to *Politics for the People*, he cast the movement as one of listening, rather than formulating: 'If we do not sympathize with their [working men's] miseries we are not fit to discuss the remedies which they propose themselves, or which others have proposed for them.'[99]

This emphasis on listening and sympathizing was consonant with the method of *The Kingdom of Christ*. The aim of the theologian was not to produce ready-made solutions to social problems, but to sound out the deepest reasons for those problems. Maurice's inattention to contemporary theoretical Socialism was perhaps a deficiency only from the position he disavowed: namely, that of politician and social reformer. He affirmed constantly the principle that theology addressed the root or ground of things. When obliged to defend himself against the claim that he had 'mixed up his name' with those who were advocates of Socialism, he emphasized that the word 'Christian' was not chosen as a qualifier: 'We believe that Christianity has the power of regenerating whatever it comes in contact with, of making that morally healthful and vigorous which apart from it must be either mischievous or inefficient.'[100] In his *Subscription no Bondage*, he had proposed the study of the Thirty-Nine Articles of Religion as revealing the ground of education.[101] Nearly thirty years later, he could tell his audience at the Working Men's College, in his lecture on 'Acquisition and Illumination', that theology 'justifies' all other studies: 'We cannot discover the Eternal and Infinite, but He discovers Himself, and in discovering Himself helps us to see what we are.'[102] But this lecture

---

[97] Maurice, *The Prayer-Book*, 284.   [98] Maurice, *Kingdom of Christ*, i. 140.
[99] 'Prospectus', 1.   [100] Maurice, *Life*, ii. 92.
[101] Maurice, *Subscription no Bondage*, 88–9.   [102] Maurice, *Friendship of Books*, 273.

alone demonstrated how intrinsic to Maurice's reflections on social being was a theological perspective, because its argument depended on a contrast of divine illumination, which binds human beings together, and egoistical acquisition, which drives them apart: 'every divine gift to individuals is precious only as it unites them with their kind'.[103]

Even so, the movement of 1848 represented a distinct development or new application of his theology. His deployment of a slightly different language in writing aimed directly at a working-class audience masked his abiding themes. A process of *translation*, in effect, was in operation. In his journalism and pamphlets, Maurice allowed his language a greater degree of flexibility and clarity than was usually the case. There was a rhetorical strategy here. He sought to avoid, wherever possible, writing as if he was concerned primarily with Anglican issues, and addressed himself directly to working men. But the primary reference of his language remained the same, and he continued to assume that his main task was to write as a Christian theologian for and about the Church.

This was evident from the very opening number of *Politics for the People*. Maurice's 'Prospectus' announced a concern to address issues of specific concern, such as the extension of the franchise and the relation of capital to labour.[104] But it went on to produce an impossibly wide conception of politics as 'whatever concerns man as a social being'.[105] It countermanded the common separation of politics and religion. But, in typically Maurician fashion, it also at once proceeded to transfigure its use of the word 'politics' by referring this wide definition to the government of God: 'The world is governed by God; this is the rich man's warning; this is the poor man's comfort . . . this is the pledge that Liberty, Fraternity, Unity, under some conditions or other, are intended for every people under heaven.'[106] Maurice's modification of the revolutionary trinity is surely significant. On this basis, his social theology does not really owe very much at all to a sociological insight into human being, *pace* the assessment made by Edward Norman.[107] It was the clothing of a theological argument about the character and destiny of human being in words that echoed the language of political controversy.

Maurice's concept of unity was used repeatedly to bring to the fore the abiding unity of human beings in God. This unity was a social challenge: it indicated an amplitude in God's creation that human division was constantly undermining. As Maurice was to write later, 'what we want, is a

---

[103] Ibid. 269.   [104] 'Prospectus', 1.   [105] Ibid.   [106] Ibid.

[107] '[In] seeking the non-religious reasons for which men hold religious ideas, and in observing the effect of the structures of society upon ecclesiastical organizations, Maurice was a precursor of the sociology of religion': Norman, *Victorian Christian Socialists*, 34.

ground in the name of the Eternal God, which shall embrace all, and at
last subdue all to itself'.[108] As a corollary of this, Maurice read social
conflict as stemming from the human tendency to turn inwards, to egoism
and selfishness. An anti-social principle was at work amongst the rich as
well as the poor, destroying bonds of unity: this 'selfish principle' sprang
from an idolatry of property, 'the assumption that the possession of
material things is the end for which men . . . must be striving'.[109] Thus,
though a degree of competition might be accounted a 'blessing', since
restrictions on it in the past had often had their origin in selfish interests,
nevertheless property was not an absolute, but a dependent concept,
subordinate to the performance of certain services for the benefit of a
whole society.[110] Here, Maurice's theological anthropology, by which
human being could be described teleologically as being *for* God, was
redefined in terms which highlighted the incompatibility of particular
features of Victorian society with Christian faith. But its theological basis
remained intact.

Furthermore, the socially destructive character of egoism implied the
presence of a real, if threatened, divine order for human society. There will
be reason to comment further on this in the following section, but here it
suffices to say that Maurice's assumption of a threefold constitution of
society, through family, nation, and Church, remained at work in his
writings from 1848 to 1852. Excessive competition had obliged working
men not to apprehend families as bound in a bond of love, but to 'count
heads' as wage-earners or competitors.[111] Freed from unrestricted competition, property could be seen as 'connected with order in the true honest
sense of the word', since it could promote mutual class interests, rather
than undermine them.[112]

The normative divine order implied in all human society could be
characterized in a particular way through the notion of fellowship. 'Society', Maurice argued, was nearly synonymous with 'Community' and with
'Fellowship'.[113] It was significant, then, that the very first article in *Politics
for the People* after the 'Prospectus' was one by Maurice himself on
'Fraternity'. He traced the re-emergence of an understanding of universal

---

[108] F. D. Maurice, 'Morality and Divinity', in 'The Sermon of the Bishop of Oxford on
Revelation, and the Layman's Answer', *Tracts for Priests and People*, no. 6 (London: Macmillan,
1861), 35.

[109] F. D. Maurice, *On the Reformation of Society, and How All Classes may Contribute to it*
(Southampton: Forbes & Knibb, 1851), 13.

[110] F. D. Maurice, *Reasons for Co-operation: A Lecture Delivered at the Office for Promoting
Working Men's Associations* (London: Parker, 1851), 21.

[111] Maurice, *Reformation of Society*, 22.

[112] Maurice, *Reasons for Co-operation*, 14.

[113] Maurice, *Reformation of Society*, 6–7.

brotherhood in writers such as Charles Dickens, and argued that it was rooted in God's self-identification with human beings through an 'elder Brother' who died for all.[114] From the standpoint of that brotherly sacrifice, all were to be addressed as brothers; men had to learn to work and act together 'by labouring strenuously in God's strength, that we may realize the true Fraternity of which this age has dreamed, and without which we believe it cannot be satisfied'.[115] Maurice's notion of fraternity or fellowship (actually much the more common term in his work) bears obvious comparison with his concept of communion. It was not so much a secularized counterpart to communion, but a repetition of the concept in a different guise. His support for co-operation derived from his conviction that it was a way of 'carrying out what seems to us the only law of fellowship among Christian men'.[116] Later, with more directly ecclesial issues in mind, he wrote: 'I believe that God has made us not to be separate creatures, but to have fellowship with one another. I believe He is working in these spirits of ours that we may have it.'[117]

Thus, the language and content of much of Maurice's social thought bore strong comparison with his reflections on theology and ecclesiology. His immersion in matters of direct concern to working men and women in these years was a logical and natural extension of his existing ecclesiological commitments. His frequent assertion that the distinction between 'secular' and 'spiritual' was valueless, or at least itself a product of the wilful, egoistical turn from God bears this out.[118] His defence of the national provision of education through church schools assumed that the teaching of religion could not be carried through effectively as one part of the curriculum amongst many, but should saturate the curriculum in its entirety: 'the object is not so much to give a certain quantity of christian or church lore, as to form christians and churchmen'.[119]

The interweaving of social, political, and theological language in Maurice's writing in these years is finely illustrated in a letter to Ludlow in which his analysis of contemporary difficulties proceeded seamlessly from political crisis to theological analysis and ecclesiological comment. It is worth quoting at length to conclude this section:

[114] 'Fraternity', *Politics for the People*, no. 1 (6 May 1848), 3.

[115] Ibid. 5. The 'men' and 'brothers' of Maurice's language here were presumably inclusive of women, but the masculine weight of terms such as this is nevertheless striking.

[116] Maurice, *Reasons for Co-operation*, 7.

[117] F. D. Maurice, *The Lord's Prayer, the Creed, and the Commandments: A Manual for Parents and Schoolmasters* (London: Macmillan, 1870), 46.

[118] 'By the Christian principle we understand that which refers everything to God; by the secular principle we understand that which refers everything to self': Maurice, *Kingdom of Christ*, 1st edn., iii. 389.

[119] Maurice, *The Education Question in 1847*, 10.

[T]he necessity of an English theological revolution . . . has been more and more pressing on my mind. We have no right to talk of Atheistic France, Atheistic Germany, true as the charge may be even now, fearfully as it may be proved hereafter. Are not we Atheistic? Is not our Christianity semi-Atheistic? We have theories of sin, of justification, of apostolical succession, schemes of divinity Protestant, Romish, semi-Romish, Anglican, Dissenting. But where is God in them all? Not first at least, not a Father; but merely the provider of a certain scheme for our deliverance, the setter-up of a Church system which is to go on without Him by help of popes, kings, doctors . . . . When we have confessed our own Atheism and repented of it, we can call upon all nations to abandon theirs. But do not let us preach a Protestantism, Catholicism, Christianity without God.[120]

THE LOCAL ROOTS OF CHRISTIAN SOCIALISM

Far from being avant-garde, for Maurice Christian Socialism was deeply traditional. Its cause was that of social harmony and stability, its values those of Christian orthodoxy, and its means the Church (albeit purified, or internally reconverted to its authentic vision) and comparable, harmonious agencies in 'secular' economics. What is perhaps surprising, in this context, is the hostility his view attracted. Yet it is not difficult to see why contemporaries misunderstood Maurice. The very title 'Christian Socialism' was bound to attract suspicion, despite Maurice's protests to the contrary. Kingsley's enthusiasm and vehemence ran away with him, in sermons and novels that looked inflammatory. The group's association with Chartist leaders and trades-unionists likewise masked its conservatism. At the same time, the idealism of the group should not be underestimated. Nor should the disparate and short-lived nature of many of its ventures conceal the genuine conviction that something was badly wrong with relations between the rich and the poor, and that social Christianity was best placed to address this.

If we leave Christian Socialism's subsequent legacy to one side, and see it instead as a characteristic response to social anxiety from within the Established Church, then a different conclusion becomes possible from the adverse judgement of scientific Socialism. Maurice was not seeking the construction of something like a permanent *national* organization or sphere of influence. Rather, in the immediate context in which he found himself he was attempting to explore the implications of Christian faith for society as whole. To put it more sharply, the *local* dimension of the movement is vital to understanding its nature, and in particular its

---

[120] Maurice, *Life*, i. 459.

subsistence within the traditional parochial structures of the Church of England.

This local dimension is perhaps underrated by historians, partly because of the very difficulty of re-imagining what west London was like in the middle of the nineteenth century. For much of the twentieth century, as today, Bloomsbury, where Maurice lived in these crucial years of the 1840s and 1850s, was virtually synonymous with affluence, literary success, and middle-class bohemianism. But in Maurice's lifetime it was a mixed area, with streets of significant poverty interspersed with the houses of the fashionable and affluent. It had its own distinctive working-class culture, a culture of craft production, particularly in the clothing industry, that was becoming increasingly debased by the introduction of 'sweated' shops. Contemporary writers saw the neighbourhood as a declining one, with the wealthy and fashionable moving further west. The journalist Albert Smith noted how 'the anomalous neighbourhood between the Foundling Hospital and Red Lion Square . . . and Gray's Inn Lane and Bloomsbury . . . was once the patrician quarter of London', but now was in decay.[121] One of Kingsley's most notorious pamphlets, *Cheap Clothes and Nasty* (1850), drew on Mayhew's *Morning Chronicle* articles to compare the East End, where the 'dishonourable trade' of 'sweated' shops was ubiquitous, with the West End, where the 'honourable' trade was 'rapidly dying out', and despair spreading amongst the tailors and other clothing workers.[122] Many of the craftsmen of the West End were a labour aristocracy, politically alert, articulate, and more organized than their counterparts in the 'sweated' trade.[123] Yet their position was declining.[124] They were a natural constituency for working-class radicalism, including many of the London Chartist leaders.[125] Other radical pressure groups also congregated in the West End. The remnant of Daniel O'Connell's supporters, the 'Old Irelanders', for example, met regularly in the Bull's Head inn in Vere Street.[126]

---

[121] A. Smith, *Sketches of London Life and Character* (London: Bogue, 1849), 84.

[122] C. Kingsley, ['Parson Lot'] *Cheap Clothes and Nasty*, Tracts by Christian Socialists, 2 (London: Bell, 1850), 2.

[123] See E. J. Hobsbawm, 'The Labour Aristocracy in Nineteenth-Century Britain', in *Labouring Men: Studies in the History of Labour* (London: Weidenfeld & Nicolson, 1968).

[124] On the general impact of the shift to semi-skilled production in London in the middle of the nineteenth century, see G. Stedman Jones, *Outcast London: A Study in the Relationship between Classes in Victorian Society* (Harmondsworth: Penguin, 1976), 19–32. See also, on the 'sweated' trades, L. D. Schwarz, *London in the Age of Industrialisation: Entrepreneurs, Labour Force and Living Conditions, 1700–1850* (Cambridge: Cambridge University Press, 1992), 179–207.

[125] D. Large, 'London in the Year of Revolution, 1848', in J. Stevenson (ed.), *London in the Age of Reform* (Oxford: Blackwell, 1977), 181.

[126] Ibid.

In this context, the sense of urgency and impending crisis in 1848 is much more comprehensible than it would have been if Maurice and the others had been looking on the labouring poor from afar. The events of 1848 in London swirled around them. Unemployment amongst the skilled trades was acute in the summer of that year, with estimates of around a third of skilled workmen out of work altogether, and the rest on reduced hours or wages.[127] In May, after the April débâcle of the national Chartist petition, there were continued disturbances, with disorderly assemblies on Clerkenwell Green and processions through the streets of the West End.[128] Highlighted by Mayhew's articles, the predicament of the workers of the West End, and their families, became a central preoccupation of the Christian Socialists. That is why much of the movement for association was, essentially, a West End phenomenon, with the creation of associations concentrated at first on the skilled trades to be found there. It was natural, too, that the Working Men's College should be located in the West End, in a failed association's premises, but significantly close to Maurice's house and within reach of many of the lecturers who taught there.

It would be easy to exaggerate this local dimension of the movement. It was never worked up into a coherent or explicit element of its social theology as such. Yet it was a natural outgrowth of the comprehensive, national vision of the Church that lay at the heart of Maurice's ecclesiology. Care of the particular communities in which the Church of England was situated, under the influence of the argument for comprehensiveness as well as the contemporary language of Socialism, thus turned conventional views of local pastoral care into a conception of the Church serving the renewal and harmonization of the local community. This was served by personal encounter, by listening, by joint study, and by prayer and preaching. It is perhaps also a partial explanation as to why Christian Socialism at this time never became anything like a national movement. Though its influence was to run deep and far eventually, its energy and idealism were made concrete in locally rooted initiatives. Tellingly, in this context it is worth touching again on Maurice's reasons for rejecting the idea of a national health league. He reminded Ludlow that he (Ludlow) had first approached him with the idea of uniting young professional men to work for the poor in the area around Lincoln's Inn. Then he extended that to a more sustained consideration of possible action, writing as chaplain to Lincoln's Inn:

---

[127] Large, 'London in the Year of Revolution', 196.
[128] Hovell, *Chartist Movement*, 293; see also Large, 'London in the Year of Revolution', 195.

[T]he Devil will not the least object to my saying the Church has a bearing upon all common life, if I take no pains that my particular Church should bear upon it at all . . . . Lincoln's Inn is a very powerful body of cultivated men in the midst of as bad a neighbourhood for health and probably education as most in London. If a small body of us could unite to do something for that place our bond would be surely a quasi-sacramental one—a much better one than that of any club or league, even if it did put D.G. on its tickets . . . . such a movement as this . . . must spread by degrees into different circles; that the Templars may come to feel their obliga-tions; King's College also; and that thus by degrees we shall have a living, primarily local, ultimately universal organisation which may not only do much more work, much more abiding work than a league, but may serve as a powerful counteraction to those godless, exclusive no-church Church unions that are springing up . . . . I speak as a clergyman to you as a lawyer.[129]

This was perhaps naïve, but it registered different connections from those associated with Christian Socialist organizations than many historians have acknowledged.

THE CHURCH AS SOCIAL COMMUNITY

Just as surely as it is necessary to read Maurice's ecclesiology into his espousal of Christian Socialism, so it is also important to emphasize the social content of his conception of the Church. To do this, the focus must widen to encompass work written throughout his life. Maurice's funda-mental vision of human being is relevant here. Men and women were made for each other and for God, and not for themselves. Human beings are, at root, spiritual beings created in God's likeness to yearn after him.[130] This fact of createdness was what accounted for the possibility of the double character of religious movements, Christian and otherwise—that is, their ability to be seen both as signs of the human turn to egoism, with its construction of systems of opinion, and as 'witnesses for the God and Father who would lead them all to His Son'.[131] But it was also a sign that human beings were not finally autonomous: they were subject to the law above them, the divine law, in which their own freedom was located. The founding of the Church, historically based in the life and ministry of Christ, also revealed the fellowship for which God had created all people, the unveiling of the order in which he had placed them and which their own actions constantly denied. Christ's teaching addressed individuals, Maurice acknowledged, but in so doing it revealed human membership of a divine society, a kingdom.[132] Whatever the spiritual wisdom to be found

---

[129] Maurice, *Life*, ii. 26–7.   [130] Maurice, *What is Revelation?*, 47.   [131] Ibid. 51.
[132] Maurice, *Social Morality*, 229–30.

in non-Christian religions, and in particular systems of political and social thought, the final and fullest expression of divine wisdom was to be found in the Church.[133] For Maurice, human being was intrinsically social, but also intrinsically ecclesial.

Maurice's language left no place for the view that sociality was second-ary and derivative. Human society was not a mere 'aggregation' of individuals, but mutually dependent.[134] The interrelatedness of all human beings was a primary theological truth, because it was an impli-cation of the sovereignty of God over human beings; and so it could be said of the kingdom that:

It was called the kingdom of God because communion with Him is the great blessedness of it. And it is the kingdom of God because men are brought into it that they may see themselves, their fellow-creatures, the whole universe, as He sees them; not partially, or each in reference to a separate centre, as they naturally do.[135]

The social character of human being was structured for Maurice through three main categories of organization and identity, the three we have already encountered in *The Kingdom of Christ*: family, nation, and Church. This threefold classification of the divine order of society remained central to Maurice's account of social institutions throughout his life, and shaped even his biblical interpretation. It formed the main axis of his most sustained reflection on the social implications of religion, his *Social Morality*, written at Cambridge in 1869, over thirty years after the first edition of *The Kingdom of Christ*.[136] It was an enormously flexible device, which could be used as a key to interpret contemporary political and social as well as religious life, but also to trace the development of the entire history of human civilization. Therein lay its weakness as a historical tool: it was far too flexible to give the reader confidence that historical phenomena treated under the category of family morality, for example, were of sufficient comparability to make Maurice's generalizations mean-ingful. It operated as a conveniently loose framework, enabling him to

---

[133] 'The grandeur of the Crescent can be understood only by the light which falls upon it from the Cross': F. D. Maurice, *The Religions of the World and their Relations to Christianity* (1847; 6th edn., London: Macmillan, 1886), 152.

[134] Maurice, *Social Morality*, 111.

[135] Maurice, *Religions of the World*, 233.

[136] Charles Cashdollar, in his *The Transformation of Theology, 1830–1890: Positivism and Protestant Thought in Britain and America* (Princeton: Princeton University Press, 1989), is therefore in error in suggesting that Maurice 'broadly adapted' his classification from Comte: p. 429. Indeed, throughout his account of Maurice, Cashdollar is much too inclined to assume that the structure of Maurice's thought in *Social Morality* was dictated by his debt to and disagreement with Comte: ibid. 428–30. Cashdollar, incidentally, makes no mention of Henry Maine (see below).

gather together in a seemingly coherent way an enormously diverse range of historical facts.

For our purposes, though, what is significant about the classification is its implicit hierarchical orientation towards its highest level, the Church, or universal society. It disclosed a characteristically nineteenth-century assumption that there is an inherent gradation in forms of human society and religion, with Christianity, for all its acknowledged faults, at the summit. In *Social Morality*, this can be discerned in the selection of historical data. In reference to the family, his material was drawn mainly from ancient society, Greeks, Romans, and Jews. Partly, this was influenced by his acknowledged debt to Sir Henry Maine's *Ancient Law*, since Maine had demonstrated how society's 'starting-point' lay in family existence, such as tribes and clans.[137] Maurice even followed Maine's use of the phrase 'patriarchal theory' to describe the idea that the history of human society echoed the biological history of individuals, who originated in a family with a father and a mother.[138] He disputed Comte's suggestion that the emphasis on monogamy in Western society was mainly a consequence of medieval society, and instead reasserted the importance of monogamous marriage and consanguinity within ancient society.[139] But the violation of 'domestic' morality in ancient society was evident in the widespread fact of slavery, although Maurice acknowledged that slavery reappeared in Western society after the Middle Ages as a child of 'the Trade age'.[140]

When he turned to 'National morality', Maurice's historical material was drawn mainly from the early medieval period. He was at pains to assert the interdependence of individual and collective identities, constituted in relations: 'The "I" and the "Thou" stand out confronting each other, making each other intelligible.'[141] It is unclear to what extent Maurice's argument was historical, and to what extent analytical. The character of social relations was defined for nations in several overlapping, developmental stages, including the growth of law, language, and government, and then the legitimate pursuit of war. Law, for example, 'sanctions' family life, but also added new, corporate feelings to society.[142] Language, the second characteristic of a nation, distinguished particular nations from each other.[143] The force of his argument for distinct national identities

---

[137] Maurice, *Social Morality*, p. x. Maine's treatise was published in 1861.

[138] Ibid. 38.   [139] Ibid. 46–57.   [140] Ibid. 82.

[141] Ibid. 115. Maurice might have been influenced by Julius Hare's lengthy discussion of 'I' and 'Thou' in A. W. and J. C. Hare, *Guesses at Truth* (1827; new edn., London: Macmillan, 1866), 97–149.

[142] Maurice, *Social Morality*, 124.

[143] Ibid. 133.

emerged in language critical of imperialism, and in his contention that
loyalty to the English constitution would best secure respect for other
nations' forms of government.[144] War was justified as a way of protecting
national identity, for the existence of nations was integral to the existence
of the kingdom Christ proclaimed: 'Unless there are nations, distinct
nations, this Kingdom loses its character; it becomes a world-empire,' a
reference to the Papacy.[145]

Now the chronology became confused again. Maurice turned to 'Universal Morality', but this at first took him back to the emergence of the
Roman Empire, an Empire that extinguished nationality in all but its
outward legal forms.[146] A periodization of sorts was evidently at work,
because he paralleled the transition from national to universal conditions
with the transition from the 'patriarchal to the legal period'.[147] But
another scale of historical development also has to be postulated, because
the real universal society, Maurice said, emerged in the centre of the false
or artificial one: namely, the kingdom proclaimed by Jesus Christ, a
kingdom meant 'for all the nations'.[148] The heart of Maurice's conception
of social morality was reached at this point. All human history, he implied,
was oriented towards the kingdom of Christ, and there was an intrinsic
relation between the character and contours of social life, and the life of
God: '[Jesus] had come to open or unveil that divine life, of which the
human life in all its social conditions and circumstances was the image; to
the end that the lower might be reformed by the higher.'[149] Persecution of
the Church followed from its establishment of a rival empire, a real
kingdom, to Rome.[150] The subjugation of the universal family of the
Church occurred under Constantine, and led to the ensuing development
of a monarchical Papacy. Maurice did not treat these developments sim-
plistically. His dialectical method and providential reading of history
enabled him to perceive the persistence of eternal principles even in fallible
or corrupt institutions and individuals. Hildebrand's reform of the Papacy,
for example, represented not merely a centralizing, autocratic impulse, but
also the conviction that the 'father of Christendom must be a Universal

---

[144] Maurice, *Social Morality*, 151, 170. It is important to remember that he was writing
some five years before the Disraeli administration embraced imperialism explicitly as a
populist cause, and that his position was in many ways akin to that of Gladstone: see
H. C. G. Matthew, *Gladstone 1875–1898* (Oxford: Clarendon Press, 1995), 124.

[145] Maurice, *Social Morality*, 180.

[146] Ibid. 218–26.

[147] Ibid. 213.

[148] Ibid. 228.

[149] Ibid. 231.

[150] Ibid. 236.

Father'.[151] Continuing through a brief survey of modern history, Maurice drew out the conclusion that social morality necessarily contained within it an appeal to universal moral values, and so to the universal society.[152]

Despite the over-schematic presentation of history in *Social Morality,* and the simplicity of Maurice's threefold classification of the elements of society, his analysis was driven by a concern to understand different aspects of morality which he took to be present simultaneously in society, and to be mutually compatible and indeed complementary: 'The Family is not lost in the Nation, nor the Nation in Human Society. They are coexistent.'[153] Within this social and historical taxonomy, there were distinct strands that sat uneasily beside each other, the history of Greece and Rome, for example, paralleling that of Israel, 'the most exclusive of nations', and the Church.[154] Indeed, Maurice's biblical commentaries can be read usefully alongside *Social Morality* for greater clarification of his interpretation of the history of Israel as the history of national identity, giving way, through idolatry and so its final abandonment of the principle of worship which had constituted it in the first place, to the Kingdom of Kingdoms.[155]

But both historical and analytical methods, however much they overlapped, converged on Maurice's understanding of the universal society, which is normative for the human condition, but also sums it up. Just as Coleridge had conceived of a 'clerisy' in *On the Constitution of the Church and State,* an educational and intellectual elite which was not theoretically identical with the clergy of the Church of England, but nevertheless contained them, so it could appear that Maurice was constructing an argument in *Social Morality* for a pattern of social relations, ascending to 'universal morality', within which the Christian Church could sit, but with which it need not be strictly identified. This was not the case. Maurice's argument left little space for any other ultimate embodiment of the universal morality than that located in the Church, or rather in the kingdom of Christ. *Social Morality* ended with a chapter on 'Human Worship', in which Maurice grounded the universal society explicitly in the Christian revelation: 'What we call the New Testament Revelation is the unveiling . . . of a perfectly Moral Being, of the Will in which all the justice, sincerity, fidelity which exist partially in any nations or men have

---

[151] Ibid. 279.   [152] Ibid. 392.

[153] Ibid. 17. *Pace* Cashdollar, Maurice's words are aimed explicitly *against* Comte's theological, metaphysical and Positivist 'ages'.

[154] Ibid. 228.

[155] The two most important texts for this purpose are *The Patriarchs and Lawgivers of the Old Testament* (1851), and *The Prophets and Kings of the Old Testament* (1853), but also useful is *The Doctrine of Sacrifice Deduced from the Scriptures* (1854; 2nd edn., London: Macmillan, 1879).

their fulfilment and their root.'[156] The summit of Maurice's analysis of social morality was the Christian Church, which, by inference, could be appreciated in its fullness in human history only by an understanding of its character and identity as 'social'. It was a witness for, and agent of, a kingdom for all: 'It must be for all kindreds and races; therefore with the sectarianism which rends Humanity asunder, with the Imperialism which would substitute for Universal fellowship a Universal death, must it wage implacable war.'[157]

MAURICE AND THE CHRISTIAN SOCIALIST TRADITION

Assessing the significance of Maurice's social theology in the context of his life and work as a whole remains peculiarly difficult. His Christian Socialism was paradoxically both consistent with his wider theological and ecclesiological interests, yet also the product of a relatively short period of mid-life activism. By 1854, when Maurice and others founded the Working Men's College, the social fear engendered by revolution on the continent of Europe and by Chartism at home had largely disappeared. Maurice's interest in Christian Socialism appeared to some to have evaporated with it. The onset of mid-Victorian prosperity, symbolized by the Great Exhibition of 1851, for a time eased the most acute pressures of poverty, unemployment, and ill health for the poor. Though concern remained high about the living conditions of the working classes in the great cities and industrial centres, the sense of impending crisis was not to appear again with such force until the 1880s. By then Maurice was dead, and a new generation of Christian Socialists had come into being, looking to him as inspiration for their attempts to grapple with the challenge which Socialism and the labour movement represented to the Christian Church.

Maurice's reputation as the founder of Christian Socialism came to be sealed by the subtle radicalizing of his message by later generations of admirers. The most attractive of these to historians has been Stewart Headlam. Controversial for his befriending of actors and actresses and his defence of the theatre, for standing bail for Oscar Wilde, and for his readiness to share a public platform with secularists and freethinkers, Headlam was nevertheless a theologically orthodox Anglo-Catholic priest who attempted to synthesize Maurice's theology into something more obviously in tune with democratic Socialism. He contributed a pamphlet on *Christian Socialism* to the Fabian Society.[158] Yet by far the

---

[156] Maurice, *Social Morality*, 403.   [157] Ibid. 414.   [158] Bettany, *Headlam*, 136.

most influential advocates of Maurice's social theology were the more moderate members of the Christian Social Union (CSU), founded in 1889. The CSU included a formidable concentration of Anglican bishops and theologians in the late nineteenth century. Amongst them were Brooke Foss Westcott, Henry Scott Holland, Charles Gore, and Edward Talbot. To all these men, and to others such as the philanthropist Octavia Hill, Maurice was a figure-head, a pioneer of a practical social theology that reconciled moderate Socialism with orthodox Christian belief. Through their commitment to particular social causes, and their occupation of positions of national influence, they effectively promoted the notion of Maurice as a prophet, an unjustly neglected figure in his own day who could help the Church of England to steer its way through the uncertain waters of social conflict that lay ahead. Edward Hicks, bishop of Lincoln, a leading member of the CSU, is a good example of a 'bridge' figure, progressive or 'New' Liberal in politics, who looked to Maurice as a symbol of the social commitment of the Church of England.[159] Probably Hicks, like so many members of the CSU, had actually read little of Maurice, if any at all; Ruskin was a more certain influence.[160]

Reception of this filtered and intensified picture of Maurice's social radicalism was assisted by the assimilation of his theology more broadly to currents within Anglican belief in the late nineteenth century. Central to this process was his recruitment to the pantheon of Liberal Anglo-Catholicism. Here, Maurice's sacramentalism, his emphasis on church order, his criticism of popular evangelical theology, and his acceptance of biblical criticism within a commitment to credal orthodoxy, were all attractive to a generation of Anglo-Catholic theologians seeking to break free of what some of them had come to regard as the unduly rigid theology of Pusey and his circle. Above all, Maurice's incarnationalism was both contributory cause and useful resource for the increasing emphasis on the Incarnation as the central Christian doctrine that was to be encountered in the most creative Anglican theologians of the late nineteenth and early twentieth centuries.[161] Yet, such a view registered a perceptible shift in the interpretation of Maurice's theological commitments. It did not represent a distortion or misreading of his theology, as we shall see in the next chapter. Rather, as the social context of Anglican conviction changed in the half-century after his death, so elements of his ecclesiology fell into the background. His Christian Socialism was

[159] G. Neville, *Radical Churchman: Edward Lee Hicks and the New Liberalism* (Oxford: Clarendon Press, 1998).

[160] Ibid. 51.

[161] On this, see A. M. Ramsey, *From Gore to Temple. The Development of Anglican Theology between* Lux Mundi *and the Second World War 1889–1939* (London: Longman, 1960).

accented, just as the force of arguments for the comprehensive and national character of the Church of England began to recede. The growth of the worldwide Anglican communion persuaded Anglicans that 'comprehensiveness' was a better description of Anglican polity than it was of the Established Church of England as such. As the political climate changed, too, it became more convenient to forget Maurice's suspicion of pressure groups, party opinion, and democracy, and to assume his advocacy of something like the collectivist and welfarist policies of the emergent labour movement.

None of this was altogether untrue to the spirit of much of Maurice's social theology. But it was a step beyond it. By the mid-twentieth century, it was common to assume, without qualification, that Maurice was the fountainhead of a tradition of Anglican social reflection that had come to exercise enormous influence on the development of British social policy in the early twentieth century. Through people like William Beveridge, R. H. Tawney, and William Temple, Maurice became symbolically a hero of English Socialism. Yet this reputation had a certain fragility. It never captured precisely enough the curious fusion of conservatism, Anglican tradition, and social imagination that marked Maurice's response to the condition of the working class. Here, as elsewhere in Maurice's work, it is unhelpful to iron out the inconsistencies, and to ignore the schematic rigidity of elements of his argument, in order to present an attractive synthesis. By the ideological standards of the twentieth century, Maurice was a curious Socialist indeed.

6

The Crisis of Belief

[Revelation] must be restored to the meaning which it has in the first chapter of the Epistle to the Romans, and everywhere else in St. Paul's writings; must therefore no longer stand in contrast to the supposed proofs derived from Nature. Revelation must be the discovery of God to a creature formed to know Him and be like Him, a revelation therefore to the reason and conscience of men, a revelation of the Will that is every moment acting on his will.

F. D. Maurice to D. J. Vaughan, 22 November 1865 (Maurice, *Life*, ii. 511)

If Maurice's rising reputation as an Anglican apologist was temporarily damaged by his association with Christian Socialism, it was scarred for the rest of his life by his dismissal from King's College, London, in 1853. Almost certainly the one controversy led to the other. The uproar over Christian Socialism, together with his Principal's suspicion, put Maurice's theology under close scrutiny. When, in mid-1853, he published a series of sermons addressed to Unitarians, under the title *Theological Essays*, it was not surprising that his theological opponents seized on the chance to attack his views. Criticism focused on his apparent denial of eternal punishment. Suspected of being a universalist, he was forced to resign from his professorial chair by the Council of King's College. The *Theological Essays* were essentially an exercise in systematic theology. They represented Maurice's attempt to answer the 'struggle of doubt' he had encountered in some working men.[1] They said little that he had not already said in print long before, but drew attention to difficult or apparently heterodox elements of his views. Marginalized by his association with Christian Socialism, Maurice was now labelled a heresiarch. Suspicion of him was to persist until his death.[2]

He remained chaplain at Lincoln's Inn, and became unpaid principal of the new Working Men's College. He continued to lecture, preach, and

---

[1] Maurice, *Life*, ii. 163.
[2] See, e.g., Liddon's association of Maurice with Benjamin Jowett in the wake of *Essays and Reviews*: Johnston, *Henry Parry Liddon*, 72–5.

publish extensively, particularly in biblical studies.[3] But the taint of the *Theological Essays* was strong in these years, especially because of the concern of orthodox churchmen and women at the growing influence of new approaches to biblical criticism. Then, in 1858, he saw his chance to vindicate himself, when the Oxford theologian, Henry Mansel delivered his Bampton Lectures on the *Limits of Religious Thought Examined* (1858). Mansel's Kantianism, given its fusion of credal orthodoxy with a denial of the human capacity to know God in any meaningful sense, alarmed Maurice, for whom the notion of communion with God was vital, informed by his reading of the Gospel of John. His criticism of Mansel, published as *What is Revelation?* (1859), brought him once more before the public mind. But its literary weaknesses damaged Maurice's cause. More-over, the intensification of public debate on the Bible in these years, prompted in part by Darwin's work, and by *Essays and Reviews* (1860), worked against him. In 1860, however, he was persuaded to become priest-in-charge of the proprietary chapel of St Peter's, Vere Street, a Crown appointment that itself provoked some minor controversy.[4]

Then, in 1866, the Knightbridge Chair of Casuistry, Moral Theology, and Moral Philosophy at Cambridge became vacant. Charles Kingsley, by then Regius Professor of Modern History, put forward Maurice's name as a candidate, and he was elected.[5] This marked the beginning of a late rehabilitation, as the climate of Anglican theology began to shift once more in his favour. The decline of the controversy over *Essays and Reviews*, the strong support Maurice received from a new generation of rising Cambridge theologians such as Fenton Hort, J. B. Lightfoot, and B. F. Westcott, and new currents of sympathy for social Christianity set the conditions for the growth of his reputation posthumously.

The main focus of this book has been on Maurice's ecclesiology. Two constitutive elements of the general theological framework that underlie his ecclesiology were highlighted earlier: namely, his sacramental and existential understanding of language, and his conviction of the mediation of God's providential ordering of the world through history. These were intrinsically related. Language was a carrier of transcendent meaning through time, referring beyond itself to a fullness it could never com-pletely capture. It was both symbolic and thoroughly historical. Maurice's

---

[3] The most noteworthy publications are: *The Patriarchs and Lawgivers of the Old Testament* (1851); *The Prophets and Kings of the Old Testament* (1853); *The Unity of the New Testament* (London: Parker, 1854); *The Doctrine of Sacrifice Deduced from the Scriptures* (1854); *The Gospel of St John* (London: Macmillan, 1856; new edn., 1878); *Sermons Preached in Lincoln's Inn Chapel*, (1856–9); *The Gospel of the Kingdom of Heaven* (1864).

[4] Maurice, *Life*, ii. 361–73.

[5] Ibid. 542–8.

conception of the Catholicity of the Church was, accordingly, to be traced through its diverse and complex modes of expression in history. But there was a third element, which in every sense—ontologically, epistemologically, chronologically, morally, and even spiritually—precedes history and language. That is the 'content' of Revelation, which includes both the concept of Revelation itself and the doctrine of the God who is the revealer. Maurice's historical ecclesiology implied, and arguably required, a specific understanding of Revelation.

In order to emphasize the changing historical context out of which Maurice's most significant work emerged, I have followed a broadly chronological scheme in this book. But there is a risk of tidying up his intellectual development. The fact that much of his published work consisted of sermons delivered at various times throughout his ministerial career guaranteed that his consideration of particular theological *topoi* did not fall into a simple chronological order. Moreover, his theological development was fundamentally complete by the mid-1830s. Thereafter, though there were some shifts in view, the basic consistency of his beliefs over time meant that his reflections on ecclesiology and on doctrine were interwoven throughout his life. Nevertheless, a general sequence of attention can be discerned, driven by particular controversies. His ordination and the rise of Tractarianism placed ecclesiological themes to the fore of his work in the 1830s and early 1840s. The social crisis of the late 1840s drew him into explicit engagement with the social implications of his theology. But in the 1850s and 1860s, his work was to be dominated by controversy over new methods of critically interpreting Christian belief, and by his own ambivalent relationship to them.

Thus Maurice came to be associated in the public mind with the mid-century 'crisis of belief'. But he always maintained that what he wrote in the last two decades of his life was consistent with his views in the 1830s and 1840s, and was not part of an assault on Christian orthodoxy. He claimed only to be restating the full implications of orthodox Christian belief, against some of its popular distortions. Five basic issues form principal sections of this chapter: the doctrine of the God who reveals himself as Trinity, the historical and theological significance of Jesus Christ, the role of Scripture as witness to the economy centred on Jesus Christ, Revelation in history, and the theological constitution of human being. A preliminary section identifies the basic character of Maurice's understanding of the theology of Revelation, after a brief discussion of the course of the mid-century controversies over criticism and belief. Inevitably some nuances in Maurice's distinctive and original approach to all of these issues have been suppressed in the interest of brevity. There is a single thread running through all the sections, however: namely, Maurice's conception of the human destiny of union with its creator. By this means, by taking the reader at this stage through a general statement of his theological position, more light will be thrown on Maurice's preoccupation with the theme of Catholicity, the universal constitution of the Church in time.

CURRENTS OF CRITICISM

The enormous vitality and ambition of the Victorian churches coexisted with acute anxiety about the health and future survival of Christianity.[6] Partly, this was a product of conviction: the sheer intensity of Victorian evangelism, and its organization by systematic means, sharpened awareness of those areas of society in which the mainstream churches felt their efforts were faltering.[7] It was also prompted by the realization that, however dominant Christianity might seem to be, it faced serious challenges. In the course of this book, various strands of this have been explored. After the French Revolution, a militant form of atheism was sometimes combined with political radicalism to produce a powerful critique of religious establishments and of Christian orthodoxy. The political impact of this radical tradition in England was muted after the reform crisis of 1828–32, but it remained potent. Social tensions in the 1830s and 1840s raised further difficulties for the churches, and were particularly pressing for the Church of England because of its close relationship with the ruling classes. But radical criticism of the churches was not confined to questions of wealth and social status. Increasingly, it fed on new currents of historical and literary criticism, raising acute questions about religious truth. Thus, the mid-century 'crisis of faith', as it is sometimes called, cannot be separated from broader elements of social and political criticism. Together, they amounted to a powerful, if incremental, challenge to the traditional authority of the Christian Church.

The rise of militant secularism illustrated this interweaving of political radicalism and religious scepticism. Early nineteenth-century critics of Christianity, such as Richard Carlile, were naturally sympathetic to radical criticism of the political and religious establishment.[8] In Chartist and

---

[6] This paradox is briefly explored in J. N. Morris, 'The Strange Death of Christian Britain: Another Look at the Secularization Debate', *The Historical Journal*, 46 (2003).

[7] There is a very large literature on Victorian evangelism. For a recent survey, see C. G. Brown, *Death of Christian Britain*, ch. 3, 'The Salvation Economy', pp. 35–57.

[8] See J. H. Wiener, *Radicalism and Freethought in Nineteenth-Century Britain: The Life of Richard Carlile* (Westport, Conn.: Greenwood Press, 1983).

Owenite circles, free-thinking was common. Many of the Chartists whom Maurice, Kingsley, and others met through Christian Socialism were free-thinkers. In the 1850s, the mantle was taken up by George Jacob Holyoake, though with little evident success. Finally, in the mid-1860s, under the more charismatic leadership of Charles Bradlaugh, the National Secular Society began to assume a higher profile.[9] Maurice was certainly aware of the arguments used by Holyoake, Bradlaugh, and others. After his dismissal from King's College, Holyoake's newspaper, the *Reasoner*, used Maurice's case as a way of seeking to discredit Christianity.[10] Yet the influence of secularism and free-thought was limited at best. Its heyday, so its historian has claimed, occurred after Maurice's death, but lasted only ten years or so, in the late 1870s and early 1880s.[11] Thereafter, it declined rapidly.

Organized secularism thus never became a serious challenge to the popularity and strength of the mid-Victorian churches. Although an important symptom of underlying anxieties about the truth of Christianity, it was hardly in a position to shake the religious mind-set of the age. But the threat it represented was magnified by the intellectual currents of criticism on which it thrived. Ironically, many of those who propounded critical or heterodox views in mid-century were religiously committed people, who at best intended only a revision of traditional doctrine, in order to assist its accommodation to the modern world. Many of them were socially conservative, too. Yet their readiness to question received views of truth placed them within the stream of scepticism also shared by political radicals and secularists. The 'crisis of belief' was complex and multi-faceted.

Public debate was influenced above all by the perception that the new currents of biblical and historical criticism were rooted in the sceptical literary culture of Germany. This was ironic, given that in the eighteenth century it was Britain, under its umbrella of limited toleration, which had exported Deism to the continent of Europe.[12] But the collapse of Deism in Britain, and the buoyancy of orthodox Anglican Trinitarianism, had pushed the memory of that episode well into the background by the early nineteenth century.[13] Now, under the impact of Enlightenment philosophy and history, pioneering approaches to the interpretation of

[9] For a summary of the history of free-thinking in the mid-nineteenth century, see E. Royle, *Victorian Infidels: The Origins of the British Secularist Movement, 1791–1866* (Manchester: Manchester University Press, 1974); see also *idem*, *Radicals, Secularists and Republicans: Popular Freethought in Britain, 1866–1915* (Manchester: Manchester University Press, 1980), 1–9.

[10] Maurice, *Life*, ii. 211.

[11] Royle, *Radicals, Secularists and Republicans*, 328.

[12] On this, see H. Reventlow, *The Authority of the Bible and the Rise of the Modern World* (London: SCM, 1984).

[13] On the strength of Anglican theology in the eighteenth century, see Nockles, *Oxford Movement, passim.*

the Bible were being undertaken in Germany rather than England. According to conventional accounts, English theological culture was aloof from all this, insulated by its lack of linguistic expertise.[14] But this is to claim too much. Through the medium of a select but influential group of scholars, key elements of the new methods and conclusions of interpretation were introduced into England. Coleridge studied at Gottingen in 1799, immersing himself in German literature, theology, and philosophy.[15] The fruits of his study were diffused through his criticism and philosophy, and found explicit articulation only in the *Confessions of an Enquiring Spirit* (1840), published posthumously. Julius Hare lived in Germany in his childhood, and later amassed a formidable private library of German literature and theology.[16] Other students of German thought included the Anglican Herbert Marsh (1757–1839), who translated Michaelis's *Introduction to the New Testament* (1801), the Dissenter John Pye Smith (1774–1851), and Thomas Hartwell Horne (1780–1862).[17] A little later still, Anglicans who took an interest (not always friendly) in German theology included Edward Bouverie Pusey, Hugh James Rose, Connop Thirlwall, and Thomas Arnold.[18]

It is no accident that several of these men had a strong influence on Maurice. They were hardly without influence or social standing. Even so, reaction to German scholarship was not generally favourable. It was not that orthodox Christian theologians in Britain were absolutely resistant to critical examination of the Scriptures. But the German tradition included what came to be seen as extreme developments of critical methodology that could not be accepted without radical modification of the terms of orthodox belief. Hare and Thirlwall's translation of Schleiermacher's *Critical Essay on the Gospel of Luke* (1821), for example, appeared to imply that the Gospel narratives had to be read as imaginative expansions of 'memorabilia', rather than as inspired paraphrases of an original Gospel.[19] But the controversy that followed was as nothing to the horror with which David Friedrich Strauss's *Life of Jesus* was greeted when it was translated by George Eliot in 1846. Strauss's use of the category of 'myth' to reinterpret the Gospels seemed entirely to dissolve the Christian revelation. Indeed, in

---

[14] '[A]t the turn of the eighteenth century, hardly anyone in England was aware of the great things that had been happening in the intellectual world of Germany': S. Neill, *The Interpretation of the New Testament 1861–1961* (London: Oxford University Press, 1964), 1.

[15] R. Holmes, *Coleridge: Early Visions* (London: Hodder & Stoughton, 1989), 218–21.

[16] Distad, *Guessing at Truth*, 15.

[17] On Marsh, see briefly Neill, *Interpretation of the New Testament*, 4–5; on Pye Smith, Corsi, *Science and Religion*, 12. Both of these men, and Horne, await a modern critical discussion.

[18] There are brief references to all of these figures in Neill, *Interpretation of the New Testament*, 7–12.

[19] Ibid. 9.

Karl Barth's momentous words, 'Strauss offered to his time the sight of the theologian who has become an unbeliever, for all to behold and without denying it.'[20]

By comparison, developments in English theology look anodyne. Maurice was by no means blind to the merits of Strauss's work. It had, he suggested, subverted the naturalistic interpretations offered by eighteenth-century critics of the Bible, and in so doing, had shown that there 'is always a dream of something transcendent'.[21] But he never paid much serious attention to the new critical methodologies. Even so, the shadow of more radical critical conclusions hung over him, and over Liberal Anglican theology, in the middle years of the century. Three blows to orthodox belief symbolized the difficulty. Darwin's *Origin of Species*, published in 1859, unavoidably raised questions for many Christians about the veracity of Genesis. The ensuing controversy was less intense than popular caricature assumes.[22] But hard on its heels came *Essays and Reviews*, essays published by a group of Broad Churchmen who sought to 'illustrate the advantage derivable to the cause of religious and moral truth' from a 'free handling' of subjects likely to suffer from 'traditional methods of treatment'.[23] The convoluted nature of that description gives some clue to the restrained, punch-pulling character of the work. All the same, it prompted a heresy trial, raised by the question of whether or not it was at all permissible for views such as those propounded in the essays by Henry Wilson and Rowland Williams to be held by clergymen of the established Church. Then, in 1862, appeared the first volume of Bishop J. W. Colenso's study of the Pentateuch, a work that has not stood the test of time well at all— 'It was the ancient school of biblical calculation topsy-turvy, used to confute and not to prove', claimed Owen Chadwick[24]—but which advanced the conclusion that the so-called Mosaic books were composed of different sources, and not entirely historical. Modern biblical scholars have little difficulty reconciling conclusions such as this with orthodox doctrinal belief, but in the mid-nineteenth century they looked little short of catastrophic for Christianity.

Overall, the crisis of faith had a double aspect. In literary terms, something evidently changed round about the middle of the nineteenth

[20] K. Barth, *Protestant Theology in the Nineteenth Century* (1972; new edn., London: SCM, 2001), 533.

[21] Maurice, *Life*, ii. 454.

[22] The standard modern account is J. R. Moore, *The Post-Darwinian Controversies: A Study of the Protestant Struggle to Come to Terms with Darwin in Great Britain and America, 1870–1900* (Cambridge: Cambridge University Press, 1979).

[23] Prefatory comments to the Ist edn., cited in Shea and Whitla (eds.), *Essays and Reviews*, 137.

[24] Chadwick, *Victorian Church*, ii. 91.

century. It became more than fashionable, conventional even, in some circles, to cast doubt on central claims of the Christian revelation. Whilst upholding broadly religious and moral positions in various ways, a cohort of Victorian men and women of letters gradually abandoned elements of traditional Christian belief. George Eliot herself is a good example. Others include Ruskin, Swinburne, Wilde, Samuel Butler, perhaps even Dickens and Tennyson. Leslie Stephen exemplified this change, and through him scepticism could be said to have become the literary orthodoxy of Blooms-bury. But theologically, the crisis proved much less damaging to orthodox Christianity than at first seemed likely. If particular forms of the doctrine of verbal inspiration had to be abandoned, that by no means required the rejection of credal orthodoxy. Responses to the new approaches varied from the robust rebuttals of Pusey and his circle to the conviction of the Cambridge circle of Hort, Lightfoot, and Westcott that a measured hand-ling of critical methodology actually supported orthodox belief, rather than undermined it.

Maurice's role in all this was paradoxical. He was seen by critics as an ally of unbelief, protesting his orthodoxy while cutting away central planks of traditional Christianity. But his effect, as well as his intention, was far from this. Like Coleridge before him, and the central tradition of Anglican theology afterwards, he sought to defend orthodox belief by demonstrat-ing the depth of its theological and devotional roots. His response to the mid-Victorian crisis of faith, then, amounted to a reinvestigation of the nature of orthodox belief. His work in the 1850s and 1860s sought to draw out the theological presuppositions of the position he had come to occupy earlier in life. He was convinced that Christianity need not fear the consequences of historical criticism. It did not need radical reinterpret-ation. But it did need careful, considered elaboration and defence. Central to this reinvestigation was the doctrine of Revelation.

WHAT IS REVELATION?

In systematic terms, Maurice's reflections on Revelation can be situated in relation to his understanding of time and eternity. On this he pursued a path well-trodden by Western theologians since Augustine. He conceived of the relation of Creator to creation as that of Absolute, timeless Being to time-bound beings; the philosophical difficulties that this undoubtedly raised were transcended by their inclusion in the mystery in which faith necessarily involved the believer. The understanding of history that this implied, with its idea of God as continually working through the history of the world, in practice did not relegate divine action to a single, creative event at the beginning of time—in effect, the Deist solution of the previous century to the philosophical difficulties of the orthodox Christian account of creation. Nor did it bracket historical events as inferior, incomplete, and insubstantial 'reflections' of the divine life. History possessed a provisional, rather than absolute, autonomy: human beings made their history themselves, but their history was also a history of God's relations with his creation. Maurice made no attempt to defend his providential reading of history philosophically. Instead, he returned again and again to the implications of the doctrine of Revelation. His understanding of history as the field of God's providence was closely connected with his understanding of Revelation as revelation *in* history. Three essential points need to be made, before a general exposition of Maurice's idea of Revelation can be undertaken.

First, Maurice's appeal to Revelation sometimes took the form of a moral argument, urging readers to take faith more seriously.[25] Underlying this was a fundamental principle of epistemology which transformed entirely the basis of his assumption about the compatibility of time and eternity. Christian theology for Maurice was always undertaken from within the community of faith, as a devotional exercise that sought, not the independent establishment of evidence, but the exploration of the consequences of believing. This was never adequately appreciated by his critics. Throughout his controversy with Henry Mansel, Maurice's assumption was that faith yielded actual knowledge of God, not as a truth of natural religion, but as a consequence of faith in the Gospel.[26] And this is a view reflected in his self-understanding as a theologian: his often-quoted claim to be a 'digger' after truth presupposed that he was already, as a theologian, in an existential relation to the object of faith: he 'dug down' into the truth in which he stood already.[27]

Second, Maurice always denied the absolute distinction between natural and revealed religion.[28] He believed that Christians could not set to one side their credal affirmations and suppose that nature could yield independently valid truths about God. But he also believed that those very credal affirmations implied that God was at work in nature, and that his

---

[25] 'Every base motive to which we address ourselves . . . puts us so much further out of communion with Him Who is the truth; makes it so much the more impossible for us, by the manifestation of the truth, to commend ourselves to every man's conscience in the sight of God': Maurice, *Sermons Preached in Lincoln's Inn Chapel*, i. 133.

[26] F. D. Maurice, *Sequel to the Inquiry, What is Revelation?* (Cambridge: Macmillan, 1860), 48.

[27] Maurice, *Life*, ii. 136.

[28] See, e.g., F. D. Maurice, 'Dr. Newman's Grammar of Assent', *Contemporary Review*, 14 (1870), 165; see also F. D. Maurice, *Moral and Metaphysical Philosophy*, i. p. xx.

wisdom and creative power were to be seen, through the eye of faith, at work in the world at large. By rejecting the separation of natural and revealed religion, he made possible a dynamic understanding of human capabilities. The nature of human beings as created beings who were naturally formed to seek God was a universal truth, presupposing the possibility of natural insight into God and his ways with the world. But the fulfilment or completion of this insight was not possible outside explicit acknowledgement of the Christian faith.[29] Thus, natural and revealed religion were related aspects of the one, overarching divine narrative.

Third, Maurice worked with a practical distinction between general and special Revelation, without ever naming it as such. His conception of Revelation as a dynamic, communicative process, expressed through his use of a dynamic vocabulary of 'discovery' and 'education', implied holding in balance both close attention to the specific events, texts, and person (Christ) of the economy of salvation, and recognition that the 'discovery' or 'unveiling' of God implies a universal, created capacity to respond to him in faith. There were, consequently, two interwoven strands of narrative in Revelation. One was the redemption for human beings wrought by God in Christ, and witnessed by Holy Scripture: there was an inherent specificity, absoluteness, and historicity in this that Maurice never denied. The other was creation's experience of God, and its growth in spiritual understanding. Though again this experience and growth was subject to history, occurring *in* history, it was also a universal process, more or less reflected in the lives of particular Christians. That these are balanced is important: undue stress on either of them can turn Maurice into a predecessor of Karl Barth's theology of Revelation or into a Platonist.[30]

Exposition of Maurice's views on Revelation must necessarily be concerned with his controversy with Henry Mansel over the latter's Bampton Lectures, *The Limits of Religious Thought Examined* (1858).[31] Maurice was horrified at Mansel's argument, which seemed to imply that it was impossible for human beings to be in communion with God. Mansel took his lead from Sir William Hamilton's dictum that 'the Unconditioned

---

[29] This coinherence of natural and revealed religion, with its presumption of a universal, creative power at work in all human society, which yet cannot be fulfilled in the wills of human beings without explicit Christian faith, was at the heart of Maurice's Boyle Lectures, *The Religions of the World* (1847).

[30] For parallels between Maurice and Barth, see Flesseman-Van Leer, *Grace Abounding*.

[31] There are two modern accounts of Mansel's philosophy of religion, neither of which strays very far from basic critical exposition of the 1858 Bampton Lectures: W. R. Matthews, *The Religious Philosophy of Dean Mansel* (Oxford: Oxford University Press, 1956); K. D. Freeman, *The Role of Reason in Religion: A Study of Henry Mansel* (The Hague: Martinus Nijhoff, 1969); see also D. Cupitt, 'Mansel's Theory of Regulative Truth', *Journal of Theological Studies*, NS, 18 (1967), and *idem*, 'Mansel and Maurice on our Knowledge of God', *Theology*, 73 (1970).

is incognisable and inconceivable; its notion being only negative of the Conditioned, which last can alone be positively known or conceived'.[32] Using this principle, expounded in part through the application of Kant's critique of metaphysics, he denied both the possibility of natural knowledge of God, and the notion that religious ideas, as held by human beings, could reflect religious truth representatively. Mansel's aim was to disable the critical use of human reason as an instrument of religious truth, in order to reaffirm the absolute authenticity of Revelation: '[T]he coexistence of the Infinite and the Finite, in any manner whatever, is inconceivable by reason; and the only ground that can be taken for accepting one representation of it, rather than another, is that one is revealed, and another is not revealed.'[33] Revelation was apprehended regulatively rather than representatively. Human beings could not know God in himself, but they could be guided in their apprehension of him and of his will for humankind by what they knew of him through his own revelation of himself in Christ and by the testimony of Scripture.

Mansel's lectures caused a sensation in Oxford, and were hailed as a decisive defence of orthodox Christianity against its contemporary philosophical assailants.[34] But others thought Mansel's critical philosophy told against itself: it was a form of agnosticism, leaving no defence in place against the simple denial of a commitment in faith.[35] Maurice's objection centred on the moral and religious implications of Mansel's understanding of the human mind as limited to its finite capacities, which seemed to undermine the doctrine of *imago Dei*. It implied that no religious experience was intelligible on its own terms.[36] To pursue Mansel's line of inquiry would be to require the revision of the creeds, the Prayer Book, and the Bible, because these contained an invitation to human beings 'to enter into an actual communion with God'.[37] Thus the essential ground of Maurice's opposition to Mansel was his understanding of Revelation as the communication and reception of an existential orientation of human beings to

---

[32] H. L. Mansel, *The Limits of Religious Thought Examined* (Oxford: Murray, 1858), p. ix.

[33] Ibid. 183.

[34] '[T]he audience could be felt breathless with excitement. The undergraduates . . . watched fascinated, as though before their eyes the greenhouse of liberal divinity was battered and crumbled into dust by the hammer-blows of reason': Chadwick, *Victorian Church*, i. 556.

[35] e.g. J. B. Mozley to R. W. Church: 'It appears to me [that Mansel's lectures are] one of those cases in which a man has been too confident of the strength of some grand general dictum, and has rested everything upon it, expressed in the boldest and most unqualified way': J. B. Mozley, *Letters* (London: Rivington, 1885), 240.

[36] See the first 'Letter to a Theological Student Preparing for Orders', subtitled 'The Cost of a Confutation', in Maurice, *What is Revelation?*, 131–40.

[37] Ibid. 140.

God. Creatureliness, despite the Fall, entailed the possibility and longing of human beings for union with God.

Maurice replied to Mansel in two works, *What is Revelation?* (1859) and *Sequel to the Inquiry, What is Revelation?* (1860). Neither has ever been regarded highly, even by Maurice's sympathizers. They are loosely constructed, padded with long quotations from Mansel, and lacking in systematic construction. Yet *What is Revelation?* contains two parts: only the second addresses Mansel's lectures directly. The first contains a series of sermons for Epiphany that are beautifully compact and clear statements of Maurice's overall position. Close examination of just one of these, on 'Christ's Parables', shows in outline most of the main features of Maurice's view.

Maurice's text was Matthew 13: 14–17, Jesus's explanation for his use of parables. He began by discounting common interpretations of this passage, including (probably as a side-swipe at Mansel) the idea that Jesus used parables because the limitations of the human intellect made it impossible for human beings to know anything of eternal things.[38] Jesus's words make it plain that it is given to 'ignorant fishermen' to have knowledge of the mysteries of the kingdom of heaven; the disciples had 'a capacity for *knowing* these mysteries, these eternal things which cannot be conceived'.[39] Thus, a starting-point for Maurice's view of Revelation is theological anthropology: human beings are made for God, and this implies the possession of a capacity, a spiritual eye or ear, for knowing God, a capacity that belongs to their very being.[40] The possession of this inherent spiritual capacity or sense is a reflection of the sacramental character of all created things: 'May not all sensible things, by a necessity of their nature, be testifying to us of that which is nearest to us, of that which it most concerns us to know, of the mysteries of our own life, and of God's relation to us?'[41] Our created, given spiritual sense is clouded by our constant tendency to turn away from God towards ourselves: it is only Christ who can remove this veil and uncover the 'common facts' of life, so that we can see that divine things are *done* in parables as well as spoken through them.[42] It is significant that the veil of which Maurice speaks in this passage is *not* material things in themselves (that is, material things are not a veil to greater spiritual realities), but the blindness of human rebellion against God—one more sign, if it were needed, that his understanding of reality is not really subsumable under the label 'Platonic'. Briefly here, Maurice touches on history, as he claims that Christ's coming,

---

[38] Maurice, *What is Revelation?*, 90.   [39] Ibid. 91; Maurice's italics.   [40] Ibid. 93.
[41] Ibid. 94.   [42] Ibid. 96.

and his use of parables, occur in a context of practical Jewish idolatry, the materializing of Jewish religion into an idolatry of law and calculation.[43]

Maurice's outline of the situation into which Revelation speaks gives way now to a sketch of what Revelation itself contains. In Matthew 13: 16, Jesus describes the disciples as 'blessed', Maurice argues, not because they have seen him as a man in the same way that they would see, for example, Caiaphas or Pontius Pilate, but because their seeing has been a spiritual as well as a material sensing of him. They have seen him as the Lord and Master of the spirit within them, 'delivering them from their own miserable conceptions, raising them above any judgments of God deduced from the objects of sense, *educating* them to know Him as He is'.[44] From this 'seeing' of Jesus comes a sense of the union between God and humankind; they have apprehended Jesus Christ as Son of Man and Son of God. The incarnation of Christ is the focal point of Revelation, and the focal point of God's ordering of the universe: 'that fact of God's union with our race in the Person of a Mediator [is] the interpretation of all other facts,—[is] the kernel mystery of the Universe'.[45] Then, in an illuminating sentence, Maurice disposes of the natural theology of the eighteenth century at the same time as affirming 'natural' theology as a deduction from faith: 'we cannot suppose that we rise to conceptions of God through the things of time and sense, [yet] we cannot help supposing that through these things He is speaking to us'.[46] Through Christ as the deliverer of human beings, and light of all, we can ascend to communion with God. The apostles proclaimed the truth of this deliverer: 'But this testimony, so far as it was received, converted all Nature, and all human acts, from dead letters into divine hieroglyphics . . . into preachers concerning the Unseen and the Eternal.'[47]

The remarkably condensed presentation of many of Maurice's leading theological themes in this sermon suggests four possible levels or dimensions of his understanding of Revelation, with his doctrine of God constituting a fifth and preliminary one. At the centre is the Incarnation, the revelation of the union of God with human being in Jesus Christ. Christ is the focal point of history and the experience of faith. In Christ the divine economy of salvation was effected. But Revelation for Maurice also embraces the medium through which revelation in Christ was attested— namely, Scripture—since the apostles' testimony was the mode of Christian proclamation. Revelation in Christ is the means by which human beings can be interpreted as creatures capable of receiving Christ and responding to him. So a third level is theological anthropology. The

---

[43] Ibid. 97–9.   [44] Ibid. 100; my italics.   [45] Ibid. 102.
[46] Ibid. 102.   [47] Ibid.

flexibility of Maurice's vocabulary of Revelation as 'discovery' serves to mediate this reflexive conception of Revelation: God 'discovers' himself to human beings who, in their own lives and experience, 'discover' him. Yet a fourth level opens up, since human beings are historical creatures, and what is revealed to them is a creative God working in and through his creation in time. Thus there is a continual 'discovery' of God to human beings in the fabric of their social lives. All of these levels or dimensions are of ultimate significance for Maurice's doctrine of the Church.

THE DOCTRINE OF GOD

Explication of the central 'motor' of Maurice's idea of Revelation, his doctrine of God, can best be undertaken through an examination of his *Theological Essays* (1853). In this highly controversial work he aimed to reconcile Unitarians to Trinitarian orthodoxy. Historians, if they have attended to the book at all, have tended to concentrate on Maurice's discussion of the doctrines of atonement and eternal punishment, to the neglect of its central concern with the Trinity.[48] This may be partly because Maurice's explicit attention to the Trinity (rather than Christology) was rare in the mid-nineteenth century.[49] Anglican discussion of Trinitarian theology in this period mostly concentrated on the doctrine of the Incarnation, motivated above all by a desire to defend or adapt traditional Christology in the light of biblical criticism.[50] Little attention was directed explicitly to the inner-Trinitarian relations until the turn of the century, when J. R. Illingworth and R. C. Moberly between them abandoned the common (but probably misplaced) derivation of psychological theories of the Trinity from Augustine, and instead explored the application of a social understanding of personality to the doctrine.[51]

---

[48] The one notable exception to this neglect is Olive Brose, who called the book 'Maurice's own "Articles of Religion", a confessional statement intended to turn the mind-set of British Christianity in a new direction': Brose, *Frederick Denison Maurice*, 213–14.

[49] Undoubtedly Maurice was writing in a period in which, in Protestant theology following Schleiermacher, the doctrine of the Trinity had been reduced to what Claude Welch called 'a doctrine of the second rank': C. Welch, *The Trinity in Contemporary Theology* (London: SCM, 1953), 3.

[50] Foremost amongst explicit treatments of the Incarnation were Robert Wilberforce's *The Doctrine of the Incarnation* (London: Murray, 1849), Henry Liddon's *The Divinity of Our Lord and Saviour Jesus Christ* (London: Rivington, 1867), Charles Gore *et al.*, *Lux Mundi* (London: Murray, 1889), and Gore's own *The Incarnation of the Son of God* (London: Murray, 1891; new edn., 1922), and *Dissertations on Subjects Connected with the Incarnation* (London: Murray, 1895).

[51] See esp. J. R. Illingworth, *The Doctrine of the Trinity* (London: Macmillan, 1907), and R. C. Moberly, *Atonement and Personality* (London: Murray, 1901). Illingworth expressly speaks of God as 'a social being, or society', and goes on to describe God as 'existing in a mode of which the family, the unit of human society, is the created and faint reflection': ibid. 143.

Often dismissed as obscure and confused, the *Essays* were a wide-ranging, cumulative argument for a faith centred on the Trinitarian God. They began and ended in a vision of charity, or love, embracing theological anthropology and eschatology. Throughout, the argument was driven by the relational nature of God as Trinity, who, as perfect love, is involved with the world he has created. As Maurice said in the penultimate chapter 'On The Trinity in Unity', 'We cannot think of a Being of perfect love as wrapt [*sic*] up in Himself.'[52] Maurice's theological anthropology assumed an original state of creatureliness as blessedness, from which all human selfishness was a self-inflicted departure. The Gospel 'discards and anathematizes' the 'horrible notion . . . that pravity [*sic*] is the law of our being, and not the perpetual tendency to struggle against the law of our being'.[53] Creation and the creator are not opposed: God indwells his creatures through his Spirit, in the incarnation of Christ, who was united in will and purpose to his Father.[54] So Maurice asserted, in language close to the Quaker sense of an 'inner light', that 'Christ is in every man— the source of all light that ever visits him'.[55] His rejection of substitutionary theories of the atonement followed from his perception of an absolute unity of will and purpose between Father and Son.[56]

The climax of the *Essays* was reached in the penultimate chapter. Here the treatment of the Trinity was prefixed by a short summary of the entire argument:

I am not speaking for the first time, of the Trinity in Unity. I have been speaking of it throughout. Each consciousness that we have discovered in man, each fact of Revelation that has answered to it, has been a step in the discovery and demonstration of this truth.[57]

Christ himself, in his unity of will with the Father, was the revelation of the ultimate Will for which both Jews and Greeks longed. As Son and Word, he expressed the mind of his Father. The Incarnation was a consequence of the Christian doctrine of God and his providential care. '[O]nly a Person can express the Will of the Absolute Being,' Maurice said, since by implication the Father himself was a 'Person'.[58] If the gap between God and his creatures was to be overcome finally, God himself must communicate his inmost life to us, through the Holy Spirit. The personalistic character of the language Maurice uses here is very striking:

To think of the Father resting in the Son, in the deepest sense knowing the Son, and of the Son knowing the Father, we must think of a uniting Spirit. And if there is

[52] F. D. Maurice, *Theological Essays* (Cambridge: Macmillan, 1853), 418.
[53] Ibid. 46.   [54] Ibid. 122–3.   [55] Ibid. 65.   [56] Ibid. 144.
[57] Ibid. 408.   [58] Ibid. 415.

such a Spirit, it must be capable of being imparted . . . We are sure that it cannot be a Spirit which exalts any one man above his fellows . . . In so far as they confess it to be the Spirit of a Father, they must confess that it is meant to make them Sons of God; in so far as they confess that it is the Spirit of Christ, they confess that it is meant to make them brothers.[59]

Economic and immanent modes of Trinitarian language are finely balanced here. The use of words such as 'relation' and 'person', and the emphasis on the filial relationship of Father and Son as type for the relation of God with humankind, occur in a context in which the shape of God's Trinitarian being emerges for Maurice primarily out of a description of the history of his interaction with his creation.

Eternal life was a corollary of the life of faith in the Trinity: '[E]ach portion of that Name into which we are baptized, answers to some apprehension and anticipation of human beings . . . the acknowledgement of that Name in its fulness [sic] and Unity, is Eternal life.'[60] 'Acknowledgement' here had an existential and devotional sense, rather than a cognitional one, as McClain pointed out was typical of Maurice's use of the term more generally.[61] Since, through the Spirit, God shared his very being of love with humankind, to know him, on Maurice's understanding, was already to participate in his divine life: 'The knowledge [of God] does not procure the life, but the knowledge constitutes the life.'[62] Thus, the theological context of Maurice's understanding of eternal life was a life of communion with God, which entailed communion with other believers, and paralleled and was grounded on the inner Trinitarian relations.

The construal of Trinitarian theology as a social doctrine of God underpinned everything Maurice held to be true of God's interaction with his creation. He conceived of God as a Unity of loving relations, a holy family, whose outpouring of love within himself is extended into his outpouring of love for his creation.[63] Creation, providence, and redemption were all to be understood as different descriptions, from different angles, of the one underlying divine initiative.

Maurice's description of the implications of a social doctrine of God for human history were pursued partly through his identification of the family as the most basic unit of human society, and a reflection of the familial character of the inner Trinitarian relations. This involved a stress on the biblical description of Father and Son. Maurice shared fully the common Patristic emphasis on the Fatherhood of God, and saw the Son's filial

---

[59] Maurice, *Theological Essays*, 419.

[60] Ibid. 409–10.   [61] McClain, *Maurice*, 80.

[62] Maurice, *Theological Essays*, 422.

[63] See his sermon on 'The Hope of the Churches', an exposition of Church unity as grounded in the Unity of the Trinity: Maurice, *Ground and Object of Hope* 54–78.

relations with the Father as analogous to human beings' relations to God.[64] Consequently, Maurice's idea of human being as social being depended entirely on his doctrine of God as a social Trinity in Unity. Rather than trace human sociality as a consequence of the contextual, historical formation and orientation of self-sufficient, natural individuals, he saw it as a deduction from Creation and Revelation. In so far as human history was the history of human interaction, it was a product of the divine making of human beings, and not a presupposition of that making. Human history itself was eloquent of the God who is its source.

THE INCARNATION OF CHRIST: THE 'KERNEL MYSTERY'

If God's divine purpose could not be perceived naturally or neutrally, how could human beings even begin to apprehend God work's in the world? Revelation, as the 'discovery' of God's own being and of his ways with the world, required a historical axis, a fulcrum on which the entire structure of faith would turn. In Maurice's theology, that function was fulfilled by the doctrine of the Incarnation, the 'kernel mystery' of the universe, in the phrase cited above.

The Incarnation was a historical fact in the simplest sense, an event *in* history occupying a definite, specifiable frame of time and space, and subject to the normal constraints of history. Christ's life presented ordinary 'human facts'.[65] Its historicity was not to be read in a narrowly reductive sense, however. To specify the Incarnation as a historical event was not to empty it of significance outside the time–space continuum. Yet, as a historical event, the Incarnation was for Maurice not a symbol alone of the union of God and man: it actually effected in history that which it symbolized. Maurice's view was, to adopt some words of J. M. Creed, 'a doctrine of a historical Incarnation', and not alone a 'doctrine of Incarnation in history'.[66] The Incarnation was a revelation of God as a person: 'This is the proclamation upon which Christendom rests. It is the proclamation, not of a doctrine, but of a Person.'[67] Christ himself, through his own loving personhood, revealed the Father as desiring a relation of love.[68] In his divinity, Christ thus revealed the truth about God. He was the source of our knowledge of God, and hence, in union with the Father, the 'keystone of Christian theology'.[69]

---

[64] See Widdicombe, *Fatherhood of God.*   [65] Maurice, *Gospel of St. John*, 25.

[66] J. M. Creed, *The Divinity of Jesus Christ* (Cambridge, 1938; new edn., London: Collins, 1964), 63.

[67] Maurice, *Acts*, 10.   [68] Maurice, *Ground and Object of Hope*, 66.

[69] Maurice, 'Dr. Lushington, Mr. Heath, and the Thirty-Nine Articles', 156.

But the incarnation of Christ also revealed the truth about human beings, since, created in the *imago Dei*, they were formed for union with God. The union of the divine and human natures in Christ was a model of the union to which all human beings were called, and for which they were made: '[I]f Christ be really the head of every man, and if He really have [*sic*] taken human flesh, there is ground for a universal fellowship among men. . . . Now the denial of a universal head is practically the denial of all communion in society.'[70] As a historical event and as the focal point of history, the Incarnation was an event of closure. It was the final, definitive action of God in the creation and redemption of the world:

[N]o man has a right to say 'My race is a sinful, fallen race,' even when he most confesses the greatness of his own sin and fall; because he is bound to contemplate his race in the Son of God, and to claim by faith in Him his share of its redemption and its glory.[71]

Yet, though complete in itself, again as a historical event the Incarnation had a history as an eschatological goal for humankind. Its revelatory significance, and its presentation of Christ as a person and so of God as Person, persist through history, as a permanent, ongoing act of revelation: 'we have to find out that God is not in a book, that He *is*, that He must reveal Himself to us, that He is revealing himself to us'.[72]

Maurice's incarnational theology was by no means unusual or eccentric for his age, at least in the main outlines presented above. His emphasis on the Incarnation accorded well with a general renewal of incarnational theology in Anglicanism from the middle of the nineteenth century, a renewal which has been variously traced to the Tractarian reaction against Evangelicalism and Free Church Calvinism, to the diverse influences of Coleridge and of critical philosophies, and to the historicism of German Idealism.[73] There were some significant parallels with the incarnational theology of the Tractarian Robert Wilberforce, since Wilberforce wrote of the Incarnation as a personal union between God and man that added a 'diviner character' to all human relations.[74] Maurice, however, would not have accepted Wilberforce's strong emphasis on the intrinsically fallen character of humanity. His position was different from that of the conservative Tractarian Henry Liddon in his famous Bampton Lectures, *The Divinity of our Lord and Saviour Jesus Christ* (1867). Liddon, like Wilberforce, claimed that there were just two sustainable positions, the 'humanitarian' (effectively a denial of the divinity) and the 'Catholic', but then claimed for

---

[70] Maurice, *Life*, ii. 258.   [71] Ibid. 408.   [72] Ibid. 455.

[73] Hilton, *Age of Atonement*; also Ramsey, *From Gore to Temple*, esp. chs. 2 and 3.

[74] R. Wilberforce, *The Doctrine of the Incarnation* (London: Murray, 1849), 10.

the Catholic view the 'full force' of the divinity, with its implication of Jesus's practical omniscience on earth.[75] Maurice, like Charles Gore and other contributors to *Lux Mundi* (1889) after him, posed a clear alternative to this sharp polarity.[76]

One of the sermons in *What is Revelation?* provides a good illustration of Maurice's view in practice. In 'Christ among the Doctors' (Luke's story of the child Christ in the Temple), he strikingly anticipated Gore's kenotic Christology, and even in some sense went beyond it. He began by noting the significance of the Church's inclusion of Christ's childhood visit to the Temple in the season of Epiphany: *every* act of Jesus is a disclosure of the glory of the Son of the Father.[77] His listening to the teachers talking and reading in the Temple would, on the presumption of his perfect manhood, be both the listening of a child, and yet listening 'in the fullest sense, reverent and awful listening'.[78] For Jesus was a child, yet a perfect one: he had none 'of that forestalling of manhood which our consciences and reason tell us is irregular and untrue'.[79] The union of divinity and humanity accorded perfectly with the natural process of intellectual growth. This was not asserted only to do justice to Jesus's humanity. How else could the divinity reveal itself except through the humanity?[80] To suggest otherwise would be epistemologically dangerous, not to say contradictory. It would create a notion of divinity as unlimited wisdom and power according to our own limited capacities: 'What we want is to know what wisdom and power are in their fullest, highest sense, not to mould and contract them by our understandings, and then fancy we make amends for the contraction by giving them the epithet "unlimited".'[81]

The kenotic notion of Incarnation implied here held divine and human natures in balance through the idea of personal growth and development. The perfect adaptation of Jesus's consciousness to his level of maturity was a perfect illustration of the completeness of the union of the two natures. The truth of Revelation was articulated through the perfection of finite, historical reality. Jesus's answers to the rabbis' questions would have been astonishing as the disclosure of the 'direct, full, original force' of the words they were using themselves. Jesus's words 'did not make veils for the sense,

[75] H. P. Liddon, *The Divinity of our Lord and Saviour Jesus Christ* (1867; 4th edn., London: Rivington, 1869), 456.

[76] Gore may have been influenced directly by reading Maurice: G. L. Prestige, *The Life of Charles Gore* (London: Heinemann, 1935), 97.

[77] Maurice, *What is Revelation?*, 18.

[78] Ibid. 20.

[79] Ibid. 22.

[80] Ibid.

[81] Ibid. 23.

but drew away a veil which concealed it'.[82] Revelation was not the unveiling of a system of ideas or even of a 'religion', but of God as Person: and as a person, human yet perfect and divine, even as a child Jesus entered into the very sense of words and understood them fully.[83] Implicit in this was that sense of sacramental depth in language to which attention was drawn in the second chapter. Jesus's omniscience was not to be construed as propositional knowledge, but as a power of penetration into the divine realities that words themselves signify. What was revealed through Jesus was perfectly adapted to his own growth towards maturity: the gradual unfolding of his human life was necessary for manifestation of the divine life.[84] Jesus's own growth was an unfolding of revelation: 'His understanding of the ways of God was more and more discovering His name to be that which the prophet had proclaimed, "He shall be called Wonderful, COUNSELLOR".'[85]

As so often, Maurice's oblique and allusive theological style prevents a systematic analysis of this 'kenotic' Christology. It is difficult to judge just how determinative it was for his incarnational theology as a whole. In the chapters on 'The Son of God' and 'The Incarnation' in the *Theological Essays*, for example, the question of Christ's consciousness and power was never directly confronted. Something along the lines of a kenotic understanding can be inferred from his double claim that the glory of God was 'concentrated' in Jesus, so that it could be diffused to many, and that human beings could not possibly know Christ as sinless unless he experienced temptation as a real human being: 'If we suppose that the Son of God had any advantage in that trial, any power save that which came from simple trust in His Father . . . we shall not feel that a real victory has been won.'[86]

This imprecision is all the more frustrating because Maurice's Christology is a clue to his ecclesiology. The balance he maintained between the divine and human natures of Christ was matched by his concern to hold in creative tension the divine and human aspects of the Church. This hidden theme of *kenosis* in Christology was paralleled by a kenotic ecclesiology.[87] As we have seen, Maurice resisted the common Protestant distinction between the visible and invisible Church. He maintained the essential and ultimate indefectibility of the Church, and yet also acknowledged that the Church constantly falls short of its divine vocation, through its members' tendency to turn inwards towards their own egoistical desires and away from God. Just as Christ's will was united to that of the Father,

---

[82] Maurice, *What is Revelation?*, 26.   [83] Ibid. 27.   [84] Ibid.   [85] Ibid. 28.

[86] Maurice, *Theological Essays*, 95–6.

[87] For an exploration of kenotic ecclesiology, see D. M. MacKinnon, 'Kenosis and Establishment', in *The Stripping of the Altars* (London: Fontana, 1969).

yet subject to the full conditions of humanity, situated in history, and not intruded into it, so the Church in like manner, as the community inhabited by the Spirit, was united with the Son in its inner reality, yet again also fully embedded in history and subject to the constraining pressures of history.

Thus, the manner in which Maurice conceived of revelation through the Incarnation did have implications for his ecclesiological theory. The role of history as carrier of Revelation was underscored in both Christology and ecclesiology. The Church's primary role was one of proclaiming and mediating in history the presence of Christ to his followers. No sharp distinction was possible between the message of the Gospel and the function of the Church.

HOLY SCRIPTURE: WITNESS TO REVELATION

Given the central role of the doctrine of the Incarnation in Maurice's theology, however, how could he respond to the new currents of criticism that seemed to question the reliability of the biblical witness? Maurice's biblical commentary was considerable, though mostly by means of published sermons. A recent monograph by John Rogerson on Maurice's Old Testament criticism helpfully characterizes his interpretative methodology, and can be used briefly to outline its relevance to his discussion of Revelation.[88] It would be impossible to offer a complete account here. All that is necessary is to demonstrate the sense in which Maurice's conception of the Bible worked alongside the account of his theology of Incarnation outlined above.

Rogerson lays down two basic principles at work in Maurice's understanding of the Old Testament. The first is a narrative approach, whereby he sees the Bible as the record of God's 'education' of the human race, and not as a set of specific doctrinal and moral propositions. The second is the assumption that God's purpose is to bless and accept the whole of humankind.[89] Tracing these principles through Maurice's relatively conservative response to the new biblical criticism, Rogerson concludes that he was a 'transitional figure'.[90] He was generally conservative on specific issues of textual and source criticism, accepting the Mosaic authorship of the Pentateuch, for example.[91] But he also departed from the (then)

---

[88] J. W. Rogerson, *The Bible and Criticism in Victorian Britain: Profiles of F. D. Maurice and William Robertson Smith* (Sheffield: Sheffield Academic Press, 1995).

[89] Ibid. 17–18.

[90] Ibid. 37.

[91] Ibid. 36.

common procedure of interpreting the Old Testament as a series of prophecies about Jesus, and instead sought to place its narrative in historical context. In so doing, his aim was to educe the central existential challenge of the Scriptures, and to represent it for believers today: 'Translating Maurice into modern idiom, we can say that the Old Testament is a record of belief within ancient Israel of God's encounter with Israel. In that record . . . God's character is revealed so that readers of the record are challenged to decide for or against the truth of that belief.'[92]

Rogerson may actually have understated Maurice's reluctance to depart from conventional exegesis.[93] His account, helpful as it is, needs to be supplemented by certain basic features of Maurice's view of Scripture as a whole and its relation to Revelation. Revelation was not itself *contained* in Scripture, but witnessed to by Scripture. Maurice accepted the doctrine of the inspiration of Scripture itself, in its formation of the testimony it had transcribed. This is not the same as verbal dictation, to which he certainly did not subscribe.[94] The distinction between inspiration and verbal dictation was widely recognized by the mid-nineteenth century.[95] What was more distinctive was Maurice's particular use of theological and ethical categories. He saw inspiration not only as a historical fact (that is, the inspiration of the writers of the sacred texts), but as a continuing process: the faithful interpreter was engaged in a process of inspirational interaction in reading the text, and being shaped by it. Read this way, the text itself was sacramental: its language expressed metaphysical truth through ordinary words, pointing to the deepest sacred realities. Commenting on his search for the resolution of his difficulties over eternal life, Maurice said: 'I fancied the Scripture language, instead of shrinking into a little corner of its own, and declining all comparison with any other, was capable of being tested by the metaphysical inquiries and beliefs of all peoples and ages.'[96] Just as the centre of Revelation was an event of incarnation that continued to be the meaning of history throughout history, the written record of that incarnation, including the national history of Israel that was its prelude, was a historical record that challenged believers throughout history.

Three further points can be made. First, Maurice's tendency to emphasize the eternal truth which the text itself conveyed operated within a

---

[92] Rogerson, *The Bible and Criticism in Victorian Britain*, 52.
[93] See Maurice's conviction that the Old Testament witnessed to humanity's yearning for a redeemer who would be Son of God and Son of Man: *Theological Essays*, 77–97.
[94] Indeed, he rejected it as 'heretical': Maurice, *Kingdom of Christ*, ii. 195.
[95] See the discussion of William Lee's lectures on *The Inspiration of Scripture* (1857) in J. R. Barth, *Coleridge*, 57–60.
[96] Maurice, *Sequel to the luquing*, 15.

powerful conception of truth as, ultimately, one. The witness of Scripture was, ultimately, self-consistent. One of Maurice's books, significantly, was titled *The Unity of the New Testament* (1854). If the Old Testament was not a record of direct prophecies of Jesus, its description of Israel's history was, for Maurice, a *praeparatio evangeli*. Yet his understanding of inspiration permitted a full acknowledgement of the diversity and occasional error of the biblical writers. Discrepancies between the three accounts of Paul's conversion in Acts 9, 22, and 26, for example, were side-stepped by an appeal to the overwhelming impact of the experience itself on Paul as the chief import of all three texts.[97] Maurice wrote about the character of the evangelists and other biblical authors in a way that acknowledged their distinctive theological concerns, yet again presupposed an essential unity.

Second, Maurice saw Scripture and Church as mutually reinforcing in communicating the primary 'given' of Revelation, Jesus Christ. The Bible and the Church interpreted each other: 'The Church exists as a fact, the Bible shews what that fact means. The Bible is a fact, the Church shews what that fact means.'[98] The revelatory significance of Scripture was inseparable from its location and use within the community of faith. This did not entail a doctrine of infallibility. Maurice's objection to Roman Catholicism included precisely the argument that it had elevated the Church above the Bible.[99] The practical demonstration of this interdependence of Church and Scripture was the liturgy, which encompassed Scripture both in its texts and through its lectionaries. There was an inspiration of prayer, in its liturgical form (the permanence of which is a guarantor of its anti-individualistic character), just as there was an inspiration of Scripture.[100] The reading of Scripture was an ecclesial activity, and the Spirit was the pledge of the perfect communion established between God and his creatures. The Church, as this communion in its earthly form, was the context for the faithful reading of Scripture.[101]

Yet, third, as if to check this, Maurice also held faithfully to the Reformation principle of *sola scriptura*. He regarded Scripture ultimately as a judge of the Church. He defended Luther's recovery of the principle of *sola scriptura*, calling it the third 'positive principle' of Protestantism, after justification through faith alone and the doctrine of election.[102] To an extent, Maurice's view has to be reconstructed from scattered comments in *The Kingdom of Christ* and elsewhere. His basic understanding seems to have been that the Bible was the authoritative source of knowledge of God. It presented a direct, unmediated knowledge of God to the believer;

[97] Maurice, *Acts*, 128–9.   [98] Maurice, *Kingdom of Christ*, ii. 214.
[99] Ibid. 214–16.   [100] Ibid. 31–2.   [101] Maurice, *The Prayer-Book*, 196–7.
[102] Maurice, *Kingdom of Christ*, i. 65–8.

far from being vulnerable to individual judgement, it was itself the arbiter of all forms of human judgement.[103] Scripture was an existential challenge for each individual; it signified a view of revelation as 'self-authenticating'.[104] It spoke directly to the person, above the confusions of sects and parties:

We who acknowledge the Bible as the high and ultimate authority, must desire that our decisions should be revised, corrected, even reversed by it, if we have adopted them from tradition, or fashioned them by our own weak, hasty inductions, without consulting it.[105]

Maurice's understanding of the relation of Revelation, Scripture, and Church presented something of a paradox, then. Scripture, on the one hand, gave unmediated access to the truth of Revelation, through its inspired witness to Christ as the centre of history. On the other hand, he also held a doctrine of inspiration within the community of the faithful, as an ongoing process of interpretation and reanimation of the truth. The institutional structure of the Church, and its credal and liturgical form, could not be set aside. Thus Maurice regretted the later developments of 'Pure Protestantism' which led to the disparagement of creeds, the Church Fathers, and the sacraments.[106] The paradox is partly stylistic. Maurice's rhetorical vehemence sometimes led him to overstate the self-authenticating character of Scripture. But the paradox was also a consequence of his determination to hold on to a historical conception of the Catholicity of the Church. The persistence of the institution of the Church through history presupposed the work of the Spirit in the Church and in Scripture.

Maurice's apparent unwillingness to confront directly the critical consequences of historical methodology earned him little gratitude from more conservative opponents, whose opinions of him were too deeply marked by the controversy over the *Theological Essays*. More liberal or radical critics, however, were bewildered by it. One of his most stringent critics was Leslie Stephen, founder of the *Dictionary of National Biography*, who found Maurice's defence of Christian orthodoxy in defiance of the new historical awareness offensive.[107] Yet it is too easy to assume it amounted to a simple evasion. As Stephen's modern biographer has pointed out, the nineteenth-century critical assumption that historical methodology would yield decisive information about the life of the real

[103] Maurice, *Kingdom of Christ*, i. 100–2.

[104] W. J. Wolf, 'Frederick Denison Maurice', in W. J. Wolf, J. E. Booty, and O. C. Thomas (eds.), *The Spirit of Anglicanism* (Edinburgh, T & T Clark, 1982), 78.

[105] Maurice, *Patriarchs and Lawgivers*, 222.

[106] Maurice, *Kingdom of Christ*, ii. 110.

[107] L. Stephen, 'Mr Maurice's Theology', *Fortnightly Review*, NS 15, (1874), 595–617.

Jesus Christ has proved illusory.[108] Theologians in the twentieth century were forced to recognize the meagre results of the quest for the historical Jesus, and to leave scope for faith accordingly.

Once again, then, complementary theological positions were held in a tense balance involving the individual and corporate reception of the inspired Word. There was an intrinsic fragility in this position. There could be occasions on which the individual interpretation of Scripture would be opposed to the interpretation of the Church, and yet both positions held with equal sincerity and determination. Maurice's approach did not present a way out of this dilemma. From a perspective of faith, the problem apparently disappeared: if the truth is one, and God is working throughout history, then divergent interpretations are ultimately reconcilable. But the practical difficulties of Maurice's view were never confronted specifically. Instead, they were transcended by the eschatological optimism built into his dialectical methodology. The task of theology was to trace the often tortuous and intricate paths throughout history that the truth of God has pursued, in all its depth and complexity. The Revelation that Christ was, the Revelation attested in Scripture, and the Revelation educed from Scripture by the Church, were finely interwoven, interconnected aspects of the one great truth, which could be seen for what it was only from the perspective of a faith prepared to acknowledge the ongoing complexity of God's relations with the world.

REVELATION IN HISTORY

Enough has perhaps been said already of Maurice's understanding of history in earlier chapters, to make it unnecessary to emphasize the revelatory character of history in his work. This fourth element of his view of Revelation can be considered through the exploration of a single instance. This is taken from *The Prophets and Kings of the Old Testament* (1853), and concerns his treatment of the history of King David. Almost any chapter from the book would suffice as a demonstration of Maurice's approach, but the story of David is especially fruitful because of the clarity of the contrast Maurice sought to draw between the providential direction of history and the sins of David.

The background theme for the volume as a whole was the development of the national character of Israel. This was grounded in the Protestant assertion that the universal Church stood only on Christ, not on a visible

---

[108] N. G. Annan, *Leslie Stephen: The Godless Victorian* (London: Weidenfeld & Nicolson, 1984), 248.

head of the Church.[109] In the absence of a visible central authority, national forms were part of the providence of God. God himself was a king and a lawgiver of nations.[110] Maurice traced a double process at work in the life of David: the providential calling of David, instanced in specific events such as his anointing, and his 'education', through the suffering he underwent in fidelity to God.[111] David was not a blind instrument of God's will: he was conscious of providential guidance.[112] Yet he was also a sinner. His wives and concubines were evidence that the Bible is 'the history of a practical education': the evils of polygamy could not be brought out at this stage of the nation's development, but became apparent later when they were clearly an obstacle to the unfolding of Revelation.[113]

Here, then, in outline was an understanding of the biblical narrative that presupposed both that the text itself was revelatory and that the historical substance to which the narrative referred was also a subject of Revelation. Text and subject mutually reinforced each other. The text was an authoritative text. Maurice never doubted, for example, the text's own attribution of authorship of the Psalms to David. Yet its subject-matter, in the books of Samuel and Kings, described the outworking of God's providential guidance through the career of King David. His interaction with God was a sign of his inward sympathy and communion with his own people: as king of Israel, then, he was a sign of God's relationship with his people.[114] But the relationship was an unfolding one. David learned his vocation as much through his mistakes and sins as through his successes. Israel, so it followed, learned its national vocation through the vicissitudes of its history. The providential meaning of these events could not be discerned without the biblical witness, and in turn the biblical witness would not be received without a prior commitment of faith in it.

THEOLOGICAL ANTHROPOLOGY: A THEOLOGY OF COMMUNION

Finally, to complete this account, there is a fifth dimension of Maurice's theology of Revelation: namely, his theological anthropology. It followed from Maurice's providential theory of history that God's purposes for humankind were to be discerned in human action. The totality of God's providence implied a voluntarist idea of agency: the free wills of individuals were subsumed within the broader divine purpose, intrinsic to it, and not obliterated by it. Human beings had a role in the reception and

---

[109] Maurice, *Prophets and Kings*, p. x.   [110] Ibid., p. vi.   [111] Ibid. 39–44.
[112] Ibid. 56–7.   [113] Ibid. 61–2.   [114] Ibid. 76–7.

communication of the truth of Revelation. Maurice saw human beings ultimately as spiritual beings, whose identity and character were discernible only in the light of God's will for humankind, supremely instanced in the Incarnation. His theological anthropology implied a theology of communion; communion with God constituted the *telos* of human existence.

Following his mentor, Coleridge, Maurice rejected the materialism of alternative contemporary approaches to human life, including utilitarianism and political economy. The selfishness of the materialist view was socially corrosive. Whilst affirming whole-heartedly the doctrinal tradition of Christian orthodoxy, Maurice sought to correct the materialism evident in the doctrine of rewards and punishments that he was convinced had crept into popular Christian culture.

For Maurice, the creation of human beings in the image of God was the fundamental principle of the Bible.[115] Since God as Trinity was a family of love, human beings were made for relationship: they were spiritual beings made in God's likeness to 'feel' after him.[116] God had made them to desire communion with him, and all that they are, including their desires, came from God himself. The status of sinful human impulses was problematic in Maurice's theology. He did not deny their existence, but plainly it is difficult to reconcile them with his optimistic ontology. They were ontologically deficient, or unreal, yet powerful. But they did not touch the real constitution of human being. This spiritual constitution justified the application of the language of rights to communion with God: 'To know that God does not depend upon our feelings, but our feelings upon God, to know that we must claim a certain spiritual position as our right before we can realise it in our apprehensions . . . this is most necessary for us.'[117]

A real human relationship to God implied the presence of a spirit that could communicate with God's Spirit. Maurice's explication of the spiritual constitution of human beings was specified generally. His description rested ultimately on biblical foundations; it did not represent an attempt to present a consistent philosophy of human being. He discouraged perplexity over the relation of religious truth to other forms of truth: 'we need not be tormented by this difficulty,' since 'Whatever in our minds is receptive of falsehood, this the Spirit will be continually warning us of . . . . Whatever is receptive of truth, this He will be unfolding.'[118] To the systematic theologian, this undoubtedly looks evasive. Maurice's formulation will not stand up to close scrutiny. But its place in a Bible-centred, devotional framework gives it some weight, none the less. That human beings have

---

[115] Maurice, *Moral and Metaphysical Philosophy,* i. 487.
[116] Maurice, *What is Revelation?,* 47.   [117] Maurice, *Life,* i. 246.
[118] Maurice, *Acts,* 170.

wills, that they are spiritual beings, and that the physical constitution of human beings complements and is integrally bound up with human identity as much as the spiritual, these were the basic foundations of Maurice's view of humankind: '[W]e are such instruments [of truth] only because the spirit in one man speaks to the spirit in his fellow, and this it does most when the Spirit of God is guiding actually both.'[119]

Given the orientation of human beings towards God, what implications does Maurice's doctrine of God have for his theological anthropology? For Maurice the relationship between the believer and God paralleled the inner relations of the Trinity. It also paralleled the relationship among believers themselves. The characteristic word Maurice used in this context was 'communion'. The communion of the faithful, with themselves and with God, was a reflection of God's own inner being as a union of three Persons. In faith, this relationship ceased to be subject to the constraints of temporality; it was eternal life. Maurice's interpretation drew on Patristic sources, and was expressed in language closer to Patristic themes of participation and deification than was common in the mid-nineteenth century (though there were some interesting parallels with the theology of Newman and Pusey).[120] As Maurice said, 'the subtlety of distinguishing eternity from time . . . I have learnt from St. Paul, Athanasius and Augustine'.[121] Hort argued that Maurice did no more than repeat Plato's doctrine on eternity, as followed by Augustine in the eleventh book of the *Confessions*.[122] Henry Mansel criticized him on precisely these grounds: Maurice had simply applied to human beings Patristic language concerning the eternity of God.[123] Actually, this was unfair, since Maurice nowhere suggested that our physicality is *itself* transformed into something 'eternal': rather, it was a *relationship* that constituted eternal life. Michael Ramsey and A. M. Allchin long ago pointed out the debt Maurice owed to the Greek and Latin Fathers, but this has never been adequately explored.[124] Contemporaries tended to read Maurice as blurring the divine–human distinction, articulating a vision of the life of faith that brought human beings into communion with God himself, but that, so

[119]   Maurice, *Acts*, 170.

[120]   See A. M. Allchin, *Participation in God: A Forgotten Strand in Anglican Tradition* (London: DLT, 1988), esp. ch. 4, 'A Life which is both His and Theirs: E. B. Pusey and the Oxford Movement'.

[121]   Maurice, *Life*, ii. 177.

[122]   A. F. Hort, *The Life and Letters of Fenton John Anthony Hort* (London: Macmillan, 1896), i. 261.

[123]   H. L. Mansel, *Man's Conception of Eternity: An Examination of Mr. Maurice's Theory of a Fixed State out of Time* (London and Oxford: Parker, 1854), 20.

[124]   A. M. Ramsey, *F. D. Maurice and the Conflicts of Modern Theology* (Cambridge: Cambridge University Press, 1951), 23, 37; Allchin, 'F. D. Maurice as Theologian', 520.

they thought, depended on a view of human nature that downgraded sin and the necessity of redemption.[125]

Drawing heavily on exegesis of St John's Gospel, however, this vision of communion as the ongoing participation of the believer in the life and love of God did not necessarily have this implication. Maurice's sense of the awfulness of sin as wilful rebellion against God, and of the reality of judgement, was strong. But it implied a different conception of the life of faith from that of his critics. Here Maurice's theology of union with God echoed Eastern Orthodox notions of *theiosis*. In *The Doctrine of Sacrifice* (1854) he took up the Pauline theme that baptism makes us sharers in the mind of Christ: 'You can claim your place in the heavenly order and harmony; He has brought you into it, breaking down the barrier of self-will which made our world an exile from it.'[126] He set this participation in the heavenly order in the context of the self-offering of the life of faith, as a communion with God: '[I]f God gives us grace not to love our lives to the death; if he makes us willing to sacrifice ourselves for His glory and the good of men, the communion may become very real even here.'[127] That 'even here', written shortly after the débâcle at King's College, implied that Maurice retained a distinction between eternal life before death and afterwards, though the distinction is hard to substantiate on his argument in the *Theological Essays*.

Maurice cannot be signed up as an early advocate of *koinonia* theology of the kind adumbrated, for example, by Jean Tillard or John D. Zizioulas.[128] It is significant that nowhere did he use the word 'communion' of the Trinitarian nature of God himself. He wrote constantly of God as 'unity', in a sense including a dynamic, relational three-in-oneness. Yet his argument stopped short of modern social Trinitarianism. It was as if he was prepared to acknowledge a parallel between the immanent Trinitarian relationships and the communion of believers with God and with each other, and yet was fearful of compromising the creatureliness of the created order by applying directly the same language he used of God to relationships of faith. This is ironic, given contemporaries' belief that compromising the distinction between creator and creatures was precisely what he was doing.

---

[125] This was particularly the view of Robert Candlish, who claimed that Maurice's eschatological doctrine in effect denied the reality of judgement, and depicted the future state (after death, that is) as nothing more than a continuation of the present: Candlish, *Examination*, 22.

[126] Maurice, *Doctrine of Sacrifice*, 224.

[127] Ibid. 241.

[128] See J. D. Zizioulas, *Being as Communion* (London: DLT, 1985); J. M. R. Tillard, *Church of Churches: The Ecclesiology of Communion* (Collegeville, Minn.: Liturgical Press, 1992).

The relevance of this perspective to Maurice's ecclesiology is note-worthy. Through baptism Christians were taken into the presence of God, joined to the communion of saints, 'an eternal and indissoluble friendship' with Christ himself.[129] Castigating the failure of the Church to proclaim the 'obligations of a common humanity' against competitive selfishness, he proclaimed that:

She can scarcely make her voice heard against schemes for reducing all things to a common stock, for establishing a fellowship upon a law of mutual selfishness, because she has not believed that the *internal communion*, the law of Love, the polity of members united in one Head, of brethren confessing a common Father, is a real one.[130]

Ecclesial life involved participation in a deep spiritual reality. In *The Kingdom of Christ*, though the Church was not absolutely coterminous with the Kingdom of God, the connection between the two was explicitly an expression of this union between God and humankind: '[T]he Catholic Church is emphatically a kingdom for *mankind*, a kingdom grounded upon the union which has been established in Christ between God and man.'[131] The Church was a society of believers through which the com-munion of humankind with God was proclaimed to all the world. Baptism was the effective and declaratory sign of this union.

Maurice's theological anthropology, with its vision of human being fulfilled only in union with God, was a vital component of his 'social' theology. As he argued to the Working Men's College in 1863, 'every divine gift to individuals is precious only as it unites them more with their kind'.[132] In his manual for parents and schoolmasters, he could not have put the working principle of his social and ethical teaching more clearly: 'I believe that God has made us not to be separate creatures, but to have fellowship with one another. I believe He is working in these spirits of ours that we may have it.'[133] In 1848, the year of revolutions, he could write in *Politics for the People* that 'we shall not rest any of us, till we have brought ourselves and our countrymen to seek for that equality which we shall have when we feel our common relation to Him, and only then'.[134]

It is perhaps natural enough that an exposition of Maurice's understand-ing of Revelation should end with a statement of his conviction

[129]   Maurice, *Kingdom of Christ*, i. 339.
[130]   Maurice, *The Prayer-Book*, 340–1; my italics.
[131]   Maurice, *Kingdom of Christ*, i. 311.
[132]   F. D. Maurice, 'Acquisition and Illumination', in *Friendship of Books*, 264.
[133]   Maurice, *The Lord's Prayer, the Creed, and the Commandments*, 46.
[134]   F. D. Maurice, 'Equality: A Dialogue between a Young Frenchman, a Statesman from America, and an English Mechanic', in *Politics for the People*, no. 6 (1848), 100.

of humankind as social being. For Maurice, the supreme revelatory significance of Christ was contained in the double dimension of salvation history: in the God-man's initiation of redemptive change and in his demonstration of the real, 'underlying', and created character of human being. The coming of the Word made flesh for Maurice was tantamount to the divine endorsement of human destiny; the Incarnation was thus at once the saving of humanity from its fallenness and the revelation of its authentic character. The dynamic, relation-seeking nature of divine love, which Maurice traced through the whole range of Christian doctrine in the *Theological Essays*, was at the root of true human community. Just as Christ was the perfection of humanity, so the 'body' he founded or left behind him as his community of followers, the Church, was the perfection of human community.

Yet Maurice's interpretation of Christian theology was certainly vulnerable to criticism. Apart from its lack of specificity, and his stylistic habit of linking abstract statements expressed with great force almost arbitrarily to particular maladies in church and social life, it also suffered from a vital but unresolved tension. On the one hand, Maurice's metaphysical presuppositions led him to emphasize the ontological connectedness of all things in their dependence on God. In this vein, his language could sound optimistic, mystical, and even ecstatic. He emphasized the permanence and unassailability of God's ordering of creation, in a way that could, taken on its own, imply that creation was no more than an imprint or reflection of the unchanging character of God. Yet, on the other hand, he was very much a biblical theologian, fully committed to the narrative of creation, fall, and redemption that constituted the doctrinal core of traditional Christian belief. The seeming ambiguity of his treatment of sin illustrates the point perfectly. He could be read as implying that sin was something of an illusion, affecting at most superficially the permanent, underlying union of humanity with God. Yet his language about sin was also intense and vehement, and shot through with a sense of shock and tragedy at the human rejection of God.

These contrasting perspectives are not fundamentally incompatible, but they are not obviously connected, either. They represented two different theological styles. They could be held together in a theological methodology that assumed the priority of the Church's corporate witness. The task of the theologian was to interpret and apply this witness to the new situations in which the Church found itself. It was to sound the depth of the faith whose shape and content were already given by the accumulated traditions of the Church.[135] This is the sense in which Maurice claimed for himself no more than the identity of 'digger'. On this supposition, strict internal consistency was unnecessary, and perhaps unavailable. The implication of his ecumenical methodology was that the truth within which the theologian could 'dig' was to be discerned at work in the whole of Christian history, and in the separated branches of the Church.

Even so, the reflexive character of this methodology left no sure guide for assessing the internal consistency of his own work. It was not a systematic elaboration of Platonism, though it contained many Platonic or Neoplatonic elements. Nor was it exclusively scriptural in its amplification of the theological implications of faith. It made much of the believer's experience of faith, as the evidence of the encounter of human beings with God; yet it did not elaborate a theory of religious experience, or produce criteria for evaluating religious experience. Maurice's language of divine order and spiritual constitution appealed again and again to scriptural warrant, as well as to human experience, but signified a conceptual field of reference that could not always be rooted decisively in either. There was no single point of departure for his theology, but a complex web of engagement across the whole range of Christian doctrine. There were, nevertheless, central principles, and repeated patterns of connection, that gave his work a formal or general consistency that could not be specified in a detailed way.

Yet it is significant, all the same, that Maurice managed to capture so well a general theological position that others after him were to state with more logical force. In registering the fact of biblical and historical criticism, at the same time as minimizing its destructive consequences, he helped delineate a way of reading Scripture and doctrine that arguably has become central to non-fundamentalist Christian responses to the modern world. His attempt to describe the self-involving character of Scripture, Church, creeds, and faith could not satisfy all of Christianity's cultured despisers. Yet it did seek to place the doctrinal authority of Christianity on a more secure basis. It neutralized something of the impact of secular hostility to religion, and did so in full recognition of the limitations and failures of the churches.

---

[135] Alec Vidler, one of the great admirers of Maurice in the twentieth century, was presumably influenced by this concept in conceiving of *Soundings: Essays Concerning Christian Understanding* (Cambridge: Cambridge University Press, 1962).

Conclusion

Maurice preached for the last time in February 1872, at St Edward's church in Cambridge, where he had recently become priest-in-charge.[1] His health had been failing for some months. He died in London in April 1872, after a short illness, and was buried in Highgate cemetery, the last resting-place also of that greater contemporary, Karl Marx. His last days were spent in conversation, in prayer, and in some devotional reading. On Easter Monday, he received communion from his friend and disciple J. Llewelyn Davies, and subsided gradually into unconsciousness, 'talking rapidly but very indistinctly' about 'the Communion being for all nations and peoples', rallying for a blessing before he died.[2] This account, preserved in his biography, may have been one of those tidied-up Victorian death-bed scenes. It was, nevertheless, fitting that a theologian for whom the vision of union with God was such a compelling theme throughout his life, should have died ruminating on communion. His death, as his son evidently saw, echoed his life. The intensity of his commitment to the Church he embraced in his twenties lasted to his final moments.

This commitment had been sustained through a period of immense change for the Church of England. When Maurice was born, it still occupied a legally entrenched position of considerable privilege. It had passed through a crisis that seemed to threaten its very existence, and emerged from the ensuing turmoil of criticism and reform stronger than ever. Yet its new-found stability, exemplified in its pastoral energy in the mid-Victorian years, was premised on a fundamental shift in the relationship between Church and State. Though it retained some of the most obvious features of Establishment, the dismantling of other key elements of the old relationship placed the Church of England in a quite different position *vis-à-vis* other churches than had been the case in earlier generations. Religious pluralism had become more than a grudgingly accepted feature of British society and government. It had become part of the very fabric of the British constitution. The steady erosion of support for the Church of England proportionate to population underlined the fragility of

---

[1] Maurice, *Life*, ii. 638.   [2] Ibid. 643.

its position. With all this awareness of the challenge of mission at home, in the working-class urban communities of Britain, as well as overseas, the language of crisis and failure was never far from the lips of Anglicans.

Maurice, like so many of his eminent Anglican contemporaries, cannot be said to have formulated a decisive or finally convincing answer, then, to the challenge thrown at Christianity by the revolutionary crisis of the late eighteenth and early nineteenth centuries. For all the attractiveness of his theology to many, it never acquired general support as a solution to the problem of social instability and religious indifference. The achievements of popular Evangelicalism, on the one hand, and popular Catholicism, on the other, were much more impressive in their purchase on the loyalties of ordinary people. The Victorians may have felt the social crisis hanging over their heads as a permanent threat, but the reality in Britain, in retrospect, was that government, society, and religion alike were capable of absorbing large shocks and rapid change without the consequence of mob violence and anarchy. Christianity surely had a significant role to play in channelling or suppressing revolutionary sentiment in mid-nineteenth-century Britain. But it did so across a broad front, and not because of the presence of an Established Church *per se*. Altogether, it can indeed be said that Christianity proved remarkably resilient in the nineteenth century, exposing the shallowness of prophets of its downfall. But the role which the moderate Anglicanism sponsored by Maurice played in all this was relatively minor.

Even so, if Maurice had been asked the question at the end of his life, it is unlikely that he would have considered his life's work a failure. Even putting to one side his pioneering work in education, with the founding of the Working Men's College and of Queen's College for women, his legacy to the Church of England was considerable. The dangers to the Church of England were real enough when he was baptized into it in 1831. With others, he helped to shape its theological and organizational renewal. Wider Anglican ambitions to Christianize society as a whole in Anglican form may have faltered, but Anglicans found new ways of surviving and adapting to social change. Maurice himself was never much interested in ecclesiastical management, and so to gauge the nature of his lasting influence, it is necessary to look elsewhere than institutional initiatives.

For most people, the dead remain for a time in the memory of those who knew them, fading as they in turn die. But for writers, for theologians, for public figures, the numbers of those who claim to have been touched by the dead may swell in number as time goes by, as their works are read, their influence and opinions discussed, and their lives constantly held up for examination. In the process, perspective becomes distorted. Memories of difficulties and controversies may fade, and other impressions come to predominate. A new view of the dead may become possible. In the case of Maurice, this happened to a greater degree than with any of his Anglican contemporaries. Why was this so?

THE GROWTH OF THE MAURICE MYTH

We have seen that Maurice led a writer's and preacher's life. He never occupied a formal position of leadership in the Church of England. His impact on the policy and administration of the Church was minimal. At his death, he was mourned greatly by the close circle of friends and followers who had been inspired by his theological vision. His son said that, Kingsley's obituary article apart, '[t]he blow had been too stunning to admit of anything but silence', but his absence was perhaps not noticed much by others.[3] Publication of his biography in 1884 rekindled public interest. But the gradual elevation of his reputation as a theologian was the result of a slow accumulation of interest in what he had stood for, as his works were read more widely, and his ideas spread through the generation of Broad Churchmen and Liberal Anglicans who came to dominate the leadership of the Church of England in the late nineteenth century. *The Kingdom of Christ* was central to this process. Gradually, the critical consensus came to settle on it as by far the most creative and original of his works. Maurice's reputation has to be seen, not so much as the result of the impact of a forceful and dynamic intellect, but as the product of a *longue durée*, a movement in Christian theology over a long period that favoured the themes and emphases on which he had concentrated.

That this was in spite of manifest weaknesses in his work cannot be denied. His elaborate, rhetorical, at times convoluted style often obscured his message. He was frustratingly difficult to place in the conventional 'party' terminology of late Victorian Anglicanism, and this pointed to a related difficulty in pin-pointing exactly where, prescriptively, his views on particular issues of Church and State might lie. In the area of Christian Socialism, this had the paradoxical effect of making him seem more attractive as a figure-head to a later generation of Christian Socialists than would have seemed likely from Maurice's ambiguous views about political and social reform in the 1850s. He was, above all, extraordinarily difficult to place theologically. The fusion of two different theological styles in his work, as described in the last chapter, gave him an unsettling ability to display varieties of intensity around particular doctrinal *foci*. He could, with ease, be made to appear more conservative or more

---

[3] Maurice, *Life*, ii 647.

progressive, according to one's predilection. He could be bracketed with the general history of English Platonism, but he could also be seen as a forerunner of twentieth-century biblical theology. Attempts to turn him into a wholly consistent theologian, a temptation followed by many who have written on him, are doomed, then, to ultimate failure.

Yet the breadth of Maurice's work was immense. He did not seek to construct a systematic theology, but to interpret an ecclesial commitment that he never felt obliged to defend a priori. In this sense, he is perhaps best considered as a Christian apologist, and as a polythematic theologian. His theological convictions took flight from multiple points of engagement, and were held in place by a consistency of sympathy and imagination that was often resistant to close analysis of what he appeared to be saying. Yet the multiplicity of foci should not obscure the fact that his central theological convictions were clustered together in a distinctive and, for its age, unique pattern. Consequently, it is important, in characterizing his work overall, to try to hold all of these convictions in view, and not to suppress or ignore certain elements that appear not to fit comfortably with others. In emphasizing his mystical conviction that union with God and communion with fellow human beings was the goal of human existence, for example, it is important not to forget that he was equally emphatic that this union and communion were secured through the institutional media of the Church. His conviction that God's wisdom was to be sought in all the various manifestations of human religion, culture, and language was counterbalanced by his conviction of Christian uniqueness and by his assumption that, in history, human selfishness had constantly turned ideas and institutions into a form of idolatry. The intensity of his language signalling a notion of the immediacy of faith, an almost ecstatic possession by faith, was balanced by his understanding of historical development.

But the polythematic quality of his work merely served to enhance interest in it as time passed. On the criticism of religious individualism, on eschatology, on Christology, on Church unity, he marked out positions that ran largely with the underlying current of British theology for a hundred years or so after his death. His fidelity to what he took to be the authentic doctrinal tradition of Christian orthodoxy proved increasingly attractive, given his readiness to concede the wisdom and truth of many different perspectives outside Christianity, as well as within it. The range of his theological interests has provided an endless supply of arresting insights on subjects that have preoccupied theologians and church people since the middle of the nineteenth century. His influence ran well beyond the Anglican churches. Already at his death, according to some witnesses, his revision of soteriological and eschatological theories was exercising a fascination for many young Nonconformist ministers who sought an escape from what they considered the sterility of an older generation's Calvinism.[4] His *Religions of the World* apparently inspired a fresh appreciation of other faiths, and helped to engineer a profound change in the method and aims of Christian mission in India.[5] The Maurician perspective come to the fore in the work of leading Free Churchmen in the late nineteenth and early twentieth centuries—men such as the Methodist John Scott Lidgett, for example.[6] Only late in the twentieth century did the stream seem to run dry, when the seeming fragmentation of theological method in the English-speaking world increasingly rendered Maurice a somewhat transitional figure. By then, he was too conservative for the radicals, and too liberal for the conservatives.

Yet, despite suffering something of an eclipse in the last two or three decades, Maurice remains a perplexing, compelling figure in modern theology. Struggling to defend his Church against successive threats, social, political, and intellectual, his convictions helped it to adjust and to survive. In isolation, these convictions often seem ill-considered, or vague, or vulnerable. Yet the overall effect of his work was always greater than the sum of its parts. His theology cannot be well understood unless it is seen in context as an appeal to traditional doctrine and institutions as the best sources of a Christian response to the rapidly changing nature of the world in which he lived. He was essentially a traditionalist who understood and could appreciate the importance of change. And this gave his theology a pliability, and an exciting quality, that was often lacking in the more thorough but prosaic theology of his contemporaries. Of all the areas of modern Christianity in which his influence has been significant, two perhaps stand out: the growth of worldwide Anglicanism and the rise of the ecumenical movement.

MAURICE AND THE ANGLICAN TRADITION

By the middle of the twentieth century, such had been the ascent of Maurice's posthumous reputation that he was generally taken to be not only the greatest Anglican thinker of his age, but a *quintessentially* Anglican figure. These are complementary but contentious claims. J. W. C. Wand,

---

[4] F. J. Powicke, 'Frederick Denison Maurice (1805–1872): A Personal Reminiscence', *Congregational Quarterly*, 8 (1930): Powicke even claimed that a 'majority' of younger ministers had a Maurician stamp when he left Spring Hill College in 1877: ibid. 172.

[5] Ibid. 179. See also the account by Cracknell, *Justice, Courtesy and Love, passim.*

[6] See esp. J. Scott Lidgett, *The Victorian Transformation of Theology* (London: Epworth Press, 1934), but also *The Spiritual Principle of the Atonement* (London: Kelly, 1898) and *The Fatherhood of God in Christian Life and Truth* (Edinburgh: T & T Clark, 1902).

bishop of London and church historian, speaking of Maurice and others, argued in 1960 that 'Anglicanism manages to be authoritative without claiming infallibility, liberal without lapsing into mere vagueness'.[7] Maurice by then had become the central figure of a widely held consensus about what Anglicanism was. Wand captured this very well in his survey. Anglicans believed in 'the virtue of reasonableness based on charity of judgment', and would contend 'that they are comprehensive rather than broad, maintaining within their own body a dialectic between high and low, between catholic and evangelical, which they regard as conducive to a deepening knowledge of the truth'.[8] This is a tribute to the influence of Maurice, without a doubt. Wand's description could almost pass as a paraphrase of Maurice's view of the Church of England. But it assumed too much. It took for granted—without, that is, demonstrating the case—the identity of Maurice's views with those of Anglicanism as a whole. And it also assumed that there was something readily identifiable and distinctive as 'Anglicanism'. Wand's description itself, in fact, was a historical statement, a product precisely of the influence of Maurice and others over time, an influence certainly open to inquiry, by no means uncontentious, and itself requiring explanation.

First, it is necessary to qualify the easy assumption that there is something as distinctive and self-evident as 'Anglicanism'. Though derived from the medieval *Ecclesia Anglicana*, the term itself was a nineteenth-century neologism, originally applied to Tractarian views, sometimes with critical overtones.[9] The 'Anglican' position, then, in the mid-nineteenth century was actually a partisan one within the Church of England. At this stage, it would have made little sense to talk about 'Anglicanism' as a systematic term describing the theology of all the Anglican churches, not only because of the depth of internal church division, but because by far the dominant church in the group of Anglican churches was the Church of England. What held the Anglican approach to church life in place above all was the particular relationship of the Church of England to the State, the very reason why the national argument assumed such prominence in Maurice's work. But, as we have seen, this relationship was undergoing attenuation in the course of the nineteenth century. Under the pressure of internal conflict and external assault, members of the Church of England were obliged to reflect on what constituted their distinctive identity in the course of the century. Impetus and urgency were added to this by the growth of

---

[7] J. W. C. Wand, *Anglicanism in History and Today* (London: Weidenfeld & Nicolson, 1961), 230.

[8] Ibid. 231.

[9] P. Avis, 'What is "Anglicanism"?', in S. W. Sykes and J. Booty (eds.), *The Study of Anglicanism* (London: SPCK, 1988), 407.

Anglican churches overseas. In that context, especially when the historical relationship of Church and State encountered in England was missing overseas, it became more and more likely that Anglicans would develop something like a sense of 'Anglicanism', as a distinctive church culture that might even lend itself to systematic, or at least coherent, description.

What, then, would constitute 'Anglicanism'? Here it was impossible to secure consensus. Continuity over time was certainly an important element. It was uncontentious to claim continuity with the Catholic church of undivided Christendom—Protestants had always denied the Catholic criticism that they were inventing a 'new' church. But there was no all-round agreement on the content of the tradition in which Anglicans stood. Sharp disagreement over the doctrine of apostolic succession illustrated this perfectly. Moreover, by their very nature, the Anglican churches did not have the centralized, institutional mechanisms of authority by which a consensus on what the Church stood for could have been secured and imposed. Cultural and linguistic commonalities were, naturally, very important. These were English-speaking churches, in the main, valuing highly the *Book of Common Prayer*. At first, though with rapid abandonment of this position, there was even something like a common doctrinal standard, secured on a minimal basis through the Thirty-Nine Articles of Religion, as well as the liturgy. Possession of the institutional criteria of traditional church order, the threefold ministry, was also important. Yet, depending on one's own theological conviction, the Church of England, and Anglicanism along with it, might be seen as close in spirit to the churches of the continental Reformation (the position of J. C. Ryle, the Evangelical bishop of Liverpool, for example), or as the natural ecumenical partner of Eastern Orthodoxy and the Roman Catholic and Old Catholic churches. Anglicanism could not be defined in relation to any one or limited number of basic positions. It was a curious hybrid of theology, culture, language, and institutions, and its plasticity in this regard is reflected even up to the present day in the persistent anxiety over what constitutes Anglican 'identity'. It is perhaps best thought of as an evolving but contested matrix, with certain dominant convictions remaining of central importance, yet never defined so closely that a wide range of disagreement over their interpretation is impossible. In this evolution, the role of history is vital, both as the context within which the Anglican churches have developed, and as the basis of a refusal (or, differently interpreted, an inability) to solidify the doctrinal and authoritative basis of Anglicanism to the point where internal division could be suppressed.

In this situation of variety and tension, it was perhaps not surprising that many Anglicans should have been drawn to arguments that seemed to offer a persuasive rationale for the very pluralism and plasticity of their church culture, and that Maurice's ecclesiological vision should have been particularly attractive. His defence of the traditional formularies of the Church of England was reassuring, yet it also had the congenial quality of leaving open the possibility of continuing disagreement. This was because his principle of comprehensiveness was expressed, as we have seen, through his understanding of the historical institutions of the Church. He showed little interest in explicating comprehensiveness as a systematic principle, yet his account of Anglican theology, education, and church life was shot through with it. Furthermore, this notion of the comprehensiveness of institutions was itself rooted in what he took to be the comprehensiveness of the Gospel. Through history, the Church protected and sustained the complex interaction between theology and social life, resisting where it could the temptation to draw the boundaries of the believing community ever more tightly. Maurice's theology could be used to justify Anglican breadth, but also to defend Anglican insistence on particular institutions. It could encourage Anglicans to be receptive to the theological insights of others from outside their own communion, yet it could also permit them to make a strong defence of the history and authority of their own church. This was quite a heady mix, however vulnerable critically. Its attractiveness was registered in the accelerating interest in Maurice's work, and particularly his ecclesiology, as the principle of comprehensiveness was translated into a pan-Anglican virtue. As that happened, the awkward fact that his own work had actually assumed, in large measure, the fact of English nationalism, Establishment, and nationality fell out of the picture.

In this way, Maurice's name and influence became assimilated to a version of Anglicanism that had become so widespread by the middle of the twentieth century that it could easily pass for an 'official' view. Famously, the Lambeth Conference of 1948 implied almost that comprehensiveness was *the* distinguishing feature of Anglican polity. Noting theological differences over episcopacy, it claimed:

[W]e acknowledge them to be part of the will of God for us, since we believe that it is only through a comprehensiveness which makes it possible to hold together . . . understandings of truth which are held in separation in other Churches, that the Anglican Communion is able to reach out in different directions, and so to fulfil its special vocation as one of God's instruments for the restoration of the visible unity of His whole Church.[10]

Unacknowledged by name, it is nevertheless difficult to read this passage without discerning in it a Mauricean debt, not least because of the

---

[10] *The Lambeth Conference 1948* (London: SPCK, 1948), part II, pp. 50–1.

implication of a special ecumenical vocation for Anglicans. Yet the modern dominance of this view, shaken recently by acute divisions over homosexuality and over women's ministry, only goes to show that a feature, historically, of Anglicanism has been its remarkable capacity to reinvent itself, and to uncover new sources of justification, and of inspiration, for what looks, in a long perspective, like a distinct subculture within world Christianity. The seriousness of internal conflict in the modern Anglican communion may have brought the attractiveness of Maurice's ecclesiology finally to an end. But that possibility can only serve to highlight the extraordinary influence it exercised for so long. Articulated as a defence of the role of the Church in promoting religious and social harmony, it represented the pained reaction of one sympathetic Anglican to the multiple crises his church faced in the early decades of the nineteenth century. It was, then, a thoroughly contextual ecclesiology. Yet it proved itself susceptible to translation and development, by which the consideration of one church's breadth could be turned into a general policy of promoting and containing internal church pluralism. In the process, it proved an extremely adaptable tool.

The flexibility of Maurice's approach was assisted, admittedly, by what on any view was a significant weakness of his method: namely, his tendency to combine sharp criticism of alternative arguments with broad-brush, general exposition of his own key principles. Time and again, as we have seen, he deployed original or unusual insights in such a way as to resist close analysis of his meaning. Stephen Sykes's influential critique of Maurice as the producer of a 'synthetic' ecclesiology gained credence from this, since Maurice could be read as arguing that comprehensiveness presumed the co-presence of mutually incompatible ecclesiologies within a greater synthesis.[11] In fact, Maurice's reflexive, inductive method did not seek so much to produce an original, systematic ecclesiological theory, as to begin from the presumption of a commonality of Christian identity across separated churches. Others could refine and sharpen his analysis. It was enough for his purpose, he might have responded, to point to the principles into which he had 'dug down' in order to defend the general position of the Anglican churches. Thus, the argument from comprehensiveness, the representative theory of ministry, the six 'signs' of the Catholic Church, the implicit but not absolute sacramentality of Church institutions were all ideas prominent in his view of the Church that would be refined and explored by later generations. The very pliability of his work was highlighted by the ease with

---

[11] Sykes, *Integrity of Anglicanism*, 16–19.

which later generations conveniently forgot his enthusiasm for the principle of nationality, and assimilated his arguments to those of his theological rivals, assuming wrongly his support for a view of Anglicanism as a
via media between Catholicism and Protestantism.[12] In this way, remarkably, his weaknesses as a theologian paradoxically may have assisted the
progress of his reputation as much as the undoubted strengths and
originality of many of the positions he adopted.

MAURICE AND THE UNITY OF THE CHURCH

But the influence of Maurice's ecclesiology was not restricted to arguments about Anglicanism. It also proved to have extensive implications for
the modern ecumenical movement. Maurice never used the word 'ecumenism', or its cognates, but if he had been tempted to, he would surely
have shared Chadwick's reservation that the modern word 'ecumenism', if
it is free from sectarian taint, is also free 'from other, and richer associations'.[13] Maurice's ecclesiological *analysis* was, in the modern sense,
'ecumenical', but his *prescription* for Church action was ecumenically
limited. Apart from his important intervention in the case of the Jerusalem
bishopric, he took little interest in practical schemes for effecting Church
unity. He saw them as contrivances, artificial if they were unrelated to the
genuine unity latent in the divided history of the Church. Conversely, his
concept of 'Catholicity' was historically grounded: the universality of the
Church in history was as important as its universality in his own age,
across diverse cultures, nations, and sectarian divisions. But 'Catholicity'
for Maurice was but a sub-theme of the greater theological theme of unity,
rooted in the doctrine of the Trinity: 'I not only believe in the Trinity in
Unity, but I find in it the centre of all my beliefs; the rest of my spirit, when
I contemplate myself or mankind.'[14] And this unitive conviction fanned
out into a myriad of recurrent themes. The unity of the Trinity was related
to the unity of will and purpose between Father and Son, to the unity of
the Trinitarian name, to the intra-Trinitarian relations as a unity of love, to
the unity of Scripture, and (through the medium of his emphasis on union
in faith with God) to the unity of God's redemptive action in history.
The unity of the Church, then, was to be conceived in terms much
more fundamental than those commonly connoted by the modern,

---

[12] For an exploration of the roots of this confusion, see J. N. Morris, 'Newman and
Maurice on the Via Media of the Anglican Church: Contrasts and Affinities', *Anglican
Theological Review*, 85 (2003).

[13] W. O. Chadwick, 'Catholicism', *Theology*, 76 (1973), 173.

[14] Maurice, *Life*, i. 41.

process-bound application of the word 'ecumenism'. It was not merely an institutional unity to which Maurice referred, but a unity that participated in the divine unity.

Maurice's distinctive apprehension of the unity of the Church in history required a Christological basis. For Maurice, as we saw in the last chapter, Christ was the focal point of creation and history; his incarnation was the hinge on which history turned. But he was at pains to suggest that Christ's ascension, far from marking an absence from history, in fact permanently and indelibly printed Christ's kingship on the whole course of history as an active, ongoing power and presence. In this light, there could only be one actual head of the Church, Christ himself. This meant, for one thing, a direct rejection of the claims of the Papacy to embody the authority of Christ.[15] It followed that it also meant the transference to the ongoing rule of Christ of all the claims about an infallible, developing authority in the Church that Newman had applied to the Papacy.[16] Christ's headship was universal in a double sense, constituted as such through the Son's agency in creation and through his universal mission to redeem humankind. The universal kingship of Christ always preceded the historical constitution of the Church, though the Church was nevertheless the corporate and *necessary* means by which Christ's presence in history was actualized. This is vividly illustrated in a passage frequently quoted from the chapter 'On the Unity of the Church' in the *Theological Essays*. Here Maurice explained the distinction between the Church and the world, asserting that the world 'contains the elements of which the Church is composed', and arguing that:

In the Church these elements are penetrated by a uniting, reconciling power. The Church is, therefore, human society in its normal state; the world, that same society irregular and abnormal. The world is the Church without God; the Church is the world restored to its relation with God, taken back by Him into the state for which He created it. Deprive the Church of its Centre, and you make it into a world.[17]

Behind this account of the unity of the Church across time lay the characteristic philosophical preoccupations of Maurice. The events of history manifested divine, eternal truths. To comprehend the development of the Church in time, it was necessary to take cognizance of truths that were for all time, and also the consequence of particular epochs of change. Once again, Maurice appeared to want to have the argument both ways. He wanted to affirm development in the life of the Church, yet also

---

[15] See Morris, 'Reconstructing the Reformation', 493.

[16] F. D. Maurice, *The Epistle to the Hebrews* (London: Parker, 1846), pp. xxxii–xxxvi.

[17] Maurice, *Theological Essays*, 396.

to assert that the 'essential idea' of Christianity was fully present from the very first, as in his response to Newman on development.[18] This may have looked like an illogical fusing of quite separate arguments about eternity and contingency. But it was a finely balanced attempt to remain faithful to two truths of faith permanently in tension: the transcendence of God, as Lord of time and matter, and his immanence in history.

Once again, *The Kingdom of Christ* is the seminal text here. In reading the history of the Christian Church as a history of schism and sectarianism, in which genuine but select aspects of the totality of truth become the 'positive principles' of different branches of Christendom, yet are thereby distorted because of the accompanying denial of other genuine principles, Maurice projected an idea of the unity of the whole Church both back-wards into the past and forwards into the future. He supposed, as a historical principle, an original unity in the life and mission of Christ himself, which was preserved in the apostolic community, albeit at times under threat. The whole history of the Christian Church was a recession from this original unity into a situation of fragmentation. But unity remained in place, nevertheless, in the real, lasting, if obscured Catholicity of the Church, rooted in the living presence of Christ in history and in his Body, the Church. And this meant that the existing churches also looked forward to a time when their divisions would disappear in a recovery of the real unity of the Church.

Thus, Maurice sketched out an ecumenical methodology—the exam-ination of theological difference, in order to apprehend the authentic principles that lay at the heart of ecclesial conflict—that has proved to be remarkably attractive to subsequent generations. H. R. T. Brandreth called his contribution to ecumenical thought 'outstanding'.[19] William Wolf described *The Kingdom of Christ* as laying down 'a theology of Christian ecumenism that has yet to come into its own', yet pointed out that a 'surprising number' of studies on the Church by Roman Catholic ecume-nists followed a methodology similar to Maurice's, citing in support a highly appreciative assessment of Maurice by Louis Bouyer.[20] Within Anglicanism itself, Maurice's influence as a theologian in the development of an ecumenical spirit, to say nothing of an ecumenical methodology, has

---

[18] Maurice, *Hebrews*, pp. lv–lxii.

[19] H. R. T. Brandreth, 'Approaches of the Churches towards each other in the Nineteenth Century', in R. Rouse and S. C. Neill (eds.), *A History of the Ecumenical Movement* (London: SPCK, 1954), 274.

[20] Wolf, 'Frederick Denison Maurice', 84–5, quoting from L. Bouyer, *The Spirit and Forms of Protestantism* (London: Narvill, 1956), 189–90. But note that Wolf's words here are a little hard to reconcile with his earlier claim that 'In many ways Maurice defined in advance our present ecumenical situation': *idem*, 'Maurice and our Understanding of "Ecumenical" ', *Anglican Theological Review*, 54 (1972), 273.

been greater, arguably, than that of any other figure before the great ecumenical pioneers of the twentieth century such as William Temple, George Bell, and Michael Ramsey.[21]

Even if we lay to one side, for the moment, the attempt to assess Maurice's historical influence, it is certainly the case, as Wolf indicates, that there are highly suggestive similarities between his theological approach to the diversity of Christian traditions and the methodology of modern ecumenism. In one of the great texts of modern Catholic ecumenism, *Divided Christendom* (1939), Yves Congar suggested a principle of the recognition and retrieval of the 'positive' insights of separated traditions which is very close to Maurice's method. As Congar argued, 'each of the great schisms which have become great Christian communities represents, in its positive aspect, certain genuine values, even if it is tragically astray in those aspects in which it is negative, exclusive, and peculiar to itself'.[22] The Anglo-Catholic report on *Catholicity* (1947) commissioned by Geoffrey Fisher, archbishop of Canterbury, outlined an account of the loss of primitive 'wholeness' as the Christian Church fragmented in history which echoed Maurice. Like him, it went on to suggest that the 'true way' of synthesis for Church unity was 'the recovery of the fulness [*sic*] of Tradition within the thought and worship and order and life of each of the sundered portions of Christendom'.[23] Modern ecumenical dialogues have often pursued a similar method. The Anglican–Roman Catholic joint statement, *Church as Communion*, outlined a view of separated traditions strikingly similar to Congar and, of course, to Maurice:

Whenever differences become embodied in separated ecclesial communities, so that Christians are no longer able to receive and pass on the truth within the one community of faith, communion is impoverished and the living memory of the Church is affected. As Christians grow apart, complementary aspects of the one truth are sometimes perceived as mutually incompatible.[24]

Maurice was just one amongst a number of significant European theological voices in the nineteenth century who, in various ways, encouraged a reconsideration of Church history and the doctrine of the

---

[21] See the significance attached to Maurice by Paul Avis in *Ecumenical Theology and the Elusiveness of Doctrine* (London: SPCK, 1986), *passim*.

[22] Y. M. J. Congar, *Divided Christendom: A Catholic Study of the Problem of Reunion* (London: Geoffrey Bles and The Centenary Press, 1939), 40. Congar's application of the principle was scarcely the same as Maurice's. Congar's principle was applied outside the Roman communion as a critical principle directed at other schismatic communities.

[23] A. M. Ramsey et al., *Catholicity: A Study in the Conflict of Christian Traditions in the West* (Westminister: Dacre Press, 1947), 45. The sympathy with Maurice's outlook is scarcely surprising, considering the presence of V. A. Demant and A. G. Hebert on the committee, along with Ramsey himself.

[24] ARCIC-II, *Church as Communion*, 22.

Church that would prove much more accommodating to the principle of reuniting separated traditions. J. A. Möhler in his *magnum opus, Symbolism* (1832), pioneered, as a Catholic, a more sympathetic (if still critical) engagement with Protestant theology.[25] The Russian A. S. Khomiakov, despite a stringent insistence on the necessity of conformity to the doctrinal standard of Eastern Orthodoxy, nevertheless elaborated a doctrine of Church unity that sought to transcend the rigidities of Orthodox ecclesiasticism of the period, and to return to the spirit of the early Church.[26] N. F. S. Grundtvig also articulated a vision of Church unity which has been immensely influential in promoting ecumenism in Scandinavia, and which has been likened to the ecclesiology of Maurice himself.[27] All these figures were evidence of new currents of thinking about the doctrine of the Church, not least of a concern to go beyond mere theological polemics, and to reassess the serious theological origins of Church division.[28]

If Maurice was significant as a progenitor of modern ecumenism, the irony of this is that he spent much of his life defending the distinctive identity and position of his own church, and did little actively to encourage specific proposals for closer relations between denominations. His influence, such as it was, lay largely in the realm of theory. And here, once again, what is striking is the concurrence of general principles that have proved immensely attractive to modern ecumenical theory with a certain imprecision in their definition. It was as if Maurice had an essential insight into the heart of the ecumenical problem, yet, either through a lack of inclination or because his method remained focused on the broad, historical reasons for Church division, could not see his way to elaborating a practical programme for Church unity. Above all was this true of his theology of communion. That there was a disjuncture in his terminology between use of the term 'union' in relation to God's own being and 'communion' in relation to human fellowship with God was a sign that

---

[25] There is a modern edition, which is based on the nineteenth-century translation by J. B. Robertson: J. A. Möhler, *Symbolism: Exposition of the Doctrinal Differences between Catholics and Protestants as Evidenced by their Symbolical Writings*, ed. M. J. Himes (New York: Crossroad Press, 1997). See also M. J. Himes, *Ongoing Incarnation: Johann Adam Möhler and the Beginnings of Modern Ecclesiology* (New York: Crossroad Press, 1997). Maurice attributed W. G. Ward's errors about Lutheranism in *The Ideal of the Christian Church* (1844) to Möhler's 'very gross misrepresentation': Maurice, *Life*, i. 362.

[26] Little of Khomiakov's work has appeared in translation in English even today. His most influential work in the West was a short pamphlet, entitled *The Church is One*, which was published by the Fellowship of St Sergius and St Alban in 1948, with an introduction by Nicholas Zernov.

[27] See especially A. M. Allchin, *N. F. S. Grundtvig: An Introduction to his Life and Work* (London: DLT, 1997), ch. 6, 'Discovering the Church', pp. 105–14.

[28] A. M. Allchin has explored some of these cross-currents in his *The Kingdom of Love and Knowledge: The Encounter between Orthodoxy and the West* (London: DLT, 1979).

his theology fell short of modern ecumenical enthusiasm for *koinonia*. His sensitivity to the historical formation of separated Christian traditions would presumably have predisposed him to agree with Nicholas Sagovsky's suggestion that the principle of *koinonia*, almost ubiquitous in modern ecumenical discussion, is useful precisely to the extent to which it is able to accommodate and encapsulate descriptions of ecclesial practice.[29] But we would rightly hesitate to assert that Maurice himself fully understood this, or that he could have foreseen the extraordinary fecundity of *koinonia* theology in an ecumenical context. The force with which the principle is advanced in, for example, the Canberra statement of the World Council of Churches, *The Unity of the Church: Gift and Calling* (1991), or in the Faith and Order document, *The Nature and Purpose of the Church* (1998), is broadly consonant with Maurice's view in theory, but obviously much more highly developed and sophisticated in practice.[30]

The emergence of an active concern for Church unity is certainly reflective of the nineteenth-century moment of theology, and of its cultural as well as theological locale. It marked the realization that Christian division was a major obstacle to mission, at a time when Christianity's intellectual as well as social credibility was threatened. What Maurice sought to confront in Britain was replicated across Europe. Under attack from political radicals, secularists, and revolutionaries, Christians were beginning to wake up to the fact that their own internal disagreements merely served to confirm the hostility of their critics. There were powerful countervailing pressures. Lingering prejudice, particularly between Catholics and Protestants, often lay behind the competitiveness and sectarianism of nineteenth-century religion. Missionary enthusiasm often sponsored further disagreement and schism, particularly in Protestant churches. The sheer vitality of Victorian religion, with its great schemes of church building and its daunting record of philanthropic endeavour, masked the possibility that disagreement between Christians might impede their ability to reach out to the unchurched. Maurice's great legacy to the emergent ecumenical movement was the perception that ecclesiastical division underlined social division, and projected distorted images of the great, separated traditions of Christianity from one side to the other.

Maurice's theology was both of its time and ahead of its time. It remained perplexing to many of his progressive friends that his reaction to the crisis of Christian authority was to join a church they considered

---

[29] N. Sagovsky, *Ecumenism, Christian Origins and the Practice of Communion* (Cambridge: Cambridge University Press 2000), 6–13.

[30] World Council of Churches (WCC), *The Unity of the Church: Gift and Calling* (text on WCC website); Faith and Order Commission, *The Nature and Purpose of the Church* (Geneva: World Council of Churches, 1998).

unwanted baggage from the past. It seemed a form of betrayal. But, defending the Church of England as he did, Maurice became a pioneer of ecumenical vision and a prophet of social responsibility, whose work was to inspire generations of Christians, Anglican and non-Anglican alike, with a conviction of the relevance and authority of Christian faith. Developing a form of apologetic in the face of secular threat, he faced the challenges of his age unapologetically. His many critics, then and now, had little difficulty pin-pointing the confusing twists and turns in his arguments, the unwarranted assertions and fragile generalizations. But for breadth of vision, imagination, and force of conviction, few could match him. These were significant theological virtues.

Select Bibliography

It is possible to include here only works specifically consulted for this book, or to which reference has been made in the footnotes. The few manuscript sources are detailed in the appropriate footnotes. A comprehensive bibliography of Maurice's writings, compiled by G. J. Gray, was included by F. Maurice in his *Life* of his father (1884), and then published separately in 1885. Additional material by and about Maurice can also be found in the bibliographies to F. M. McClain, *Maurice, Man and Moralist* (1972), and D. Young, *F. D. Maurice and Unitarianism* (1992).

WORKS BY F. D. MAURICE CONSULTED FOR THIS BOOK

The Metropolitan Quarterly Magazine (4 nos., in 2 vols., London, 1825–6); articles by F. D. Maurice:
'The Age of Folly', nos. 1–4.
'John Milton's *A Treatise on Christian Doctrine*', no. 1.
'The New School of Cockneyism', nos. 1 and 3.
'A Supplementary Sheet to Bentham's Book of Fallacies', no. 2.
'On Pastoral Poetry', nos. 3 and 4.
'The Diary of Mr. Papster from the year 1790 to 1827', no. 3.
'The Prose of Poets', no. 4.
'Montgomery's "Pelican Island" ', *Westminster Review*, 8 (1827).
'Theobald Wolf Tone's Memoirs', *Westminster Review*, 9 (1828).
The Athenaeum (London, 1828–); articles by F. D. Maurice:
'Sketches of Contemporary Authors, No. 1', 16 January 1828.
'No. 2. Mr Jeffrey and the Edinburgh Review', 23 January 1828.
'No. 3. Mr Southey', 29 January 1828.
'No. 4. Mr Cobbett', 12 February 1828.
'No. 5. Mr Wordsworth', 19 February 1828.
'No. 6. Mr Moore', 22 February 1828.
'No. 7. Mr Brougham', 29 February 1828.
'No. 8. Percy Bysshe Shelley', 7 March 1828.
'No. 9. Sir Walter Scott', 11 March 1828.
'No. 10. Sir James Mackintosh', 18 March 1828.
'No. 11. Maria Edgworth', 28 March 1828.
'No. 12. Lord Byron', 8 April 1828.
'No. 13. Mr James Mill', 18 June 1828.
'No. 14. Mr Crabbe', 30 July 1828.
'Review of S. L. Blanchard's *Lyric Offerings*', 30 July 1828.
'Review of T. Davies's *Estimates of the Human Mind*', 6 August 1828.
'Review of A. & J. C. Hare's *Guesses at Truth*', 13 August 1828.
'London University and King's College', 15 October 1828.

'Spanish and Italian Refugees', 5 November 1828.

'The Spanish Exiles', 26 November 1828.

'The Universities of Europe and America. Cambridge No. I', 3 December 1828.

'The Universities ... Cambridge No. II', 17 December 1828.

'Review of J. C. Hare's *The Children of Light*', 31 December 1828.

Eustace Conway; or, the Brother and Sister (London: Bentley, 1834).

Subscription no Bondage, or the Practical Advantages Afforded by the Thirty-Nine Articles as Guides in all the Branches of Academical Education (Oxford: Parker, 1835).

The Kingdom of Christ, or Hints on the Principles, Ordinances, and Constitution of the Catholic Church in Letters to a Member of the Society of Friends, 1st edn. (3 vols., London: Darton & Clark, 1838).

Has the Church, or the State, the Power to Educate the Nation? (London: Rivington, 1839).

Reasons for Not Joining a Party in the Church: A Letter to the Ven. Samuel Wilberforce (London: Rivington, 1841).

The Kingdom of Christ, or Hints to a Quaker Respecting the Principles, Constitution and Ordinances of the Catholic Church (2nd edn., London: Rivington, 1842; 4th edn., London: Macmillan, 1891).

Three Letters to the Rev. W. Palmer (London: Rivington, 1842; 2nd edn., 1842).

On Right and Wrong Methods of Supporting Protestantism: A Letter to Lord Ashley (London: Parker, 1843).

'Introduction' to *William Law, Remarks on the Fable of the Bees* (Cambridge: Macmillan, 1844).

A Few Words on the Irish Colleges (London: Houlston & Stoneman, 1845).

The New Statute and Mr Ward: A Letter to a Non-Resident Member of Convocation (Oxford: Parker, 1845).

Thoughts on the Rule of Conscientious Subscription, or the Purpose of the Thirty-Nine Articles, and our Present Perils from the Romish System in a Second Letter to a Non-Resident Member of Convocation (Oxford: Parker, 1845).

The Epistle to the Hebrews (London: Parker, 1846).

'The Government Scheme of Education', *English Journal of Education*, NS I (1847).

The Education Question in 1847: A Letter Addressed to the Editor of the English Journal of Education (London: Bell, 1847).

Letter on the Attempt to Defeat the Nomination of Dr. Hampden (London: Pickering, 1847).

Moral and Metaphysical Philosophy, Part 1: Ancient Philosophy, Anterior to the Time of Christ (London: Griffin, 1847; revised, 1850; 2 vol. edn., Macmillan, 1873).

The Religions of the World and their Relations to Christianity (London: Parker, 1847; 6th edn., Macmillan, 1886).

Thoughts on the Duty of a Protestant in the Present Oxford Election: A Letter to a London Clergyman (London: Parker, 1847).

The Lord's Prayer: Nine Sermons (London: Parker, 1848; 3rd edn., with *Prayer-Book*, Macmillan, 1880).

Politics for the People (weekly, 6 May–29 July 1848; London: J. W. Parker):

'Prospectus', 1 (6 May 1848).

'Fraternity', 1 (6 May 1848).

'Dialogues in the Penny Boats. No. 1. Between a Templar, a Silk Mercer, a Coalwhipper, and Myself', 2 (13 May 1848).

'Liberty: A Dialogue between a French Propagandist, an English Labourer, and the Editor', 4 (27 May 1848).

'The Universities and the Working Men: A Dialogue in the Penny Boats between a Student from Oxford, a Carpenter, and Myself', 5 (Supplement for May 1848).

'Equality: A Dialogue between a Young Frenchman, a Statesman from America, and an English Mechanic', 6 (3 June 1848).

'Rough Notes of Some Lectures on Modern History', 7 (10 June 1848).

'A Dialogue in the Penny Boats. No. 3. Education', 9 (24 June 1848).

'Recollections and Confessions of William Milward', 10 (Supplement for June 1848).

Queen's College, London: Its Object and Method: A Lecture Delivered in the Hanover Square Rooms (London: Rivington, 1848).

The Prayer-Book Considered Especially in Reference to the Romish System: Nineteen Sermons (London: Parker, 1849; 3rd edn., with *The Lord's Prayer*, Macmillan, 1880).

The Church a Family: Twelve Sermons on the Occasional Services of the Prayer-Book (London: Parker, 1850).

A Letter to the Right Hon. and Right Rev. The Lord Bishop of London, in Reply to the Article in no. CLXXII of the Quarterly Review, entitled 'Queen's College, London' (London: Parker, 1850).

Tracts on Christian Socialism (London: Bell, 1850):

'I. Dialogue between Somebody (a person of respectability) and Nobody (the writer)'.

'II. History of the Working Tailors' Association'.

'VII. A Dialogue between A. & B., Two Clergymen, on the Doctrine of Circumstances as it Affects Priests and People'.

The Patriarchs and Lawgivers of the Old Testament (London: Parker, 1851; 2nd edn., London: Macmillan, 1855).

Reasons for Co-operation: A Lecture Delivered at the Office for Promoting Working Men's Associations (London: Parker, 1851).

Tracts on Christian Socialism (London: Bell, 1851):

'VIII: A Clergyman's Answer to the Question 'On What Grounds Can You Associate with Men Generally?''

On the Reformation of Society, and How All Classes may Contribute to it (Southampton: Forbes & Knibb, 1851).

The Prophets and Kings of the Old Testament (London: Macmillan, 1853; 3rd edn., 1871).

Sermons on the Sabbath-Day (London: Macmillan, 1853).

Theological Essays (Cambridge: Macmillan, 1853).

The Word 'Eternal' and the Punishment of the Wicked: A Letter to the Rev. Dr. Jelf, Canon of Christ Church and Principal of King's College (Cambridge: Macmillan, 1853).

The Doctrine of Sacrifice Deduced from the Scriptures (1854; 2nd edn., London: Macmillan, 1879).

Lectures on the Ecclesiastical History of the First and Second Centuries (Cambridge: Macmillan, 1854).

Moral and Metaphysical Philosophy, Part II: Philosophy of the First Six Centuries (London: Griffin, 1854; 2 vol. edn., Macmillan, 1873).

The Unity of the New Testament (London: Parker, 1854).

Administrative Reform, and its Connexion with Working Men's Colleges: An Address (London: Macmillan, 1855).

Plan of a Female College for the Help of the Rich and of the Poor (Cambridge: Macmillan, 1855).

Learning and Working (Cambridge: Macmillan, 1855).

The Gospel of St John: A Series of Discourses (London: Macmillan, 1856; new edn., 1878).

Sermons Preached in Lincoln's Inn Chapel, (1856–9; new edn., London: Smith Elder, 1860).

The Indian Crisis: Five Sermons (London: Macmillan, 1857).

Moral and Metaphysical Philosophy, Part III: Mediaeval Philosophy (London: Griffin, 1857; 2 vol. edn., Macmillan, 1873).

The Worship of the Church a Witness for the Redemption of the World (London: Macmillan, 1857).

What is Revelation? (London: Macmillan, 1859).

Sequel to the Inquiry, What is Revelation? (London: Macmillan, 1860).

The Faith of the Liturgy and the Doctrine of the Thirty-Nine Articles (London: Macmillan, 1860).

'Lord Macaulay', *Macmillan's Magazine*, 1 (1860).

'On the Revision of the Prayer-Book and the Act of Uniformity', *Macmillan's Magazine*, 1 (1860).

Review of vols. v and vi of Froude's *History of England*, *Macmillan's Magazine*, 2 (1860).

'History and Casuistry', *Macmillan's Magazine*, 2 (1860).

Tracts for Priests and People (by various) (London: Macmillan, 1861–2):

   '2. The Mote and the Beam: A Clergyman's Lessons from the Present Panic'.

   '6. The Sermon of the Bishop of Oxford on Revelation, and the Layman's Answer. II. Morality and Divinity'.

   '10. Politics Ancient and Modern, II: Do Kings Reign by the Grace of God?'

   '14. Introductory Letter to the Author' [prefaced to 'The Incarnation and Principles of Evidence', by R. H. Hutton].

Dialogues between a Clergyman and a Layman on Family Worship (London: Macmillan, 1862).

'Dr. Lushington, Mr. Heath, and the Thirty-Nine Articles', *Macmillan's Magazine*, 5 (1862).

Moral and Metaphysical Philosophy, Part IV: Modern Philosophy (London: Griffin, Bohn & Co., 1862; 2 vol. edn., London: Macmillan, 1873).

The Gospel of the Kingdom of Heaven: A Course of Lectures on the Gospel of St. Luke (London: Macmillan, 1864; new edn., 1893).

What Message have the Clergy for the People of England? A Letter to the Rt Hon and Rt Rev the Bishop of London, in Reference to the Controversy on the Future State of Sinners (London: Macmillan, 1864).

The Commandments Considered as Instruments of National Reformation (London: Macmillan, 1866).

The Workman and the Franchise: Chapters from English History on the Representation and Education of the People (London: Strahan, 1866).

The Conscience (London: Macmillan, 1868).

The Ground and Object of Hope for Mankind (London: Macmillan, 1868).

'The Irish Church Establishment', *The Contemporary Review*, 7 (1868).

'The Dean of Cork and the Irish Establishment', *The Contemporary Review*, 7 (1868).

'On Church and State', eight letters to the *Daily News*, August and September 1868.

Review of 'A Few Words on Irish Church Questions' by W. G. Clark, *Cambridge University Gazette*, no. 3 (11 Nov. 1868).

Social Morality (London: Macmillan, 1869).

'Dr. Newman's Grammar of Assent', *Contemporary Review*, 14 (1870).

'A Few More Words on the Athanasian Creed', *Contemporary Review*, 15 (1870).

'The Thirty-Nine Articles and the Broad Church', *The Spectator*, 2 April 1870.

The Lord's Prayer, the Creed, and the Commandments: A Manual for Parents and Schoolmasters (London: Macmillan, 1870).

'Meditations and Prayers Concerning the Church and Mankind', in A. Ewing (ed.), *Present-Day Papers on Prominent Questions in Theology*, 1st ser. (London; Oaldy, Isbister & Co., 1870).

'The Use of the Word "Revelation" in the New Testament', in A. Ewing (ed.), *Present-Day Papers on Prominent Questions in Theology*, 2nd ser. (London: Strahan 1871).

The Friendship of Books (London: Macmillan, 1893).

The Acts of the Apostles: A Course of Sermons (London: Macmillan, 1894).

CONTEMPORARY AND NEAR-CONTEMPORARY SOURCES (PRE-1914)

Arnold, T., *Principles of Church Reform* (1833); ed. M. J. Jackson and J. Rogan (London: SPCK, 1962).

—— *Fragments on Church and State: Written in 1827–1840 and Published as Appendices to the First Edition of the Fragment on the Church* (London: Fellowes, 1845).

Ashwell, A. R., and Wilberforce, R. G., *Life of Samuel Wilberforce* (3 vols., London: Murray, 1880–2).

Bunsen, F., *A Memoir of Baron Bunsen* (London: Longmans, Green, 1868).

Burke, E., *Collected Works*, ed. F. H. Willis (Oxford: Oxford University Press, 1906).

Candlish, R. S., *Examination of Mr. Maurice's Theological Essays* (London: Nisbet, 1854).

Carlyle, T., *The French Revolution: A History* (1837; London: Oxford University Press, 1907).

—— 'Chartism' (1839); in *Selected Essays* (London: Dent, 1915).

Chalmers, T., *Church Establishments Defended* (London: Waddon, 1833).

Church, R. W., *The Oxford Movement: Twelve Years 1833–45* (1891; new edn., Chicago: University of Chicago Press, 1970).

—— *Occasional Papers* (London: Macmillan, 1897).

Clark, Samuel, *Memorials from Journals and Letters*, ed. with intro. by E. J. H. Clark, (London: Macmillan, 1878).

Coleridge, S. T., *Aids to Reflection* (1825; new edn., New York: Chelsea Publishing House, 1983).

—— *On the Constitution of Church and State* (1830; new edn., London: Everyman, 1972).

—— *Confessions of an Enquiring Spirit* (1840; New York: Chelsea Publishing House, 1983).

Conybeare, W. J., 'Church Parties', *Edinburgh Review*, 98 (October 1853); ed. R. A. Burns in S. Taylor (ed.), *From Cranmer to Davidson: A Church of England Miscellany*, Church of England Record Society, 7 (Woodbridge: Boydell Press, 1999).

Cornish, F. W., *The English Church in the Nineteenth Century* (London: Macmillan, 1910).

Croker, J. W. [Anonymous], 'Revolutionary Literature', *Quarterly Review*, 89 (1850–1).

Davies, J. Llewellyn, 'Secularism and Mr. Maurice's Theology', *Contemporary Review*, 24 (1874).

—— 'Frederick Denison Maurice', *The Contemporary Review*, 45 (1884).

Engels, F., *The Condition of the Working Class in England in 1844* (1845; ET London: Allen & Unwin, 1892).

Erskine, T., *The Brazen Serpent, or Life coming through Death* (1831; 3rd edn., Edinburgh: David Douglas, 1879).

Farrar, F. W., *Chapters on Language* (London: Longman, 1865).

—— *The History of Interpretation* (London: Macmillan, 1886).

Froude, J. A., *Life of Carlyle: Carlyle's Life in London*, i (1884; new edn., London: Longmans, 1897).

Froude, R. H., *Remains of the Late Reverend Richard Hurrell Froude* (4 vols., London: Rivington, 1838–9).

Gibbon, E., *Autobiography* (1796; Oxford: Oxford University Press, 1972).

Gladstone, W. E., *The State in its Relations with the Church* (London: Murray, 1838; 4th edn., 1841).

—— *Church Principles Considered in their Results* (London: Murray, 1840).

Gore, C., *The Incarnation of the Son of God* (1891; new edn., London: Murray, 1922).

—— *Dissertations on Subjects Connected with the Incarnation* (London: Murray, 1895).

—— et al., *Lux Mundi* (London: Murray, 1889).

Hare, J. C., *Vindication of Luther against Recent English Assailants* (London: Parker, 1855).

—— and Hare, A. W., *Guesses at Truth* (1827; new edn., London: Macmillan, 1866).

Headlam, S. D., *Christian Socialism: A Lecture*, Fabian Society Tract no. 42 (London: Fabian Society, 1892).

Hook, W. F., *A Letter to the Rt. Rev. the Lord Bishop of Ripon, on the State of Parties in the Church of England* (London: Rivington, 1841).

Hooker, R., *The Laws of Ecclesiastical Polity* (1594–7; London: Everyman, 1907).

Hope, J. R., *The Bishopric of the United Church of England and Ireland at Jerusalem* (London: Stewart, 1841).

Hort, A. F., *Life and Letters of Fenton John Anthony Hort* (London: Macmillan, 1896).

Hort, F. J. A., 'Coleridge', in *Cambridge Essays* (London: Parker, 1856).

Hutton, W. H., *The Age of Revolution: 1648–1815* (London: Rivington, 1908).

Illingworth, J. R., *The Doctrine of the Trinity* (London: Macmillan, 1907).

Jelf, R. W., *Grounds for Laying before the Council of King's College, London, Certain Statements Contained in a Recent Publication, Entitled, 'Theological Essays', by the Revd F. D. Maurice, MA* (Oxford and London: Parker, 1853).

Johnston, J. O., *Life and Letters of Henry Parry Liddon* (London: Longmans, 1905).

Jowett, B. (*et al.*), *Essays and Reviews* (London: Parker, 1860).

Keble, J., *On Eucharistical Adoration* (Oxford: Parker, 1857).

—— *Difficulties in the Relations between Church and State* (Oxford: Parker, 1877).

Kingsley, C., *Cheap Clothes and Nasty,* (Tracts by Christian Socialists, 2, by 'Parson Lot' (London: Bell, 1850).

—— *The Message of the Church to Labouring Men* (London: Parker, 1851).

—— 'Frederick Denison Maurice: In memoriam', *Macmillan's Magazine*, 26 (1872).

Kingsley, F. E., *Charles Kingsley: His Letters and Memories of his Life* (1877; new edn., London: Macmillan, 1899).

Liddon, H. P., *The Divinity of our Lord and Saviour Jesus Christ* (1867; 4th edn., London: Rivington, 1869).

—— *Life of Pusey* (5 vols., London: Longmans, 1893–7).

Lidgett, J. Scott, *The Spiritual Principle of the Atonement* (London: Kelly, 1898).

—— *The Fatherhood of God in Christian Life and Truth* (Edinburgh: T & T Clark, 1902).

Ludlow, J. M., *King's College and Mr. Maurice, no.1: The Facts* (London: Nutt, 1853).

—— 'Dissent from, and Dissent in the Church', in *Dissent and the Church*, Tracts for Priests and People, 9 (London: Macmillan, 1861).

—— 'Some of the Christian Socialists of 1848 and the Following Years, I', *The Economic Review*, 3 (1893).

—— 'Thomas Hughes and Septimus Hansard', *The Economic Review*, 6 (1896).

—— *The Autobiography of a Christian Socialist*, ed. A. D. Murray (London: Frank Cass, 1981).

—— and Jones, L., *The Progress of the Working Class 1832–1867* (London: Alexander Strahan, 1867).

Macaulay, T. B., 'Gladstone on Church and State', in *Critical and Historical Essays* (1843; new edn., London: Longmans, 1850).

Mansel, H. L., *Man's Conception of Eternity: An Examination of Mr. Maurice's Theory of a Fixed State out of Time* (London and Oxford: Parker, 1854).

—— *The Limits of Religious Thought Examined* (Oxford: Murray, 1858).

—— *The Witness of the Church to the Promise of Christ's Coming* (Oxford: Parker, 1864).

Marx, K., *The Revolutions of 1848*, ed. D. Fernbach (Harmondsworth: Penguin, 1973).

—— *Early Writings*, ed. L. Colletti (Harmondsworth: Penguin, 1975).

Masterman, C. F. G., *Frederick Denison Maurice* (London: Mowbray, 1907).

Maurice, F., *The Life and Letters of Frederick Denison Maurice* (1884; 2nd edn., London: Macmillan, 1884).

Mill, J. S., *Autobiography* (1873; ed. J. Stillinger, new edn., Oxford: Oxford University Press, 1969).

Moberly, R. C., *Atonement and Personality* (London: Murray, 1901).

Mohler, J. A., *Symbolism: Exposition of the Doctrinal Differences between Catholics and Protestants as Evidenced by their Symbolical Writings* (1832), ed. M. J. Himes, (New York: Crossroad Press, 1997).

Mozley, J. B., *Letters* (London: Rivington, 1885).

—— 'Professor Maurice's Theological Essays', in *Essays Historical and Critical*, ii (London: Rivington, 1892).

Newman, J. H., *Parochial and Plain Sermons* (1834–42; new edn., London: Longman, 1891).

—— *An Essay on the Development of Christian Doctrine* (1845), ed. J. Cameron (Harmondsworth: Penguin, 1974).

—— *Apologia Pro Vita Sua* (1864; London: Oxford University Press, 1964).

—— *The Via Media of the Anglican Church* (London: Pickering, 1877).

—— *Letters and Diaries of John Henry Newman*, v, ed. T. Gornall (Oxford: Clarendon Press, 1981).

—— *Letters and Diaries of John Henry Newman*, vi, ed. G. Tracey, (Oxford: Clarendon Press, 1984).

Owen, R., *Book of the New Moral World* (London: Wilson, 1836).

Palmer, W., *Treatise on the Church* (London: Rivington, 1838).

—— *Narrative of Events Connected with the Tracts for the Times* (Oxford: Parker, 1843).

Palmer, W., [of Magdalen], *Aids to Reflection on the Seemingly Double Character of the Established Church, with Reference to the Foundation of a 'Protestant Bishopric' at Jerusalem* (Oxford: Parker, 1841).

—— *A Letter to a Protestant-Catholic* (Oxford: Parker, 1842).

Pattison, M., *Essays*, ed. by H. Nettleship (Oxford: Clarendon Press, 1889).

Prothero, R. E., *Life and Correspondence of Dean Stanley* (1893; London: Nelson, 1909).

Pusey, E. B., *Scriptural Views of Holy Baptism*, Tracts for the Times, nos. 67–9 (Oxford: Parker, 1836).

—— *A Letter to his Grace the Archbishop of Canterbury on Some Circumstances Connected with the Present Crisis in the English Church* (London: Parker, 1842).

—— *The Holy Eucharist, a Comfort to the Penitent* (Oxford: Parker, 1843).

Rigg, J. H., *Modern Anglican Theology* (London: Heylin, 1857).

—— *A Comparative View of Church Organizations* (1887; 2nd edn., London: Charles Kelly, 1891).

Rousseau, J.-J., *The Social Contract* (1762; Harmondsworth: Penguin, 1968).

Shorthouse, J. H., 'Frederick Denison Maurice', *The Nineteenth Century*, 15 (1884).

Smith, A., *Sketches of London Life and Character* (London: Bogue, 1849).

Stanley, A. P., *The Life and Correspondence of Thomas Arnold* (London: Fellowes, 1844).

—— *The Unity of Evangelical and Apostolical Teaching: Sermons Preached Mostly in Canterbury Cathedral* (London: Murray, 1859).

—— *Essays Chiefly on Questions of Church and State* (London: Murray, 1870).

Stephen, Leslie, 'Mr Maurice's Theology', *Fortnightly Review*, NS 15 (1874).

—— 'F. D. Maurice', in *Dictionary of National Biography*, xxxvii (1894).

Storr, Vernon F., *The Development of English Theology in the Nineteenth Century, 1800–1860* (London: Longmans, 1913).

Strachey, E., 'Recollections of Frederick Denison Maurice', *Cornhill Magazine*, 3rd ser., 2 (1897).

Talbot, E. S., 'Frederick Denison Maurice', *Macmillan's Magazine*, 50 (1884).

Trench, M., *Letters and Memorials of Richard Chevenix Trench, Archbishop* (London: Kegan Paul, 1888).

Trench, R. C., *On the Study of Words* (1851; new edn., London: Parker, 1855).

Tulloch, J. R., *Movements of Religious Thought in Britain during the Nineteenth Century* (1885; new edn., Leicester: Leicester University Press, 1971).

Wade, J., *Unreformed Abuses in Church and State: With a Preliminary Tractate on the Continental Revolutions* (London: Effingham Wilson, 1849).

Ward, W., *William George Ward and the Oxford Movement* (London: Macmillan, 1889).

Ward, W. G., *Ideal of a Christian Church* (London: Toovey, 1844).

Westcott, B. F., *Lessons from Work* (London: Macmillan, 1901).

Wilberforce, R., *The Doctrine of the Incarnation of our Lord Jesus Christ* (London: Murray, 1849).

—— *The Doctrine of the Holy Eucharist* (London: Mozley, 1854).

LATER SOURCES (POST-1914)

Aarsleff, H., *The Study of Language in England 1780–1860* (1967; new edn., Westport, Conn.: Greenwood Press, 1978).

Akenson, D. H., *The Church of Ireland: Ecclesiastical Reform and Revolution 1800–1885* (New Haven and London: Yale University Press, 1971).

Allchin, A. M., *The Spirit and the Word* (London: Faith Press, 1963).

—— 'F. D. Maurice as Theologian', *Theology*, 76 (1973).

—— *The Kingdom of Love and Knowledge: The Encounter between Orthodoxy and the West* (London: DLT, 1979).

—— 'The Understanding of Unity in Tractarian Theology and Spirituality', in G. Rowell (ed.), *Tradition Renewed* (London: DLT, 1986).

—— *Participation in God: A Forgotten Strand in Anglican Tradition* (London: DLT, 1988).

—— *N. F. S. Grundtvig: An Introduction to his Life and Work* (London: DLT, 1997).

Allen, P., *The Cambridge Apostles: The Early Years* (Cambridge: Cambridge University Press, 1978).

Allen, P. R., 'F. D. Maurice and J. M. Ludlow: A Reassessment of the Leaders of Victorian Christian Socialism', *Victorian Studies*, 11 (1968).

Altholz, J. L., *The Religious Press in Britain, 1760–1900* (Westport, Conn.: Greenwood Press, 1989).

Annan, N. G., *Leslie Stephen: The Godless Victorian* (London: Weidenfeld & Nicolson, 1984).

ARCIC-II (Anglican-Roman Catholic International Commission II), *Church as Communion* (London: Catholic Truth Society/Church House Publishing, 1991).

Arx, J. P. von, *Progress and Pessimism: Religion, Politics and History in Late Nineteenth Century Britain* (Cambridge, Mass.: Harvard University Press, 1985).

Aston, N., 'Horne and Heterodoxy: The Defence of Anglican Belief in the Late Enlightenment', *English Historical Review*, 108 (1993).

Avis, P., *Ecumenical Theology and the Elusiveness of Doctrine* (London: SPCK, 1986).

—— *Gore: Construction and Conflict* (Worthing: Churchman, 1988).

—— 'What is "Anglicanism"?', in S. W. Sykes and J. Booty (eds.), *The Study of Anglicanism* (London: SPCK, 1988).

—— *Anglicanism and the Christian Church: Theological Resources in Historical Perspective* (Edinburgh: T & T Clark, 1989).

—— 'Anglican Conciliarity and the Lambeth Conference', *Theology*, 101 (1998).

—— *Church, State and Establishment* (London: SPCK, 2001).

Backstrom, P. N., *Christian Socialism and Co-operation in Victorian England: Edward Vansittart Neale and the Co-operative Movement* (London: Croom Helm, 1974).

Banton, M., 'Kingsley's Racial Philosophy', *Theology*, 78 (1975).

Barth, J. R., *Coleridge and Christian Doctrine*, new edn. (New York: Fordham University Press, 1987).

Barth, K., *Protestant Theology in the Nineteenth Century* (1972; London: SCM, new edn., 2001).

Bebbington, D. W., *The Nonconformist Conscience: Chapel and Politics, 1870–1914* (London: Allen & Unwin, 1982).

Bellamy, J., and Saville, J. (eds.), *Dictionary of Labour Biography*, ix (Basingstoke: Macmillan, 1993).

Best, G. F. A., *Temporal Pillars: Queen Anne's Bounty, the Ecclesiastical Commissioners and the Church of England* (Cambridge: Cambridge University Press, 1964).

Bettany, F. G., *Stewart Headlam: A Biography* (London: Murray, 1926).

Bettenson, H. (ed.), *Documents of the Christian Church* (Oxford: Oxford University Press, 1950).

—— *The Later Christian Fathers* (Oxford: Oxford University Press, 1970).

Binyon, G. C., *The Christian Socialist Movement in England: An Introduction to the Study of its History* (London: SPCK, 1931).

Birley, R., 'Maurice and Education', *Theology*, 76 (1973).

Booty, J. E. (ed.), *John Jewel's Apology of the Church of England* (London: SPCK, 1963).

Boulger, James D., *Coleridge as Religious Thinker* (New Haven: Yale University Press, 1961).

Bouyer, L. *The Spirit and Forms of Protestantism* (London: Harvill, 1956).

Brandreth, H. R. T., 'Approaches of the Churches towards each other in the Nineteenth Century', in R. Rouse, and S. C. Neill, (eds.), *A History of the Ecumenical Movement* (London: SPCK, 1954).

Brent, R., *Liberal Anglican Politics: Whiggery, Religion, and Reform, 1830–1841* (Oxford: Clarendon Press, 1987).

Briggs, A., *The Age of Improvement 1783–1867* (1959; new edn., London: Longman, 1979).

Brock, M., *The Great Reform Act* (London: Hutchinson, 1973).

Brock, M. G., and Curthoys, M. C. (eds.), *The History of the University of Oxford*, vi: *Nineteenth-Century Oxford, Part 1* (Oxford: Clarendon Press, 1997).

Bromley, J., *The Man of Ten Talents: A Portrait of Richard Chevenix Trench, 1807–86* (London: SPCK, 1959).

Brose, O. J., *Church and Parliament: The Reshaping of the Church of England 1828–1860* (London: Oxford University Press, 1959).

—— *Frederick Denison Maurice: Rebellious Conformist* (Athens, Oh.: Ohio University Press, 1971).

Brown, C. G., *The Death of Christian Britain* (Cambridge: Cambridge University Press, 2000).

Brown, R., *Chartism* (Cambridge: Cambridge University Press, 1998).

Brown, S. J., *The National Churches of England, Ireland and Scotland 1801–1846* (Oxford: Oxford University Press, 2001).

Brundage, A., *The People's Historian: John Richard Green and the Writing of History in Victorian England* (Westport, Conn.: Greenwood Press, 1994).

Bryant, C., *Possible Dreams: A Personal History of British Christian Socialists* (London: Hodder & Stoughton, 1996).

Brynn, E., *The Church of Ireland in the Age of Catholic Emancipation* (New York and London: Garland, 1982).

Burdon, C., *The Apocalypse in England: Revelation Unravelling, 1700–1834* (London: Macmillan, 1997).

Burns, R. A., ' "Standing in the Old Ways": Historical Legitimation of Church Reform in the Church of England, c.1825–65', in R. N. Swanson (ed.), *The Church Retrospective*, Studies in Church History, 33 (Woodbridge: Boydell, 1997).

—— *The Diocesan Revival in the Church of England c.1800–1870* (Oxford: Oxford University Press, 1999).

Burrow, J. W., *A Liberal Descent: Victorian Historians and the English Past* (Cambridge: Cambridge University Press, 1983).

Bushaway, R. W., *By Rite: Custom, Ceremony and Community in England 1700–1880* (London: Junction Books, 1982).

Butler, B. C., *The Idea of the Church* (London: DLT, 1962).

Butler, M. (ed.), *Burke, Paine, Godwin and the Revolution Controversy* (Cambridge: Cambridge University Press, 1984).

Butler, P., *Gladstone: Church, State and Tractarianism: A Study of his Religious Ideas and Attitudes 1809–59* (Oxford: Clarendon Press, 1982).

Cashdollar, C. D., *The Transformation of Theology, 1830–1890: Positivism and Protestant Thought in Britain and America* (Princeton: Princeton University Press, 1989).

Chadwick, H., *The Vindication of Christianity in Westcott's Thought* (Cambridge: Cambridge University Press, 1961).

Chadwick, W. O., *From Bossuet to Newman* (1957; new edn., Cambridge: Cambridge University Press, 1987).

—— *The Victorian Church* 2 vols. (London: A. & C. Black, 1966, 1970).

—— 'Catholicism', *Theology*, 76 (1973).

Chadwick, W. O., *The Popes and European Revolution* (Oxford: Clarendon Press, 1981).

—— *Michael Ramsey: A Life* (Oxford: Oxford University Press, 1990).

Chitty, S., *The Beast and the Monk: A Life of Charles Kingsley* (London: Hodder & Stoughton, 1974).

Christensen, T., 'F. D. Maurice and the Contemporary Religious World', in G. J. Cuming (ed.), *Studies in Church History, 3* (Leiden: Brill, 1966).

—— *The Origins and History of Christian Socialism 1848–1854* (Aarhus: Universitetsforlaget, 1962).

—— *The Divine Order: A Study of F. D. Maurice's Theology* (Leiden: Brill, 1973).

Clark, G. K., *Churchmen and the Condition of England, 1832–1885* (London: Methuen, 1973).

Clark, J. C. D., *English Society 1660–1832: Religion, Ideology and Politics during the Ancien Régime* (1985; 2nd edn., Cambridge: Cambridge University Press, 2000).

Clayton, J. W., 'Reason and Unity in F. D. Maurice', *Anglican Theological Review,* 54 (1972).

Cocksworth, C. J., *Evangelical Eucharistic Thought in the Church of England* (Cambridge: Cambridge University Press, 1993).

Cole, G. D. H., *British Working Class Politics 1832–1914* (London: Labour Book Service, 1941).

Coleman, B. I., *The Church of England in the Mid-Nineteenth Century: A Social Geography* (London: Historical Association, 1980).

Collison, R. L., *Encyclopaedias: Their History Throughout the Ages* (New York: Hafner, 1964).

Colloms, B., *Charles Kingsley: The Lion of Eversley* (London: Constable, 1975).

Congar, Y. M. J., *Divided Christendom: A Catholic Study of the Problem of Reunion* (London: Geoffrey Bles and The Centenary Press, 1939).

—— *Diversity and Communion* (London: SCM, 1984).

Coppa, F. J., *The Modern Papacy since 1789* (London: Longman, 1998).

Corsi, P., *Science and Religion: Baden Powell and the Anglican Debate, 1800–1860* (Cambridge: Cambridge University Press, 1988).

Coulson, J., 'Newman on the Church—His Final View, its Origins and Influence', in J. Coulson and A. M. Allchin (eds.), *The Rediscovery of Newman: An Oxford Symposium* (London: SPCK, 1967).

—— *Newman and the Common Tradition: A Study in the Language of Church and Society* (Oxford: Clarendon Press, 1970).

Cracknell, K., *Justice, Courtesy and Love: Theologians and Missionaries Encountering World Religions 1816–1914* (London: Epworth Press, 1995).

Creed, J. M., *The Divinity of Jesus Christ* (Cambridge, 1938; new edn., London: Collins, 1964).

Cullen, A. D., *The Victorian Mirror of History* (London: Yale University Press, 1985).

Cunliffe-Jones, H., 'A New Assessment of F. D. Maurice's "The Kingdom of Christ" ', *Church Quarterly,* 4 (1971).

Cupitt, D., 'Mansel's Theory of Regulative Truth', *Journal of Theological Studies,* NS, 18 (1967).

—— 'Mansel and Maurice on our Knowledge of God', *Theology,* 73 (1970).

—— 'The Language of Eschatology: F. D. Maurice's Treatment of Heaven and Hell', *Anglican Theological Review,* 54 (1972).

Currie, R., Gilbert, A. D., and Horsley, L., *Churches and Churchgoers: Patterns of Church Growth in the British Isles since 1700* (Oxford: Oxford University Press, 1977).

Daunton, M. J., *Progress and Poverty: An Economic and Social History of Britain 1700–1850* (Oxford: Oxford University Press, 1995).

Davie, D., *Essays in Dissent: Church, Chapel and the Unitarian Conspiracy* (Manchester: Carcanet, 1995).

Davies, W. M., *An Introduction to F. D. Maurice's Theology* (London: SPCK, 1964).

Dickinson, H. T. (ed.), *Britain and the French Revolution 1789–1815* (London: Macmillan, 1989).

Dinwiddy, J. R., *From Luddism to the First Reform Bill* (Oxford: Blackwell, 1986).

Distad, N. M., 'Julius Charles Hare and the "Broad Church" Ideal', in P. T. Phillips (ed.), *The View from the Pulpit: Victorian Ministers and Society* (Toronto: Macmillan, 1978).

—— *Guessing at Truth: The Life of Julius Charles Hare* (Shepherdstown, W. Va.: Patmos Press, 1979).

Dowland, D. A., *Nineteenth-Century Anglican Theological Training: The Redbrick Challenge* (Oxford: Clarendon Press, 1997).

Doyle, W., *Origins of the French Revolution*, 3rd edn. (Oxford: Oxford University Press, 1999).

Dulles, A., *The Catholicity of the Church* (Oxford: Clarendon Press, 1985).

Ellis, I., *Seven against Christ: A Study of* Essays and Reviews (Leiden: Brill, 1980).

Elton, G. R. (ed.), *The Tudor Constitution*, 2nd edn. (Cambridge: Cambridge University Press, 1982).

Emsley, C., *British Society and the French Wars, 1793–1815* (London: Macmillan, 1979).

—— (ed.), *Britain and the French Revolution* (Harlow: Longman, 2000).

Engell, J., 'Coleridge and German Idealism: First Postulates, Final Causes', in R. Gravil, and M. Lefebvre, (eds.), *The Coleridge Connection* (London: Macmillan, 1990).

Evans, E. J., *The Contentious Tithe: The Tithe Problem and English Agriculture 1750–1850* (London: Routledge & Kegan Paul, 1976).

Evans, G. R., and Wright, J. R. (eds.), *The Anglican Tradition: A Handbook of Sources* (London: SPCK, 1991).

Eyck, F., *Religion and Politics in German History: From the Beginnings to the French Revolution* (Basingstoke: Macmillan, 1998).

Faith and Order Commission, *The Nature and Purpose of the Church* (Geneva: World Council of Churches, 1998).

Fenwick, J., and Spinks, B., *Worship in Transition: The Twentieth-Century Liturgical Movement* (Edinburgh: T & T Clark, 1995).

Flegg, C. G., *'Gathered under Apostles': A Study of the Catholic Apostolic Church* (Oxford: Clarendon Press, 1992).

Flesseman-Van Leer, E., *Grace Abounding: A Comparison of F. D. Maurice and Karl Barth* (London: King's College, 1968).

Forbes, D., *The Liberal Anglican Idea of History* (Cambridge: Cambridge University Press, 1952).

Forrester, D., *Young Doctor Pusey: A Study in Development* (London: Mowbray, 1989).

Foster, J., *Class Struggle and the Industrial Revolution: Early Industrial Capitalism in Three English Towns* (London: Weidenfeld & Nicolson, 1974).

Frappell, L. O., 'Coleridge and the "Coleridgeans" on Luther', *Journal of Religious History*, 7 (1973).

Freeman, K. D., *The Role of Reason in Religion: A Study of Henry Mansel* (The Hague: Martinus Nijhoff, 1969).

French, H. W., 'The Victorian Broad Church, Seedbed of Twentieth-Century Religious Pluralism and Implicit Religion: An Historical Perspective', *Implicit Religion*, 1 (1998).

Gardner, C., 'Frederick Denison Maurice', *Hibbert Journal*, 28 (1930).

Garland, M. M., *Cambridge before Darwin: The Ideal of a Liberal Education, 1800–1860* (Cambridge: Cambridge University Press, 1980).

Gascoigne, J., *Cambridge and the Enlightenment* (Cambridge: Cambridge University Press, 1989).

Gash, N., *Politics in the Age of Peel: A Study in the Technique of Parliamentary Representation, 1830–1850* (London: Longman, 1953).

Gilbert, A. D., *Religion and Society in Industrial England: Church, Chapel and Social Change 1740–1914* (London: Longman, 1976).

Gilley, S. W., 'Nationality and Liberty, Protestant and Catholic: Robert Southey's Book of the Church', in S. Mews (ed.), *Studies in Church History: Religion and National Identity*, 18 (Oxford: Blackwell, 1982).

—— 'The Ecclesiology of the Oxford Movement', in P. Vaiss, (ed.), *From Oxford to the People* (Leominster: Gracewing, 1996).

Gleadle, K., *The Early English Feminists: Radical Unitarians and the Emergence of the Women's Rights Movement, 1831–51* (Basingstoke: St Martin's Press, 1995).

Gloyn, C. K., *The Church in the Social Order: A Study of Anglican Social Theory from Coleridge to Maurice* (Forest Grove, Ore.: Pacific University Press, 1942).

Godechot, J., *The Counter-Revolution: Doctrine and Action 1789–1804* (London: Routledge, 1972).

Gray, D., *Earth and Altar: The Evolution of the Parish Communion in the Church of England to 1945* (Norwich: Canterbury Press, 1986).

Greaves, R. W., 'The Jerusalem Bishopric, 1841', *English Historical Review*, 64 (1949).

—— 'The Working of the Alliance: A Comment on Warburton', in G. V. Bennett and J. D. Walsh (eds.), *Essays in Modern English Church History: In Memory of Norman Sykes* (London: A. & C. Black, 1966).

Green, V. H. H., *Religion at Oxford and Cambridge* (London: SCM, 1964).

Griffin, J. R., 'John Keble, Radical', *Anglican Theological Review*, 59 (1971).

—— 'The Radical Phase of the Oxford Movement', *Journal of Ecclesiastical History*, 27 (1976).

Grimsley, R., *The Philosophy of Rousseau* (Oxford: Oxford University Press, 1973).

Grylls, R. G., *Queen's College, 1848–1948: Founded by F. D. Maurice* (London: Routledge, 1948).

Hall, R. O., 'Revised Reviews: F. D. Maurice's "The Doctrine of Sacrifice" ', *Theology*, 64 (1961).

Hammond, J. L., and Hammond, B., *The Town Labourer, 1760–1832* (London: Longman, 1917).

Harrison, B. H., and Trinder, B., *Drink and Sobriety in an Early Victorian County Town: Banbury 1830–1860*, English Historical Review Special Supplement, 4 (1969).

Harrison, J. F. C., *A History of the Working Men's College, 1854–1954* (London: Routledge & Kegan Paul, 1954).

Hart, J., 'Religion as Social Control', in A. P. Donajgrodski (ed.), *Social Control in Nineteenth-Century Britain* (London: Croom Helm, 1977).

Harvey, V. A., *The Historian and the Believer* (London: SCM, 1967).

Hebert, A. G., *Liturgy and Society: The Function of the Church in the Modern World* (London: Faber, 1935).

Hedley, D., 'Coleridge's Intellectual Intuition, the Vision of God, and the Walled Garden of "Kubla Khan" ', *Journal of the History of Ideas*, 59 (1998).

—— *Samuel Taylor Coleridge's* Aids to Reflection: *A Romantic Philosophy of Religion* (Cambridge: Cambridge University Press, 2000).

Heeney, B., 'Harry Jones and the Broad Church Pastoral Tradition in London', in P. T. Phillips (ed.), *The View from the Pulpit: Victorian Ministers and Society* (Toronto: Macmillan, 1978).

Hempton, D., *Religion and Political Culture in Britain and Ireland: From the Glorious Revolution to the Decline of Empire* (Cambridge: Cambridge University Press, 1996).

Higham, F., *F. D. Maurice* (London: SCM, 1947).

Hilton, B., *The Age of Atonement: The Influence of Evangelicalism on Social and Economic Thought, 1795–1865* (Oxford: Clarendon Press, 1988).

Himes, M. J., ' "A Great Theologian of our Time": Möhler on Schleiermacher', *Heythrop Journal*, 37 (1996).

—— *Ongoing Incarnation: Johann Adam Möhler and the Beginnings of Modern Ecclesiology* (New York: Crossroad Press, 1997).

Hinchliff, P. B., *Benjamin Jowett and the Christian Religion* (Oxford: Clarendon Press, 1987).

—— *God and History: Aspects of British Theology 1875–1914* (Oxford: Clarendon Press, 1992).

—— *Frederick Temple, Archbishop of Canterbury: A Life* (Oxford: Clarendon Press, 1998).

Hobsbawm, E. J., *The Age of Revolution* (London: Weidenfeld & Nicolson, 1962).

—— 'The Labour Aristocracy in Nineteenth-Century Britain', in *Labouring Men: Studies in the History of Labour* (London: Weidenfeld & Nicolson, 1968).

—— and Rudé, G., *Captain Swing* (London: Lawrence & Wishart, 1969).

Hodkin, H., 'The Theological Teaching of F. D. Maurice', *Theology*, 34 (1937).

Holmes, J. D., *The Triumph of the Holy See: A Short History of the Papacy in the Nineteenth Century* (London: Burns & Oates, 1978).

Holmes, R. *Coleridge: Early Visions* (London: Hodder & Stoughton, 1989).

—— *Coleridge: Darker Reflections* (London: Harper Collins, 1998).

Holt, R. V., *The Unitarian Contribution to Social Progress in England* (1938; new edn., London: The Lindsey Press, 1952).

Hope, N., *German and Scandinavian Protestantism, 1700–1918* (Oxford: Oxford University Press, 1995).

House of Bishops, *Apostolicity and Succession* (London: General Synod of the Church of England, 1994).

Hovell, M., *The Chartist Movement* (1918; new edn., Manchester: Manchester University Press, 1966).

Illingworth, A. L., *The Life and Work of John Richardson Illingworth* (London: Murray, 1917).

Inglis, K. S., *Churches and the Working Classes in Victorian England* (London: Routledge & Kegan Paul, 1963).

Irvine, C., *Worship, Church and Society* (Norwich: Canterbury Press, 1993).

Isichei, E., *Victorian Quakers* (Oxford: Oxford University Press, 1970).

Jacob, W. M., *The Making of the Anglican Church Worldwide* (London: SPCK, 1997).

Jann, R., *The Art and Science of Victorian History* (Columbus, Oh.: Ohio State University Press, 1985).

Jasper, D. (ed.), *The Interpretation of Belief: Coleridge, Schleiermacher and Romanticism* (London: Macmillan, 1986).

—— 'Living Powers: Sacred and Secular Language in European Romanticism', in S. E. Porter (ed.), *The Nature of Religious Language* (Sheffield: Sheffield Academic Press, 1996).

Jasper, R. C. D., *Prayer Book Revision in England 1800–1900* (London: SPCK, 1954).

—— *The Development of the Anglican Liturgy 1662–1980* (London: SPCK, 1989).

Jenkins, C., *F. D. Maurice and the New Reformation* (London: SPCK, 1938).

Jenkins, T. D., 'Church and Intellectuals, Nation and State', *Theology*, 98 (1996).

—— *Religion in Everyday English Life: An Ethnographic Approach* (Oxford: Berghahn, 1999).

Jones, D. J. V., *The Last Rising: The Newport Chartist Insurrection of 1839* (Cardiff: University of Wales Press, 1999).

Jones, G. S., *Outcast London: A Study in the Relationship between Classes in Victorian Society* (Harmondsworth: Penguin, 1976).

Jones, H. S., *Victorian Political Thought* (Basingstoke: Macmillan, 2000).

Jones, P., *The 1848 Revolutions* (London: Longman, 1991).

Jones, P. D'A., *The Christian Socialist Revival 1877–1914: Religion, Class and Social Conscience in Late Victorian England* (Princeton: Princeton University Press, 1968).

Joyce, P., *Work, Society and Politics: The Culture of the Factory in Later Victorian England* (Brighton: Harvester, 1980).

—— *Visions of the People: Industrial England and the Question of Class 1848–1914* (Cambridge: Cambridge University Press, 1991).

Jump, J. D. (ed.), *Alfred Tennyson:* In Memoriam, Maud *and Other Poems* (London: Dent, 1974).

Kasper, W., *Theology and Church* (London: SCM, 1989).

Kent, J. H. S., *Wesley and the Wesleyans: Religion in Eighteenth-Century Britain* (Cambridge: Cambridge University Press, 2002).

Kenyon, J. P. (ed.), *The Stuart Constitution 1603–1688*, 2nd edn. (Cambridge: Cambridge University Press, 1986).

Khomiakov, A. S., *The Church is One* (1863), ed. by N. Zernov (London: Fellowship of St Alban & St Sergius, 1948).

Kittel, G. (ed.), *Theological Dictionary of the New Testament* (Grand Rapids, Mich.: Eerdmans, 1964).

Klinck, D., *The French Counterrevolutionary Theorist, Louis de Bonald (1754–1840)* (New York: Lang, 1996).

Kneale, W. C., 'Time and Eternity in Theology', *Proceedings of the Royal Aristotelian Society,* (1960–61).

Koss, S., *Nonconformity in Modern British Politics* (London: Batsford, 1975).

The Lambeth Conference 1948 (London: SPCK, 1948).

Large, D., 'London in the Year of Revolution, 1848', in J. Stevenson (ed.), *London in the Age of Reform* (Oxford: Blackwell, 1977).

Lebrun, R. A., *Throne and Altar: The Political and Religious Thought of Joseph de Maistre* (Ottawa: University of Ottawa Press, 1965).

Lidgett, J. Scott, *The Victorian Transformation of Theology* (London: Epworth Press, 1934).

Litvack, L., *John Mason Neale and the Quest for Sobornost* (Oxford: Clarendon Press, 1994).

Lossky, V., *The Mystical Theology of the Eastern Church* (1957; new edn., Cambridge: James Clarke, 1991).

Lubenow, W. C., *The Cambridge Apostles, 1820–1914: Liberalism, Imagination and Friendship in British Intellectual and Professional Life* (Cambridge: Cambridge University Press, 1998).

McAdoo, H. R., *The Spirit of Anglicanism: A Survey of Anglican Theological Method in the Seventeenth Century* (London: A. & C. Black, 1965).

—— and Stevenson, K., *The Mystery of the Eucharist in the Anglican Tradition* (Norwich: Canterbury Press, 1995).

McClain, F. M., *Maurice, Man and Moralist* (London: SPCK, 1972).

—— 'Maurice and Sara Coleridge: Baptism and Human Nature', *Anglican Theological Review,* 54 (1972).

—— Norris, R., and Orens, J., *F. D. Maurice: A Study* (Cambridge, Mass.: Cowley, 1982).

MacCulloch, D., *Thomas Cranmer: A Life* (New Haven and London: Yale University Press, 1996).

McDowell, R. B., *The Church of Ireland 1869–1969* (London: Routledge & Kegan Paul, 1975).

McGrath, A. (ed.), *The SPCK Handbook of Anglican Theologians* (London: SPCK, 1998).

Mackinnon, D. M., 'Kenosis and Establishment', in *The Stripping of the Altars* (London: Fontana, 1969).

McLellan, D., *The Thought of Karl Marx* (1971; 2nd edn., London: Macmillan, 1980).

McLeod, D. H., *Class and Religion in the Late Victorian City* (London: Croom Helm, 1974).

—— *Religion and Society in England, 1850–1914* (London: Macmillan, 1996).

McManners, J., *The French Revolution and the Church* (London: SPCK, 1969).

—— *Church and Society in Eighteenth-Century France,* i: *The Clerical Establishment and its Social Ramifications* (Oxford: Clarendon Press, 1998).

Marsh, P. T., *The Victorian Church in Decline: Archbishop Tait and the Church of England, 1868–1882* (London: Routledge & Kegan Paul, 1969).

Masterman, N. C., *John Malcolm Ludlow: The Builder of Christian Socialism* (Cambridge: Cambridge University Press, 1963).

—— 'F. D. Maurice, Progressive or Reactionary?', *Theology,* 76 (1973).

Mather, F. C., *High Church Prophet: Bishop Samuel Horsley (1733–1806) and the Caroline Tradition in the Later Georgian Church* (Oxford: Clarendon Press, 1992).

Mathias, P., *The First Industrial Nation: An Economic History of Britain 1700–1914* (1969; new edn., London: Methuen, 1983).

Matthew, H. C. G., 'Edward Bouverie Pusey: From Scholar to Tractarian', *Journal of Theological Studies,* 32 (1981).

—— *Gladstone 1809–1874* (Oxford: Clarendon Press, 1986).

—— *Gladstone 1875–1898* (Oxford: Clarendon Press, 1995).

Matthews, W. R., *The Problem of Christ in the Twentieth Century: An Essay on the Incarnation* (Oxford: Oxford University Press, 1950).

—— *The Religious Philosophy of Dean Mansel* (Oxford: Oxford University Press, 1956).

Moore, J. R., *The Post-Darwinian Controversies: A Study of the Protestant Struggle to Come to Terms with Darwin in Great Britain and America, 1870–1900* (Cambridge: Cambridge University Press, 1979).

—— (ed.), *Religion in Victorian Britain,* iii: *Sources* (Manchester: Manchester University Press, 1988).

More, P. E., and Cross, F. L. (eds.), *Anglicanism* (London: SPCK, 1935).

Morgan, R. (ed.), *The Religion of the Incarnation: Anglican Essays in Commemoration of 'Lux Mundi'* (Bristol: Bristol Classical Press, 1989).

Morris, J. N., 'A Disappearing Crowd? Collective Action in Late Nineteenth-Century Croydon', *Southern History,* 11 (1989).

—— *Religion and Urban Change: Croydon, 1840–1914* (Woodbridge: Boydell, 1992).

—— 'Reconstructing the Reformation: F. D. Maurice, Luther, and Justification', in R. N. Swanson, (ed.), *The Church Retrospective,* Studies in Church History, 33 (Woodbridge: Boydell, 1997).

—— 'A "Fluffy-Minded Prayer Book Fundamentalist"? F. D. Maurice and the Anglican Liturgy', in R. N. Swanson, (ed.), *Continuity and Change in Christian Worship,* Studies in Church History, 35 (Woodbridge: Boydell, 1999).

—— 'A Social Doctrine of the Trinity? A Reappraisal of F. D. Maurice on Eternal Life', *Anglican and Episcopal History,* 69 (2000).

—— 'Newman and Maurice on the Via Media of the Anglican Church: Contrasts and Affinities', *Anglican Theological Review,* 85 (2003).

—— 'The Strange Death of Christian Britain: Another Look at the Secularization Debate', *Historical Journal,* 46 (2003).

—— 'The Text as Sacrament: Victorian Broad Church Philology', in R. N. Swanson (ed.), *The Church and the Book,* Studies in Church History, 38 (Woodbridge: Boydell, 2004).

Morrow, J. (ed.), *Young England: The New Generation* (London: Leicester University Press, 1999).

Needham, N. R., *Thomas Erskine of Linlathen: His Life and Theology 1788–1837* (Edinburgh: Rutherford House Books, 1990).

Neill, S., *The Interpretation of the New Testament 1861–1961* (London: Oxford University Press, 1964).

Nettleship, L. E., 'William Fremantle, Samuel Barnett and the Broad Church Origins of Toynbee Hall', *Journal of Ecclesiastical History*, 33 (1982).

Neville, G., *Radical Churchman: Edward Lee Hicks and the New Liberalism* (Oxford: Clarendon Press, 1998).

Newsome, D., 'Justification and Sanctification: Newman and the Evangelicals', *Journal of Theological Studies*, NS 15 (1964).

—— *Bishop Westcott and the Platonic Tradition* (Cambridge: Cambridge University Press, 1969).

—— *Two Classes of Men: Platonism and English Romantic Thought* (London: Murray, 1974).

Nias, J. C. S., *Gorham and the Bishop of Exeter* (London: SPCK, 1951).

Nichols, A., *From Newman to Congar: The Idea of Doctrinal Development from the Victorians to the Second Vatican Council* (Edinburgh: T & T Clark, 1990).

—— *The Panther and the Hind: A Theological History of Anglicanism* (Edinburgh: T & T Clark, 1993).

Nockles, P. B., 'An Academic Counter-Revolution: Newman and Tractarian Oxford's Idea of a University', *History of Universities*, 10 (1991).

—— *The Oxford Movement in Context: Anglican High Churchmanship 1760–1857* (Cambridge: Cambridge University Press, 1994).

—— ' "Church and King": Tractarian Politics Reappraised', in P. Vaiss (ed.), *From Oxford to the People: Reconsidering Newman and the Oxford Movement* (Leominster: Gracewing, 1996).

—— ' "Lost Causes and ... Impossible Loyalties": The Oxford Movement and the University', in M. G. Brock and M. C. Curthoys (eds.), *The History of the University of Oxford, v: Nineteenth-Century Oxford, Part 1* (Oxford: Clarendon Press, 1997).

Norman, E. R., *The Victorian Christian Socialists* (Cambridge: Cambridge University Press, 1987).

O'Donovan, O., *On the 39 Articles: A Conversation with Tudor Christianity* (Oxford: Latimer House Publications, 1986).

Oloffson, F., *Christus Redemptor et Consummator: A Study in the Theology of B. F. Westcott* (Uppsala: Acta Universitatis Uppsaliensis, 1979).

Pals, D. L., *The Victorian 'Lives' of Jesus* (San Antonio, Tex.: Trinity University Press, 1982).

Parker, C., *The English Historical Tradition since 1850* (Edinburgh: John Donald, 1990).

Parsons, G. (ed.), *Religion in Victorian Britain, ii: Controversies* (Manchester: Open University, 1988).

—— 'A Forgotten Debt: John Colenso and the Life of Blanco White', *Faith and Freedom*, 51 (1998).

Patrick, G. A., *F. J. A. Hort: Eminent Victorian* (Sheffield: Almond Press, 1987).

Paz, D. G. (ed.), *Nineteenth-Century English Religious Traditions: Retrospect and Prospect* (Westport, Conn.: Greenwood Press, 1995).

Phillips, P. T., *The Sectarian Spirit: Sectarianism, Society and Politics in Victorian Cotton Towns* (Toronto: University of Toronto Press, 1982).

—— 'The Concept of a National Church in Late Nineteenth-Century England and America', *Journal of Religious History*, 14 (1986).

—— *A Kingdom on Earth: Anglo-American Social Christianity 1880–1940* (University Park, Pa.: Penn State University Press, 1996).

Pinnington, J., 'Anglican Openness to Foreign Protestant Churches in the Eighteenth Century: A Gloss on the Old Priest and New Presbyter Thesis of Norman Sykes', *Anglican Theological Review*, 51 (1969).

—— 'Church Principles and the Early Years of the Church Missionary Society: The Problem of the German Missionaries', *Journal of Theological Studies*, 20 (1969).

—— *Kingdom and Commonwealth: The Christian Social Union and its Legacy to Radical Social Thought in the Church of England* (Croydon: Jubilee Group, 1997).

Powicke, F. J., 'Frederick Denison Maurice (1805–1872): A Personal Reminiscence', *Congregational Quarterly*, 8 (1930).

Prest, J. M., *Liberty and Locality: Parliament, Permissive Legislation, and Ratepayers' Democracies in the Mid-Nineteenth Century* (Oxford: Clarendon Press, 1990).

Prestige, G. L., *The Life of Charles Gore* (London: Heinemann, 1935).

Preston, R., *Religion and the Persistence of Capitalism* (London: SCM, 1979).

Prickett, S., 'Coleridge, Newman amd F. D. Maurice', *Theology*, 76 (1973).

—— *Romanticism and Religion: The Tradition of Coleridge and Wordsworth in the Victorian Church* (Cambridge: Cambridge University Press, 1976).

Ramsey, A. M., *The Gospel and the Catholic Church* (London: Longman, 1936).

—— *F. D. Maurice and the Conflicts of Modern Theology* (Cambridge: Cambridge University Press, 1951).

—— *From Gore to Temple: The Development of Anglican Theology between* Lux Mundi *and the Second World War 1889–1939* (London: Longman, 1960).

—— et al., *Catholicity: A Study in the Conflict of Christian Traditions in the West* (Wesminster: Dacre Press, 1947).

Raven, C. E., *Christian Socialism 1848–54* (1920; new edn., London: Frank Cass, 1968).

Ravitch, N., *The Catholic Church and the French Nation, 1589–1989* (London: Routledge, 1990).

Reardon, B. M. G., *Religious Thought in the Victorian Age* (London: Longman, 1980).

—— *Religion in the Age of Romanticism: Studies in Early Nineteenth-Century Thought* (Cambridge: Cambridge University Press, 1985).

Reckitt, M. B., *Maurice to Temple: A Century of the Social Movement in the Church of England* (London: Faber, 1947).

Reisman, D. (ed.), *Democratic Socialism in Britain: Classic Texts in Economic and Political Thought, 1825–1952*, ii: *The Christian Socialists: Frederick Denison Maurice, Charles Kingsley & John Malcolm Ludlow* (London: Pickering & Chatto, 1996).

Reventlow, H., *The Authority of the Bible and the Rise of the Modern World* (London: SCM, 1984).

Richter, D. C., *Riotous Victorians* (London: Ohio University Press, 1981).

Robinson, J. A. T., 'Kingdom, Church and Ministry', in K. M. Carey (ed.), *The Historic Episcopate in the Fullness of the Church* (Westminster: Dacre Press, 1954).

Rogerson, J. W., *The Bible and Criticism in Victorian Britain: Profiles of F. D. Maurice and William Robertson Smith* (Sheffield: Sheffield Academic Press, 1995).

Rouse, R., and Neill, S. C., *A History of the Ecumenical Movement 1517–1948* (London: SPCK, 1954).

Rowell, G., *Hell and the Victorians: A Study of the Nineteenth-Century Theological Controversies concerning Eternal Punishment and Future Life* (Oxford: Oxford University Press, 1974).

Rowlands, J. H. L., *Church, State and Society: The Attitudes of John Keble, Richard Hurrell Froude and John Henry Newman* (Worthing: Churchman, 1989).

Royle, E., *Victorian Infidels: The Origins of the British Secularist Movement, 1791–1866* (Manchester: Manchester University Press, 1974).

—— *Radicals, Secularists and Republicans: Popular Freethought in Britain, 1866–1915* (Manchester: Manchester University Press, 1980).

—— *Revolutionary Britannia? Reflections on the Threat of Revolution in Britain, 1789–1848* (Manchester: Manchester University Press, 2000).

Sachs, W. L., *The Transformation of Anglicanism: From State Church to Global Communion* (Cambridge: Cambridge University Press, 1993).

Sagovsky, N., *Ecumenism, Christian Origins and the Practice of Communion* (Cambridge: Cambridge University Press, 2000).

Sampson, R. V., 'The Limits of Religious Thought: The Theological Controversy', in P. Appleman, W. A. Madden, and M. Wolff (eds.), *1859: Entering an Age of Crisis* (Bloomington, Ind.: Indiana University Press, 1959).

Sanders, C. R., *Coleridge and the Broad Church Movement* (Durham, NC: Duke University Press, 1942).

Schwarz, L. D., *London in the Age of Industrialisation: Entrepreneurs, Labour Force and Living Conditions, 1700–1850* (Cambridge: Cambridge University Press, 1992).

Secor, P., *Richard Hooker, Prophet of Anglicanism* (Tunbridge Wells: Burns & Oates, 1999).

Sell, A. P. F., *The Philosophy of Religion 1815–1980* (London: Routledge, 1988).

—— *Philosophical Idealism and Christian Belief* (Cardiff: University of Wales Press, 1995).

Shannon, R. T., 'John Robert Seeley and the Idea of a National Church', in R. Robson (ed.), *Ideas and Institutions of Victorian Britain* (London: Bell, 1967).

Sharma, S. K., *Charles Kingsley and the Victorian Compromise* (New Delhi: Vani Prakashan, 1989).

Shea, V., and Whitla, W. (eds.), *Essays and Reviews: The 1860 Text and its Reading* (Charlottesville, Va.: University Press of Virginia, 2000).

Slee, P., *Learning and a Liberal Education: The Study of Modern History in the Universities of Oxford, Cambridge and Manchester, 1800–1914* (Manchester: Manchester University Press, 1986).

Smith, M. A., *Religion in Industrial Society: Oldham and Saddleworth 1740–1865* (Oxford: Oxford University Press, 1994).

Smith, P., *The Young England Movement* (High Wycombe: University Microfilms, 1971).

Snell, K. D., and Ell, P. S., *Rival Jerusalems: The Geography of Victorian Religion* (Cambridge: Cambridge University Press, 2000).

Soffer, R. N., 'History and Religion: J. R. Seeley and the Burden of the Past', in R. W. Davis and R. J. Helmstadter (eds.), *Religion and Irreligion in Victorian Society* (London: Routledge, 1992).

Southgate, W. M., *John Jewel and the Problem of Doctrinal Authority* (Cambridge, Mass.: Harvard University Press, 1963).

Speller, J. L., 'Alexander Nicoll and the Study of German Biblical Criticism in Early Nineteenth-Century Oxford', *Journal of Ecclesiastical History,* 30 (1979).

Spurr, J., *The Restoration Church of England, 1646–1689* (New Haven and London: Yale University Press, 1991).

Stevenson, J., *Popular Disturbances in England, 1700–1870* (London: Longman, 1979).

Sykes, N., *Old Priest and New Presbyter: The Anglican Attitude to Episcopacy, Presbyterianism and Papacy since the Reformation* (Cambridge: Cambridge University Press, 1956).

Sykes, S. W., *The Integrity of Anglicanism* (Oxford: Mowbray, 1978).

—— *Unashamed Anglicanism* (London: DLT, 1995).

Taylor, A. J. (ed.), *The Standard of Living in Britain in the Industrial Revolution* (London: Methuen, 1975).

Taylor, S., 'William Warburton and the Alliance of Church and State', *Journal of Ecclesiastical History,* 43 (1992).

Thomis, M. I., *The Luddites: Machine-Breaking in Regency England* (Newton Abbot: David & Charles, 1970).

Thompson, D. M., (ed.), *Nonconformity in the Nineteenth Century* (London: Routledge & Kegan Paul, 1972).

—— 'The Liberation Society 1844–1868', in P. Hollis (ed.), *Pressure from Without in Early Victorian England* (London: Edward Arnold, 1974).

—— 'F. D. Maurice', in S. P. Mews (ed.), *Modern Religious Rebels* (London: Epworth Press, 1993).

Thompson, E. P., *The Making of the English Working Class* (1963; 2nd edn., Harmondsworth: Penguin, 1968).

—— *Witness against the Beast: William Blake and the Moral Law* (Cambridge: Cambridge University Press, 1993).

—— *Customs in Common* (London: Merlin, 1991).

—— and E. Yeo (eds.), *The Unknown Mayhew* (Harmondsworth: Penguin, 1973).

Thompson, K. A., *Bureaucracy and Church Reform: The Organizational Response of the Church of England to Social Change, 1800–1965* (Oxford: Clarendon Press, 1970).

Tillard, J. M. R., *Church of Churches: The Ecclesiology of Communion* (Collegeville, Minn.: Liturgical Press, 1992).

Tillotson, K., *Novels of the Eighteen-Forties* (1954; new edn., Oxford: Clarendon Press, 1983).

Together in Mission and Ministry: The Porvoo Common Statement (London: Church House Publishing, 1993).

Toon, P., *Evangelical Theology 1833–1856: A Response to Tractarianism* (London: Marshall, Morgan & Scott, 1979).

Torrance, T. F., *Scottish Theology from John Knox to John McLeod Campbell* (Edinburgh: T & T Clark, 1996).

Touchefeu, Y., *Antiquité et le christianisme dans la pensée de Jean-Jacques Rousseau* (Oxford: Voltaire Foundation, 1999).

Treloar, G. R., *The Nature and Role of History in the Life and Thought of J. B. Lightfoot (1828–1889) as Churchman and Scholar* (Tübingen: Mohr Siebeck, 1998).

Turner, D., *The Darkness of God: Negativity in Christian Mysticism* (Cambridge: Cambridge University Press, 1995).

Van Kley, D. K., *The Religious Origins of the French Revolution: From Calvin to the Civil Constitution, 1560–1791* (New Haven: Yale University Press, 1996).

Vidler, A. R., *The Orb and the Cross: A Normative Study in the Relations of Church and State with Reference to Gladstone's Early Writings* (London: SPCK, 1945).

—— *The Theology of F. D. Maurice* (London: SCM, 1947).

—— *Prophecy and Papacy: A Study of Lamennais, the Church, and the Revolution* (London: SCM, 1954).

—— *The Church in an Age of Revolution* (Harmondsworth: Penguin, 1961).

—— *Soundings: Essays Concerning Christian Understanding* (Cambridge: Cambridge University Press, 1962).

—— *F. D. Maurice and Company: Nineteenth-Century Studies* (London: SCM, 1966).

Vincent, A., and Plant, R., *Philosophy, Politics and Citizenship: The Life and Thought of the British Idealists* (Oxford: Blackwell, 1984).

Vincent, J., *The Formation of the Liberal Party, 1857–1868* (London: Constable, 1966).

Virgin, P., *The Church in an Age of Negligence: Ecclesiastical Structure and Problems of Church Reform 1700–1840* (Cambridge: James Clarke, 1988).

Vovelle, M., *The Revolution against the Church: From Reason to the Supreme Being* (Cambridge: Polity, 1991).

Walsh, J. D., Haydon, C., and Taylor, S. (eds.), *The Church of England, c.1689–c.1833: From Toleration to Tractarianism* (Cambridge: Cambridge University Press, 1993).

Wand, J. W. C., *Anglicanism in History and Today* (London: Weidenfeld & Nicolson, 1961).

Want, C., 'Frederick Denison Maurice and *Eustace Conway*', *Anglican Theological Review*, 54 (1972).

Ward, W. R., *Religion and Society in England, 1790–1850* (London: Batsford, 1972).

—— *Christianity under the Ancien Régime, 1648–1789* (Cambridge: Cambridge University Press, 1999).

Waterman, A. M. C., *Revolution, Economics and Religion: Christian Political Economy, 1798–1833* (Cambridge: Cambridge University Press, 1991).

—— 'A Cambridge "Via Media" in Late Georgian Anglicanism', *Journal of Ecclesiastical History*, 42 (1991).

Watts, M., *The Dissenters*, ii: *The Expansion of Evangelical Nonconformity* (Oxford: Clarendon Press, 1995).

Watts, R., *Gender, Power and the Unitarians in England 1760–1860* (London: Longman, 1998).

Webster, A. B., 'Church Order and Re-Union in the Nineteenth Century', in K. M. Carey (ed.), *The Historic Episcopate in the Fullness of the Church* (Westminster: Dacre Press, 1954).

Welch, C., *The Trinity in Contemporary Theology* (London: SCM, 1953).

—— *Protestant Thought in the Nineteenth Century*, i: *1799–1879* (New Haven: Yale University Press, 1972).

Welch, P. J., 'Anglican Churchmen and the Establishment of the Jerusalem Bishopric', *Journal of Ecclesiastical History*, 8 (1957).

Widdicombe, P., *The Fatherhood of God from Origen to Athanasius* (Oxford: Clarendon Press, 1994).

Wiebe, D., 'Comprehensiveness: The Integrity of Anglican Theology', in M. D. Bryant (ed.), *The Future of Anglican Theology* (New York and Toronto: Edwin Mellen Press, 1984).

Wiener, J. H., *Radicalism and Freethought in Nineteenth-Century Britain: The Life of Richard Carlile* (Westport, Conn.: Greenwood Press, 1983).

Wiener, M. J., *English Culture and the Decline of the Industrial Spirit, 1850–1980* (Cambridge: Cambridge University Press, 1981).

Wigmore-Beddoes, D. G., *Yesterday's Radicals: A Study of the Affinity between Unitarianism and Broad Church Anglicanism in the Nineteenth Century* (Cambridge: James Clarke, 1971).

Wilkinson, A., *Christian Socialism: From Scott Holland to Tony Blair* (London: SCM, 1998).

Williams, R., *Culture and Society, 1780–1850* (London: Chatto, 1958).

—— *The Country and the City* (London: Chatto, 1973).

Williams, R. D., *The Wound of Knowledge* (London: DLT, 1979).

—— 'Liberation Theology and the Anglican Tradition', in R. D. Williams and D. Nicholls, *Politics and Theological Identity* (London: Jubilee Group, 1984).

Winslow, D. F., *Thomas Erskine: Advocate for the Character of God* (Lanham, Md.: University Press of America, 1993).

Wolf, W. J., 'Maurice and our Understanding of "Ecumenical" ', *Anglican Theological Review*, 54 (1972).

—— 'Frederick Denison Maurice', in W. J. Wolf, J. E. Booty, and O. C. Thomas, *The Spirit of Anglicanism: Hooker, Maurice and Temple* (Edinburgh: T & T Clark, 1982).

Wolffe, J., *God and Greater Britain: Religion and National Life in Britain and Ireland, 1843–1945* (London: Routledge, 1994).

Wood, H. G., *Frederick Denison Maurice* (Cambridge: Cambridge University Press, 1950).

Woodhouse-Hawkins, M., 'Maurice, Huntington, and the Quadrilateral: An Exploration in Historical Theology', in J. Robert Wright (ed.), *Quadrilateral at One Hundred* (Oxford: Mowbray, 1988).

Woodward, L., 'The Rise of the Professional Historian in England', in K. Bourne and D. C. Watt (eds.), *Studies in International History* (Hamden, Conn.: Archon Books, 1967).

World Council of Churches, *The Unity of the Church: Gift and Calling* (World Council of Churches website: first published, 1991).

Young, D., 'F. D. Maurice and the Unitarians', *Churchman*, 98 (1984).

—— 'Rev. Michael Maurice, 1766–1855', *Transactions of the Unitarian Historical Society*, 19 (1989).

—— 'F. D. Maurice's Debt to the Unitarians', *Faith and Freedom*, 43 (1990).

—— ' "A Reverence for the Earth": F. D. Maurice and his Unitarian Roots', *Journal of the Association of Open University Graduates* (1990/1).

—— *F. D. Maurice and Unitarianism* (Oxford: Clarendon Press, 1992).

Zernov, N., *Three Russian Prophets: Khomiakov, Dostoevsky and Soloviev* (London: SCM, 1944).

Zizioulas, J. D., *Being as Communion* (London: DLT, 1985).

UNPUBLISHED THESES

Byrne, G., 'Consulting the Faithful: The Role of the Laity in the Government of the Church of England 1861–1904' (M.Phil. thesis, Cambridge University, 1998).

Cox, J. W., 'God Manifesting Himself: A Study of Some Central Elements in the Theology of F. D. Maurice' (Ph.D. thesis, Cambridge University, 1972).

Jackson, P. W., 'F. D. Maurice's Educational Theory: A Philosophical Examination' (Ph.D. thesis, King's College, London, 1983).

Lethaby, J. I., ' "A Less Perfect Reflection": Perceptions of Luther in the Nineteenth-Century Church of England' (Ph.D. thesis, Cambridge University, 2001).

Redfern, A. L. J., 'Oversight and Authority in the Ninteenth-Century Church of England: A Case Study of Bishop Samuel Wilberforce' (Ph.D. thesis, University of Bristol, 2001).

Roberts, M. J. D., 'The Role of the Laity in the Church of England c.1850–1885' (D.Phil. thesis, Oxford University, 1974).

Index